Panoma Canal

The Legacy
of the
Monroe Doctrine

The Legacy of the Monroe Doctrine

A REFERENCE GUIDE TO U.S. INVOLVEMENT IN LATIN AMERICA AND THE CARIBBEAN

David W. Dent

Greenwood Press
Westport, Connecticut • London

Library of Congress Cataloging-in-Publication Data

Dent, David W.
   The legacy of the Monroe doctrine : a reference guide to U.S.
involvement in Latin America and the Caribbean / David W. Dent.
     p. cm.
  Includes bibliographical references and index.
  ISBN 0–313–30109–3 (alk. paper)
   1. Latin America—Foreign relations—United States. 2. United
States—Foreign relations—Latin America. 3. Caribbean Area—
Foreign relations—United States. 4. United States—Foreign
relations—Caribbean Area. I. Title.
F1418.D458 1999
327.7308—dc21   98–15326

British Library Cataloguing in Publication Data is available.

Library of Congress Catalog Card Number: 98–15326
ISBN: 0–313–30109-3

First published in 1999

Greenwood Press, 88 Post Road West, Westport, CT 06881
An imprint of Greenwood Publishing Group, Inc.

Printed in the United States of America

The paper used in this book complies with the
Permanent Paper Standard issued by the National
Information Standards Organization (Z39.48–1984).

10 9 8 7 6 5 4 3 2 1

Copyright Acknowledgments

The author and publisher gratefully acknowledge permission to reprint the following material:

Cartoons by Thomas F. Flannery. Reprinted by permission of Thomas F. Flannery and *The
Baltimore Sun*.

Maps reprinted by permission of Environmental Systems Research Institute, Inc.

Contents

Contents

Preface

This reference work is designed to provide a synthesis of the major themes in the history of U.S. involvement in Latin America and the Caribbean since the independence of the Latin American nations. Particular emphasis is placed on the Monroe Doctrine—the nineteenth-century principle that the United States would not tolerate foreign intervention in the Western Hemisphere—and its chronology of corollaries and interpretations, clearly one of the most durable foundations of American foreign policy. This work contains an introduction and twenty-four separate country-chapters, each with a timeline and relatively brief analysis that highlight the most important features of U.S. involvement in the area. Each country-chapter, from Argentina to Venezuela, emphasizes the individuals (private and governmental) and events that shaped the relationship during four historical eras: the nineteenth century; the early twentieth century (until the end of World War II); the Cold War; and the post–Cold War. Within each period the focus is on milestones and important legacies in the history of inter-American relations. For example, the discussion of major wars—Mexican War, Triple Alliance War, War of the Pacific, Spanish-American War, Chaco War, and Soccer War—emphasizes the role of the United States in the causes and consequences of each conflict, including diplomatic efforts at mediation. Because of the richness and complexity of the material contained in *The Legacy of the Monroe Doctrine*, it will serve as a convenient reference tool for those interested in learning more about the United States and Latin America.

Latin America and the Caribbean have not been tranquil places during the twentieth century. Several revolutions have given rise to leaders and political transformations that have threatened U.S. interests and challenged the ability of leaders in Washington to cope with these events and work with their leaders. In each case where a major revolution occurred—Mexico, Bolivia, Guatemala, Cuba, Chile, Nicaragua, and Grenada—the role of the United States is of paramount interest. The involvement of the United States in Latin America and the Caribbean is also related to the creation and preservation of "friendly dictators," some of whom were servile in their support of the United States if they were allowed to maintain themselves in power, regardless of how this was accomplished or how humanely they treated their opposition. Many tyrants emerged from the Spanish colonial experience and the political turmoil of the nineteenth century; others came of age during the revolutions and international conflicts of the twentieth century. The reasons for U.S. involvement with Latin American dictators varied, and often the friendships soured over time and the United States played a role in their removal, but they nevertheless served the interests of the United States—at least as they were perceived by many of their defenders in Washington.

Another important theme of this book is the application of the Monroe Doctrine to the history of U.S. involvement in Latin America. The "doctrine" actually arose from an address crafted by John Quincy Adams and delivered by President James Monroe in 1823; it became a central guideline in how the United States dealt with other nations in the Western Hemisphere and the encroachment of foreign powers after Latin American independence. At the core of President Monroe's message was the belief that it was important for the United States to become a protector of Latin America's newly acquired freedom. The idea that the United States could enforce a "hands-off" policy was dubious from the beginning, but as the address evolved into a powerful tool for justifying U.S. involvement in Latin American affairs, it became highly useful for policymakers in Washington. At times it served the needs of Latin American political leaders as well. For example, in the 1920s Peruvian president Augusto Leguía hung a portrait of James Monroe in the presidential palace to reflect his feelings toward the United States. By eulogizing Monroe in speeches and monuments, Leguía and other Latin Americans thought they could obtain economic and political advantages for themselves and their countries. The Monroe Doctrine could work both ways, but it was also avoided by some and criticized by others, particularly as Monroe's message became associated with more forceful diplomacy and the use of a "big stick" that resulted in continual U.S. intervention and military occupation during the first three decades of the twentieth century.

There are many of Monroe's ghosts in this book, people with power over inter-American relations who carried the spirit of 1823 in their hearts and minds. Although some of those who applied the Monroe Doctrine by means of a series of corollaries/interpretations to different aspects of U.S. relations with the Western Hemisphere were knowledgeable about the history, people, and culture of the region, many were ignorant (few spoke the language of the host country) and arrogant, rarely cared about the consequences of their efforts, and blundered to the point of doing considerable harm to the relationship. Those who became involved in Latin America often expressed negative stereotypes and racial prejudices that were passed from one generation to another. At times the same gap in knowledge and understanding of the United States existed among Latin American public figures, although it never seemed as noteworthy as it was among policy-makers in Washington.

My attempt to synthesize a vast amount of inter-American history in a short amount of space was a daunting task. It meant that some details concerning a particular country and its relationship with the United States could not be covered as extensively as others. Moreover, certain individuals who played roles in the drama had to be either left out or treated only briefly. This was necessary in the interest of making the book a true reference tool that will serve the best interests of the general reader, not the specialist in inter-American relations. As a result, the reader will find a selected list of readings at the end of each chapter that can be used to explore topics related to the subject in greater detail.

This reference book would not have been possible without the assistance of friends and colleagues. I owe an enormous debt to Larman C. Wilson, who read the entire manuscript and offered encouragement, information, and important insights. Tom Mullen provided me with clippings from a wide variety of sources that I used for critical subjects. Paul Sondrol shared his expertise on Paraguay's history of authoritarianism, and Jack Binns, former U.S. ambassador to Honduras, helped clarify the chapters on El Salvador and Honduras. Gary Brana-Shute read the chapter on Guyana and offered useful suggestions. Sue Mundell of the Hispanic Division of the Library of Congress was instrumental in helping me locate hard-to-find books, and I am grateful to her and the other staff members of the Hispanic Division who were consistently helpful in the most difficult stages of the research. Kelly Smith, one of my former students, provided research assistance on the chapters about Chile and Haiti. Finally, I appreciate the invitation from Barbara Rader at Greenwood Press to tackle this challenging project. It allowed me to embark on a stimulating and rewarding journey into the story of events and individuals who have shaped the inter-American relationship. In no way are any of the above-mentioned individuals to be held responsible for the material selected, the views expressed on certain subjects, or the limitations and defects found in this volume, which are entirely my own.

The end of the Cold War has forced the United States and Latin America to forge a new relationship and prepare for the next century. I hope that *The Legacy of the Monroe Doctrine* will provide the reader with the necessary information to comprehend the important legacies—and policy blunders—that are part of the fabric of hemispheric relations.

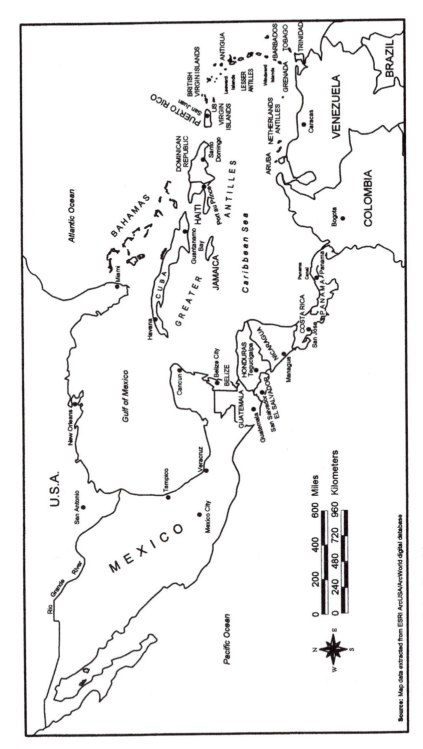

Central America and the Carribbean

Source: Map data extracted from ESRI ArcUSA/ArcWorld digital database

South America

1

Introduction

Latin Americans believe that if the United States claims the right to prevent foreign intervention, the least it can do is *not* intervene itself.

—Cole Blasier, *The Giant's Rival* (1987)[1]

MONROE'S MESSAGE

It was to be a routine message, on a variety of subjects of importance to the nation, delivered by the fifth president (1817–1825) of the United States, James Monroe. President Monroe was not an imaginative thinker but was experienced in battle and foreign affairs and had mastered the details of his address in a slow and methodical fashion. The world had gone through profound changes since Monroe took office, but in the "era of good feelings" he experienced no sense of urgency as he prepared to deliver his message to Congress on December 2, 1823. A farm boy from Virginia, James Monroe resembled the twentieth century's Gerald Ford with his six-foot stature, fair complexion, and country-boy heartiness. He lacked the intellectual capacity of Thomas Jefferson or John Quincy Adams, and he did not have the oratory skills of Henry Clay, but as his second term was coming to a close he realized the importance of making a statement that extended the foreign policy principles of former presidents Washington and Jefferson. However, in addressing the issue of the safety and security of the newly independent Latin American nations, Monroe feared that he might come to be known as an architect of war if his speech echoed with belligerency.

Monroe's words would have to balance two opposing currents of thought that were prevalent in Washington at the time: isolationism, and interventionism and territorial expansion. Isolationism is a foreign policy principle that advocates minimal participation in the internal affairs, or external wars, of other nations and the avoidance of entangling treaties that involve security commitments. Those who advocate isolationism are usually wary of international law and organizations, believing that noninterference is the best policy. Interventionism has many guises, but at its core is a belief that various forms of intervention or involvement are necessary remedies for protecting national interests, whether economic, political, or security. The original Monroe Doctrine was an isolationist policy, opposed to extrahemispheric intervention in the Americas. However, as the United States became more powerful, it was amended through various corollaries and interpretations to authorize Washington to engage in the unilateral use of force to deal with a myriad of situations in Latin America and the Caribbean region. With the support of his cabinet Monroe's message would address both domestic political issues, but without arousing hostility abroad.

Monroe tried to justify his new policy through a simple distinction between the "good" politics of republicanism (representative democracy) in the Western Hemisphere and the "bad" monarchies then widespread in the Old World (Europe). However, the essence of Monroe's address was not democracy-building in Latin America, but a rhetorical ploy to keep Spain, France, Russia, and England from acquiring new territorial possessions in the Americas. Unlike dozens of presidents who followed him, Monroe also recognized the importance of candor in articulating the principles he wished to convey to the nation and the world.

John Quincy Adams, secretary of state, was the figure most responsible for the content of Monroe's speech that pertained to Latin America. Adams held no romantic notions about the political future of the Latin American republics. A practicing Calvinist, he put little faith in countries of Catholic religion and Latin temperaments. Adams was proud of his Anglo-Saxon heritage and felt that "It was one thing to tell Europe to keep its hands off the Western Hemisphere," according to James Humes, "but it was another to join hands with those weak Latin governments in the spirit of equality and fraternal affection."[2] Most of his diplomatic life had been spent in Europe, where he learned to speak several languages and formulate a view of the world that fit the changing times. His first priority was to deter the European powers from encroaching on the Western Hemisphere, and he firmly believed that whatever strategic doctrine was formulated, it should not involve a joint declaration with the British.

The early nineteenth-century struggles in Latin America to break free of European domination and achieve statehood were varied in terms of causes, intensity, and length, but they eventually freed a vast territory—stretching from California and Florida in North America all the way to the southern tip of South America—from Spanish and Portuguese control. Slave revolts against French settlers resulted in political freedom for Haiti in 1804, the first in the hemisphere. There was no war of independence in Brazil because the colonial government declared independence in 1822 after moving the Portuguese monarchy to Rio de Janeiro. With the exceptions of Cuba and Puerto Rico—two Caribbean possessions that Spain ruled until 1898—most of the Spanish colonies achieved their independence between 1810 and 1826. However, the elimination of two great colonial empires in the Western Hemisphere did not put an end to foreign domination. After independence, the weak and poorly governed Latin American countries faced a new form of colonialism as the region was opened up to public and private interests from the United States and Europe. The basic principle of "hands off" the Western Hemisphere, expressed in the Monroe Doctrine in 1823, was inspired by U.S. policymakers' perception of neocolonial economic pursuits and threats to U.S. security by the major European powers at the time.

On December 1, the day before President Monroe was scheduled to deliver his address, Adams handed the president a fifty-two-paragraph statement; however, only three paragraphs—buried deep within the speech—ultimately came to constitute the Monroe Doctrine. With the collapse of the Spanish Empire, President Monroe and his advisors worried—with some justification—about the possibility of a reversal of the independence movement in the Western Hemisphere by one, or several, European powers. In what would amount to an artificial separation of the world into "spheres of influence," and a warning "whisper" to the monarchies of Europe, the three operative phrases of the Monroe Doctrine occurred in the seventh, fiftieth, and fifty-first paragraphs of the address (see Appendix).

The first proposition (paragraph 7, the **noncolonization principle**) declared that the "American continents, by the free and independent condition which they have assumed and maintain, are henceforth not to be considered as subjects for future colonization by any European powers." The second proposition (paragraph 50, the **warning against European meddling**), and the heart of the doctrine, stated that "We owe it, therefore, to candor and to the amicable relations existing between the United States and those powers to declare that we should consider any attempt on their part to extend their system to any portion of this hemisphere as dangerous to our peace and safety." The third proposition (paragraph 51, the **noninterference—or isolation—principle**) in the original message emphasized that "Our policy in regard to Europe, which was adopted at an early stage of the wars which have so long agitated that quarter of the globe, nevertheless remains the same, which is, not to interfere in the internal concerns of any of its powers."[3] The perceived threats from Europe in 1823 were greatly exaggerated by Americans at the time, but Monroe's message ultimately became operational policy for those who chose to assign their own meaning to the spirit of 1823. "We must admit," according to Dexter Perkins, "that the message of 1823 was directed against an imaginary menace.

Not one of the Continental powers cherished any designs of reconquest in the New World in November or December of 1823."[4]

From President Monroe's message in 1823 came the nation's first, and historically most significant, presidential doctrine, one that would give Monroe a kind of political immortality that no other American president has acquired. As Humes points out, "No president, not even the venerable Washington, the learned Jefferson, or the saintly Lincoln, has a national sacred dogma attached to his name."[5] In many ways it was not even a Latin American policy, because it emphasized European relations and the proper role of the United States in dealing with the monarchies of the time. It contained neither a diplomatic accord nor an international legal foundation, but it grew into one of the most powerful symbols ever created to lend authority to a wide variety of foreign policy positions. Over the years it acquired a mythic grandeur that stretched far beyond what the crafters of the original message had envisioned. The Monroe Doctrine continues to generate interest as an important subject of investigation. As of 1998 the Library of Congress listed over 425 works devoted to the Monroe Doctrine, a number that far exceeds that devoted to any other presidential doctrine in the history of U.S. foreign policy.

A Critical Analysis

Monroe delivered his address in writing and with little fanfare and enthusiasm, unlike Theodore Roosevelt and other U.S. presidents who have used the "bully pulpit" of the presidency, a term referring to a forceful style of speaking from a platform. Once it became known as the Monroe Doctrine in the 1840s its flaws as a policy regarding Latin America soon were revealed, although this did not detract from the popularity of the message at home and abroad. The Monroe Doctrine's five basic flaws were either the result of faulty assumptions inherent in the message or the result of the way in which top officials used the doctrine to justify their actions and soothe the concerns of the American public about things strategic and political in Latin America.

A Unilateral Doctrine

The Monroe Doctrine was a unilateral pronouncement of foreign policy principles designed to conform to the interests of the United States in a hemisphere it hardly understood. There was no consultation with the newly independent states in the Americas while it was being drawn up, and no effort to obtain their cooperation in enforcing it throughout the Americas. The United States alone reserved the right to both interpret and implement it to best suit its own foreign policy interests. As G. Pope Atkins points out, "Unilateralism was indicated by the rejection of a prior British proposal for a joint declaration and by rebuffing subsequent Latin American suggestions for formal alliance against Europe."[6] Not until the 1930s did the United States agree to modify the Monroe Doctrine from a unilateral doctrine of U.S. policy to a basis for multilateral inter-American collective security. However, during the Cold War the United States resurrected the Monroe Doctrine and used it to justify numerous unilateral interventions. The times when North American presidents insisted on "go-it-alone" policies of intervention in defiance of the United Nations and the Organization of American States (OAS) revealed the depth of Monroeist sentiment in Washington.

A Doctrine Based on Limited Knowledge

The Monroe Doctrine was put forth during an era in which very few special agents had anything more than a rudimentary knowledge of Latin America and its people. Although Latin America was officially recognized as important to the United States as early as 1808, understanding of the Americas developed in a vacuum in which Washington policymakers based many of their decisions on little information and myopic visions of the people and international politics of the region. "It is a striking fact," says historian Arthur Whitaker, "that of the three men—James Monroe, John Quincy Adams, and Henry Clay—who were to play the leading roles in shaping American policy and opinion in the next decade [1815–1825], *not one possessed any special training or qualifications for the task*" (emphasis mine).[7] Monroe had a good reading and speaking knowledge of Spanish, but none of the three had ever set foot in Latin America. As the United States became more involved in, and assumed greater responsibility for, Latin America, information from special agents' reports and first-hand encounters increased, as did negative stereotypes. Historian John J. Johnson contends that "both our public and private dealings with the Latin American republics have resulted to a significant degree from widely accepted stereotyped negative images of their people, religion, and value systems."[8] These negative perceptions have been incredibly durable, often reinforced and transmitted by each successive generation on the basis of faulty cultural assumptions.

Once the Monroe Doctrine became established, those who found the spirit of Monroe useful did not worry about the need for or accuracy of information about Latin America. Indeed, even during the 1980s the ignorance about Central America among foreign policy bureaucrats in Washington was appalling. Much of what was decided about Central America was based on what had transpired in previous conflicts such as World War II and the Vietnam War. As Gaddis Smith points out,

> None of those in the [Reagan] administration who made high policy toward Central America knew very much about the region, nor did they consider such knowledge relevant or necessary. In that sense they

were true heirs to the original Monroe Doctrine. Never had policies developed in the doctrine's name been concerned with real Latin American conditions, but only as they were perceived as inviting or blocking extra-hemispheric intervention threatening the United States.[9]

The doctrine was rarely referred to during the Central American conflict of the 1980s and was not specifically invoked to justify the U.S. invasion of Grenada in 1983 or Panama in 1989. Once Mikhail Gorbachev helped to extricate the Soviet Union from the Western Hemisphere, starting in the late 1980s, and following the subsequent collapse and fragmentation of other extra-hemispheric threats, the Monroe Doctrine essentially ceased to exist. As spiritual heirs to the original pronouncement, policymakers in Washington formulated policies on the basis of faulty assumptions and inappropriate models drawn from other contexts, and often repeated the mistakes made by their predecessors. A common factor in these policy tragedies—some absurd and others disastrous in their consequences—was the general indifference to Latin American political and social reality.

What haunted Monroe's ghosts was not so much the symbols and history of U.S. involvement in Latin America; it was more the belief that Latin America didn't matter as long as foreign powers could be denied a strategic foothold within geographic proximity of the southern boundary of the United States. Over 30 major corollaries and interpretations have modified, extended, or reinforced Monroe's original message (see Table 1.1). The Monroe Doctrine also contributed to the belief in Washington that the United States could conduct a moral foreign policy in Latin America, based on the notion that using excessive power to force other countries to behave in a principled way for the sake of hemispheric security was noble. This has proven to be a dangerous assumption because U.S.-backed efforts to promote democracy, human rights, and social justice have often been accompanied by forceful measures to bolster security by expelling other foreign powers and ideas. At times this crusading moralism was counterproductive, with disastrous consequences for the conduct of foreign relations. There are limits to the pursuit of principled foreign policy, and misguided noble ideals can sometimes be a poor guide to foreign policy.

No Legal Foundation

Throughout its lifetime the Monroe Doctrine contained no legal basis for conducting a hemispheric policy. Efforts by Latin American governments to transform the doctrine into a binding inter-American commitment were rejected by the United States until well into the twentieth century. European governments dismissed the Monroe Doctrine as irrelevant and having no legal foundation, particularly during the nineteenth century when the United States lacked the power to enforce it. When the Monroe

Doctrine was violated—as during the British seizure of the Malvinas Islands in 1833, and during the French takeover of Mexico in the 1860s—the United States reacted like a helpless giant. In an effort to "detoxify" Monroe's message in preparation for the Good Neighbor Policy in 1928, State Department official J. Reuben Clark demonstrated that the Monroe Doctrine had no validity in international law. By the 1930s successive Inter-American Conferences weakened the Monroe Doctrine by winning the assent of other states in the hemisphere to form regional or multilateral security.

A Destructive Catchword

At first Latin American governments welcomed the Monroe Doctrine as a protective shield against European expansion in the Western Hemisphere. However, after the Mexican War (1846–1848) and the indifference of Washington to predatory *filibusteros* (private mercenaries or adventurers from the United States) that plagued Latin America in the 1850s and intermittently thereafter, most Latin American governments viewed the doctrine with intense hostility. For over a century and a half, interventionists (collective and unilateral) and isolationists (liberal and conservative) alike have invoked the Monroe Doctrine for a myriad of purposes, both domestic and foreign. Monroe's message served the needs of U.S. presidents, foreign investors, *filibusteros*, and others who needed a slogan to justify their actions. In Latin America and the Caribbean, the Monroe Doctrine was frequently criticized for its faulty assumptions and demeaning references to Latin Americans by top officials in Washington. However, it is important to note that opportunistic rulers (both democrats and dictators) in Latin America and the Caribbean also found the Monroe Doctrine useful for winning concessions from the United States.

Rationalization for U.S. Intervention

For over 150 years the Monroe Doctrine served as a rationalization for U.S. intervention and coercive diplomacy in dealing with Latin America. Although Monroe's original message was based on keeping Europe out of the Western Hemisphere, it said nothing about the United States keeping its own "hands off" the region. Acting on its own initiative, the United States constantly violated the sovereignty of independent nations in the name of its own national security or some other interest. Whenever policymakers in Washington determined that an extra-hemispheric power might intrude into Latin America, they claimed that the United States had the right, and moral duty, to carry out its own interventionary action. Between 1895 and 1930 the United States assumed the role of hemispheric policeman, imposing its control over Central America and the Caribbean in the name of peace, democracy, stability, and economic protection (see Table 1.2). The persistent efforts by Latin Americans to establish nonin-

Table 1.1
Monroe Doctrine Interpretations/Corollaries

Date	President	Secretary of State	Country/ Region	Interpretation (or Corollary)
1823	Monroe	Adams	Americas	No colonization of Americas by European powers
1825	Adams	Clay	Americas	No specific obligations
1826	Adams	Clay	Americas	Third-Power intervention
1828	Adams	Clay	Americas	No specific commitment
1845	Polk	Buchanan	Americas	No colonization in North America without U.S. consent
1848	Polk	Buchanan	Americas	No transfer of territory
1861	Lincoln	Seward	Mexico	No return to mother country of colony
1865	Lincoln	Seward	Mexico	No establishment of monarchy
1868				[Calvo Doctrine is established]
1870	Grant	Fish	Americas	No transfer of territory
1895	Cleveland	Olney	Venezuela	Olney declares the United States sovereign in the Western Hemisphere
1896				[Porfirio Díaz criticizes Olney Corollary]

Year	President	Secretary of State	Region	Event
1902	Roosevelt	Hay	Americas	[Drago Doctrine is established]
1904	Roosevelt	Hay	Dominican Republic	Chronic wrongdoing might lead to European intervention; "big stick" diplomacy inaugurated
1912	Taft	Knox	Mexico	Lodge Corollary declares no private foreign interests are allowed in Magdalena Bay, Baja California
1914	Wilson	Bryan	Americas	Attempts to multilateralize the Monroe Doctrine
1914	Wilson	Bryan	Americas	Recognition: unilateral interpretation and intervention
1920	Wilson	Colby	Americas	Regional understanding of United States (Article 21 of League of Nations Covenant)
1923	Coolidge	Hughes	Panama	Unilateral interpretation; no foreign interests near Canal
1928	Coolidge	Kellogg	Americas	Clark memo attempts to repudiate Roosevelt Corollary to the Monroe Doctrine
1928				[Sandino calls for abolition of Monroe Doctrine]
1933	Roosevelt	Hull	Americas	Good Neighbor Policy is enunciated
1933	Roosevelt	Hull	Americas	Collective efforts to establish a regional defense system

Table 1.1 (continued)
Monroe Doctrine Interpretations/Corollaries

Date	President	Secretary of State	Country/Region	Interpretation (or Corollary)
1936	Roosevelt	Hull	Americas	Multilateral issues of common concern to American states
1945	Truman	Byrnes	Americas	Collective intervention; Rodriguez Larretta Doctrine; Braden Corollary to the Good Neighbor Policy
1950	Truman	Byrnes	Americas	Kennan Corollary justifies harsh methods of rule to repel communist attacks in the hemisphere
1954	Eisenhower	Dulles	Guatemala	Leftist Arbenz regime is seen as threat to Monroe Doctrine
1961	Kennedy	Rusk	Cuba	Collective responsibility, but United States may take unilateral actions if Latin America defaults
1962	Kennedy	Rusk	Americas	Spirit is invoked to gain hemispheric/OAS support during Cuban missile crisis
1965	Johnson	Rusk	Dominican Republic	Spirit of Monroe Doctrine is invoked to prevent "second Cuba" in the Caribbean
1970	Nixon	Rogers	Chile	Spirit is invoked to justify destabilization of Chilean government

10

1977	Carter	Vance	Americas	Carter tries to repudiate Kennan Corollary to Monroe Doctrine in a speech declaring our fear of communism is over
1982	Reagan	Haig	Falklands Islands	Supporters of Argentine position during the war bring up Monroe Doctrine
1983	Reagan	Shultz	Grenada	Spirit is invoked to remove Cuban influence on the island
1984	Reagan	Shultz	Central America	Spirit is invoked to remove communist influences from Central America in the Contra wars against Nicaragua
1987	Reagan	Shultz	Nicaragua	Reagan invokes Monroe Doctrine in State of Union address to justify his Nicaragua policy
1993	Clinton	Christopher	Cuba	Monroe Doctrine "dies" when Soviet brigade leaves Cuba

Prepared with the assistance of Larman C. Wilson.

Table 1.2
Levels of U.S. Involvement in Latin America

Country	Nineteenth Century	Twentieth Century	Incidents of Military Intervention Since 1823
Argentina	Low	Medium	2
Brazil	Low	Medium	1
Bolivia	Low	Medium	2
Chile	Medium	Medium	2
Colombia	Medium	Medium	8
Costa Rica	Low	Medium	0
Cuba	High	High	12
Dom. Republic	High	High	8
Ecuador	Low	Low-Medium	1
El Salvador	Low	Medium-High	2
Grenada	Low	Medium	1
Guatemala	Low	High	1
Guyana	Low	Medium	0
Haiti	Medium	High	8
Honduras	Low	Medium-High	4

Jamaica	Low	Medium	0
Mexico	High	High	15
Nicaragua	High	High	18
Panama	High	High	23
Peru	Medium	Medium-High	2
Paraguay	Low	Medium	1
Trinidad	Low	Medium	0
Uruguay	Low	Medium	0
Venezuela	Low	Medium	0

Note: **Levels of involvement**--high, medium, and low--represent a more encompassing measure of intervention than the column listing specific incidents of military intervention. In this broader measure, involvement includes such acts as economic sanctions or pressures applied to international lending agencies such as the International Monetary Fund (IMF), drug policy certification, building political institutions in the name of democracy, supplying proxy armies to engage in anticommunist subversion, diplomatic non-recognition, covert intervention to change unacceptable political leaders or to determine the outcome of elections, coercing treaty rights to authorize military intervention or other forms of involvement, and armed intervention that is either unilateral or by invitation by the host government in Latin America or the Caribbean. A *low* level of involvement represents a general absence of armed military intervention and other forms of intervention. Low levels of involvement are generally associated with South America and English-speaking Caribbean countries during the nineteenth century. *High* levels of involvement are generally associated with close geographical proximity to the United States or the Panama Canal, combined with frequent usage of Monroe Doctrine rhetoric. *Medium* levels of involvement usually include a mixture of both military intervention and other forms of involvement in the internal affairs of the country. With only a few exceptions, medium levels of involvement are associated with South American and English-speaking Caribbean countries during the twentieth century, particularly during times of war (including the Cold War).

tervention as an international legal principle were rebuffed by the United States until the 1930s.

MONROE'S GHOSTS: THE EVOLUTION OF A LATIN AMERICAN POLICY

By the last decade of the nineteenth century, the United States had gotten the British to defer to the Monroe Doctrine during the first Venezuelan crisis (1895) and had driven Spain out of the Caribbean during the Cuban-Spanish-American War (1898). For the next twenty years policymakers in Washington viewed Germany as the major threat to the hemisphere. This was an era known for protective imperialism; it was a time when the United States, under three presidents (Roosevelt, Taft, and Wilson), put teeth in the Monroe Doctrine to help solidify U.S. influence over the Americas. The United States was no longer the smug protector of the status quo in the Caribbean, as it had been during most of the nineteenth century; it was now time to assume the role of a full-fledged imperial power. After the second Venezuelan crisis (1902–1903) there was no serious German challenge to the United States in the Caribbean. Nevertheless the image of a predatory Germany persisted, and top officials in Washington soon realized that they could capitalize on the fear of Germany to assert U.S. dominance in the region. The United States took control over Cuba, Puerto Rico, Panama, Haiti, and the Virgin Islands, and it made repeated interventions in the Dominican Republic and throughout Central America. By the 1920s the Monroe Doctrine was a battered instrument of U.S. Latin American policy, but for those in Washington in charge of Caribbean policy it had served as potent medicine to administer to Germans and others lurking in the United States' "backyard." It facilitated pro-American regimes that accommodated U.S. economic interests, and it eliminated an assortment of rebels who wanted greater control over their own political destiny. It provided the excitement of a foreign policy based on bravado and fear; however, the instruments of control and domination were altered after 1930, and the residue of resentment in Latin America would haunt Monroe's ghosts for generations. In the 1920s the Monroe Doctrine was cited by those who opposed the League of Nations, as it was by those who supported the United Nations years later.

The Monroe Doctrine was "rediscovered" during the Cold War era and was put to use by U.S. presidents worried about the expansionist goals of the Soviet Union and Cuba. President Eisenhower and his top advisors made generous use of the Monroe Doctrine when Guatemala became the target of a CIA plan to overthrow President Jacobo Arbenz in 1954. John Peurifoy, the U.S. ambassador who played a key role in the removal of Arbenz, declared later that "In proving that communism can be defeated,

Lest We Forget...

we relied on the traditional American principle of honesty in the conduct of foreign affairs and the American doctrine of continental liberty from despotic intervention, first enunciated by President Monroe 131 years ago."[10] However, this was not the kind of candor Monroe had had in mind, and it contributed to criticism of the United States after 1954. Secretary of State John Foster Dulles called the Guatemala intervention a "glorious victory." Years later this statement prompted the following criticism from Mexican author Carlos Fuentes:[11]

A "glorious victory" for what? For the unilaterally proclaimed Monroe Doctrine—this Monroe Doctrine that periodically and conveniently pops out of the ghost closet of the U.S. government until it meets . . . the Brezhnev Doctrine; this Monroe Doctrine that would ban extracontinental interventions in this hemisphere but not extracontinental interventions by the United States in other hemispheres and most assuredly not in this one, its backyard, its most immediate sphere of influence, Latin America; this Monroe Doctrine that ironically and conveniently forgets that if a Monroe Doctrine had been in effect in 1776, the United States would not exist.

Members of Congress cited the Monroe Doctrine as justification for undermining the Cuban Revolution in 1960. In the 1960s liberals cited the Monroe Doctrine to improve U.S.–Latin American relations and to advance President Kennedy's Alliance for Progress (a massive assistance program designed to improve Latin America economically and politically while at the same time thwarting Castro's revolution in Cuba). In the 1980s President Reagan and his conservative followers used the Monroe Doctrine to support the president's anti-Sandinista campaign in Nicaragua and U.S. policy in El Salvador. In his State of the Union address in January 1987, President Reagan tried to build bipartisan support at home by saying, "Our commitment to a Western Hemisphere safe from aggression [from abroad] did not occur by spontaneous generation on the day we took office. It began with the Monroe Doctrine."[12]

As a founding myth of the United States, the Monroe Doctrine spawned generation after generation of policymakers who relied on Monroe's message to formulate a policy toward Latin America. With the end of the Cold War, the Monroe Doctrine is no longer a guiding principle of American foreign policy, yet its spirit remains embodied in the legacies of U.S. involvement in the Americas.

NOTES

1. Cole Blasier, *The Giant's Rival: The USSR and Latin America*, rev. ed. (Pittsburgh: University of Pittsburgh Press, 1987), p. 184.

2. James C. Humes, *My Fellow Americans: Presidential Addresses That Shaped History* (New York: Praeger, 1992), p. 33.

3. Ibid., pp. 35–36; Donald Marquand Dozer, *The Monroe Doctrine: Its Modern Significance* (New York: Alfred A. Knopf, 1965), pp. 3–7.

4. Dexter Perkins, *A History of the Monroe Doctrine*, rev. ed. (Boston: Little, Brown, 1963), p. 50.

5. Humes, *My Fellow Americans*, p. 36.

6. G. Pope Atkins, *Encyclopedia of the Inter-American System* (Westport, CT: Greenwood Press, 1997), p. 340.

7. Arthur Preston Whitaker, *The United States and the Independence of Latin America, 1800–1830* (New York: Russell & Russell, 1962), p. 147. Emphasis mine.

8. John J. Johnson, *Latin America in Caricature* (Austin: University of Texas Press, 1980), p. 9.

9. Gaddis Smith, *The Last Years of the Monroe Doctrine: 1945–1993* (New York: Hill and Wang, 1994), p. 188.

10. Gaddis Smith, "Monroe Doctrine," in Bruce W. Jentleson and Thomas G. Paterson, eds., *Encyclopedia of U.S. Foreign Relations*, vol. 3 (New York: Oxford University Press, 1997), p. 164.

11. Carlos Fuentes, "Three Dates of Change in Latin America," *Harpers* (August 1980), p. 29.

12. *Public Papers of the Presidents of the United States: Ronald Reagan, 1987* (Washington, DC: U.S. Government Printing Office, 1989), Vol. 1, p. 57.

SUGGESTED READINGS

Atkins, G. Pope. *Encyclopedia of the Inter-American System*. Westport, CT: Greenwood Press, 1997.

———. *Latin America in the International Political System*, 4th Edition. Boulder, CO: Westview Press, 1998.

Cockcroft, James D. *Latin America: History, Politics, and U.S. Policy*, 2nd Edition. Chicago: Nelson-Hall Publishers, 1996.

Jentleson, Bruce W., and Thomas G. Paterson, eds. *Encyclopedia of U.S. Foreign Relations*, 4 vols. New York: Oxford University Press, 1997.

Kryzanek, Michael J. *U.S.-Latin American Relations*, 3rd Edition. Westport, CT: Praeger, 1996.

Schoultz, Lars. *Beneath the United States: A History of U.S. Policy Toward Latin America*. Cambridge, MA: Harvard University Press, 1998.

Shavit, David. *The United States in Latin America*. Westport, CT: Greenwood Press, 1992.

Smith, Gaddis. *The Last Years of the Monroe Doctrine: 1945–1993*. New York: Hill and Wang, 1994.

Wilson, Larman C., and David W. Dent. *Historical Dictionary of Inter-American Organizations*. Lanham, MD: Scarecrow Press, 1998.

2

Argentina

TIMELINE OF U.S. RELATIONS WITH ARGENTINA

1816	Argentina declares independence from Spain
1822	U.S. diplomatic relations are established
1831	U.S. naval vessels clash with Argentina over Falkland/Malvinas Islands
1833	British capture Malvinas/Falkland Islands
1845–1848	Joint French-British blockade of Buenos Aires
1864–1870	Triple Alliance War
1940–1945	Argentina refuses to declare war on Axis powers until end of World War II
1946	U.S. ambassador Spruille Braden publishes "Blue Book on Argentina"
1946–1955	Juan D. Perón serves two terms as president
1955	Perón is overthrown by the military
1962	Arturo Frondizi is ousted in military coup
1965	Argentina supports U.S. invasion of Dominican Republic
1973	Perón returns to Argentina
1974	Perón wins presidency but dies in same year; Isabel Perón, his widow and vice-president, replaces him
1976	Isabel Perón is overthrown by the military
1976–1982	Dirty War results in thousands of deaths during military dictatorship
1978	President Carter criticizes Argentina for human rights abuses
1981	Argentine military assists with Contra training

1982	Falklands/Malvinas War results in 3,115 killed and wounded
1983	Raúl Alfonsín is elected president
1989	Carlos S. Menem (Peronist) is elected president
1991	Argentina supports Persian Gulf War
1995	Menem is reelected president for second term
1997	President Clinton visits Argentina as part of his trip to South America to promote free markets and democracy

INTRODUCTION

In general, Argentina and the United States experienced cordial relations throughout the nineteenth century. The main exceptions to this pattern were the unwillingness of the United States to apply the Monroe Doctrine to keep Europeans out of the Río de la Plata (River Plate) region and the British seizure of the Falkland/Malvinas Islands in 1833. However, no country in South America caused Washington as much torment as Argentina during most of the twentieth century, when the two countries sparred over trade preferences and market access, Pan-Americanism, Argentine neutrality during times of war, U.S. intervention, and definitions of regional security. Argentine foreign relations reveal a century-old tradition of uniqueness and prominence in world affairs that presumes and accepts confrontation with the United States. This tradition is no longer valid, but it continues to influence the world view held by Argentines and their leaders.

U.S.-Argentine relations have also been influenced by geography and history: Buenos Aires is roughly the same distance from New York as New York is from Moscow, and Argentina's capital of 12 million is not on the average American's path to anywhere. Given its distant location, low level of trade and investment, and close ties to Europe, Argentina realized early on that it was unrealistic to expect protection from the United States. Moreover, there is a pervasive French, Italian, Spanish (Iberian), and German influence that has contributed to a disdain for American democracy and culture in Argentina, although there have been times at which political leaders expressed admiration for all things American. Argentina refused to take sides during both world wars, expressed sympathy for Nazi ideology and Germany, and consistently opposed U.S. initiatives during Pan-American meetings.

During the Cold War, Argentina resisted U.S. efforts to introduce anti-communism into the inter-American system and in bilateral relations with leftist governments. For example, Argentina opposed the diplomatic and covert military attacks on Guatemala in 1954, the trade and diplomatic embargo of Cuba after 1959, Carter's boycott of the 1980 Olympics in Moscow, and U.S. hostility toward Nicaragua during the Sandinista era. In terms of power politics, Argentina often sought its own regional influence and felt no need to join any system of security protection from the United States. After a while it became obvious to Argentine leaders that the Monroeist principles of noncolonization and nonintervention, which they had originally endorsed, would not reach Buenos Aires—or at least would have little applicability in such a distant location.

ARGENTINA AND THE UNITED STATES IN THE NINETEENTH CENTURY

The United States and Argentine Independence

The difficulties that Argentina experienced during its first century of independence were typical of those experienced by other new states in the Western Hemisphere: boundary disputes, the danger of foreign intervention, the personal ambitions of caudillos or military dictators, and interstate frictions that were likely to lead to armed conflicts. In order to formulate more effective Latin American policies, President Monroe felt he needed to know more about the capacity and willingness of the South Americans to establish and maintain an independent form of government. He reasoned that this information would establish the basis for recognizing Argentina's legitimacy, and the best way to keep it from falling into the hands of a European monarchy.

To impress the United Provinces of the River Plate (Argentina's official name at the time) with U.S. friendship and interest in their struggle for independence, Monroe sent the South American Commission (1817–1818) to gather information on the political status of the newly independent republics located in southern South America (Southern Cone). The diplomatic reports expressed different perspectives—some positive, some negative—on the political situation but were not persuasive enough to convince the Monroe administration to offer formal diplomatic recognition. This brand of cautionary diplomacy displeased the Argentines and made future bilateral relations more difficult to achieve.

Argentina and the Monroe Doctrine

The independence (1816) and recognition of Argentina had little to do with the deliberations that led to President Monroe's message to Congress in late 1823 spelling out the principles that would later come to be known as the Monroe Doctrine. With recognition in 1822 and the promises put forth in the Monroe Doctrine, Argentina looked favorably at the Latin American policy of the United States, expecting to benefit from the principles of noncolonization and nonintervention. After the euphoria that accompanied Argentina's early reactions to Monroe's address, Argentine leaders grew repeatedly disappointed by the refusal of the United States to invoke the Monroe Doctrine when clear violations occurred.

There were three occasions between 1823 and 1850 on which the Argentine leaders expected the United States to invoke the Monroe Doctrine to protest European (British and French) intervention and occupation in the Río de la Plata (River Plate, in English) region. The first occurred between 1825 and 1828 when the Argentine government tried to invoke the principles of Monroe in their conflict with Brazil over the status of Uruguay. Secretary of State Henry Clay refused President Bernardo Rivadavia's request, claiming that the United States wished to remain neutral and, furthermore, that Monroe's principles did not seem to apply to the case. The second episode occurred between 1831 and 1833 and concerned the Falkland/Malvinas Islands (see below). Finally, the United States did nothing to prevent the British from occupying the islands and claiming sovereignty in 1833 in clear violation of the Monroe Doctrine. During the rule of Juan Manuel de Rosas in the 1840s, Argentina faced several interventions by France and Great Britain in La Plata Estuary that did not end until Rosas signed an agreement with the European powers in 1850. Rosas had no luck in convincing the Polk administration that Anglo-French intervention in the Río de la Plata threatened the peace and security of the hemisphere and that the acceptance of the principle of nonintervention required U.S. action. Polk was more interested in moving the United States westward under the banner of Manifest Destiny (a belief in the superiority of the United States that often justified territorial expansion) than in forcing a showdown over such a faraway place as Argentina. In his annual message to Congress in 1845, President Polk said he was willing to apply the Monroe Doctrine only to North America.

The Falklands/Malvinas Crisis, 1831–1833

The Falkland Islands (the Argentines call them Las Islas Malvinas) have been the source of conflict between the United States and Argentina on two occasions. In both cases the United States sided with Great Britain. The first U.S. dispute with Argentina over the Falkland Islands developed in 1831 when the Argentine governor captured three U.S. vessels and charged them with illegal seal hunting. In retaliation, the commanding officer of the USS *Lexington* landed a small force, raided and looted the islands, and then brought the governor and most of his men as prisoners to Montevideo. This naval bluster led the Argentines to sever diplomatic relations with the United States and gave the British the opportunity, without objection from the Jackson administration, to establish their own colony. In January 1833 the British flag went up to signal the newly acquired sovereignty. Though the Argentines protested both the U.S. intervention and the British occupation, the United States refused to consider the British acquisition of territory a violation of the noncolonization principle of the Monroe Doctrine. The inability to resolve conflicting claims of sovereignty would lead to a major war between Argentina and Britain that lasted for twenty-five days in 1982.

Between 1862 and 1916, Argentina experienced dramatic economic growth and modernization as a major producer of beef and grains. Power rested in the hands of a small group of wealthy farmers and merchants who were often at odds with U.S. foreign policy. By 1910 Argentina had become a powerful agricultural nation, which contributed in part to its exaggerated claims of national superiority. Some Argentines went so far as to predict that Argentina would surpass the level of material accomplishment of the United States; others envisioned a destiny that would result in Argentina becoming the "colossus" of the Southern Hemisphere and, thus, having no need for civilizing instruction from the United States. Argentina soon became a major player in the world economy, but many differences existed between the United States and Argentina that would subsequently cause friction in the twentieth century.

The Triple Alliance War, 1865–1870

The Triple Alliance War (sometimes referred to as the Paraguayan War) was one of the bloodiest in the history of the Western Hemisphere. It involved three South American countries—Brazil, Argentina, and Uruguay—against Paraguay. After Paraguayan dictator Francisco Solano López declared war against Brazil in 1864—ostensibly to forestall a Brazilian takeover of Uruguay—Brazil, Argentina, and Uruguay signed a secret pact (backed by British bankers) to carry on the war against López until his downfall (see Chapter 21). In 1866 Secretary of State William Seward tried to mediate an end to the war, but his offer was turned down. The U.S. minister in Rio de Janeiro, James W. Webb, had insisted that Latin Americans had a duty to seek protection and advice from the United States, which had the right to intervene in all international conflicts in the Western Hemisphere. Webb's assertive arguments for the "moral protection" principle of the Monroe Doctrine were not well received because no South American government agreed with Webb's assumptions.

Opposition to U.S. Intervention I: The Calvo Clause

In an effort to create legal blocks to U.S. and European intervention in the hemisphere, Argentine jurists asserted the leadership among Latin American states to prevent foreign intervention and loss of national sovereignty. In 1868 jurist Carlos Calvo proposed to revise international law to prevent North American and European powers from intervening and to ensure that civilized levels of justice would be administered to their nationals. Calvo's doctrine was in direct response to the North American belief that the Latin Americans were too primitive to correctly administer justice to resident aliens (primarily investors) in their countries. Calvo's Clause stated that "*Under no circumstances* does the resident alien enjoy the right to have his own government interpose in his behalf. Not even a denial of justice could warrant intervention, for it would convey a privileged status to aliens not enjoyed by the nationals."[1] Many Latin American countries have used Calvo's Clause in contracts with international corporations; however, the principle has been widely rejected outside of Latin America, including in the United States.

ARGENTINA AND THE UNITED STATES DURING THE EARLY TWENTIETH CENTURY

Opposition to U.S. Intervention II: The Drago Doctrine

After the European blockade and bombardment of Venezuela in 1902 (see Chapter 25), Argentine foreign minister Luis M. Drago put forth the international principle "that the public debt cannot occasion armed intervention nor even the actual occupation of the territory of American nations by a European power." Such a situation (territorial occupation), he declared, seems "obviously at variance" with the principles of the Monroe Doctrine, "sustained and defended with so much zeal . . . by the United States, [and] a doctrine to which the Argentine Republic has heretofore solemnly adhered."[2] Drago's diplomatic note contributed to the Roosevelt Corollary to the Monroe Doctrine, a significantly revised interpretation in which the United States decided it would exclude European intervention in the Caribbean by intervening itself. The Drago Doctrine received wide support throughout Latin America; at the Second Hague Peace Conference in 1907 it was accepted after the United States managed to tone down the anti-interventionist language in the proposal. At the Pan-American Conference in Buenos Aires in 1936, after the United States gave up its interventionist policies, the Drago Doctrine was adopted as a fundamental principle for the Americas. As an economic corollary to the Monroe Doctrine, it represented an Argentine effort to curb the growing power of the United States, precisely at the time when the greatest amount of intervention in the Caribbean Basin and Central America was taking place.

The United States and Argentina during World War I

At the start of World War I, President Wilson tried to convert the Monroe Doctrine from a unilateral policy of the United States into a multilateral Pan-American treaty under which all member states would settle their internal differences by peaceful means. Of the three ABC powers (Argentina,

Brazil, and Chile) that Wilson tried to convince of the importance of converting the Monroe Doctrine, Argentina was the most enthusiastic, but the crisis of war in Europe and Chile's reluctance doomed the proposal. After the war, President Wilson again tried to implement his idea of a mutual guarantee of independence of territorial integrity to his Fourteen Points speech (a plan for peace after World War I) and in the Covenant of the League of Nations. Wilson's failure was clearly associated with the difficulties in justifying military intervention in the name of the Monroe Doctrine.

Argentina and the Good Neighbor Policy

The economic and strategic need for intervention declined after World War I as Britain, France, and Germany lost much of their capability for economic expansion abroad, and no existing naval power threatened the security of the Panama Canal. By the beginning of the Good Neighbor Policy under President Hoover, there was little need for intervention to prohibit European financial investment in Latin America and the Caribbean. Nevertheless, the three Republican administrations that followed Woodrow Wilson began to worry about how decades of intervention and exploitation might affect the growing economic nationalism in Latin America. After years of military intervention and occupation, the American public had grown weary of references to the Monroe Doctrine as justification for policing the Western Hemisphere. Anti-imperialists in the United States criticized the economic exploitation of the region and demanded the rejection of the Monroe Doctrine. At the fifth Pan-American Conference held in Havana, Cuba, in 1928, the Argentine representative delivered a blistering attack on the United States and the Monroe Doctrine, a clear sign of the poor state of inter-American relations.

Between 1923 and the inauguration of Franklin D. Roosevelt in 1933, Republican diplomats made efforts to remove the Monroe Doctrine's corollaries that had contributed to the negative reactions to intervention in Latin America. As chairman of the Senate Foreign Relations Committee in 1923, Henry Cabot Lodge was given the task of speaking on the meaning of the Monroe Doctrine after one hundred years as a bedrock principle of American foreign policy. As a lifelong Republican, a friend of Theodore Roosevelt, and an advocate of a forceful foreign policy, Lodge proclaimed that the Monroe Doctrine "is no more to be disturbed or questioned or interpreted by other nations than [is] the independence of the United States."[3] Although the U.S. Senate tried to preserve the Monroe Doctrine after World War I, the State Department in the 1920s and the Roosevelt administration in the 1930s called for a thorough reexamination of the principles of Monroeism, beginning with the Clark Memorandum of 1928. The so-called Clark Memorandum was the result of an internal analysis of the history of the Monroe Doctrine written by Under Secretary J. Reuben Clark at the direction of Secretary of State Frank Kellogg. This remarkable policy reevaluation stated that the Roosevelt Corollary was not a legitimate part of the original doctrine and that Monroe's message had been formulated in terms of the United States versus Europe, not the United States versus Latin America. President Herbert Hoover accepted the report, but it was not made public until 1930. Nevertheless, aspects of intervention remained despite the rhetoric applied to hemispheric nonintervention, and the Good Neighbor Policy did not take form until Franklin D. Roosevelt assumed office in 1933. Although at the time of the Clark Memorandum there was not much security threat to the United States or Latin America, the policy statement represented a move toward nonintervention and helped make the case for the withdrawal of U.S. armed forces from Nicaragua, Haiti, and the Dominican Republic.

The United States and Argentina during World War II

Prior to World War II, Argentina was convinced that its future was more closely linked to Europe than to the United States. During this period Argentina was governed by a conservative military government that expressed open admiration for Germany and Italy and resisted U.S. efforts at hemispheric solidarity against the coalition of fascist states (Axis powers) that lost World War II. Argentina's refusal to break completely with Germany until the end of World War II would serve as a backdrop to the major feud that arose with the United States during 1945–1946. At the Chapultepec Conference in Mexico City in early 1945, which was designed to strengthen the inter-American system and address the Argentine problem, the Argentine government accepted the invitation to rejoin the American community of nations, declared war against the Axis powers (March 27, 1945), and agreed to adhere to the provisions mapped out in the Act of Chapultepec. By calling for common action against an aggressor from outside or inside the Western Hemisphere, the Act of Chapultepec expanded the Monroe Doctrine's unilateral guarantee against outside intervention in the Americas into a mutual (or collective) security system. It also made it possible for Argentina to be admitted to the San Francisco Conference and thus become a charter member of the United Nations. Although Argentina's admission to the United Nations marked a return to some degree of normalcy in Argentine-American relations, it wasn't long before diplomatic hostilities broke out again.

Diplomatic Dilemmas: Braden versus Perón

U.S. ambassador Spruille Braden's feud with Argentine president Juan Perón went through several stages between 1945 and 1946. Braden had considerable experience in Latin American affairs, both as a businessman and as a diplomat, but his views on the meaning of intervention and sovereignty and his abrasive and outspoken diplomatic style inhibited efforts to achieve hemispheric solidarity. During a four-month period as ambassador to Argentina in 1945, Braden publicly attacked Perón for not expelling Axis-controlled firms from the country and preventing Argentina's return to constitutionalism. In retaliation, Perón branded Braden as another agent of North American imperialism. Meanwhile, personnel changes in the State Department in Washington paved the way for Braden's rise to the position of assistant secretary of state for Latin American affairs. The conflict between Braden and Perón did not end with his transfer to Washington; Braden continued his war against Perón and Argentine fascism with long-distance public attacks and other forms of persuasion.

Several months after assuming his State Department post, Braden circulated a State Department manuscript—"Blue Book on Argentina"—that denounced Argentine links to the Nazis during World War II. The "Blue Book" not only failed to undermine Perón's electoral success but it severely damaged Argentine-American relations and the Good Neighbor Policy. While Braden continued his public statements attacking the Argentine government, his "Blue Book" became a symbol of Yankee arrogance, and throughout Latin America the U.S. policy toward Argentina was condemned as a return to the era of intervention.

The long feud with Argentina did not end until 1947, when General George C. Marshall replaced James F. Byrnes and Spruille Braden resigned, thus terminating the years of "get-tough" policies toward Buenos Aires. Braden retired from public life but during the Cold War became an uncompromising anticommunist. He became a founder of the anticommunist John Birch Society and served as public relations director for the United Fruit Company during the time when it was engaged in the overthrow of the democratically elected reformist Jacobo Arbenz in Guatemala (see Chapter 13). In his book *Diplomats and Demagogues* (1971), Braden called President Kennedy's pledge not to invade Cuba during the missile crisis of 1962 a clear defeat of the Monroe Doctrine.

ARGENTINA AND THE UNITED STATES DURING THE COLD WAR

The Perón Era, 1946–1955

During his first term in office (1946–1952), Juan Perón maintained a neutral "third position" in the Cold War, a stance that policymakers in Washington found aggravating. Shortly after his inauguration, Perón—a professed anticommunist—established diplomatic relations with the Soviet Union. These continued throughout the Cold War. However, Perón did little to promote Argentine-Soviet relations until economic difficulties arose in 1953. Perón's economic nationalism angered the foreign business community during this first term, but in his second term he reversed his stand and welcomed investments by Standard Oil of New Jersey, Kaiser, and others. U.S. relations with Argentina improved until his second term ended in a military coup in 1955. By the time the United States had established its containment doctrine in dealing with world communism in the late 1940s, the regionalist policymakers in Washington were gone and Latin America's economic development became secondary to U.S. security in the Western Hemisphere.

Argentina and the Alliance for Progress

Latin American governments were unsuccessful in obtaining a "Marshall Plan for Latin America" after World War II because, according to Secretary of State George Marshall, U.S. funds were scarce and the security threat in Europe was considerably greater than in Latin America. President Kennedy's Alliance for Progress was launched in March 1961. It was a long-term economic assistance program designed to promote economic growth, social modernization, and political democratization. Arturo Frondizi, elected president of Argentina in 1958, became one of the strongest supporters of the Alliance for Progress and in return was aided by the United States. However, Frondizi upset the United States and the Argentine military by maintaining relations with Castro's Cuba and by offering his services to mediate the growing differences between Cuba and the United States. Frondizi's diplomatic tightrope was designed to accomplish two things for Argentina: (1) by serving as mediator between the United States and Cuba, he could demonstrate Argentine independence in world affairs; and (2) by steering a middle path, he could also calm nationalists—in the military, in the labor movement, and within his own political party—who feared Castro's revolutionary policies. However, pressure from the United States and his own military forced him to break relations with Cuba in February 1962 and caused his removal from office by the military two months later. During the Cold War, democratic regimes were important to the United States, but only if they adopted anticommunist rhetoric and expressed opposition to Castro's Cuba.

In the decade preceding the military coup of March 1976, Argentina faced cyclical economic crises, weak and quasi-legitimate governments, and public cynicism regarding the effectiveness of Argentine democracy. The military overthrew the elected government in 1966 and imposed an authoritarian regime headed by General Juan Carlos Onganía. In what was referred to as the Argentine Revolution, the military tried to implement a state-led development strategy emphasizing economic self-reliance and other economic measures to solve Argentina's development problems.

However, economic development policies eventually provoked popular protests among civilian opposition groups, revolutionary guerrilla groups, and the export-dependent business community. The turmoil from the military's "revolution" paved the way for the return of the aging dictator Juan D. Perón and his sweeping electoral victory in 1973. When Perón died in 1974, his wife, Isabel, assumed the presidency from her position as vice-president; but her lackluster performance contributed to her removal from the presidency in March 1976.

The "Dirty War," 1976–1982

In 1976 the Argentine military stepped in once again, and a new cycle of militarism and brutal dictatorship was launched, replete with death squads and torture centers. In what became known as the Dirty War, the military declared and waged a war against politicians and "subversives" that left thousands dead or "disappeared" by the early 1980s. The key military figure in the 1976 coup and the repression that followed was General Jorge Rafael Videla, a close associate of General Pinochet in Chile and Honduran general Gustavo Álvarez Martínez. Videla justified the coup on grounds of civilian corruption, deceit, and treason; in public statements he promised to restore law, order, stability, and social discipline. In what the military called a war against subversion and terrorism, persons suspected of leftist views or "subversive" acts were arrested, tortured, kidnapped, killed, or "disappeared." One year after Videla's coup, Amnesty International estimated that 15,000 people had disappeared and that many were being held in secret detention camps. Some victims of military and police brutality reported that secret detention centers displayed swastikas and photographs of Hitler, Mussolini, and Franco, fascists from previous wars who were admired by the military government.

At first, policymakers in Washington welcomed the military takeover. Ambassador Robert Hill looked favorably on what had happened and claims that U.S. secretary of state Henry Kissinger told the coup leaders to proceed with their dirty war.[4] Ambassador Hill later became disturbed at the extent of the brutality and human rights violations of the military in Argentina, despite the fact that he had helped plan the removal of Arbenz from power in Guatemala in 1954, an event that led to over three decades of a similar "dirty war" in Central America.

The Carter Administration and Human Rights

By the time Jimmy Carter arrived in Washington in 1977, most of Latin America was a graveyard of democracies and the U.S. Congress had passed legislation requiring human rights considerations before granting foreign aid. President Carter's human rights–based Latin American policy was influenced by the work of the Commission on United States–Latin American Relations, a group of prominent business and academic leaders concerned about reordering relationships in the hemisphere. Published in 1975, the report—*The Americas in a Changing World*—provided a comprehensive critique of U.S.–Latin American policy going back to the Truman administration and a condemnation of the principles inherent in the Monroe Doctrine. It recommended that the United States bring military interventions and covert action to a close, work toward normalizing relations with Cuba, and sign and ratify a new treaty with Panama granting it full control over the canal.[5]

In his efforts to condemn past sins and provide for a moral rebirth, President Carter indicated that his administration would stop supporting repressive dictatorships, emphasize the protection of human rights, and begin to treat the Latin American nations in a less paternalistic way. His human rights campaign in Latin America hit the hardest in Argentina, Nicaragua, Brazil, and Chile, where authoritarian dictatorships and repressive military regimes tried to ingratiate themselves with the United States by claiming strong anticommunism.

Within a month after taking office, Carter cut military aid to Argentina and Uruguay by two-thirds, opposed economic assistance, and pursued a vigorous campaign of public diplomacy that included support for critical resolutions in the United Nations and the Organization of American States. In contrast to previous administrations that often criticized U.S. ambassadors for raising the issue of human rights in private discussions, the Carter administration instructed diplomats to apply human rights standards as part of American foreign policy. To counter the criticism of Argentina in the United States and elsewhere, General Videla hired one of the best public relations firms in Washington—Deaver and Hannaford—and established close ties with various anticommunist alliances around the world. The Carter administration was not able to remove the military government in Argentina, but the Reagan administration lightened up on its criticism of the government and bargained with the military for assistance in raising support for its anticommunist efforts against the Nicaraguan revolutionary movement (Sandinistas) in the early 1980s.

The Falklands/Malvinas War

The war between Argentina and Britain in 1982 put severe strains on the inter-American system and U.S.-Argentine relations because the United States supported the British effort to regain the islands after the Argentine military government invaded the British-held islands. The basis of the war involved (1) Argentina's legal and historical claim to title since achieving independence in 1816, (2) the failure of years of intermittent negotiations over Argentine control of the islands, and (3) the apparent efforts of Argentina's military government to encourage nationalism and turn attention away from a disastrous economic situation in April 1982. The military government (under General Leopoldo Galtieri) ordered the invasion, assuming that the United States would remain neutral, the British would not come to the defense of the islands, and the Latin American states would be sympathetic to Argentina's claim of sovereignty, regardless of its chosen methods. It was a desperate and risky gamble by a government that was isolated in the international community.

At first, the British troops stationed on the islands were quickly overcome and the islands were occupied by Argentine forces. Both the United Nations and the Organization of American States (OAS) met to decide on a response, and a debate took place over which body had the proper jurisdiction to handle the dispute. Argentina preferred the latter, the Organization of Consultation meeting on the basis of the Rio Treaty, thus eliminating all but one of the Commonwealth Caribbean states since they were not parties to the treaty and would side with the British (or so Argentina thought). What provoked the Argentines' anger at the United States was that at first the United States sided with the OAS but later shifted its position in support of the British, who favored the United Nations Security Council. In a move reminiscent of 1833, the United States gave military aid to the British and imposed economic sanctions on Argentina. The pro-UN/British and anti-OAS/Argentine stance of the United States seriously undermined U.S.-Argentine relations and ultimately weakened the OAS as a peacekeeping body.

Although the war lasted only 45 days, 255 British troops were killed and 777 seriously wounded in the battle to regain the Falklands. The cost to Argentina was considerably greater; 746 troops were killed and 1336 wounded in defending their effort to regain sovereignty over the Islas Malvinas. The war cost the two countries $2–3 billion, and the fact that the Reagan administration sided with Britain generated widespread Latin American criticism of the United States, but the animosity did not linger. The war put an end to the human rights violations associated with the Dirty War by discrediting the military junta and contributing to its replacement by a freely elected president. However, the Falklands remained a British possession.

The Reagan Administration and Argentina

Argentina was part of a regional trend toward the resurgence of democracy in South America between 1979 and 1985, as Ecuador, Peru, Bolivia, Uruguay, Argentina, and Brazil moved from military to civilian rule. After the Carter administration's human rights crusade had worsened U.S.-Argentine relations, the Reagan administration decided to correct this by shifting U.S. support for "moderate authoritarians," regimes that supposedly deserved U.S. support because of their anticommunist orientation. However, other motives also served the interests of the Reagan administration. First, the Reagan administration needed the support of military governments in South America to assist with the struggle against communism in Central America. Second, after the Pentagon declared the South Atlantic a "zone of growing strategic importance," the Reagan administration felt it needed to court military governments to prevent any possible Soviet attempts to block vital sea lanes and cripple the mineral and energy needs of the West. The Reagan administration abandoned Carter's high-profile human rights policy and replaced it with "quiet diplomacy." In terms of relations with Argentina, this meant that human rights issues were largely ignored in dealing with the military governments prior to the return to civilian rule. Reagan's new policy did lead to improved relations, but it also led to Argentina's involvement in Central America. Prior to the Falklands/ Malvinas War, the Argentine military worked with the CIA and the Honduran military to provide technical and financial assistance to the Nicaraguan Contras. With $15 million in U.S. government funds, major Nicaraguan Contra leaders were trained by the Argentine military in Buenos Aires and then later sent to Honduras to lead another "dirty war" in Central America.

The U.S.-Argentine relationship during the Reagan administration remained artificial, as was demonstrated by the miscalculation of U.S. support for Argentina after its invasion of the Falkland Islands in 1982. The United States did not stay neutral and supported Britain instead of Argentina in the conflict. This misjudgment on behalf of the Argentine military seriously damaged the Reagan administration's policy toward the rest of the region, where an effort was being made to convince Congress that the military leaders of South America were useful allies. Now it was clear to Argentina and the rest of South America that when the chips were down, the United States would not side with its hemispheric allies.

The humiliation of the Argentine military in the Falklands/Malvinas War contributed to Argentina's decision to hold democratic elections and establish new domestic and foreign policies. Argentina's first president to assume power in the aftermath of the "dirty war" and the loss to the British over sovereignty in the Falklands was Raúl Alfonsín, who defeated the Peronists on the Radical Party ticket in 1983. His central task was to figure out how to reinsert Argentina into world affairs, given the tumultuous nature of its foreign policies since World War II. To reach this goal Argentina would have to redefine its relations with the United States, a highly charged matter in domestic politics. Alfonsín also inherited severe economic problems—a huge foreign debt, rampant inflation, and stagnant growth—and was forced to deal with public anger over the years of inept and violent military rule. He organized the first human rights trials in Latin America and reversed the Amnesty Law that the military had enacted, but the military retaliated by staging three unsuccessful uprisings against him during his time in office. Argentina's relations with the United States cooled significantly as Alfonsín opposed Reagan administration policy in Central America, pursued a more Third World focus in foreign policy, and allowed his economic ministers to criticize the United States publicly.

Nevertheless Alfonsín received favorable political attention from the United States because he symbolized the reemergence of democracy in South America, and Washington backed him verbally when military rebellions occurred against him in 1987 and 1988. In addition, the Reagan administration supported Argentina by expressing opposition to coups and through an assortment of democracy assistance projects such as conferences on democratic transition, party-building efforts, legislative training, and constitutional reform. Overall the programs did not amount to much, but they provided enough domestic capital to pursue other foreign policy objectives.

POST–COLD WAR U.S.-ARGENTINE RELATIONS

The "Menemization" of Argentine Foreign Policy

In Argentina the 1990s have been dominated by Carlos Saúl Menem, a reform Peronist who has been twice-elected (1989 and 1995) president of Argentina on the Justicialista Party ticket. Using old-style politics, Menem has implemented the most radical privatization program ever undertaken in Latin America, reducing public employment and government spending and opening the Argentine economy to foreign competition. The primary architect of Menem's neoliberal economic policies (reforms based on privatization and reducing the size of government) was Domingo Cavallo, a Harvard-trained economist whose prescriptions for Argentina's ailing economy emphasized privatizing the state sector to produce revenue, but with little concern for improving efficiency or fostering greater competition. However, Menem's political style—a form of authoritarianism and cordial relations with the United States—did not deter his landslide reelection in 1995 despite economic difficulties and strikes against privatization of the state sector, opposition to his pardons of those involved in the "dirty war," corruption scandals, and dependency on international lending agencies such as the World Bank and the International Monetary Fund.

Argentina and the United States: From Bush to Clinton

During the presidencies of George Bush and Bill Clinton, Argentina supported the United States and its foreign policy more than any other Latin American country. When President Menem's foreign minister declared that Argentina wanted to have "carnal relations with the United States," he was reversing years of Argentine opposition to U.S.–Latin American policy. President Menem, of Muslin-Syrian ancestry, was the only Latin American leader to send troops to the Persian Gulf War. He criticized Fidel Castro's government in Cuba and endorsed U.S. intervention in Haiti to restore President Jean-Bertrand Aristide. Although his neighbors often accuse him of subordinating Argentina's foreign policy to U.S. interests, Menem's alliance with Washington has had its rewards in getting some relief from its huge foreign debt by having its payments rescheduled, securing financial assistance from international financial institutions, and opening the door to arms sales for the first time since the Falklands/Malvinas War. As a member of the Southern Cone Common Market (MERCOSUR), Argentina has been able to attract investment capital from major automobile manufacturers such as Ford, General Motors, Chrysler, Honda, Toyota, and Fiat.

President Menem and his economic advisors deserve credit for creating a stronger and more competitive economy, but Argentines have had to pay dearly for Menem's neoliberal economic policies. First, they have endured unemployment, reduced wages, and the elimination of a well-established social saftey net. Second, Menem tends to justify his authoritarian style as a political necessity to move forward and get things done. This tradeoff may not foster domestic political legitimacy or good relations with the United States. Although the United States has lost interest in anticommunism in the aftermath of the Cold War, it still must confront situations in countries like Argentina where military nationalists resist pressure to introduce human rights considerations as part of "democratization" efforts because they fear a deliberate effort to weaken or eliminate the armed forces in Latin America. Some of those in the Latin American military confronted with military budget cuts, policies of arms control, and a new emphasis on environmental problems and illicit drug trafficking fear not only a plan to eliminate the armed forces and undermine sovereignty, but a strategic effort to restore U.S. imperial control over the region. The Clinton administration may be committed to the promotion of free markets and democracy in places like Argentina, but it may eventually have to chose between unappealing alternatives—ones that are similar to those that many of Monroe's defenders have had to face during times of both war and peace.

CONCLUSION

U.S.-Argentine relations have been based on conflicting views of power and diplomacy in the Americas. Argentina's geographic distance from the United States and its colonial ties to Europe created a pattern of involvement in which top officials in Washington were not too likely to perceive a security threat from European activity in the region. In contrast, Argentina's close ties to Germany during World War II, and to the Soviet Union during the Cold War, were indeed perceived as security threats to the

United States; but the United States could do little to counter a nationalist government—civilian and military—that wished to pursue an independent foreign policy in defiance of the United States. Argentina's twentieth-century dictators were no match for those in Central America and the Caribbean who followed the cues from Washington in exchange for economic and military assistance. Although the current government in Buenos Aires has adopted pro-American foreign policies in the aftermath of the Cold War, Argentina's traditional view of itself as a key player in the hemisphere, and a general feeling of opposition to the United States, will make it difficult to maintain cordial relations indefinitely.

NOTES

1. Quoted in Edward J. Williams, *The Political Themes of Inter-American Relations* (Belmont, CA: Duxbury Press, 1971), p. 77. Emphasis in original.

2. Quoted in Harold F. Peterson, *Argentina and the United States, 1810–1960* (New York: State University of New York, 1964), p. 258.

3. Quoted in Randall Bennett Woods, *The Roosevelt Foreign Policy Establishment and the "Good Neighbor": The United States and Argentina, 1941–1945* (Lawrence: Regents Press of Kansas, 1979), p. 4.

4. James D. Cockcroft, *Latin America: History, Politics, and U.S. Policy.* 2nd Edition (Chicago: Nelson-Hall, 1996), pp. 593–594.

5. This summary of the report's recommendations is provided in Gaddis Smith, *The Last Years of the Monroe Doctrine, 1945–1993* (New York: Hill and Wang, 1994), p. 141.

SUGGESTED READINGS

Armony, Ariel C. *Argentina, the United States, and the Anti-Communist Crusade in Central America, 1977–1984.* Athens, Ohio: Ohio University Press, 1998.

Falcoff, Mark. *A Tale of Two Policies: U.S. Relations with the Argentine Junta, 1976–1983.* Philadelphia: Foreign Policy Research Institute, 1989.

Milenky, Edward S. *Argentina's Foreign Policies.* Boulder, CO: Westview Press, 1978.

Tulchin, Joseph S. *Argentina and the United States: A Conflicted Relationship.* Boston: Twayne Publishers, 1990.

3

Bolivia

TIMELINE OF U.S. RELATIONS WITH BOLIVIA

1825	Bolivia achieves independence from Spain
1848	U.S. diplomatic relations are established
1879–1884	War of the Pacific
1900–1932	Tin replaces silver as major export commodity
1932–1935	Chaco War
1937	Bolivian petroleum industry is nationalized
1952	Bolivian revolution begins under Movimiento Nacional Revolucionario (MNR)
1952–1964	Major reforms are instituted under MNR rule
1964	General René Barrientos takes power
1967	Ché Guevara is captured and executed with help of U.S. military
1970	General Juan José Torres González takes power
	Cocaine trafficking begins
1971	General Hugo Banzer Suárez seizes power
1980	"Cocaine coup" brings Luis García Meza to power
1985	Víctor Paz Estenssoro is elected president
1985–1990	Cocaine trade flourishes
1986	Under Operation Blast Furnace, 160 U.S. troops come to Bolivia
1989	Jaime Paz Zamora is elected president
1993–1997	Gonzálo Sánchez de Lozada serves as president
1997	Former dictator Hugo Banzer Suárez is elected president
	Ché Guevara's remains are uncovered in Vallegrande and transported to Cuba for reburial

INTRODUCTION

Major factors in U.S.-Bolivian relations have included (1) Bolivia's economic dependency on mining and the trafficking of illicit drugs, (2) the detrimental effects of two wars—the War of the Pacific and the Chaco War—with its neighbors, and (3) U.S. investment and control of key industries. From independence in 1825 to 1938, Bolivia lost over half of its original territory to its bordering states: Chile, Peru, Brazil, Paraguay, and Argentina. One of two countries in South America that have no seacoast (the result of territorial losses to neighbors), Bolivia has put considerable emphasis on international organizations and friendly relations with the United States to obtain economic assistance and political guarantees for national security and to regain its outlet to the sea.

With a record of chronic problems in governance, financial mismanagement, and economic stagnation, Bolivia has had to rely on foreign capital and financial advisors, as well as public assistance from the United States, to survive. During times of war Bolivia has solicited diplomatic assistance from the United States to mediate disputes and gain economic leverage. For most of the Cold War period Bolivia built close ties with the U.S. military, a relationship that often affected the success of democratic rule in Bolivia and efforts to combat drug trafficking. The negative effects of U.S. economic, political, and military involvement in Bolivia have contributed to outbreaks of anti-Americanism, regardless of the charitable motives of policymakers in Washington. Bolivia's revolution in 1952 stemmed from domestic grievances built up over a half century of foreign domination and economic exploitation by a small band of wealthy tin barons, but it has remained unfinished as a thoroughly social revolution. With a population sharply divided along racial, cultural, and geographic lines, Bolivia has struggled since independence to establish a sense of national unity to pacify regional/racial tensions that have made governing so difficult.

BOLIVIA AND THE UNITED STATES DURING THE NINETEENTH CENTURY

The United States and Bolivian Independence

During the colonial period Bolivia was an important mining region called Upper Peru. It included the highland community of Potosí, site of the seventeenth century's richest silver mines and a major source of Spanish wealth and power. Bolivia achieved its independence from Spain in 1825 and installed Antonio José de Sucre as president, a position he was to hold for life but in fact held only for several years. Between 1825 and 1880 Bolivia was run by a series of quasi-military strongmen, or caudillos, from regional strongholds. Mariano Melgarejo (1862–1871), the most notorious despot of the nineteenth century, stripped over 100,000 Indian peasants of their land titles and sold off large segments of national territory as if it were his own personal property. Despite attempts to adopt U.S. and French constitutional traditions, Bolivia has suffered from a long history of political instability and military takeovers. Since 1825 there have been at least 190 coups, often the result of struggles among rival elite factions to control the central government and the bounty that it controlled.

Bolivia and the Monroe Doctrine

Faced with intense rivalries with its not-so-friendly neighbors, Bolivia was forced to play balance-of-power politics but suffered tragically with each confrontation. The Monroe Doctrine served no purpose in preventing Bolivia's predatory neighbors from nibbling away at its national territory. There were times when Bolivia (and Peru) turned to the United States for help, claiming the possibility of European intervention in the Andean region. Even during the twentieth century when German and Soviet influence expanded into Bolivia, the Monroe Doctrine did not come into play—either because the United States saw no threat to its security or because the Bolivians realized that invoking Monroe's words would serve no national purpose.

The Rise of the Tin Barons

Bolivia's economic links to the international capitalist system evolved as the result of its dependency on the export of silver and tin. After the silver mines were depleted in the middle of the nineteenth century, Bolivians turned to tin mining in an effort to meet world demand. As tin exports expanded, a new mining elite appeared. It was supported by foreign capitalists and linked to the traditional elite and oriented to free enterprise capitalism. With wars in Europe and elsewhere during the first half of the twentieth century, the weapons industry (as well as the invention of the tin vacuum-packed can) helped produce a surge in the world demand for tin.

Until the Bolivian revolution in 1952, control of Bolivia's tin mining business remained in the hands of a small group of local capitalists known collectively as the "tin barons." With no restrictions on foreign investment, and the growing demand for tin, it is surprising that Bolivians themselves emerged as the dominant mine-owners. The backbone of the small group of tin barons was Simón Patiño, who at the peak of his power controlled 10 percent of world tin output. To avoid export taxes and other regulations, Patiño moved his corporate headquarters to Delaware in 1924. Although Patiño spent most of his time in Paris or New York, he remained Bolivia's dominant miner and its most powerful capitalist until his death in the 1940s. The tin barons who controlled the other half of production included the Aramayo family and the European-born Mauricio Hochschild. However, through financial deals with foreign bankers and refinery owners, the tin barons allowed the tin industry to gradually fall under the control of foreigners. The most powerful foreign owners of Bolivian mines were the Guggenheim brothers' American Smelting and Refining Company (ASARCO, incorporated in 1899) and W. R. Grace's international mining company. Foreign control of Bolivia's tin mines contributed to the emergence of a leftist, anti-imperialist trade union movement that became the focus of political conflict between the Bolivian military, miners (angry over low wages and deplorable working conditions), and major political parties.

The War of the Pacific

The War of the Pacific (1879–1884) was waged by Chile against Bolivia and Peru over territory and control of the Atacama Desert, a 600-mile strip of the Pacific coast rich in guano and nitrates, fertilizers used to improve agricultural production in Europe and the United States. Bolivia's possession of Antofagasta meant the control of valuable nitrate and silver lands, but because of geographic barriers and political instability it was unable to exercise effective control (see Chapters 5 and 22). From the very beginning of hostilities, Bolivia and Peru turned to the United States to help block Chile's expansionist desires in South America. The Bolivian minister in Washington offered the prospect of lucrative guano (dried excrement from seabirds) and nitrate concessions to U.S. investors in exchange for official protection. After two U.S.-mediated peace treaties in 1883 and 1884, the war came to a formal close, but Bolivia was left landlocked, without access rights to the Pacific Ocean. It languished in remorse and resentment at both Chile and the United States for what it considered unfair diplomacy and the loss of valuable territory. Unfortunately the *salida al mar* (outlet to the sea) issue would poison relations among Bolivia, Chile, and Peru well into the twentieth century, and it would also give rise to other wars and political disturbances (see Chapters 5 and 22).

BOLIVIA AND THE UNITED STATES DURING THE TWENTIETH CENTURY

During the first two decades of the twentieth century Bolivia experienced substantial economic growth based on its growing share of the world tin market, which rose from 12 percent in 1900 to 22 percent in 1925. The added income enabled Bolivia to build railroads and other forms of communication. A rubber boom stimulated interest in its eastern territory bordering on Brazil, drawing North American capitalists in search of rubber plantations. After Bolivians heard of President Wilson's "peace without victory" speech in 1917 in which he said that every nation had the right of a direct outlet to the sea, they reversed course and severed diplomatic relations with Germany in 1917, hoping that this gesture would benefit Bolivia economically and politically.

The Chaco War

The Chaco War (1932–1935) was an exceptionally violent and long-lasting conflict between Bolivia and Paraguay for possession of a desolate and seemingly worthless region called the Chaco Boreal. Since gaining their independence in the 1820s, both nations had claimed the region but were unable to settle the territorial question of ownership, despite the assistance of outside actors including the League of Nations, inter-American conferences, and a number of American states acting individually and, at times, together. The Chaco War was the bloodiest war in twentieth-century South America with over 80,000 deaths and some 250,000 injuries. Many of those who participated in the peace talks, including the United States, recognized that the failure of international peace mechanisms to prevent war in this case meant that it might be impossible to avoid war in Europe and elsewhere in the world.

The core of the dispute involved feelings of lost territory and control on the part of both nations reaching back to the nineteenth century. Bolivia, having lost its route to the sea in the War of the Pacific, thought it could secure a passage to the Atlantic via the Paraguay River, gain control over vast oil reserves (a mistaken belief since few known reserves existed in the region), and redeem its national honor, which had been sullied by losses of national territory in past wars. Paraguay's motives arose from efforts to maintain sovereignty over territory it had settled, and strong desires to restore its national honor, which had been lost in the Paraguayan War in the 1860s.

Bolivia's neighbors—Argentina, Brazil, Chile, and Peru—viewed the conflict as a threat to their own economic and security interests and worried about being drawn into war. They hosted several inter-American conferences but failed to prevent the outbreak of hostilities, being afraid that any form of coercion would be considered a form of intervention. This attitude undermined inter-American solidarity and principles of peaceful settlement and mutual security throughout the Americas. The United States cited the Chaco War to emphasize its opposition to the League of Nations and its preference for a regional or inter-American solution to conflict resolution. The war also provided the United States with opportunities to sell trucks, airplanes, and munitions, especially to Bolivia. Paraguay resented these sales and charged that the United States' oil interests (primarily Standard Oil) were secretly funding Bolivia's war effort, while at the same time Great Britain and Argentina were behind Paraguay's armed forces. After three years of conflict—compounded by both sides' financial ruin and battlefield exhaustion—both sides turned to outside intervention to help end the war. This brought about a cease-fire in 1935, but the war did not formally end until 1938 with Paraguay as the military victor. The peace treaty that both parties signed was mediated and ratified by a commission made up of representatives from the United States and five Latin American states.

Although Paraguay was allowed to keep about three-quarters of the disputed area, and Bolivia gained port facilities and rights of passage through Paraguay, the war had far-reaching consequences. Bolivia's "Chaco generation" of veterans organized peasant leagues, labor unions, and new reformist and revolutionary political parties that helped bring about the 1952 revolution. However, Paraguay suffered from continual political instability, a succession of military governments, and major setbacks in economic development. U.S. ambassador Spruille Braden played an important diplomatic role in the Chaco Peace Conference, as did Argentine foreign minister Carlos Saavedra Lamas, who was awarded the Nobel Peace Prize in 1936 for his leadership role at the Conference.

Bolivia and the Good Neighbor Policy

President Roosevelt's new policy of respect for the interests of Latin Americans (Good Neighbor Policy) was challenged by the seizure of U.S. oil companies in Bolivia in 1937, the first of several tests of the interplay between the U.S. pledge of nonintervention and the protection of foreign investors. In March 1937 the Bolivian government annulled the petroleum concession of Standard Oil of Bolivia (a subsidiary of Standard Oil of New Jersey) and confiscated its properties. Bolivia's case was based on claims that the oil company had opposed Bolivia during the Chaco War, avoided tax payments, and engaged in the illegal export of oil. The Roosevelt administration reacted with caution, wishing to practice the policy of the good neighbor, although being well aware that the oil fields in Bolivia were producing little oil and were of limited value. This approach was successful when Bolivia agreed to a $1.5 million settlement followed by a $25 million loan from the United States for economic assistance.

BOLIVIA AND THE UNITED STATES DURING THE COLD WAR

The United States and the Bolivian Revolution

The Bolivian revolution of 1952 presented the United States with the difficult task of having to cope with a social revolution during the early years of the Cold War. Led by Víctor Paz Estenssoro's Revolutionary Nationalist Movement (Movimiento Nacional Revolucionario, or MNR), the revolution set out to destroy the elitist power structure by nationalizing 80 percent of the nation's mining industry, approving a broad agrarian reform program, declaring universal voting rights, and purging the old army of its more traditional and undemocratic elements. The causes of the Bolivian revolution were largely domestic, although Paz and his followers were inspired by the social welfare components of the Mexican revolution and the political stability that arose from its one-party dominant system. What bothered the United States about the Bolivian revolution was not so much the MNR's vaguely leftist program but the background of its leaders; some had been Nazis during World War II, and others were Marxists and strongly critical of U.S. hegemony.

Despite suspicions of the political ideology of the MNR leaders, the United States formally recognized Bolivia's revolutionary government after a two-month delay. Bolivians realized the importance of U.S. recognition, and they promised a government that would respect private property and international agreements. Recognition required Bolivia to assure the United States that compensation would be paid for the expropriated mining properties, and that the government was not communist and supportive of dictators. The Eisenhower administration wanted a noncommunist Bolivia and used economic and military assistance to curb political radicalism and economic nationalism. In return for serving as a bulwark against communism, Bolivia received $200 million in economic and military assistance from the United States between 1952 and 1964.

The favorable response on the part of the United States was also due to the efforts of Milton Eisenhower, the president's brother, who denounced American business leaders for calling the Bolivians communists because of their land reform and mine nationalization programs. In his book *The Wine Is Bitter*, Milton Eisenhower defends the Bolivian revolution by stating that the Paz Estenssoro government "may have been inexperienced, sometimes critical of us, and more inclined to socialism than Americans generally prefer. But they were not Communists." He went on to stress that "We should not confuse each move in Latin America toward socialism with Marxism, land reform with Communists, or even anti-Yankeeism with pro-Sovietism."[1] Eisenhower continued to advise presidents of both parties until his death in 1985, but his Cold War admonitions seemed to fall on deaf ears.

During the Kennedy administration U.S. military and economic assistance to Bolivia continued to expand, due in large part to the perceived threat of communist influence and the close personal ties between President Paz (then in a second term, 1960–1964) and John F. Kennedy. In an effort to comply with Kennedy's Alliance for Progress, Paz Estenssoro pushed through economic reforms to restructure the tin industry and the state mining corporation to attract domestic and foreign capital, but his efforts produced confrontations with organized labor that required the deployment of troops around the mines. In a strange twist of events, the Bolivian revolution did not reduce the country's dependence on the United States or the magnitude of U.S. influence in Bolivian internal affairs. Bolivian reliance on U.S. grants and loans, markets, and top officials soon superseded its earlier dependence on the tin mines, mine entrepreneurs, and British markets.

Despite the fact that the MNR reforms dismantled most of the old power structure, the Bolivian revolutionaries were unable to create a viable new order. Thus, the revolution remained incomplete after 12 turbulent years. By 1964 growing internal conflicts over economic restructuring served to expand the power of the military. After prodding by the U.S. embassy, Paz decided to run again for the presidency, but the military forced him to accept an air force general, René Barrientos, as his running mate in the 1964 elections. Returned to power after an easy election, Paz lasted only three months before he was overthrown by Barrientos with the support of labor and opposing factions of the MNR. To consolidate power after the coup, Barrientos promised peasants that he would not harm their interests if they promised to remain loyal to the military, which was by now a key political player.

Bolivia and the Death of Ché Guevara

Determined to defeat revolutionary communism in the Western Hemisphere, President Lyndon B. Johnson infused a great deal of his thinking and rhetoric in Monroeist principles, but without invoking the Monroe Doctrine by name. His foreign policy advisors were mostly Cold Warriors who devised a conceptual strategy according to which any group or individual "inspired" by a foreign regime or ideology (Cuba or the Soviet Union) and intent on changing a Latin American government was considered an instrument of foreign aggression, thereby justifying the use of force and covert action—including assassination. In these advisors' view, whenever political or revolutionary struggles involve national forces inspired from abroad by training, money, and propaganda, they cease being internal and become international or external. The efforts to isolate Cuba in the mid-1960s also included the use of the Central Intelligence Agency and U.S. military forces against Castro's revolutionary colleague—Ernesto "Ché" Guevara—and international insurgents in rural Bolivia in 1967.

Ché's Bolivia campaign was designed to bring the Cuban revolution to Bolivia as well, but it faced the opposition of local communists, constant hostility from the Bolivian peasantry, and a collaborative anti-insurgency effort carried out by the United States and the Bolivian armed forces. The United States provided some arms and a team of CIA agents—including Felix Rodríguez, a veteran of the Bay of Pigs invasion—to improve the Bolivian military's feeble rural forces. It also flew in 17 members of a new elite counterinsurgency corps (Green Berets) to instruct a Bolivian battalion in field intelligence and counterinsurgency warfare. Using infrared photographic "sensors" that detect human body heat from long distances, those in pursuit of the Argentine-born revolutionist had little trouble locating Ché and his comrades. After his capture in October 1967, the decision to execute Ché came from Bolivia's president, René Barrientos, and his military advisors, not U.S. intelligence; Washington wanted to keep the guerrilla leader alive and take him to Panama for interrogation. His death on October 9, 1967, put an end to a crusade that the U.S. government had long considered a major challenge to its hegemony in the Western Hemisphere.

One of the architects of the Cold War during the 1960s was Walt W. Rostow, President Johnson's national security advisor. Rostow was an astute foreign policy analyst who became the chief architect of military escalation to counter communist revolutions. He hated revolutionary leaders such as Ché Guevara, Fidel Castro, and Ho Chi Minh. On October 9, 1967, he called a meeting to announce to the National Security Council staff in Washington that Guevara had been executed in Bolivia. In an excited state of euphoria, Rostow took great pleasure in slowly announcing Ché's death: "I have important news; the Bolivians have executed Ché; they finally got the SOB. The last of the romantic guerrillas."[2]

The Cocaine Coup and Narcomilitarism

Bolivia ranks second to Peru in coca-leaf production and is a major link in the international cocaine trade (see Table 22.1 in Chapter 22). The paradox of Bolivia's role in hemispheric drug trafficking is that despite billions of dollars in profits yielded by the tons of coca paste sent abroad on a weekly basis, it remains one of the poorest countries in the Western Hemisphere. The growing importance of the international cocaine trade after the fall of General Banzer in 1978, and the continuing U.S. pressure on Bolivia to curtail the drug trade, contributed to what became known as the "cocaine coup" of July 1980, led by General Luis García Meza.

One of Bolivia's leading drug barons, Roberto Suárez Gómez, called a meeting of top *narcotraficantes* (drug traffickers) and offered several members of the Bolivian armed forces a bribe of $1.3 million to lead the coup—and promises of vast profits if the coup succeeded. This arrangement brought to power the narcomilitary regime of General García Meza in what was one of the bloodiest coups in Bolivia's history. After taking power, García Meza's government became known for its brutality and corruption. Colonel Luis Arce Gómez, a cousin of Roberto Suárez, was appointed head of the interior ministry, but he soon became known as the "Minister of Cocaine" because of his corruption and links to the drug trade.

The Carter administration was outraged by the 1980 coup, and U.S.-Bolivian relations deteriorated rapidly until the middle of the decade. After "cocaine generals" were installed at the highest levels of the Bolivian government, the United States suspended all antinarcotics efforts, removed its team of Drug Enforcement Agency advisors, and suspended about $127 million in foreign assistance. After being criticized and threatened by García Meza, U.S. ambassador Marvin Weisman left the country. During the last months of the Carter administration several conditions were established for normalizing relations, but none were met and U.S.-Bolivian relations remained distant and cool.

The Reagan Administration and the Bolivian Political Morass

President García Meza anticipated that the Reagan administration would overlook Bolivia's human rights violations and lack of democracy and reestablish normal relations. However, despite some sympathy for García Meza among hardliners in the Reagan administration, Carter's policy of pressuring the military to reduce drug production and trafficking, shift toward civilian rule, and improve human rights continued, although in a less visible manner. Disagreements developed between the drug dealers and the military, the economy began a sharp decline, and after only one year in power García Meza and his close collaborators were overthrown in another bloodless coup.

U.S.-Bolivian relations remained cool despite efforts by President Hernán Siles Zuazo (1982–1985) to clean up corruption, curb the power of the military, and put an end to drug trafficking. The Reagan administration was not pleased with the Siles Zuazo presidency because he was a leftist with connections with foreign governments that were considered security threats to the United States, but the U.S. embassy worked to keep civilian rule afloat. Siles did manage to capture and extradite the fugitive Nazi, Klaus Barbie, to France in 1983, and he removed a number of high-ranking military figures linked to the drug trade and corruption; but his economic reforms were negated by labor unrest, congressional opposition, and several coup attempts. When Siles Zuazo was kidnapped by the military in 1984, his wife called U.S. ambassador Edwin Corr to tell him of the abduction and to request his aid in preventing the planned assassination. The U.S. ambassador intervened, telling the generals that "if there's a coup, you'll have problems with the United States."[3] After word got out that Siles had contacted drug baron Suárez about helping to pay off Bolivia's public debt, and that $500 million had been offered, an impeachment drive against the president and his "narco-democracy" began. Siles was pressured to finish his term early and hold elections in 1985; this brought Víctor Paz Estenssoro back to power for a fourth term. The cocaine industry continued to flourish, however, as the rest of Bolivia's economy disintegrated, particularly the collapse of the tin market in 1985 and again in 1993.

Money Doctors for Bolivia's Ailing Capitalism

Bolivia has a long history of employing foreign economic advisors (money doctors) to solve its financial and economic woes. From the Kemmerer missions (led by Princeton University economist Edwin Kemmerer) in the 1920s to the more recent economic stabilization measures and long-term market-oriented reforms of the 1980s, Bolivia has become dependent on money doctors from the United States to advise on how best to acquire foreign loans and construct a capitalist system. Bolivia's success in conquering hyperinflation (at one point it reached 24,000 percent per year) in 1985–1987 was attributed to Jeffrey Sachs, a Harvard economist. The dramatic success of Sach's anti-statist and free market experiment in Bolivia earned him praise from around the world, including the title of "the Indiana Jones of economics" by the *Los Angeles Times*. In contrast to the "Chicago Boys" who advised Chilean dictator Augusto Pinochet (see Chapter 5), Sachs only advises "democratic" governments. Under the direction of Sachs, Bolivia achieved some economic stability, including a tremendous drop in inflation, but at the price of continued poverty, economic stagnation, and high employment rates.

Operation Blast Furnace

Bolivia has become a showcase for the Andean drug war due to its willingness to comply with Washington's need to display resolve against narcotics trafficking. In July 1986, at the invitation of President Paz, hundreds of U.S. military personnel were sent into Bolivia in a joint counternarcotics campaign to stop the processing and transportation of cocaine. Known as Operation Blast Furnace, the intervention helped the Reagan administration publicize the seriousness of a problem that had become a major domestic and hemispheric issue. Bolivia's major concern was not so much the demand for drugs in the United States as it was the influence of drug traffickers on Bolivian politics and its inability to obtain badly needed financial assistance from the United States on grounds related to the narcotics trade. With at least 20 U.S. agencies now operating in Bolivia, and over $200 million in annual assistance to finance counternarcotics missions, Bolivia is now one of the principal sites for U.S. anti-drug activities in the Andes. Bolivia has not had to face a drug-rural insurgency connection nexus, but joint efforts like Operation Blast Furnace have proved to be only a temporary solution to a much more deeply rooted problem.

BOLIVIA AND THE UNITED STATES AFTER
THE COLD WAR

Recent U.S. involvement in Bolivia has been based on support of economic reforms, the survival of democracy, and the continuing effort to combat the growing cocaine trade. Bilateral relations have been friendly, but strains still exist over the continuing power of the Bolivian military and the pace of reforms tied to debt reduction, privatization, and the openness toward foreign investment. Themselves "addicted" to the funds they receive from Washington to fight the drug war, Bolivian governments must confront domestic political forces that resent the degree of control the United States has over the nation.

From Dictator to Democrat: The Return of General Hugo Banzer

Bolivians voted in 1997 to return Hugo Banzer to the presidency, a position he held for eight years after a bloody coup in 1971. During his first presidency (1971–1979) Banzer decided to adopt the model of military rule then employed in Brazil, and later in Chile and Argentina. In accordance with the new military ideology, Banzer believed that democratic rule ultimately led to social chaos and was dangerous to the development of a modern capitalist economy. He felt that the masses needed to be "depoliticized" and "re-educated" in order to become more submissive and compliant. Only then could rapid modernization and peaceful development occur.

Banzer's more recent political metamorphosis makes some observers wonder whether he is still an autocrat or a democrat. By ignoring Washington's political advice and entering into a coalition with a left-wing party, the Revolutionary Leftist Movement (MIR) headed by Jaime Paz Zamora (because of his involvement in drug trafficking, Paz is ineligible for a U.S. visa), Banzer has annoyed top officials in the United States. Tensions in U.S.-Bolivian relations have not prevented Banzer from pushing ahead with his own brand of populism and economic nationalism despite Bolivia's need for U.S. investment and trade. Banzer has promised to continue his predecessor's economic reforms, but with more emphasis on helping the poor with education and health care programs; and he has assured the United States that he is committed to eliminating both corruption and narcotrafficking. As a member of the Andean Pact regional trade group, and an associate member of MERCOSUR, Banzer hopes to take advantage of Bolivia's central location bordering on Brazil, Argentina, Chile, and Peru.

CONCLUSION

Since the time of the Monroe Doctrine, U.S.-Bolivian relations have been characterized as generally friendly but interspersed with periods of tension during times of war or domestic crises arising out of military dictatorships, drug trafficking, and the failure of economic reforms. Although Bolivia means little to the United States in terms of foreign investment and bilateral trade, its location and central place in the current drug wars requires continuing attention from U.S. government agencies. Bolivia has made some headway in strengthening democracy, fighting corruption, and exporting tin and energy resources to the U.S. market, but the obstacles—political and economic—that Bolivia faces will not be easily overcome, with or without trade arrangements that lower tariffs, and U.S. assistance.

NOTES

1. Milton S. Eisenhower, *The Wine Is Bitter: The United States and Latin America* (Garden City, NY: Doubleday, 1963), pp. 67–68.

2. David Halberstam, *The Best and the Brightest* (New York: Random House, 1972), p. 197.

3. Quoted in Thomas Carothers, *In the Name of Democracy: U.S. Policy toward Latin America in the Reagan Years* (Berkeley: University of California Press, 1991), p. 128.

SUGGESTED READINGS

Bagley, Bruce M., ed. *Drug Trafficking Research in the Americas: An Annotated Bibliography.* Boulder, CO: Lynne Rienner, 1997.

Bagley, Bruce M., and William O. Walker III, eds. *Drug Trafficking in the Americas.* Boulder, CO: Lynne Rienner, 1994.

Leons, Madeline Barbara, and Harry Sanabria, eds. *Coca, Cocaine, and the Bolivian Reality.* Albany, NY: State University of New York Press, 1997.

Malloy, James M., and Eduardo Gamarra. *Revolution and Reaction: Bolivia 1964–1985.* New Brunswick, NJ: Transaction Books, 1988.

Menzel, Sewall H. *Fire in the Andes: U.S. Foreign Policy and Cocaine Politics in Bolivia and Peru.* Lanham, MD: University Press of America, 1996.

4

Brazil

TIMELINE OF U.S. RELATIONS WITH BRAZIL

1822	Brazil proclaims independence from Portugal
1822–1831	Emperor Pedro I rules Brazil
1824	United States recognizes Brazil's independence
1831–1889	Emperor Pedro II rules Brazil
1876	Pedro II visits United States for centennial celebrations
1888	Slavery is abolished in Brazil
1889	Brazilian military overthrows monarchy to begin republic
1890	United States recognizes republic
1891–1894	Marshal Floriano Peixoto serves as president
1893–1894	Rio Bay naval revolt
1894	Charles Flint's twelve-ship fleet of mercenaries sails for Rio Bay
1895	Brazil names new Senate building after President Monroe
1902–1912	Rio Branco period of cordial bilateral relations
1906	Brazil and United States exchange ambassadors
1917	Brazil enters World War I
1930	Getúlio Vargas assumes power; rules until 1945
1942	Brazil enters World War II
1945–1946	Adolf Berle Jr. becomes U.S. ambassador to Brazil
1945	Vargas is overthrown by the military
1945–1951	General Eurico G. Dutra serves as elected president
1947	President Truman visits Brazil to sign Rio Treaty
1949	Superior War College (ESG) is founded

1951–1954	Vargas serves as elected president; commits suicide in 1954
1956–1960	Juscelino Kubitschek serves as elected president
1960	Jânio Quadros is elected president; resigns in 1961
1961	Quadros rejects "Berle's bride"
	João Goulart assumes presidency
1964	The military overthrows Goulart
1964–1985	Generals rule Brazil
1978	President Carter visits Brazil
1982	President Reagan visits Brazil
1985	Democracy returns to Brazil
1992	President Bush attends Earth Summit in Rio de Janeiro
	President Fernando Collor is impeached
1995	Fernando Henrique Cardoso is elected president
1997	President Clinton visits Brazil

INTRODUCTION

Brazil and the United States—two unequal giants in the Western Hemisphere—have maintained an outwardly friendly, but sometimes distant and strained, relationship since the early part of the nineteenth century. In an effort to establish a privileged relationship with the United States, Brazilian officials have endorsed the Monroe Doctrine and interventionism in Central America and the Caribbean, served as an intermediary between the other Latin American nations and the United States, sided with the United States during World Wars I and II, and provided a pillar of stability in South America. For Brazilian officials, endorsement of Washington's Latin American policies was more a recognition of diplomatic prudence and power politics than submissiveness to inequalities in power. If Brazil could promote closer trade links with the large U.S. market, counterbalance the power of Argentina, and enhance its desire for worldwide power and prestige, then a policy of alliance with the United States was considered a beneficial and prudent strategy. Brazil seemed willing to recognize the hegemony of the United States in the Western Hemisphere as long as it was allowed to pursue its own dominant position in South America.

Brazil remained a monarchy after proclaiming independence from Portugal and didn't abolish slavery until 1888, but the United States managed to maintain peaceful relations as each pursued its own political and economic interests. For the United States, the kind of government in Brazil mattered little—whether monarchy, democratic civilian government, dictatorship, or a small military group (junta)—as long as other more important interests and objectives could be achieved. Between the end of the monarchy in 1889 and 1968, the United States consistently wooed the Brazilian military, even when it intervened in internal politics, because it appeared to be a defender of stability and provided a bulwark against communist advances in the Americas. In economic relations, Brazil was viewed by U.S. policymakers as a market for manufactured goods, a source of raw materials, and a favorable place to invest.

BRAZIL AND THE UNITED STATES DURING THE NINETEENTH CENTURY

Brazil and the Independence of Latin America

Brazil's transition to independence was bloodless and much less chaotic than the devastating wars that took place in the rest of Latin America. After Napoleon's armies invaded Portugal in 1807, the British navy escorted the Portuguese court to Brazil in 1808. There was no war of independence in Brazil because the colonial government headed by Pedro I, crown prince of Portugal, declared independence from Portugal in 1822 as a monarchical empire. President Monroe's distaste for monarchy delayed formal recognition of Brazil until 1824, but he had no doubt that Brazil would eventually move toward republicanism and recognize the commercial benefits of an alliance with the United States. In general, the United States kept its distance from Brazil in the nineteenth century, believing that Brazil's continuing support for slavery and the institution of the monarchy were somehow out of place with the rest of the Americas. The first U.S. consul to Rio de Janeiro, Condy Raguet (1822–1827), arrived with instructions to persuade the Brazilians to abolish the slave trade, support the Monroe Doctrine, and improve bilateral trade and commerce. However, he made little progress in fulfilling these instructions, with the exception of winning Brazilian admiration for Washington's "hands off" the Americas message to the Europeans.

Brazil and the Monroe Doctrine

Although the Spanish American nations never officially recognized the Monroe Doctrine, few went as far as Brazil in giving it a cordial welcome. Less than two months after President Monroe's message of 1823, the Brazilian government recognized the new doctrine—based in large part on the belief that it would protect Brazil's newly proclaimed independence and provide a protective shield against European aggression—but insisted on giving it a collective perspective rather than an interpretation by one state. Brazil became the only Latin American government in the nineteenth century to express appreciation and outright support for the Monroe Doctrine.

Later, during the Rio Branco period (1902–1912), Brazil used the Monroe Doctrine to cement closer relations with the United States and to strengthen its international position in the world. Brazil even responded favorably to the Roosevelt Corollary (1904) to the Monroe Doctrine, justifying U.S. intervention, an interpretation loathed by the rest of Latin America at the time because of the repeated violations of their sovereignty in the name of Monroe. Brazil actually favored Roosevelt's reference to the use of "international police power" to deal with "chronic wrongdoing" because it believed it might apply to its unruly neighbors, Paraguay and Uruguay.

The Brazilian Monarchy and the United States

The Brazilian monarchy was dominated by Dom Pedro I (1822–1831) and his son, Dom Pedro II (1831–1889). For the most part the Brazilian empire was stable and conservative, but Brazil and the United States remained apart due to its distant location, monarchy, and retention of slavery (Brazil was the last Latin American country to abolish slavery in 1888). Emperor Pedro II visited the United States in 1876 to attend the centennial exhibition at Philadelphia. He received a perfunctory reception by President Grant, but his visit left a positive and lasting impression. Despite periods of war and turmoil, relations between the United States and Brazil remained friendly and cordial for the duration of the empire. Offers from Washington to settle the Paraguayan War were turned down by Brazil, but Pedro II pleased the United States when he decreed the opening of the Amazon River to the merchant ships of all nations. When the empire was overthrown in 1889 the United States was the first to recognize the new government (1890) and congratulated the Brazilians on their adoption of republican institutions, but many in Washington also mourned the end of a stable and friendly regime.

Brazil and the U.S. Civil War

The U.S. Civil War (1861–1865) presented another opportunity for European powers to challenge the hegemony of the United States in the Western Hemisphere. Since the naval powers of Europe had never recognized the Monroe Doctrine, new colonies or protectorates could be more easily obtained while the United States was embroiled in its own civil war. Brazil granted the Confederate states the status of belligerents, but the Emperor's government also displayed a friendly outlook toward the Northern government. Although the Monroe Doctrine had nothing to do with ending the French occupation of Mexico in 1867, it may have saved Brazil from the expansionist plans of European powers since monarchy and slavery still existed at the time. Samuel F. Bemis argues that "the Monroe Doctrine was one of the principal barriers" to the "mad romantic dreams for monarchy for the Americas."[1] Napoleon's hand-picked and subservient emperor (Maximilian) in Mexico dreamed of a double Hapsburg empire (the great dynastic power that dominated Europe from 1282 to 1918) based on the marriage of his younger brother to a Brazilian princess. Once the U.S. Civil War ended in 1865, thousands of American Southerners migrated to Brazil in hopes of continuing their way of life in another land. Brazil still has a small community of descendants of the thousands of Southerners (*Confederados*) who fled to Brazil after the war rather than face the unpleasantries of Reconstruction.

The Rio Bay Naval Revolt and Flint's Fleet

The Brazilian government faced a naval revolt in 1893–1894 that brought the United States and Brazil closer together and served as a prelude for the era of U.S. intervention between 1895 and 1930. The Rio Bay naval revolt also provided an opportunity for American entrepreneur Charles Flint to influence U.S. policy toward Brazil. His mercenary flotilla—known as Flint's Fleet—joined the battle to protect U.S. business interests in Brazil during the last decade of the nineteenth century. But Flint's Fleet was more than simply the privatization of American foreign policy in the wake of Pan-Americanism, trade expansion, and a renewal of Manifest Destiny and the Monroe Doctrine. It also marked a watershed in the shift from the nineteenth-century *filibusteros* who often won concessions through bribery and cajolery, to the twentieth-century "entrepreneurs" who used the power of the U.S. state to get their way in Latin America.

Charles R. Flint was a successful merchant in New York, perhaps the largest rubber dealer in the United States, a powerful private voice for trade expansionism, and one of the chief U.S. delegates to the Pan American Conference in 1889. Although he was younger than 40 years old at the time, Flint had decades of business experience in Latin America, particularly in shipping (he was the son of one of Maine's largest sailing-ship builders) and the sale of arms. His greatest commercial interests in Latin America were in Brazil, and they needed protection. The origin of Flint's Fleet centered on the transfer of leadership in Brazil from Deodoro da Fonseca to Vice-President Marshal Floriano Peixoto in November 1891. A supporter of industrialization and friendship with the United States, Floriano faced a naval mutiny that ultimately changed the course of U.S.-Brazilian relations. The revolt of the Brazilian navy, led by José Custódio de Mello and Saldanha da Gama, started with monarchists intent on toppling the new republic. The naval revolt threatened international shipping in Brazilian ports and soon prompted a forceful U.S. naval demonstration on behalf of Floriano's government. According to Steven Topik, the U.S. military response in Rio Bay represented "the greatest concentration of U.S. gunboats in American history to that point" and "led directly to the expansionist policy that would continue the buildup of the New Navy, yield the Olney Doctrine in Venezuela, and lead to the Spanish-American War."[2]

As Floriano faced increasing turmoil and chaos in Brazil, it became imperative that he gain the support of the United States, but his requests for additional ships were turned down because of their unavailability by President Cleveland. Charles Flint was the perfect choice to help save the government under siege in Brazil. He had a long and vested interest in U.S.-Brazilian relations and commerce, knowledge of shipping and the arms trade, experience in Latin American naval warfare, close ties with U.S. policymakers, and the necessary connections with international financiers who could finance the flotilla. There were times when Flint operated virtually as Brazil's minister to the United States. Flint's mercenary squadron gained public attention by outfitting its ships with the most sophisticated and experimental weapons of the time, some of which had never been tested in warfare. Flint and Salvador de Mendonça—co-organizer of Flint's Fleet—were masters of favorable publicity and propaganda. Flint established a literary bureau to control the news coming from and going to Brazil. Mendonça published articles in U.S. newspapers in which he described the perilous adventure in terms of defending the Monroe Doctrine. Flint's Fleet suffered numerous mishaps and arrived late, but it aroused great fear with its new dynamite gun; by preventing the naval rebels and the Federalists from joining forces to defeat Floriano, Flint's Fleet played a critical role in ending the threat to the Brazilian government. Although Flint's mercenary squadron did not militarily defeat the rebels, they surrendered out of fear of the destructive potential of the dynamite gun.

The success of Flint's Fleet expanded the meaning of the Monroe Doctrine and created a closer relationship between Brazil and the United States. During the following year, the United States was acknowledged by Brazilians with celebrations and honors. At the inauguration of Brazil's new president—Prudente de Morais—the cornerstone to the James Monroe and Monroe Doctrine monument was laid in Brazil, testimony to the efforts of Charles Flint and the American naval effort in Brazil. In 1895, Brazil's new senate building in Rio de Janeiro was named the Palacio Monroe in honor of the important principles of noncolonization and nonintervention. In the end, the events in Rio Bay between 1893 and 1894 demonstrated that even a domestically inspired attempt at restoring a monarchy now fit within the expanding interpretations of the Monroe Doctrine. It was certainly the most bizarre chapter of the naval revolt in Rio Bay, but it also turned out to be the decisive factor in saving Floriano's government and fostering closer ties between Brazil and the United States.

BRAZIL AND THE UNITED STATES IN THE EARLY
TWENTIETH CENTURY

The United States did not intervene in South America, at least not in the same way that it did in Central America and the Caribbean. This regional difference, according to President Theodore Roosevelt, was based on the understanding that the southern half of South America had advanced so far that countries like Brazil could be treated as friends and equals, no longer requiring the guidance of the United States. The accuracy of Roosevelt's observation can be questioned, but threat perception and geographic distance seem to have been on the president's mind.

Foreign Minister Baron de Rio Branco

Brazilian foreign minister Rio Branco worried about the inability of Latin American governments to pay their foreign debts, even though Brazil was on excellent terms with its foreign creditors. This problem surfaced in 1902–1903 when Britain, Italy, and Germany resorted to their own brand of "gunboat diplomacy" to coerce Venezuela into paying claims it owed to European citizens (see Chapter 25). Although the Europeans stressed that they were not interested in acquiring territory, their attempt to collect debts by force produced adverse reactions throughout Latin America. President Theodore Roosevelt used the episode to inaugurate his own corollary to the Monroe Doctrine, a new phase of diplomacy characterized by frequent intervention in the Caribbean and Central American regions. After the Venezuelan blockade incident, Rio Branco applauded the "great service" provided by the Monroe Doctrine in checking European territorial ambitions in the Western Hemisphere. In contrast to most of his Spanish-American counterparts, Rio Branco argued that the United States should be regarded as a benevolent guardian interested in protecting Latin America against external interference, and not an imperialist aggressor. Rio Branco endorsed the Roosevelt Corollary to the Monroe Doctrine, and he made Brazilian-American friendship the cornerstone of his foreign policy. By supporting U.S. Latin American policy, Rio Branco hoped to offset British influence in the Río de la Plata region and reduce the negative impact of border disputes among Brazil's neighbors. The developing rivalry with Argentina also contributed to the perceived pro-U.S. stance of Brazilians at the time.

In return, the United States recognized the importance of cultivating friendly relations with Brazil. Secretary of State Elihu Root tried to counter the distrust and fear in the Americas by reassuring Latin Americans that the United States had no selfish or aggressive motives in its Latin America policy and only wished for peace and prosperity for all. When he took office in 1905, Root's rhetoric offered a stark contrast to the bluster and racist comments of Theodore Roosevelt and Secretary of State John Hay. In urging officials at the State Department to show friendship and respect to Latin American diplomats, Root wrote in 1905:

> The South Americans now hate us, largely because they think we despise them and try to bully them. I really like them and intend to show it. I think their friendship is really important to the United States, and the best way to secure it is by treating them like gentlemen. If you want to make a man your friend, it does not pay to treat him like a yellow dog.[3]

In an obvious "diplomatic tilt" toward Brazil, Root suggested to Brazilian ambassador Joaquim Nabuco in a private conversation that the United States, with the assistance of Brazil and Mexico, take on the responsibility for affirming the Monroe Doctrine throughout the hemisphere. Several weeks later President Roosevelt indicated he wished to have Brazil, rather than Argentina, exercise the main influence in South America. On the basis of these unofficial soundings, Rio replaced Caracas or Buenos Aires as the site for the 1906 Pan-American Conference. U.S.-Brazilian relations were solidified further when Root decided to personally lead the American delegation to the conference in Rio, the first time that a serving secretary of state had left the United States. In 1906, Brazil became the first South American country to exchange envoys at the rank of ambassador with the United States.

It is important to point out that Root's Pan-Americanism was more public rhetoric than a genuine elevation of the importance of Brazil to the United States. Root's reference to "South America" in his address mentioned above was a deliberate effort to treat Brazil differently from "Latin America." Unlike the less-developed and unruly republics of Central America and the Caribbean, Brazil was considered peaceful, politically conservative, and law-abiding. Root's journey to South America was aimed at persuading the Latin American nations to attend the forthcoming peace conference at The Hague. While in Rio de Janeiro, Root spoke at the James Monroe palace emphasizing the role of all nations of the hemisphere in securing world peace. The United States could not have found a more compliant ally than Brazil; it was the only country in the hemisphere to support the United States during the Spanish American War, the chronic use of force in the Caribbean and Central America, the separation of Panama from Colombia in 1903, and Washington's position toward the leaders of the Mexican revolutionary government in 1914.

Brazil and World War I

As the crisis in Europe deepened between 1914 and 1917, the United States struggled to remain neutral but ultimately realized that with Germany's unrestricted submarine warfare it would have to intervene. President Wilson realized that U.S. intervention in Europe would violate the Monroe Doctrine's "sacred" injunction to stay out of Europe's battles; but in a bold effort to put his own stamp on the Monroe Doctrine, the president tried to elevate it to a universal principle on January 22, 1917:

> I am proposing, as it were, that the nations should with one accord adopt the doctrine of President Monroe as the doctrine of the world: that no nation should seek to extend its policy over any other nation, but that every people should be free to determine its own policy, its own way of development, unhindered, unthreatened, unafraid, the little along with the great and powerful.[4]

Once the United States declared war on Germany, President Wilson made strenuous efforts to get Brazil to join the Allies in defeating Germany, hoping to set a precedent that the other Latin American governments would follow. Although a large number of German colonists lived in southern Brazil, Germany's naval encroachments threatened Brazil's extensive merchant marine, and Brazil found it easy to follow the wishes of the United States; after the war, Brazil took a pro-U.S. position at the Paris Peace Conference and became a staunch supporter of the League of Nations. Despite Brazil's wartime collaboration with the United States, Washington refused to grant its request for a special-status relationship and shifted its focus again to themes of hemispheric solidarity, often neglecting Brazil as unimportant to U.S. policy concerns.

The Vargas Period, 1930–1954

Getúlio Vargas came to power in a military coup in 1930 and ruled for fifteen years before being overthrown by the military in 1945. He returned to power in 1951, but during a bitter political crisis three years later he committed suicide. A caretaker administration finished his term of office. Under Vargas's first period of rule Brazil came under a semi-dictatorship, flirted briefly with Hitler's Germany, and then became a close wartime ally of the United States. Brazil was the first nation to sign a reciprocal trade agreement with the United States as part of Roosevelt's Good Neighbor Policy. The Roosevelt administration promoted the Monroe Doctrine and continental solidarity, frequently pressuring Brazil to enter the war as an example to the rest of Latin America. In 1936 President Roosevelt attended the Inter-American Conference for the Maintenance of Peace in Buenos Aires, the first occasion that an American president met with Latin American leaders outside the United States.

President Roosevelt strongly supported the authoritarian government of Getúlio Vargas and collaborated with it closely throughout the war. Although Washington considered Vargas's government a dictatorship, it was viewed as a benevolent one with considerable popular support. Vargas equated democracy with disorder, criticized liberalism, and praised fascist virtues, but the United States still considered Brazil a cornerstone of the Good Neighbor Policy and a key ally. Argentine anti-Americanism also contributed to the belief that maintaining friendly relations with Brazil was important to hemispheric unity. The key to friendly relations between Brazil and the United States and Brazil's role as a fighting ally was Oswaldo Aranha (1938–1944), Vargas's foreign minister, who remained firmly committed to democratic procedures while at the same time serving an authoritarian government.

Brazil and World War II

Until World War II, Brazil had established a professional military based on the educational and training programs of Germany and France, and it used their manuals, instructors, and equipment. The war changed this pattern, as President Roosevelt sought Brazil's support for U.S. actions against the Axis threat by strongly encouraging Brazilian leaders to join the war effort as an example to the rest of Latin America. During the war years Adolf A. Berle Jr., assistant secretary of state for Latin American affairs (1938–1944) and ambassador to Brazil (1945–1946), was Roosevelt's key Latin American advisor. Berle believed that the Brazilian military represented a positive force for democracy, free elections, and representative government. He painted a favorable picture of Vargas during his tenure, claiming that although the Brazilian government was a dictatorship it had kept all its international obligations, and since Getúlio Vargas was a popular figure in Brazil his regime could hardly be a police state.

Despite the fact that the Brazilian government was a dictatorship during the war, the United States—being more interested in stability and order than in promoting democracy—supported the Vargas regime and collaborated closely with it throughout the war. Vargas flirted with fascism prior to World War II, but eventually he succumbed to U.S. pressure to align Brazil with the Allies in the war effort. Cut off from German and French contacts because of the war, the Brazilian armed forces came to rely more and more on the United States for training, techniques, and equipment. The fear of a German invasion of Brazil—combined with Nazi activity in neighboring Argentina—contributed to several joint military arrangements and U.S. financial assistance for a large steel industry in Brazil. After a German submarine attack on a Brazilian ship, Brazil declared war on Germany in August 1942. To support the war, Brazil sent an expeditionary force— Força Expedicionária Brasilerira (FEB)—of 25,000 men to fight in Europe, a move that raised the professionalism of the Brazilian officer corps and heightened its political orientation. According to Gerald Haines, "The irony of a dictatorship sending an army across the seas to liberate oppressed people was not lost on the Força Expedicionária Brasileira (FEB)."[5] The contacts with American military forces and the war experience helped the FEB officers forge a much closer, or "special," relationship with the United States and convince policymakers in Washington that the Brazilian military represented an apolitical force that supported the democratic process; however, this outlook ceased to exist after the election of Jimmy Carter in 1978.

The harmony and cooperation in Brazilian-American relations during World War II changed in 1945 as many of the key players in Washington who carried out Latin American policy were replaced, including Nelson Rockefeller (assistant secretary of state for Latin American affairs, 1944–1945) and Edward R. Stettinius Jr. (secretary of state, 1944–1945). Both were sympathetic to Latin America in their own way, but their links to corporate America led them to believe that private enterprise provided the best way to promote national economic development (this was not an attractive option to many Brazilian policymakers who were accustomed to state-sponsored programs during the war effort). In 1945 Spruille Braden, an outspoken diplomat with several businesses in Chile, became responsible for Latin American affairs in the U.S. State Department. With Braden and Berle now in charge, U.S. Latin American policy took a new turn and was marked by more blatant forms of intervention and hints that the Good Neighbor Policy had served its purpose now that the war was over. After World War II, the United States turned away from the government-sponsored economic aspects of the Good Neighbor Policy to an emphasis on private investment as the key to inter-American relations. The progressive disengagement of the United States in matters of economic assistance in Latin America contributed to Brazil's decision to adopt a more independent, nationalistic foreign policy in the 1960s and 1970s. Nelson Rockefeller and Henry Kaiser—giants of corporate America—came to Brazil after 1945 to demonstrate that U.S.-style democratic capitalism could have a positive effect on economic development and international relations. They invested in rural development, agriculture, and automobile manufacturing and helped determine the nature of U.S.-Brazilian economic relations from 1945 to 1960.

After Roosevelt's death in 1945, Berle and Braden joined the chorus of those who opposed dictatorships in Latin America and assumed efforts to squeeze Vargas from power. Ambassador Berle decided to give a speech (which was cleared in an earlier draft by Vargas himself) to opposition journalists stating that the United States would not support dictatorships in the hemisphere. Berle's speech, indicating pleasure that Brazil was proceeding to restore constitutional democracy, caused an uproar by appearing to approve of opposition plots to depose Vargas. Within one month of the scheduled elections, the Brazilian military removed Vargas in a bloodless coup and then proceeded to oversee the election of General Eurico Gaspar Dutra (Vargas's war minister). This political act delighted the Truman administration because it was interpreted as a sign of the growing democratization of Brazil.

BRAZIL AND THE UNITED STATES DURING THE COLD WAR

During the early Cold War years, Brazil maintained an open-door policy toward foreign capital and was a consistent supporter of the United States in the United Nations and other international organizations. President Dutra (1945–1951) severed relations with the Soviet Union, outlawed the Brazilian Communist Party, and took repressive measures against leftists and reformers. Although it was not an automatic supporter, Brazil voted more consistently with the United States in international organizations during the period 1946–1955 than any other Latin American country, except Somoza's Nicaragua. When the Inter-American Treaty on Reciprocal Assistance (Rio Treaty) was signed in Brazil in 1947, declaring a regional version of the Monroe Doctrine and a pledge to consult immediately in cases of extrahemispheric aggression against an American state, Brazilian delegates sided with the United States on every issue.

President Truman arrived on the battleship *Missouri* for the ceremonial conclusion of the conference. He was cheered as the inheritor of Roosevelt's Good Neighbor Policy and was invited to speak to the Brazilian Congress, where he emphasized the importance of a united front against communism. While Brazilians were clearly sympathetic to President Truman's desire to protect small and weak nations from foreign aggression, this was not their primary concern. They wanted a "special relationship" with the United States to assist with their own economic development (including internal stability), and to ensure their nation's continual dominance in South America—particularly against their traditional rival, Argentina. Although Truman's division of the world by political ideology (the Truman Doctrine) was not directed specifically at Brazil, it represented the spirit of Monroeism by stressing resistance to all efforts to impose an alien political system or foreign domination on a region vital to the security of the United States. Both the Truman and Eisenhower administrations were convinced that communism and the Soviet Union represented a threat to the United States and its hegemonic position in the Western Hemisphere, and Brazil was needed as a key ally in this effort.

The Escola Superior de Guerra (Superior War College)

One of the most important links between the United States and Brazilian militaries was the Escola Superior de Guerra (ESG), created in 1949 to train civilian and military elites in Cold War ideology and national security needs. Modeled after the National War College in the United States, its curriculum placed heavy emphasis on anticommunism and counterinsurgency. Participants in the courses discussed national development needs, particularly in relation to Brazil's defense against the alleged communist threat in the hemisphere. Military officers as well as businessmen were taught the value of "civic action" programs. Graduates of the ESG became the leading proponents of anticommunism and private foreign investment within Brazil. Those who attended ESG classes soon became the center of conspiracy against the government, particularly after President Jânio Quadros resigned and João Goulart assumed the presidency in the early 1960s. ESG graduates were instrumental in the 1964 coup against Goulart and staffed almost all the most important positions during the long period of military government that followed. The ESG was led by officers who had participated in the FEB during World War II and formed a close bond with U.S. military officers. Having been taught Cold War theories developed in the United States, the enemy for ESG graduates was not a nation or group of nations but a hostile ideology. Officials in Washington maintained that the ESG experience exposed Brazilian officers to democracy in action and bureaucratic efficiency.

One of the most consistent aspects of U.S. policy toward Brazil during the early Cold War was the cultivation of the military as a valuable asset in the battle against communism. This was a relatively easy task because the Brazilian military was always considered the final arbiter in domestic politics and the ultimate custodian of political power. The Brazilian military overthrew the monarchy in 1889, installed Vargas in the presidency in 1930, deposed him in 1945, and forced him to resign in 1954; engineered the counter-coup of 1955 that allowed Juscelino Kubitschek to take the presidency; carried out a coup against Goulart in 1964 with the backing of the United States; and ruled the longest of any Latin American military during the Cold War, from 1964 to 1985. The formation of the ESG provided the critical link between the Brazilian military and the United States. It instilled the necessary Cold War ideology, and the Brazilian generals found plenty of U.S. assistance to carry out their mission.

Brazil and the Alliance for Progress

The election of Juscelino Kubitschek (1956–1960) marked the beginning of a Brazilian foreign policy of greater independence from the United States. Unable to secure maximum financial assistance for his economic development programs, Kubitschek created Operation Pan America (OPA), an opportunity to encourage a new U.S.-Latin American policy emphasizing economic development. The OPA was not a radical departure in Brazilian foreign policy because it embodied aspirations for greater hemispheric unity, Cold War anticommunism, and trade expansionism. By stressing the importance of economic development as a deterrent to communist revolution in Latin America, Kubitschek's OPA included the creation of the Inter-American Development Bank (IDB), social development loans, and more economic assistance with fewer strings attached. However, Brazil and the United States differed over economic development strategies. The United States wanted Latin Americans to rely on their own private initiative, whereas Brazilians believed in a hemisphere-wide economic plan. Despite Kubitschek's efforts, disputes with the United States and the International Monetary Fund (IMF) led to OPA's failure.

The "unwritten alliance" between Brazil and the United States that reached back to the turn of the century was unraveling as Brazil struggled to project a more independent foreign policy. Beginning in the late 1950s, Brazil's foreign policy included the following: a more active involvement in international organizations, increased emphasis on hemispheric solidarity and economic integration, increased trade and diplomatic ties with the communist bloc, and closer ties with the Third World. After the Cuban revolution and President Kennedy's election, efforts were made to reverse the negative trends in U.S.–Latin American relations left over from the Eisenhower years. In an effort to mobilize hemispheric unity in the battle against both poverty and communism, Kennedy proposed two dramatic initiatives—the Peace Corps and the Alliance for Progress—within his first two months in office. Kennedy's strategy was to use economic development and social reform to direct the growing nationalism of developing countries in democratic directions. By shifting the emphasis of U.S. aid programs from military assistance to economic development programs such as the Alliance for Progress, Kennedy hoped to prevent violent revolutions in Latin America.

After Castro's revolution, what mattered the most to U.S. policymakers was not so much the development of a democratic Brazil as it was the creation of a bulwark against communism and the spread of Castroism in Latin America. When it seemed expedient to do so, the United States supported democratic elections in Brazil; but Washington also played a major role in deposing the two democratically elected Brazilian presidents who followed Kubitschek between 1960 and 1964. When Brazil's presidents appeared to be leaning too far to the left and pursuing a more independent foreign policy, they were considered threats to the security of the hemisphere—and in need of replacement.

Jânio Quadros (1960–1961) angered Washington with his refusal to visit the United States before his inauguration, his informal talks with the communist bloc nations, and his decoration of Ché Guevara with Brazil's highest medal, the Cruzeiro do Sul. Relations deteriorated further when Adolf Berle, Kennedy's special envoy, visited Brazil with an offer of $300 million in foreign aid in exchange for backing the Bay of Pigs invasion of Cuba in 1961. President Quadros expressed his disgust with "Berle's bribe" and promptly rejected the offer. When Quadros resigned unexpectedly in August 1961, his vice-president, João Goulart, assumed the presidency, but Brazil's more independent foreign policy continued.

The 1964 Coup against Goulart

At least two years before the military coup that deposed Goulart in April 1964, the United States and Brazil had serious clashes over Cold War security issues and economic reform efforts. The key players in the coup against President Goulart were members of the Brazilian military who had developed close links with policymakers in Washington stretching back to World War II. Those who assisted with the coup, or did nothing to stop it, included U.S. ambassador Lincoln Gordon, Defense Attaché Vernon A. Walters, and Assistant Secretary of State Thomas Mann. Most U.S. officials admitted privately that Goulart was not a communist but that his foreign policy suggested the possibility of a communist takeover in Brazil if things were not "corrected." Colonel Walters, who had served as liaison officer with the Brazilian Expeditionary Force in Italy during World War II, was on friendly terms with the military conspirators and was fully aware of the details surrounding the coup. Walters communicated what he knew about the coup to Ambassador Gordon, who in turn informed Assistant Secretary Mann of the military conspiracy. In case the conspiracy against Goulart failed, the U.S. military had made contingency plans, including intervention if there were any signs of Soviet movement into Brazil. Some of the U.S. military officers operating out of Panama were convinced of a Soviet takeover. U.S. Army lieutenant Colonel Robert Schuler compared the Brazilian crisis to the prior challenges to the Monroe Doctrine during the Venezuela crisis in 1902–1903. The Central Intelligence Agency was also instrumental in supporting the military conspirators and in generating hemisphere-wide propaganda in support of the new military government of Marshall Humberto Castello Branco in 1964.

The Brazilian coup of 1964 was considered a major event in Washington because it fit neatly into the Cold War prescription against communism in the Western Hemisphere. Those who saw military rule as the only alternative to chaos and communism also believed that military rule would be short-lived and serve as a transition to a more reliable civilian presidency. However, the majority of officers favored a strong "apolitical" government that would rule Brazil for a much longer time, despite opposition from Castello Branco himself. The Cold War doctrine of national security that had been taught at the Escola Superior de Guerra (ESG) formed the basis of authoritarian rule in Brazil after the coup. In Castelo Branco's government during the 1960s, fully 80 percent of the core group of Brazilian policymakers were graduates of the ESG or U.S. military schools.

The Generals Take Control, 1964–1985

Since the 1946 constitution had given the Brazilian military the responsibility of maintaining law and order and guaranteeing the effective functioning of government, those who engineered the coup of 1964 never doubted that they had acted constitutionally in removing Goulart. However, few Brazilians anticipated the length and harshness of military rule. Instead of a transitional regime that would usher in a return to democracy, the military consolidated its power and ruled for over 20 years. Military rule reversed the populist trends toward economic nationalism—the law limiting the remittance of profits by foreign firms was revoked—and the earlier efforts to steer a more independent foreign policy. With the military firmly in power, the United States did not have to worry about demoralized foreign investors, the legitimacy of the Alliance for Progress, demands for populist economic policies, and communist "disruption" in Latin America's largest country. In return for Brazilian realignment with the United States under the generals, Washington increased its economic and military aid to substantial levels.

To solidify its newly acquired dependency on the United States, Brazil severed its relations with Cuba, spearheaded the diplomatic and economic isolation of Cuba at OAS meetings, and was a key supporter of the U.S. intervention in the Dominican Republic in 1965. Believing that it was once again stopping communism in Latin America, Brazil provided the commanding officer and most of the 2,500 Latin American troops that were subsequently employed in the OAS "peacekeeping" operation. However, the United States provided the majority of military force. The commitment to military counterinsurgency, repression, and favorable conditions for foreign investment set the stage for numerous "dirty wars" that would sweep across Latin America in the 1970s. Brazil's military rulers provided logistical and financial support to the military coups that followed in Bolivia, Uruguay, Chile, and Argentina. However, President Carter (1977–1981) was unsympathetic toward military governments, most notably that of Brazil, and battled with Brazil over trade issues, human rights, nuclear energy, international lending policies, and the reduction of U.S military assistance. The deterioration of U.S.-Brazilian relations during the Carter years was reversed by President Reagan (1981–1989), who was convinced that "moderate authoritarians" such as existed in Brazil deserved backing from the United States.

The Return of Democracy

Brazil's return to democratic rule was a gradual process that began in the late 1960s and ended in 1985. Until the early 1970s, military economic policy centered on providing an "economic miracle" at the expense of any effort to return Brazil to democracy. Emphasizing economic expansion and efforts to curb inflation, the Brazilian military enjoyed the support of many key groups in Brazil. Critics of the military authoritarian government who had not gone into exile were subject to threats and torture. In an effort to eliminate internal subversion, the military imposed press censorship, prohibited innovative teaching techniques of Paulo Freire, banned almost all political activity, outlawed old political parties and created new ones, and tightly controlled elections. By creating a two-party democratic facade, the military was able to control national politics in the name of a "revolution" for democracy. Some endorsed the coup—industrialists, technocrats, and urban dwellers—since they envisioned economic benefits from the regime and the anticommunist ideology of the military coincided with their own political beliefs. However, the military's economic miracle came to an abrupt halt in 1973 when the OPEC (Organization of Petroleum Exporting Countries) oil embargo sent prices of petroleum skyrocketing and inflation began to rise. With the economy on a serious downturn, the military leaders decided to move toward an *abertura*, an opening toward the return of democratic rule, and their departure from the political arena.

BRAZIL AND THE UNITED STATES IN THE AFTERMATH OF THE COLD WAR

The return of civilian rule in 1985 and the end of the Cold War have brought important changes to the Brazilian-U.S. relationship. The civilian politicians who have held power since 1985 have had to struggle with a huge foreign debt, bouts of hyperinflation and official corruption, expanding a trade-based economy, and working out a competitive, rather than complementary, economic status with the United States. Any effort to bring the generals to justice for human rights violations has been undermined by the residual power of the Brazilian military. Although the United States remains Brazil's largest market, its biggest supplier of goods and services, and a major source of investment and finance, recent trends indicate frictions and disagreements over trade policies. President Fernando Henrique Cardoso (1995–   ) personifies the important changes in economic development strategy taking place in Brazil (and Latin America) and in U.S.-Brazilian relations. During the 1960s Cardoso taught at the University of São Paulo, opposed the military government, and was a firm believer in neo-Marxist principles favoring socialism and a powerful state. He has since disavowed his earlier economic and political views, being convinced that a modified capitalist model is the solution to Brazil's economic woes.

As the end of the century approaches, relations between the United States and Brazil have become less important than was the case during the Cold War. There are several reasons for this change, despite a long history of collaboration and close ties, both politically and militarily. First, the end of the Cold War has reduced the need of the United States to cultivate the Brazilian military or worry about security matters in South America. Second, Brazil's success in forming the Southern Cone Common Market (MERCOSUR) with Argentina, Paraguay, and Uruguay has offset the dominance of the United States (and Canada and Mexico) in the North American Free Trade Agreement (NAFTA). Third, there is a growing gulf between how the two countries' governments see each other. Although presidents Carter (1978), Reagan (1984), Bush (1992), and Clinton (1997) have visited Brazil to promote American interests, most Americans know and care little about Brazil, and what they do comprehend often generates hostility. Brazilians feel that the United States either tries to prevent Brazil from becoming a world power or does little to provide assistance in overcoming its persistent economic, environmental, and technological difficulties.

CONCLUSION

Today Brazil is a formidable world power, larger than the continental United States, with a population (165 million) and economy that exceeds that of Russia, and the major player in a new trade bloc called the Southern Cone Common Market (MERCOSUL in Portuguese). The United States has never intervened directly to expel an alien force from Brazil, but the rhetoric and emotions associated with the Monroe Doctrine have served the foreign policy needs of both countries in ways that would have surprised even the most ardent Monroeists of the 1820s. Despite the changing nature of the historical relationship, and the tendency of American policymakers to neglect Brazil, the United States remains central to many aspects of Brazilian economic life, the largest investor and dominant foreign business presence in the country. The end of the Cold War and Brazil's efforts to consolidate democracy have helped improve the bilateral relationship between the two giants of the hemisphere. The fact that Brazil and Argentina have both forsworn nuclear weapons programs (neither obtained the bomb), once considered a threat to peace in the hemisphere, has also served to improve the relationship. Unlike U.S.-Mexican relations, the absence of a shared border with the United States and Brazil means that the bilateral relationship is free of domestic economic and political problems.

NOTES

1. Samuel Flagg Bemis, *The Latin American Policy of the United States: An Historical Interpretation* (New York: W. W. Norton, 1971), pp. 111–112.

2. Steven C. Topik, *Trade and Gunboats: The United States and Brazil in the Age of Empire* (Stanford, CA: Stanford University Press, 1996), p. 121.

3. Quoted in Joseph Smith, *Unequal Giants: Diplomatic Relations between the*

United States and Brazil, 1889–1930 (Pittsburgh, PA: University of Pittsburgh Press, 1991), p. 52.

4. Quoted in Gaddis Smith, "Monroe Doctrine," in Bruce W. Jentleson and Thomas G. Paterson, eds., *Encyclopedia of U.S. Foreign Relations*, vol. 3 (New York: Oxford University Press, 1997), p. 162.

5. Gerald K. Haines, *The Americanization of Brazil: A Study of U.S. Cold War Diplomacy in the Third World, 1945–1954* (Wilmington, DE: Scholarly Resources Books, 1989), p. 41.

SUGGESTED READINGS

Cobbs, Elizabeth Anne. *The Rich Neighbor Policy: Rockefeller and Kaiser in Brazil.* New Haven, CT: Yale University Press, 1992.

Dawson, Cyrus B., and James M. Dawsey. *The* Confederados: *Old South Immigrants in Brazil.* Tuscaloosa.: University of Alabama Press, 1997.

Haines, Gerald K. *The Americanization of Brazil: A Study of U.S. Cold War Diplomacy in the Third World, 1945–1954.* Wilmington, DE: Scholarly Resources Books, 1989.

Smith, Joseph. *Unequal Giants: Diplomatic Relations between the United States and Brazil, 1889–1930.* Pittsburgh: University of Pittsburgh Press, 1991.

Topik, Steven C. *Trade and Gunboats: The United States and Brazil in the Age of Empire.* Stanford, CA: Stanford University Press, 1996.

5

Chile

TIMELINE OF U.S. RELATIONS WITH CHILE

1810	Chile declares independence from Spain
1822	United States recognizes Chile's independence
1832	United States establishes diplomatic relations
1842	Chile leads world in copper production
1850s	Railroads and telegraph lines are built by U.S. engineers
1879–1884	War of the Pacific
1884	Treaty of Ancón ends War of the Pacific
1891	*Baltimore* incident
1914–1918	Chile remains neutral during World War I
1943	Chile breaks diplomatic relations with Axis powers
1948	Communist Party is proscribed until 1956
1953	Chile signs defense pact with the United States
1958–1964	Jorge Alessandri serves as elected president
1964–1970	Eduardo Frei serves as elected president
1965	Chileanization of U.S. copper companies begins
1970	Salvador Allende is elected president
1971	Allende nationalizes foreign-owned copper mines
1973	Allende is overthrown in coup supported by CIA
1973–1989	The military rules under General Augusto Pinochet
1973–1977	Nixon and Ford presidencies remain friendly toward Chile
1976	Orlando Letelier is assassinated in Washington, D.C.
	Kennedy Amendment ends military aid to Chile

1977–1981	Carter presidency emphasizes human rights
1981–1989	Reagan presidency emphasizes quiet diplomacy
1983–1985	Reagan administration shifts to promoting democracy
1988	Dictator Pinochet is defeated in plebiscite
1989	Democracy returns with election of Patricio Aylwin
1994–1998	Eduardo Frei, son of former president, serves as elected president
1997	Clinton administration allows sale of F-16 fighters to Chile
1998	Pinochet retires as head of the military and assumes permanent Senate seat
	President Clinton visits Chile and declares that "the day of the dictators is over"

INTRODUCTION

Although it is small in population and somewhat isolated from the rest of South America, Chile has had frequent confrontations with the United States over trade and commerce, security, access to raw materials, intervention, and political ideology. William Sater describes this troublesome relationship between the two nations as one of "empires in conflict."[1] The rivalry between Chile and the United States in the nineteenth century was fueled by the size of Chile's navy (the largest in Latin America) and its territorial gains from the War of the Pacific (1879–1884). After the *Baltimore* incident in 1891 in which two U.S. sailors were killed in a drunken brawl, the United States forced Chile to pay an indemnity that generated deep anti-Yankee sentiment in Chile. The demand for sodium nitrate and copper contributed to the rise of a foreign-dominated economy, first by the British and later by the United States. Chile's distant location and Washington's tendency to waffle during times of European encroachment weakened the validity of the Monroe Doctrine and alienated the Chileans.

When Americans invested heavily in the large copper mines at El Teniente and Chuquicamata at the turn of the century, that helped forge an important economic and political link between Washington and Santiago, producing heightened security concerns during times of war. However, foreign control over lucrative mining enterprises frequently boiled over into nationalist resentment against U.S. corporations. Once U.S. companies came to dominate Chile's major source of foreign exchange, it became possible to exercise a greater degree of control over Chilean foreign policy.

During the Cold War, the United States pressured Chile to conform to its anticommunist foreign policy by demanding that it outlaw its Communist party, integrate its military into the inter-American collective security structure, and subject its democratic system to electoral manipulation and covert action that eventually destroyed Chilean democracy in 1973.

The military coup against President Salvador Allende ushered in 17 years of harsh military rule under General Augusto Pinochet. Between 1973 and 1988, thousands of Chileans were killed or "disappeared" by the military junta that seized power. It was primarily on the basis of the harsh repression in Chile that the Carter administration and the Democratic-controlled Congress elevated human rights in the making of U.S. policy toward Latin America and the Caribbean in the 1970s, although this was reversed after President Reagan took office in 1981. Later, Reagan shifted his rhetoric to "democracy promotion" in Chile as a counterbalance to his policy toward Nicaragua, and he watched as democracy gradually returned to Chile with the electoral defeat of dictator Pinochet in 1988. With the end of the Cold War and the return of Chilean democracy, U.S.-Chilean relations have improved; there is emphasis on free trade and investment rather than ideological hostility, human rights abuses, and ownership of vital economic resources.

CHILE AND THE UNITED STATES DURING THE NINETEENTH CENTURY

Independence and the Monroe Doctrine

Chile fought for its independence from Spain between 1810 and 1818, but the United States did not establish formal diplomatic relations until 1832. In the spirit of Monroe's defensive imperialism, President Andrew Jackson (1829–1837) signed a number of commercial treaties with Chile, Mexico, Peru-Bolivia, Spain, and Venezuela, but Spanish interest in Peru and Chile continued despite the Monroe Doctrine. Washington refused to act during times of European intervention, claiming that it did not wish to alienate Spain and that at such a distance there hardly seemed a security threat to the United States. For example, Secretary of State Seward irritated Chileans by claiming that as long as European nations did not intend to seize or occupy land in the Western Hemisphere, there was no need to invoke the Monroe Doctrine. Through the latter half of the nineteenth century Chileans remained ambivalent toward Monroe's principles; they criticized the United States for assuming the role of hemispheric policeman and refusing to stand by its declared policies, but at the same time they expected Washington to halt Spanish intervention. On two occasions—in the 1860s and the 1880s—the United States failed to stand behind the Monroe Doctrine in Chile. This indifference to any form of protective imperialism allowed the Chileans to establish their own sphere of influence and dominate the Pacific Coast of South America until World War I.

Once the United States became embroiled in its own civil war, fears surfaced over the possibility of European intervention in the Americas. Prior to the Emancipation Proclamation in 1862, President Abraham Lincoln contemplated colonizing Latin America and Africa with freed slaves to defuse the heated abolition issue in the United States, but Secretary of State Seward's opposition to slavery squelched this option. President Lincoln thought that abolishing slavery would reduce European interest in the Americas. Between 1861 and 1866 Thomas Henry Nelson served as U.S. minister to Chile, where he tried to improve relations by emphasizing the Monroe Doctrine, democracy, and the fact that the United States was not interested in acquiring territory in Latin America.

Chile's mineral wealth—mainly in copper and nitrates—played a major role in its domestic and international politics after independence. By 1842 Chile led the world in copper production, and mining wealth began to shape its political economy and relations with the outside world. U.S. economic penetration of Chile started with American railroad and bridge builders such as Henry Meiggs and William Wheelwright during the 1850s and 1860s. Wheelwright built the first railroad in South America—from the Chilean port of Caldera to the silver and copper mines of Copiapó—and in 1850 constructed Chile's (and South America's) first telegraph line. For years he ran a steamship service along the western coast of South America. The ambitious Henry Meiggs also built railroads in Chile, mined and exported Bolivian guano, founded a bank in La Paz, and constructed railroads in Peru.

The War of the Pacific, 1879–1884

Once it was discovered that fertilizers could be produced from sodium nitrate (*salitre*), the large deposits in the Atacama desert created a mining frenzy that generated great wealth and a major war. The War of the Pacific was fanned by the great commercial value of nitrates and copper, Chilean imperialism, and inept political leadership in Bolivia and Peru. After Chilean laborers and entrepreneurs flocked to the northern desert to mine the nitrate, treaties were signed among the three nations to allow for taxation, revenue sharing, and territorial demarcation. When it became apparent that there was considerable wealth in the Atacama desert, Bolivia and Peru entered into a secret treaty of alliance in the event that Chile might attempt to expand its control over the nitrate fields. Both Bolivia and Peru violated the 1874 treaty permitting Chile to carry on its mining activities, thereby provoking a major confrontation. After Chilean troops occupied Antofogasta, both Peru and Bolivia declared war on Chile. With superior naval and army forces, Chile defeated both Peru and Bolivia and was clearly the victor by 1884. The War of the Pacific ended with the Treaty of Ancón between Peru and Chile in 1883 and an armistice between Bolivia and Chile in 1884. As a result of the war Bolivia was left landlocked, without a land outlet to the Pacific Ocean; Peru ceded the province of Tarapacá outright to Chile, which thereby increased its national territory by one-fourth. The war gave Chile clear access to nitrate revenues, and within ten years its national income increased nearly fourfold. However, Chile's possession of Tacna and Arica poisoned relations with Peru until the territory question was settled in 1929. Under the terms of the final settlement Chile returned Tacna to Peru in exchange for a $6 million cash settlement, and Arica remained under Chilean jurisdiction.

Once Chilean forces moved north and occupied Tacna and Arica during the early phases of the war and were preparing to attack Peru's capital, Lima, the United States decided to invoke the Monroe Doctrine in order to stave off the possibility of European intervention. When Germany suggested that it join with them and Britain to negotiate a peace settlement between the three contending parties, the United States brought up George Washington's dictum against involvement in entangling alliances. In an effort to settle the war, U.S. secretary of state William Evarts sent envoys to mediate the dispute, but they were unsuccessful. James G. Blaine replaced Evarts in 1881, but his tenure was brief and his assertive nationalism, racist remarks, and interventionism proved to be counterproductive.

In one of the worst cases of diplomatic ineptitude, Blaine sent two diplomats—Hugh J. Kilpatrick and Stephen A. Hurlbut—to Chile and Peru to engineer a peaceful settlement of the war. Hurlbut tried to have the U.S. Navy intervene in the war, but he exceeded his instructions from President Garfield by demanding that Peru cede to the United States territory for the Chimbote coaling station without the president's permission. Kilpatrick was replaced by his wife after he fell ill and died during his brief stint in Chile. Blaine replaced Kilpatrick and Hurlbut with two new envoys (including his son, Walker), but their instructions were limited on account of Blaine's replacement—Frederick Frelinghuysen—after the death of Garfield and the ascendancy of Chester A. Arthur as president in 1881. Frelinghuysen initiated a policy shift that emphasized mediation and compromise rather than confrontation. In the end, the United States convinced Peru to cede land to Chile and Santiago to moderate its demands to terminate the conflict. The War of the Pacific helped Chile develop its own sphere of influence in South America after the war, but relations worsened with the United States because of the diplomatic incompetence and arrogance displayed during the dispute.

The *Baltimore* Incident, 1891

After five months at sea the USS *Baltimore* docked in Valparaíso, Chile, in October 1891. In a brawl at the True Blue Saloon, two U.S. sailors were killed by a mob after fighting with a Chilean sailor. During the melee 17 U.S. sailors were beaten severely and another 30 were jailed by Chilean authorities. Tensions escalated as each side searched for ways of blaming the other for an incident that came close to provoking a war between the

United States and Chile. After receiving a report on the affair, Admiral Winfield Scott Schley concluded that the Chileans were to blame. He passed this on to President Benjamin Harrison, who demanded an apology and the payment of reparations for what he concluded was an insult to the U.S. military. Chile misperceived the level of concern of the Harrison administration and tried to ignore the diplomatic demands. As Washington's patience wore thin, Chilean foreign minister Manuel Matta sent a telegram to Chile's minister in the United States, claiming that President Harrison was either stupid or lying in his report blaming Chile for the incident. After the message was leaked to a Santiago newspaper, the news filtered back to the United States, where it further inflamed the situation.

In January 1892 Chile finally released the results of its own investigation, concluding that U.S. sailors were to blame for instigating the riot, that the Valparaíso police had acted properly, and that the whole affair had been nothing more than a drunken brawl. The United States refused to accept this interpretation, and in a speech to Congress in 1892 President Harrison suggested that the United States prepare for war against Chile if the incident was not settled "properly." However, after Chile determined that its South American neighbors were not on its side in the affair, it decided to dissociate itself from the Matta telegram and agreed to third-party arbitration. Santiago then sent word to Washington that it hoped that Matta's remarks had not destroyed the historical friendship between the two countries. The diplomatic debacle was resolved after the United States interpreted this gesture as an apology and further pleased the Chileans by granting an earlier request to recall U.S. minister Patrick Egan in September 1893.

THE UNITED STATES AND CHILE DURING THE EARLY TWENTIETH CENTURY

The Conquest of Copper

During the first two decades of the twentieth century, mining engineers and entrepreneurs opened operations in Chile that would gradually become a defining feature of the relationship between the United States and Chile. William Braden, a mining engineer from Indianapolis, founded the Braden Copper Company in 1904 to mine the rich Rancagua mine in north-central Chile. Four years later he sold the company to Guggenheim Enterprises, a family of entrepreneurs with mining interests in California and Mexico. In 1915 the Guggenheims transferred control of the company to Kennecott Copper Company. By 1925, U.S. copper companies controlled most of the copper and nitrate mines in Chile. Although Chileans recognized the wealth to be gained in mining enterprises, Braden was unsuccessful in convincing Chileans to invest in their copper mines. Consequently, American capitalists gained a powerful foothold in what would later become the principal resource of the Chilean economy. As the Guggenheims and Braden reaped huge profits from the mines, Chileans grew increasingly resentful of U.S. ownership of *their* primary source of foreign exchange. Between 1906 and 1929, U.S. mining corporations expanded production tenfold and owned 90 percent of Chilean copper operations.

Chile, the United States, and World War I

At first the outbreak of war in Europe in 1914 did not significantly affect U.S.-Chilean relations. After the United States declared war in April 1917, President Woodrow Wilson (1913–1921) tried to enlist Latin American countries on the side of the United States. With strong ties to Germany, France, and Britain, Chile decided to remain neutral during the war, claiming that it was better to provide nitrates to the Allies than to issue a declaration of war. More important in Chile's decision to avoid entering World War I was domestic opposition to the war, significant currents of pro-German sentiments, and a residual anti-Americanism from the nineteenth century. Chile's mineral wealth should have brought prosperity during the war, but Chile gained little from its neutrality and its economy suffered from devalued nitrates. Chile's refusal to enter the war annoyed the United States, and the inability to resolve the Tacna-Arica dispute further strained U.S.-Chilean relations after World War I. During the 1920s the United States acted as a mediator in the heated border controversy, but the final settlement in 1929 was a result of direct negotiations between Peru and Chile *without* the United States.

The Good Neighbor Period and World War II

President Franklin D. Roosevelt's Good Neighbor Policy was popular in Chile and helped to improve bilateral relations until the outbreak of World War II, when relations again turned sour. The United States tried to pressure Chile into breaking relations with the Axis powers, but Santiago resisted due to the influence of its strong German community and the perceived security threats to its long coastline. However, after the United States exposed subversive German activity in Chile, it broke relations with the Axis powers in January 1943. It did not formally declare war on Japan until early 1945, a precondition for attending the San Francisco conference that gave rise to the United Nations. Chile received Lend-Lease (Roosevelt's program to extend aid to all countries considered vital to American defense) war materials from the United States and joined in the defense of South America. U.S.-owned copper companies kept copper prices low during the war years, which was a boon to Washington, but Chile lost hundreds of millions of dollars in lost revenues and taxes, and postwar inflationary pressures further devalued the price of copper.

CHILE AND THE UNITED STATES DURING THE COLD WAR

Chile and the U.S. Military

After World War II, the United States spent most of its time fostering Chile's integration into the newly established inter-American security system. The establishment of the Inter-American Defense Board led Chile to join the United States and other western hemispheric nations in signing the 1947 Inter-American Treaty of Reciprocal Assistance and the Charter of the Organization of American States in the following year. Chile did not send troops to the Korean War, and it resisted U.S. pressure to impose a price ceiling on copper. In 1953 Chile signed the Mutual Defense Assistance Pact, allowing its military to receive U.S. military training, grants, and low-interest loans. Until Salvador Allende—candidate of a socialist-communist coalition—almost won the Chilean presidency in 1958, Washington assumed it would not have to worry about combating communism in Chile.

The CIA Comes to Chile

Shortly after Allende nearly won the presidency in 1958, the Central Intelligence Agency (CIA) moved into Chile to combat the influence of the Chilean Communist Party (it had been outlawed by the government from 1948 to 1958) and undermine any attempt on the part of a socialist-communist alliance from coming to power, legally or illegally. After the success of the Cuban revolution in 1959, Washington became even more concerned about the spread of communism southward to Chile. A combination of covert action, economic and military assistance, and international pressure was put in place to protect U.S. copper companies, prevent Allende from coming to power, and keep the Cubans and Soviets out of South America.

Chile and the Alliance for Progress

Chile became a showcase of President Kennedy's Alliance for Progress, a ten-year aid program for Latin America designed to demonstrate the advantages of democratic reform over Fidel Castro's revolutionary path, which was then gaining popularity in the Americas. With a history of commitment to pluralist democracy, a centrist political party (Christian Democratic Party), and compliant leaders, Chile became an important target for Alliance reforms and American largesse. The CIA spent $2.6 million in support of Eduardo Frei Montalva's (1964–1970) successful campaign for the presidency in 1964. Speaking of a "Revolution in Liberty," Frei successfully promoted economic growth, land reform, and Chile's purchase of majority ownership of the U.S.-owned copper companies. The United States sent civilian financial advisors and provided the Chilean military with generous assistance in the form of grants and equipment. By the late 1960s the Frei administration faced a host of difficulties at home and abroad. Frei's reforms angered both the left and the right inside Chile, and the Nixon administration reduced U.S. assistance to Chile as part of its "low-profile" policy for Latin America.

Salvador Allende and the Nixon Administration

Once it became evident that the left had a chance of winning the 1970 presidential election in Chile, the Nixon administration reversed its "low-profile" strategy and became deeply involved in Chile. The CIA was authorized to spend $300,000 for an anti-Allende propaganda campaign, while U.S. businesses funneled $600,000 to Jorge Alessandri, the candidate of the right. Despite the covert efforts of the CIA and heavy involvement of the U.S. corporate community to prevent Allende from being elected, he emerged from the contentious elections as the winner, but by only 1.2 percent over his closest opponent. President Nixon then ordered the CIA to prevent Allende from being approved by the Chilean Senate, and when that failed, to continue a program of destabilization. According to Paul Sigmund, "The CIA program included propaganda, economic destabilization, and a top-secret (even the [U.S.] ambassador was kept uninformed), ultimately unsuccessful, effort to promote a military coup."[2]

President Allende's domestic and foreign policies brought added pressure from the Nixon administration. On the domestic front, Allende tried to redress decades of social and economic inequality by confiscating and dividing large landed estates, and by implementing income redistribution measures of benefit to the lower classes. He blamed foreign capitalists and multinational corporations for looting Chile's resources and put in place measures to eliminate foreign control of its mines and other economic activities in the hands of foreigners. Allende believed the solution to the nation's problems required the complete political and economic independence of Chile, resistance to imperialism, and the formation of closer ties with Latin America.

Allende's determination to eliminate monopolies and the nationalization of foreign-owned mines and factories—while committed to pluralist democracy and freedom—provoked anger and resentment inside the Nixon administration. However, President Nixon and Henry Kissinger, his national security advisor, worried less about the fate of American economic holdings in Chile than about the spreading effects of a leftist government on South America and the strategic interests of the United States around the globe. Despite Allende's solid socialist credentials, President Nixon considered Allende a "communist" (Allende had always worked with the Chilean communists), someone who could not at the same time be a democrat. Henry Kissinger worried about the spread of communism (domino effect) if a freely elected Marxist government was allowed to rule Chile, disregarding the fact that Salvador Allende had become president of Chile through a democratic process. The ideological hysteria displayed by Nixon and Kissinger was not matched, however, by the foreign policy bureaucracy in Washington. The CIA and departments of state and defense indicated that Allende posed no threat to the region and that the United States had no vital interests within Chile, although most agreed that Allende's victory symbolized a psychological defeat for the United States.

In retaliation for Allende's policies of nationalization and his independent foreign policy, the United States reduced economic aid (but not military aid) to Chile and pressured the World Bank, the Inter-American Development Bank, and private lenders to deny loans to Chile. During a top-level meeting at the White House, Nixon told his foreign policy advisors he wanted to "make the Chilean economy scream" in an effort to undermine Allende. President Allende tried to avoid the squeeze by obtaining loans from the Soviet Union and European and Latin American countries. While U.S. economic pressures caused economic difficulties for his administration, Allende generated his own problems—runaway inflation and increasing violence on the left and right—in pursuit of his goals of economic and political restructuring. A CIA-supported truckers strike that lasted for months worsened the domestic turmoil and provoked the Chilean military (supported with U.S. financial assistance) to move against Allende's democratically elected government. On September 11, 1973, Allende was overthrown in a bloody military coup led by General Augusto Pinochet Ugarte. His suicide-death sparked an avalanche of criticism and controversy over the role of the United States in the sordid affair, particularly the role of the CIA, the U.S. military, and multinational corporations (such as the International Telephone and Telegraph Company) in the "destabilization" campaign and Allende's replacement by a military junta.

The Pinochet Dictatorship, 1973–1989

Few of those who supported the coup against Allende imagined that the Chilean military would remain in power for 17 years in what was portrayed as a heroic effort to "save democracy" and repudiate the actions of the Soviet Union in Chile. Pinochet's military-authoritarian regime involved harsh repression and killings (including two U.S. citizens) that provoked outrage in the United States. The violence that followed the coup was uncharacteristic of Chile: from one thousand to six thousand people were killed or "disappeared," thousands were arrested, and by the 1980s as many as three hundred thousand Chileans lived in exile. In the year following the coup, information disclosed about CIA involvement in Chile led to a full-scale investigation, which in turn led Congress to cut aid to Chile. The June 1976 Kennedy Amendment ended U.S. military aid and sales to Chile, pending human rights improvements. The Nixon and Ford administrations favored the new government, but the Carter administration did not, emphasizing the brutality of the regime, its human rights violations, and the destruction of democracy there.

Pinochet's efforts to destroy what he called the "enemies of Chile" reached far beyond Chile's borders. Orlando Letelier, Allende's former ambassador to the United States, and a female American companion were killed by a car bomb in Washington, D.C., in September 1976, and others critical of the dictator were killed in other countries. The United States was able to trace Letelier car bombers to Chile and sought an investigation and justice, but at first with little assistance from the junta. The Letelier assassination became a major issue in U.S.-Chilean relations, as it served to mobilize the United States against the dictatorship and its human rights abuses. After the Carter administration imposed military and economic sanctions on Chile, General Pinochet extradited a U.S. citizen who had organized the attack; along with several Cuban Americans who had carried out the bombing, he was sent to prison. Ronald Reagan, who began his presidency emphasizing quiet diplomacy and the virtues of the Pinochet dictatorship, removed Carter's sanctions, and the Letelier assassination became a low-key issue in Washington.

The Chicago Boys

The University of Chicago and the Catholic University of Chile signed an agreement in March 1956 that provided scholarships for Chilean students pursuing the study of economics at the University of Chicago. Under the guidance of Milton Friedman and Arnold Harberger, conservative economists who emphasized free-market reforms, Chile soon developed a network of young civilian technicians anxious to apply their American-acquired economic knowledge to their homeland. Known as the "Chicago Boys," they were employed by Pinochet to aid in the consolidation of authoritarian rule while removing all traces of Allende's socialist economics. The Chicago Boys became defenders of the dictatorship by claiming that postponing democratic rule was needed to allow General Pinochet the opportunity to achieve economic freedom and a market-based economy.

The Reagan Administration and Return of Democracy

By the mid-1980s the Reagan administration stopped extolling the benefits of Pinochetismo and shifted toward a greater concern for Chilean democracy. As the threat from the "evil empire" declined and the rest of Latin

America shed military rule, the Pinochet government became more of an embarrassment and policy liability to the United States. Reagan's change in Chilean policy was also aided by a broad-based Chilean democratic movement opposed to the Pinochet regime. In response to U.S. threats to block World Bank and Inter-American Development Bank loans to Chile, Pinochet lifted the state of siege—justifying press censorship and indefinite detentions—in June 1985. The United Nations Human Rights Commission passed a resolution (adopted unanimously) criticizing Chile's human rights situation, adding further pressure on the dictatorship.

As Chile's 1988 presidential election (a renewal of President Pinochet's eight-year term, as called for in the 1980 Constitution) approached, the U.S. Congress appropriated $1 million for democracy promotion in Chile through the National Endowment for Democracy (NED), a quasi-public institution designed to assist with democratization efforts abroad. An additional $1.2 million in funds for "get-out-the-vote" and voter registration efforts was appropriated through the U.S. Agency for International Development (USAID). U.S. funding of Pinochet's opposition, however, was not without controversy, as many Chileans remembered the heavy investment in preventing Allende from being democratically elected in 1964 and 1970. Democracy finally returned to Chile after the 1988 vote went against Pinochet by 55 to 43 percent, and in December 1989 a Christian Democrat, Patricio Aylwin Azócar, was elected president of Chile. Chile's return to democracy after 17 years of dictatorship was more an internal victory for Chileans, however, than a tribute to Washington's democratization efforts.

The Dilemmas of Democratization

After President Aylwin was inaugurated in March 1990, Pinochet remained as head of the army until his retirement in early 1998. U.S.-Chilean relations improved after the end of the Pinochet dictatorship, the arms ban was lifted, and a free trade agreement with the United States seemed to be within reach. U.S. investment in Chile increased dramatically, and the past tension and mutual distrust were replaced by cooperation and assistance. Nevertheless, Chile's two successor regimes (Patricio Aylwin and Eduardo Frei Jr., son of the former president) found governing difficult with Pinochet in charge of the military. After all, he was a powerful political player responsible for the deaths of thousands of political opponents, but with self-imposed immunity for past crimes. General Pinochet's legacy is still being hotly debated inside and outside Chile. Pinochet's supporters portray him as a "national father" who transformed Chile into an economic powerhouse; his opponents still consider him a bloody dictator. A recent government poll showed that over 70 percent of Chileans remember Pinochet as a military dictator. President Clinton's inability to secure "fast-track" authority from Congress after his South American trip in 1997 bothered

Chile, since it had anticipated a free trade agreement similar to the North American Free Trade Agreement (NAFTA) among Canada, the United States and Mexico. Chile has not refrained from criticizing the United States over its harsh Cuba policy, nor did it hesitate from joining the Southern Cone Common Market as an associate member in 1996 to build closer ties with Argentina and Brazil. However, during his visit to Chile in 1998 as part of the Second Summit of the Americas gathering, President Clinton spoke of the importance of deepening democracy and distributing its benefits to all citizens throughout the hemisphere. With the exception of Castro's Cuba, he asserted that "the day of the dictators is over" in the Americas. He made no mention of the CIA-induced military coup against democratically elected Salvador Allende in 1973 and the dark days when the United States supported ruthless dictators in Latin America on a regular basis.

CONCLUSION

U.S. relations with Chile represent a microcosm of numerous policies that have been employed to deal with Latin American countries over the past two centuries. Unlike its implications for other countries geographically closer to the United States, the Monroe Doctrine had little to do with U.S. involvement in Chile, regardless of threats to its independence from foreign powers. Beginning in the late nineteenth century, mining companies invested heavily and profited handsomely from contracts signed with weak and compliant governments in Santiago. With only a few exceptions U.S. relations with Chile remained cordial until the 1960s, when Chilean nationalism and the Cold War clashed, disrupting a democratic system that had served Chile since 1833 (interrupted only twice by military takeovers) and ultimately leading to 17 years of brutal dictatorship, often with Washington's support. The mixture of self-interest and idealism, often the source of conflict between two unequal empires, will likely continue to influence U.S.-Chilean relations.

NOTES

1. William F. Sater, *Chile and the United States: Empires in Conflict* (Athens: University of Georgia Press, 1990).

2. Paul E. Sigmund, "Chile," in Bruce W. Jentelson and Thomas G. Paterson, eds., *Encyclopedia of U.S. Foreign Relations*, vol. 1 (New York: Oxford University Press, 1997), p. 240.

SUGGESTED READINGS

Jensen, Poul. *The Garotte: The United States and Chile, 1970–1973*, 2 vols. Aarhus, Denmark: Aarhus University Press, 1989.

Muñoz, Heraldo, and Carlos Portales. *Elusive Friendship: A Survey of U.S.-Chilean Relations.* Boulder, CO: Westview Press, 1991.

Sater, William F. *Chile and the United States: Empires in Conflict.* Athens: University of Georgia Press, 1990.

Sigmund, Paul E. *The United States and Democracy in Chile.* Baltimore, MD: Johns Hopkins University Press, 1993.

Whelan, James R. *Out of the Ashes: The Life, Death, and Transfiguration of Democracy in Chile, 1833–1988.* Washington, DC: Regnery/Gateway, 1989.

6

Colombia

TIMELINE OF U.S. RELATIONS WITH COLOMBIA

1819	Colombia achieves independence from Spain
1822	Colombia is recognized by the United States
1826	Panama Conference is organized by Simón Bolívar
1830	Simón Bolívar dies
	Colombia separates from Gran Colombia
1846	Bidlack-Mallarino Treaty is signed (ratified in 1848)
1850	Clayton-Bulwer Treaty
1899–1902	War of a Thousand Days
1903	Hay-Herrán Treaty is signed but not ratified
	Panama is separated from Colombia by the United States
1914	Thompson-Urrutia Treaty is signed (ratified by United States in 1922)
1939–1945	United States pressures Colombia to purge German nationals during World War II
1948	Organization of American States (OAS) is created
	Jorge Eliécer Gaitán is assassinated
1950	Laureano Gómez becomes president
1952	Military pact is signed with the United States
1953	General Gustavo Rojas Pinilla assumes dictatorial powers
1957	Rojas dictatorship is overthrown
1958–1962	Alberto Lleras Camargo serves as elected president
1958	National Front power-sharing experiment begins
1961	Colombian leaders endorse Alliance for Progress
1964	National Liberation Army (ELN) is formed

1966	Revolutionary Armed Forces of Colombia (FARC) is formed
1966–1970	Carlos Lleras Restrepo serves as elected president
1974–1978	Alfonso López Michelsen serves as elected president
1978	President Turbay and Carter administration quarrel over human rights violations
1979–1987	Colombia plays key role in solving Central American crisis
1980–1990	United States increases funding of anti-drug programs
1985	President Belisario Betancur (1982–1986) begins extraditing key drug traffickers to the United States under 1977 extradition treaty
1994–1998	Ernesto Samper serves as elected president
1996	Colombia is "decertified" due to lack of progress in drug war
1997	Colombia is decertified for second time
1998	U.S. military reports that Colombian rebels are winning the war against Colombian government
	President Clinton "certifies" Samper government despite human rights violations and escalating drug-related violence

INTRODUCTION

Due to its location astride the top of South America, bordered by Panama (its northern province until 1903), Venezuela, Ecuador, Peru and Brazil, Colombia has played an important role in the Latin American policy of the United States since independence. Colombia's strategic importance to the United States in the nineteenth century stemmed from the possibility of constructing an interoceanic link across Panama. During times of war in the twentieth century, Colombia's value to the United States increased due to the fact that it is the only South American country with coastlines on two oceans, the Caribbean-Atlantic and the Pacific.

Colombia is only one of two cases in which the United States managed to take territory from Latin America after independence. In a deliberately provoked war with Mexico in 1846–1848, the United States seized over one-half of its territory. In the political battle over a canal route at the turn of the century, the United States helped generate a separatist revolt that resulted in Colombia's loss of Panama. In both cases the United States compensated the losing countries; Mexico was paid $15 million for its loss in 1848, and Colombia was paid $25 million—but not until almost two decades after the loss of Panama (see Table 6.1).

Despite chronic political violence and periods of intense internal war, Colombia has managed to avoid either U.S. military intervention or occupation, or frequent or long periods of direct military rule. Since independence Colombia has had only three military governments, the last one

Table 6.1
Territorial Expansion of the United States in Latin America and the Caribbean, 1845–1917

Territory*	Date Acquired	Square Miles	How Acquired
Texas	1845	390,143	Annexed as independent nation after separating from Mexico
Mexican Cession	1848	529,017	Conquest from Mexico
Gadsden Purchase	1853	29,640	Purchase from Mexico
Puerto Rico	1899	3,435	Conquest from Spain
Panama Canal Zone	1904	553	Treaty with Panama after taking territory from Colombia (returned to Panama by treaty in 1978, but to take effect 1-1-2000)
Corn Islands	1914	4	Treaty with Nicaragua (returned to Nicaragua by treaty in 1978)
Virgin Islands	1917	133	Purchase from Denmark

Source: Mary Beth Norton, et al., *A People and History of the United States, Vol. 1: To 1877.* Third Edition (Boston, MA: Houghton-Mifflin, 1990), p. A-24.

*The United States has also acquired military bases in the Caribbean under bilateral lease arrangements such as those with Cuba (Guantánamo Bay, 1903--), and Trinidad (1941-1974).

between 1953 and 1958. The ability of powerful party elites—Liberal and Conservative—to reach some form of accommodation with the United States has been one factor in explaining this fact. Moreover, the absence of serious security threats from Germany or the Soviet Union allowed the United States and Colombia to avoid the acrimony so common elsewhere in Latin America.

The fact that Colombian elites came to the conclusion, after the loss of Panama, that a constructive foreign policy should center on cautious co-operation with the United States—because of its proximity and power—laid the foundation for generally friendly relations throughout most of the twentieth century. Colombia's essentially pro-American foreign policy—with only minor differences over U.S. intervention in other Latin American countries, human rights, multinationals, and illicit drug trafficking—makes it a somewhat unique case. The Monroe Doctrine was not needed to justify U.S. intervention in Colombia since there was no burden of having to respond to violent revolutions, rebellious and nasty dictators, and nationalist repercussions from years of Yankee domination.

COLOMBIA AND THE UNITED STATES IN THE NINETEENTH CENTURY

The United States and Colombian Independence

Colombia's independence was complicated by (1) the fact that it separated from Spain as part of a larger political entity called the United Provinces of New Granada, and (2) the length and intensity of the liberation struggle, from 1811 to 1819. The United States had little contact with Colombia while it was a colony of Spain and maintained a policy of cautious neutrality until it formally recognized Colombia (including Venezuela and Ecuador) in 1822. Unofficially, major political figures in the United States such as Alexander Hamilton, Thomas Jefferson, James Monroe, Thomas Paine, and William Henry Harrison expressed support for Latin American independence. Washington's official policy of strict neutrality clashed with the efforts of Colombian rebels to gain the support of the United States to help defeat royalist forces. Manuel Torres, a long-time resident of the United States, lobbied hard from 1818 to 1820 for weapons, U.S. recognition, and a reciprocal commercial agreement. The reluctance of the United States to side with those in the independence movement stemmed in large part from its interest in acquiring Florida from Spain, rather than challenging Spain over liberation struggles among its colonies. By 1822 the United States was ready to recognize Colombia, and Torres was received by the Monroe administration as the first official Colombian and Latin American representative to the United States. Although Gran Colombia (the union of Colombia, Ecuador, and Venezuela) was dissolved in 1830, Colombia (known as New Granada until 1863) would have to endure chronic political instability and civil wars throughout the rest of the nineteenth century. This pattern of early development complicated and frustrated U.S.-Colombian relations, culminating in the War of a Thousand Days (1899–1902) and the loss of Panama in 1903.

Colombia and the Monroe Doctrine

President Monroe's message was initially received with great enthusiasm in Bogotá; however, Simón Bolívar recognized the ambiguities in Monroe's words, fearing the dangers of European imperialism less than the merits of being included in a U.S. sphere of influence. Alarmed at the rumors of a French effort to colonize territory and the reestablishment of a monarchy in 1824, Colombia requested a treaty of alliance with the United States based on the Monroe Doctrine. John Quincy Adams rejected the Colombian initiative, arguing that in order to undertake military resistance to a European incursion there would have to be assistance from the British. It was a strange way to retreat from the bold language of the year before, but it seemed to indicate a reluctance to translate the broad generalities of Monroe's message into more concrete terms. Each of the requests for an alliance with the United States was turned down by policymakers in Washington, ostensibly on grounds that it was not wise to get involved in the affairs of the nations to the south. Later, efforts to link the Monroe Doctrine with the canal question proved to be ineffectual.

Between 1848 and 1850 the United States signed the Bidlack-Mallarino Treaty (ratified in 1848) and the Clayton-Bulwer Treaty (1850) to establish rights of transit across the isthmus of Panama. The Bidlack-Mallarino Treaty provided the United States with the exclusive right of transit across Colombia's northern province (Panama) in return for U.S. guarantees of Colombia's sovereignty; the Clayton-Bulwer Treaty addressed British encroachments in Nicaragua, the site of a competing canal across the isthmus (see Chapter 13). The Clayton-Bulwer Treaty was the most controversial—it was attacked by those who claimed that it violated the noncolonization principle of the Monroe Doctrine—but remained in force until the second Hay-Pauncefote Treaty in 1901, a treaty that removed the requirement that any canal constructed would have to be completed jointly by the United States and Britain.

COLOMBIA AND THE UNITED STATES IN THE EARLY TWENTIETH CENTURY

The Loss of Panama and the Politics of Compensation

The United States was not about to let Colombia stand in the way of a U.S.-built canal project, regardless of previous promises or even obligations under international law. As far as Theodore Roosevelt's administration was concerned, Colombia's rejection of the Hay-Herrán Treaty of 1903 could be overcome by stirring up a revolt among Panamanian separatists, then simply renegotiating a new treaty with an "independent" Panama. The Hay-Herrán Treaty would have given the United States the right to construct the canal in Colombia, plus other generous benefits. In an expression of his irritation at the recalcitrant Colombians, President Roosevelt told Secretary of State John Hay in August 1903 that "I do not think that the Bogotá lot of Jackrabbits should be allowed permanently to bar one of the future highways of civilization."[1] The loss of Panama was a traumatic event for the nation, one that resulted in anti-Americanism because of President Roosevelt's role in the secession from Colombia (see Chapter 20). The bitter feelings and antagonism toward the United States increased as negotiations over compensation dragged on, impeding friendly relations for at least a generation. From the middle of the nineteenth century until 1903, Colombia had expected to reap the financial benefits from an interoceanic canal through its northern province.

After World War I, President Wilson resubmitted to the U.S. Senate the treaty with Colombia that he hoped, when approved, would heal the rift caused by the loss of Panama in 1903. Wilson faced the opposition of senators Albert Fall and Henry Cabot Lodge, two Republicans who wanted to use the treaty as a lever for oil concessions and who objected to any apology for the U.S. role in Colombia's loss of its northern province. According to Joseph Tulchin, "The public debate outraged Colombians who resented the arrogance with which the Americans discussed another sovereign nation."[2] After the Colombians announced that their government would control all petroleum rights, the U.S. Senate, for domestic political reasons, refused to act on the treaty for the remainder of Wilson's term. The U.S. Senate finally ratified the Thompson-Urrutia Treaty in 1921, awarding Colombia compensation of $25 million. After almost two decades the matter of Panama was settled, but the sordid affair would be remembered as one of the most volatile episodes in U.S.-Colombian relations. It left a bitter legacy that complicated future matters, particularly trade expansion and petroleum exploitation.

The Polar Star Doctrine

It was during the final diplomatic negotiations over the indemnification treaty that Colombian president Marco Fidel Suárez (1918–1921) proclaimed the "Polar Star Doctrine," by which he meant that Colombia should look northward to its powerful English-speaking neighbor for economic support and democratic political guidance. It was a piece of prudent statecraft perfectly tailored to the interests of the United States in Colombia, but unfortunately Suárez's efforts to improve relations with the United States contributed to the domestic political crisis that drove him from office before the treaty was ratified. Despite the lack of popularity of the Polar Star Doctrine, U.S.-Colombian relations improved considerably over the next 50 years. With few exceptions, Colombia followed the Polar Star Doctrine with remarkable consistency through the 1980s. The success of this foreign policy was buttressed by the fact that Colombia's powerful coffee oligarchy was fond of the doctrine.

Colombia and the Good Neighbor Policy

The United States faced the possibility of a government takeover of U.S. oil concessions during the 1930s as Colombian Liberals attempted mild socialist reforms, but Colombian governments did not follow the pattern of nationalization that occurred in Mexico and Bolivia during the Good Neighbor Policy. Fortunately for the United States, the Good Neighbor Policy of Franklin D. Roosevelt overlapped with Colombian administrations that adopted programs that dovetailed with U.S. strategic and economic interests during the war years. Although his close collaboration with the Pulpo del Norte (Octupus of the North; the United States) helped to fuel criticism from the Conservative opposition, President Eduardo Santos (1938–1942) complied with the wishes of the United States during the early years of World War II. Colombian cooperation came through the nationalization of German-controlled airlines, the expulsion of thousands of Germans from Colombia, the severing of relations with the Axis powers, and permitting the U.S. embassy to operate a counterespionage system throughout the country. Santos was attacked bitterly by Conservative Laureano Gómez, whose newspaper, *El Siglo*, ran continuous stories praising the Nazi cause and denouncing the United States.

THE UNITED STATES AND COLOMBIA DURING THE COLD WAR

Colombia emerged from World War II polarized by political divisions that would soon plunge the country into a long period of internal war called *la violencia* (violence), a cataclysmic event sparked by the assassination of popular Liberal leader Jorge Eliécer Gaitán in April 1948. The wave of violence unleashed by political hostility had little to do with communism—it grew out of the hereditary hatreds between Liberals and Conservatives—but before the violence was over, 200,000 people lay dead and Colombia experienced its first military takeover in the twentieth century. Although short-lived, the Gustavo Rojas Pinilla dictatorship (1953–1957) alienated the major sectors of Colombian society, eventually contributing to his overthrow in 1957, and aided in the establishment of the National Front (NF) in 1958. The NF was a constitutional arrangement of alternation between the two major parties for a period of 16 years.

Colombia and the U.S. Military

Contacts between the U.S. military and Colombia's armed forces can be traced to the War of a Thousand Days. Prior to World War II, U.S.-Colombian military relations involved assistance with the Leticia conflict with Peru and the coordination of efforts to defend the Panama Canal. During World War II, Colombia allowed the United States to construct air and naval bases on its territory, strengthened by a military training mission and Bogotá's commitment to the Allied cause. This collaboration continued after the war with the signing of mutual security pacts along with U.S. military assistance. When the School of the Americas opened in Panama in the late 1940s, Colombia was among the first Latin American countries to send recruits for training. It was the only Latin American country to commit troops (a 1,000-man army infantry battalion) to fight as part of the United Nations force in Korea, and in 1952 it hosted the first U.S. military counterinsurgency training school in Latin America. Colombian troops gained valuable experience from the Korean conflict, skills that were later used to confront rural insurgencies at home.

Colombia and the Alliance for Progress

The Cold War and the effects of the Cuban Revolution shaped Colombian-U.S. relations during the 1960s. Colombia's dominant political figures (Liberals Alberto Lleras Camargo and Carlos Lleras Restrepo) during the 1960s cooperated fully with the Alliance for Progress in an effort to forestall social revolution and promote economic growth. Colombia became a "showcase" for Alliance reforms, launching needed reforms while receiving large amounts of both economic and military assistance from the United States. Although Lleras Camargo was a firm believer in the New Deal and Kennedy's Alliance for Progress, he differed with the United States by emphasizing the importance of acting through the Organization of American States and refusing to associate the Monroe Doctrine with the principle of collective defense spelled out in the OAS charter. Lleras Camargo believed that the chronic use of force by the United States to achieve its foreign policy goals in Latin America demonstrated the emergence of a new form of imperialism. Despite these policy differences, between 1960 and 1975 Colombia received $1.5 billion in U.S. aid in loans and grants, in most cases tied to the purchase of U.S. goods. U.S.-Colombian military aid and cooperation increased with the growing problem of narcotrafficking in the 1980s, and by the early 1990s Colombia ranked first in U.S. military assistance to Latin America.

Colombia and the United States: From Reagan to Bush

From the early 1980s to the 1990s, the defining factor in U.S.-Colombian relations has been the huge flow of illegal drugs to the United States from

Colombia and the difficulties that each country has faced in dealing with the problem. To strengthen the U.S. anti-narcotics efforts at home and abroad in early 1986, the Reagan administration declared drug trafficking a "lethal" threat to U.S. national security, thus setting the stage for an expanded role of the U.S. military in drug interdiction at U.S. borders and abroad. In the same year the U.S. Congress passed the Anti-Drug Abuse Act. This mandated the annual International Narcotics Control Strategy Report to assess the situation in the drug-producing and drug-trafficking nations around the world, including Colombia and 18 others in Latin America and the Caribbean Basin.

Drug trafficking, however, is not the only problem affecting Colombian-U.S. relations. Between 1980 and 1990 the expanding guerrilla movement, communism, and the Central American crisis served to worsen the drug problem echoing throughout the region. During the Central American crisis, Colombia opposed President Reagan's aggressiveness in dealing with El Salvador and Nicaragua, and it became one of the leading voices within the Contadora peace process (made up initially of Colombia, Mexico, Panama and Venezuela), arguing that a negotiated settlement and the withdrawal of all foreign military influence were preferable to Washington's strategy. However, in dealing with rural insurgencies and drug cartels, Colombia and the United States recognized the importance of cooperation in devising a common strategy to counter the problem.

The Drug-Insurgency Nexus

Colombia's preeminent position in the Latin American drug trade is largely the result of its location (midway between the coca-producing countries of Bolivia and Peru and the major routes leading to the U.S. market), its remote forests and jungles where processing laboratories and airstrips can be hidden, the strong entrepreneurial skills of the Colombian people, and the availability of exiles living in major U.S. cities willing to collaborate with trafficking operations. Since the 1970s, Colombian presidents have had to face the difficult task of solving three interrelated problems: economic decline, the growing guerrilla movement, and drug trafficking. Each of the post–National Front presidencies, beginning with Alfonso López Michelsen (1974–1978), has had to face rural guerrillas and drug cartels that hold significant control over the national economy, thereby undermining the ability of government authorities to deal effectively with these forces. Although U.S. presidents have made some headway in addressing the demand side of the drug problem, the United States still prefers the law-and-order approach, emphasizing militarized interdiction efforts, extradition of drug traffickers from Latin America, and a variety of measures to reduce supply from the region. Guerrilla involvement with the major drug cartels, and the massive social and economic damage that drugs cause in the United States, have made the Colombian cocaine industry an especially potent threat to the fabric of American society.

Currently, Colombia is the world's largest producer of cocaine and second-largest grower of coca leaf after Peru (see Table 22.1). Because of the high demand for drugs such as cocaine, marijuana, and heroin—and vast profits—the drug cartels have been able to hire private armies, bribe local judges and politicians, distort national development programs, and contribute to corruption and human rights abuses. The economic impact of drug production in Colombia is evident in its providing of employment, foreign exchange, and stabilizing economies beset by declining prices of primary exports like coffee and petroleum. After the death of Pablo Escobar (known as the godfather of the Medellín cartel), the neighboring Cali cartel quickly became the world's largest in the refining, smuggling, and distribution of cocaine. However, the Cali cartel's grip on world control was weakened in 1995 by the arrest of its leaders and the revelation that it had contributed to the successful election campaign of President Ernesto Samper.

THE UNITED STATES AND COLOMBIA AFTER
THE COLD WAR

U.S.-Colombian relations have deteriorated since the end of the Cold War, due in large part to the expanding problem of narcotics-linked terrorism and differences over the extradition of captured drug kingpins. During the presidency of César Gaviria (1990–1994), Colombia struggled against the twin demons of drugs and the expanding of power of the Army of National Liberation (Ejército de Liberación Nacional, or ELN) and the Revolutionary Armed Forces of Colombia (Fuerzas Armadas Revolucionarias de Colombia, or FARC). Both of these leftist guerrilla groups have been in operation since the mid-1960s—drawing their inspiration from Marxism and Castroism—and have grown to more than 20,000 insurgents by the end of the 1990s. The greater threat seems to be from FARC, since it is estimated to have 15,000 members and supports itself mainly through drug-trafficking operations, kidnappings, and bank robberies. Although Gaviria had campaigned against the extradition treaty with the United States, which caused considerable tension within Colombia, his close and active cooperation in dealing with the drug trade as president won him strong support from Washington.

After winning the 1994 presidential election, Ernesto Samper (1994–1998) fell under a cloud of suspicion that he had received $6 million from the Cali cocaine cartel so that they could avoid long jail terms. Despite protests and corroborating statements from his closest associates, Samper has repeatedly denied that any drug money was funneled to his campaign. However, the chief accountant of the Cali cartel—Guillermo Pallomari—

testifying in a drug trial in Miami in July 1997 offered further evidence of the link between the Cali cocaine trafficking ring and the Samper campaign by claiming he had arranged for the large cash donation and was present at a secret dinner in Cali in 1994, hosted by members of the Cali cartel and attended by Samper, then a presidential candidate. On hearing that Samper would win the Colombian presidential elections, according to Pallomari, the boss of the Cali ring boasted, "We've got ourselves a president!" Despite being cleared of charges that Cali drug dealers financed his election, Samper was pressured to leave office by the Clinton administration and leading business and industrial groups in Colombia because of the extent of his narco-corrupted government. But the pressure was to no avail.

In response to the Anti-Drug Abuse Act, Colombia was "decertified" (a law that requires a determination whether a country is making sufficient efforts to eradicate illicit drugs) by the United States in 1996 and 1997 because of its insufficient effort in the eradication of illicit drugs. To further express its concern about Colombia and drugs, the Clinton administration canceled President Samper's visa in July 1996 in hopes of generating more pressure on the president to resign. Although his vice-president resigned two months later, claiming he could no longer be associated with such a drug-corrupted government, President Samper refused to leave office, defying the United States and strong opposition inside Colombia. After more than a decade of anti–drug abuse legislation, the United States finds itself even more entangled in the controversies over the interconnection between drug cartels and several guerrilla groups in Colombia and the impact of drug trafficking on the national security of the United States.

In late 1997 the United States announced that it had approved more than $50 million in equipment to help Colombia's military fight leftist guerrillas involved in drug trafficking. This White House initiative reversed the termination of military assistance to Colombia in 1994, after the U.S. General Accounting Office (GAO) found that such aid had gone to units accused of violating human rights and was being used to fight leftist guerrillas rather than drug traffickers. General Barry R. McCaffrey, head of President Clinton's anti-drug campaign, visited Colombia and announced that the additional aid—contingent on an agreement by the Colombian police and armed forces to observe human rights—was not to be used for counterinsurgency efforts. Despite the fact that the State Department, the National Security Council, and the Drug Enforcement Agency counseled McCaffrey against a visit that would involve meeting with drug-tainted President Ernesto Samper, the White House drug czar carried his campaign to Colombia, citing the importance of the drug war to the national security of the United States. Those who doubt the sincerity, or ability, of the Colombian government to improve human rights concerns among military units point to the fact that despite many accusations, not a single Colombian soldier has been sentenced for torture. Despite the hemisphere's worst human rights record in 1998, the Clinton administration lifted Colombia's status as a pariah nation in the fight against drugs.

By 1998, the United States confronted another problem in its relations with Colombia. As Colombian rebel forces made increasing gains in attacking the Colombian army throughout the countryside, the United States faced the difficult choice of adding to the 200 U.S. military "advisors" to fight the leftist guerrillas, a move that some feel could easily lead to the "Vietnamization" of U.S. policy in Colombia. The security situation in Colombia has contributed to growing tension within the Clinton administration and the Pentagon over how best to confront the Marxist insurgency, financed by millions of dollars from the drug trade. Colombia's anti-rebel campaign has been hampered by an inept and poorly equipped military and a weakened government unable to function effectively. A 1997 U.S. Defense Intelligence Agency (DIA) report concluded that Colombian rebels controlled more than 40 percent of the country.

CONCLUSION

The United States and Colombia have clashed over a number of issues that have strained relations between the two countries, but in general the foreign policies of Colombia have been of benefit to Washington. The importance of transportation and trade issues in the nineteenth century were focused on Panama, Colombia's northern province. In an effort to counter British and French influence in the isthmus, the United States conspired to undermine the power of both European powers by putting teeth in the Monroe Doctrine and establishing hegemony over the region. After the loss of Panama, Colombians decided that it was more important to cooperate with the United States, and suffer challenges to the nation's sovereignty, than to oppose top officials in Washington and their policies devised to deal with Latin America. One of the important lessons that emerges from the U.S. relationship with Colombia is the importance of acquiescing to the foreign policy interests of the United States, rather than challenging or opposing the power Washington wields in the region.

NOTES

1. Quoted in Stephen J. Randall, *Colombia and the United States: Hegemony and Interdependence* (Athens: University of Georgia Press, 1992), pp. 85–86.

2. Joseph S. Tulchin, *The Aftermath of War: World War I and U.S. Policy toward Latin America* (New York: New York University Press, 1971), p. 140.

SUGGESTED READINGS

Gugliotta, Guy. *Kings of Cocaine: Inside the Medellín Cartel—An Astonishing True Story of Murder, Money, and International Corruption*. New York: Simon and Schuster, 1989.

Lael, Richard L. *Arrogant Diplomacy: U.S. Policy toward Colombia, 1903–1922*. Wilmington, DE: Scholarly Resources, 1987.

Menzel, Sewall H. *Cocaine Quagmire: Implementing the U.S. Anti-Drug Policy in the North Andes–Colombia*. Lanham, MD: University Press of America, 1997.

Randall, Stephen J. *Colombia and the United States: Hegemony and Interdependence*. Athens: University of Georgia Press, 1992.

———. *The Diplomacy of Modernization: Colombian-American Relations, 1920–1940*. Toronto: University of Toronto Press, 1997.

7

Costa Rica

TIMELINE OF U.S. RELATIONS WITH COSTA RICA

1821	Costa Rica achieves independence from Spain
1856–1857	Costa Rica joins British-backed force against William Walker
1858	U.S. diplomatic relations are established
1859	Costa Rica and Nicaragua propose a reverse Monroe Doctrine
1871	Minor Cooper Keith begins railroad from the Caribbean to San José
1899	Costa Rica's first free democratic elections are held
	United Fruit Company is founded
1917	General Federico Tinoco seizes power
1919	Tinoco resigns under pressure from Wilson administration
1940–1944	Rafael Angel Calderón serves as elected president
1944–1948	Teodoro Picado serves as elected president
1948	Otilo Ulate is elected president
	José Figueres successfully leads Army of National Liberation against government
1949	New constitution abolishes the military
1953–1958	José Figueres serves as elected president (first term)
1970–1974	José Figueres serves as elected president (second term)
1978	Costa Rica breaks relations with Nicaragua
1979	Sandinista offensive against Somoza starts from Costa Rica
1982	Luis Alberto Monge is elected president
1983–1984	Contra forces operate out of northern Costa Rica
1986	Oscar Arias is elected president

1987	Arias peace plan for Nicaragua is proposed
	Arias wins Nobel Peace Prize
1989	Rafael Calderón is elected president
1994	José Figueres Jr. is elected president
1997–1998	Costa Rican government is faced with serious conflicts with Costa Rican squatters on U.S.-owned estates and ranches
1999	Costa Rica celebrates 100 years of democratic rule

INTRODUCTION

Costa Rica is less well known than the other countries of Central America, often confused with Puerto Rico, and rather distinct from its neighbors. It has managed to avoid most of the wars, repressive dictatorships, military coups, assassinations, revolutions, and economic woes that have afflicted its neighbors—a remarkable achievement in Central America. Those who visit Costa Rica today are surprised to find a democratic and peaceful country with a level of social development rarely found in Third World nations. After decades in which bananas and coffee provided most of the national income, eco-tourism is now the number one generator of foreign exchange. Home to national parks, biological reserves, and wildlife refuges, Costa Rica easily holds the world's number one rank for its commitment to environmental protection.

Costa Rica's relationship with the United States is based on its political geography (it is a small mountainous country located between Panama and Nicaragua, with harbors and coasts along the Caribbean Sea and Pacific Ocean), its export economy based on coffee and bananas, a long history of democratic institutions (including the absence of a military after 1948), and a foreign policy that has emphasized neutrality and peaceful resolution of regional conflicts. For the most part, the history of U.S.–Costa Rican relations has been cordial, based on commercial dependency and a shared political outlook. However, imbalances in power and contrasting definitions of political and security interests have contributed to several disruptive conflicts between Washington and Costa Rican policymakers in San José. In response to the daring *filibustero* William Walker in the 1850s, Costa Rica joined a British-backed regional armed force to expel Walker's U.S.-backed regime from Nicaragua. After World War II, Cold War anti-communism worsened tensions between the United States and Costa Rica. Washington considered Costa Rican governments to be troublemakers because they traded with Cuba, aided Nicaraguan revolutionaries, refused to join a Central American defense force and other Pentagon projects, opposed U.S.-supported intervention schemes, and pushed for a peaceful solution to the conflicts in Central America during the 1980s.

The full force of U.S. involvement that occurred in other parts of Central America never materialized in Costa Rica; it has never been invaded by the United States, and the Monroe Doctrine has not been needed, or utilized, by either country. Plagued by economic difficulties in the early 1980s, it became impossible for Costa Rica to resist U.S. pressure in convincing Costa Rica to create a Southern Front against the Sandinista revolutionaries in Nicaragua. Its small size and limited foreign policy autonomy have caused Costa Rica to place a great deal of emphasis on the Organization of American States (OAS) and its principles of neutrality, nonintervention and peaceful resolution of conflicts.

COSTA RICA AND THE UNITED STATES IN THE NINETEENTH CENTURY

Domestic and international issues—the location of a transisthmian canal, banana and coffee production, railroad building, Central American unification, and U.S. expansionism—played a role in U.S.–Costa Rican relations throughout the nineteenth century. Costa Rica managed to escape the patterns of elite rule and the degree of economic dependency that hampered the rest of Central America after the Central American Federation collapsed in 1838, a failed effort to unify all of Central America between 1823 and 1838. The United States and Great Britain fought to protect economic, political, and security interests in Central America, enticed by the possibility of constructing a canal through one of the small countries of the region. Coffee-for-export became the major source of foreign revenue, particularly in Costa Rica, Guatemala, and Nicaragua. Costa Rica managed to overcome the debilitating effects of Liberal-Conservative turmoil and military rule to hold its first fair and free elections in 1899. This early democratic development took place without any support or encouragement from the United States, a tribute to the determination of Costa Ricans to control their fate without the guiding hand of local dictators or meddling foreigners.

The United States and Costa Rican Independence

Costa Rica gained its independence from Spain in 1821 but agreed to join the Central American Federation in 1823. Although the attempt at federation only lasted until 1838, it established a legacy by which domestic and regional issues have often blended together and fostered other problems of a political and economic nature. The failure of union had many explanations, but Costa Rica often displayed little interest in getting entangled with the political turmoil in Nicaragua and Panama that greater Central American unity would have required. Until World War I, Costa Rica remained of little concern to the United States.

Costa Rica and the Monroe Doctrine

Costa Rica is one of the rare cases in U.S.–Latin American relations in which policymakers in Washington have not invoked the Monroe Doctrine to justify U.S. involvement or protect U.S. interests in the country. Even when coping with Latin America's first Cold War, leftist government in Costa Rica under Teodoro Picado (1944–1948), the United States did not resort to the Monroe Doctrine or intervene militarily. The Costa Ricans never embraced the Monroe Doctrine like the Brazilians, or others, to pry concessions from the United States.

After Mexico's loss of territory in the Mexican-American War (1846–1848) and William Walker's filibustering activities during the 1850s, Costa Ricans worried about talk from Washington of expanding "territorial limits" in the name of Manifest Destiny and the Monroe Doctrine. In an interesting response to U.S. expansionism and use of the Monroe Doctrine after 1845, Costa Rica and Nicaragua proposed a reverse Monroe Doctrine in the form of a manifesto requesting that England and France assist them in protecting their respective territories from further intervention from the United States. The United States tried unsuccessfully to foster union movements in Central America throughout the nineteenth century on the grounds that federation would offer political strength to the Central American republics and help prevent encroachments of European powers.

Costa Rica and William Walker

During the 1850s, *filibusteros* (predatory adventurers) from the United States moved into Mexico and Central America intent on spreading slavery southward and obtaining transit concessions across the isthmus. William Walker was the most notorious of these North American adventurers, leading expeditions to Mexico (Baja California) and Nicaragua to acquire additional slave territory on behalf of the Southern slave owners. As the United States replaced Britain as the most influential power in Central America during the 1850s, Costa Rica and other Central American countries began to worry about the impact of the increasingly aggressive policies that appeared to threaten their continuing independence and sovereignty.

William Walker and his *filibusteros* had grandiose plans for the Central American venture. After conquering Nicaragua and moving into northern Costa Rica, Walker planned to use wealthy U.S. investors and cheap Nicaraguan labor to construct canals from the Atlantic to the Pacific, using Lake Nicaragua and the San Juan River. A romantic figure, Walker envisioned himself the supreme leader of a new federal republic of Central

American states and Cuba along with a profitable slave system. Walker and his troops found more than they could handle when they attacked northern Costa Rica in 1856, losing a historic battle against 9,000 Costa Ricans led by Juan Santamaría. Two more defeats, one in Nicaragua and the other in Honduras, put an end to Walker's idea of a southern empire. After being stopped by a British naval ship in 1860 he was turned over to the Hondurans, who promptly placed him before a firing squad.

At the center of these controversial efforts was James Buchanan, an aggressive expansionist and pro-slavery president (1857–1861) who struggled to create U.S. protectorates over Mexico and Nicaragua that were unsuccessful. Buchanan was one of many opponents of the Clayton-Bulwer Treaty of 1850 (see Chapter 13), arguing that it precluded the possibility of a Central American canal constructed, owned, and operated exclusively by the United States, not a joint venture with Great Britain. Between 1855 and 1856, Guatemala, Costa Rica, and Nicaragua asked for both arms and the protection of the powerful European maritime powers as a shield against the United States and the Monroe Doctrine. Although Buchanan predicted that Central America would eventually become part of the United States, his expansionist plans and calls for the use of military force were thwarted by Northern senators who opposed the acquisition of more slave states for the Union. Had Buchanan's diplomatic efforts not been entangled in the issues of abolition and sectionalism, it is quite possible he would have achieved greater U.S. control over Cuba, Nicaragua, Mexico, and Panama.

The King of Central America

After several decades of expanding coffee production and the use of mules to ship coffee beans to the small Pacific port of Puntarenas, Costa Rica realized that it needed a railroad from the central highlands to the Pacific Ocean. With the major markets being in Europe and along the eastern seaboard of the United States, it was not profitable to continue shipping the long way around Cape Horn at the tip of South America. In the early 1870s, President Tomás Guardía contracted with Minor Cooper Keith to build a railroad linking the prime coffee-growing region with the Atlantic coast. Despite Keith's success as a railroad engineer in South America, the Costa Rican project was a monumental undertaking. But Keith was a charismatic and somewhat larcenous individual who had no trouble doing business with the dictators who governed the region. It took Keith almost 20 years to complete the 120-mile railroad, struggling with rough terrain, tropical diseases, mutinies by disgruntled workers, and bankruptcy. Over five thousand workers (mostly Jamaicans), including three of Keith's brothers, died during the ordeal, either from malaria, yellow fever, or exhaustion. Although he came to Costa Rica to build a railroad, Keith soon recognized the wealth that could be made in the cultivation and export of bananas. During the construction of the railroad, Keith planted banana trees as a ready source of income. Later he expanded his banana business into Guatemala, present-day Panama, and Colombia, building railroads, port facilities, banks, and trade and transport companies. By the end of the century Minor Cooper Keith was one of the most powerful figures in modern Central American history. According to historian Paul Dosal, "Minor Keith was not just the man who built or acquired most Central American railroads and founded the world's largest banana company; he was also known as the uncrowned king of Central America, the green pope, and the Cecil Rhodes [a British imperialist who made his fortune in South African diamonds] of Central America."[1]

Minor Keith was not only well connected with power brokers in Washington but also maintained close ties with Costa Rican politicians and British bankers. To make sure he had the blessings of Costa Rica's elite, Keith married the daughter of a family whose father had twice occupied the presidency and whose mother's family ties were distinguished as well as extensive. Keith received extremely lucrative grants and tax concessions while his railroad and banana empire expanded. In return for renegotiating bank debts with British bankers, the Costa Rican government granted him 800,000 acres of land adjoining the railway route. In 1899 Keith merged his Tropical Trading and Transport Company with the Boston Fruit Company to form the giant United Fruit Company. By the early twentieth century, coffee and banana production provided massive profits for those very few at the top and opened Costa Rica to powerful foreign investment; it also generated enormous social and economic problems later in the century.

However, Keith's Atlantic Railroad and United Fruit never came to monopolize Costa Rica like they did Guatemala and Honduras. The foreign presence (and the large black population) was more isolated on the coast, the Costa Rican government owned the other half of the nation's railroad system from San José to Puntarenas, and reformer politicians carried out needed social reforms. By the turn of the century bananas, coffee, and minerals formed the backbone of Central American export activity, a pattern that lasted until after World War II. Financial losses and landslides forced the Atlantic Railroad to close in 1990, a few days short of its 100th anniversary.

COSTA RICA AND THE UNITED STATES IN THE TWENTIETH CENTURY

The Central American Court of Justice

After the United States obtained treaty rights to proceed with the building of the Panama Canal in 1903, the importance of Central America to the security of the United States increased considerably. What worried the United States was the tendency of Central American dictators to intervene in one anothers's affairs, causing continual political turmoil and revolutionary activity. To remedy the situation the United States called a conference of all five Central American republics to take place in Washington in 1907; at the meeting a series of treaties aimed a promoting peace and cooperation in the region would be signed. One treaty required that the Central American republics submit all future conflicts between them to a Permanent Central American Court of Justice. Others attempted to place restrictions on the use of their respective territories as a base for revolutionary movements and to prevent unconstitutional regimes from coming to power by adopting the Tobar Doctrine, a policy of collective nonrecognition of governments established by revolutions or by other-than-democratic means. Although the United States was not a party to the treaties, it tried to follow the nonrecognition principle in recognizing Central American governments. President Woodrow Wilson borrowed from the Tobar Doctrine for his recognition policy, but it fostered considerable distrust and hatred of the United States after it became commonly viewed as a pretense for U.S. intervention in the region. After the Court ruled in 1917 that the Bryan-Chamorro Treaty (between the United States and Nicaragua) was injurious to Costa Rica, Nicaragua ignored the decision and withdrew from the body (on advice from the United States), and it ceased to exist in 1918. Costa Rica and others soon departed from the Tobar principles in recognizing new governments. This contributed to its demise and a new era of dictatorships in El Salvador, Guatemala, and Honduras in the early 1930s.

Woodrow Wilson, World War I, and the Tinoco Dictatorship

After the difficulties of dealing with the turbulent early phase of the Mexican revolution, President Wilson, a professionally trained political scientist, decided to use Costa Rica as a case for teaching the political arts to Latin Americans. At the time the United States was being drawn into World War I, Costa Rica experienced an illegal seizure of power in 1917 that produced internal strife, international conflict, and the threat of direct U.S. intervention. The coup against democratically elected President Alfredo González Flores was carried out by Federico Tinoco, sparked by González's close ties to Costa Rica's large German colony, and economic and tax reforms to modernize the economy that challenged the coffee oligarchy and the United Fruit Company. President Wilson, fearful of what political disturbances might do to the security of the Panama Canal, and convinced of the illegitimacy of Tinoco's government, invoked his policy of nonrecognition. State Department official Herbert Stabler was assigned the task of

devising a policy toward Tinoco that would reflect Wilson's political philosophy. Stabler recommended that the United States "will not give recognition to him or to any government which he may form, since he
[Tinoco] came to power through a revolutionary, illegal and unconstitutional act."[2]

Although Tinoco had the support of the United Fruit Company and the
coffee growers, he could not survive the diplomatic pressure and economic
sanctions against his government by Washington. Tinoco refused to bend
to the heavy-handed arm twisting, and President Wilson remained steadfast
in his determination to "teach" Tinoco a lesson in democratic governance,
even when his nonrecognition policy clashed with U.S. economic and strategic interests. Wilson prevailed despite a Senate resolution favoring recognition of Tinoco after he declared war against Germany, support for
Tinoco among U.S. business interests, and warnings from Secretary of State
Robert Lansing that the U.S. nonrecognition of Tinoco ran directly contrary to its interests in prosecuting World War I. Nevertheless, Wilson held
to his belief that the principles of nonrecognition and democracy promotion
were more important than treating Costa Rica in terms of national interest.

Wilson's nonrecognition of Tinoco did not help promote peace in Costa
Rica; it further harmed the economy, made the dictatorship more repressive, and stimulated rebellion and internal violence. Although the United
States did not intervene directly in Costa Rica despite pleas from González's
supporters, Tinoco had only 30 months before being forced to step down
in August 1919. The Tinoco affair is noteworthy because it was one of the
few examples of a destabilization campaign directed against a dictator by
the United States in the twentieth century. Moreover, Wilson's reaction to
Tinoco was considered a form of blatant intervention and left bitter memories that lasted for decades. It also demonstrated that U.S. efforts at democracy promotion had little effect on Costa Rica—although after the
Tinoco military dictatorship was overthrown in 1919, constitutional rule
became the norm through the period of the Good Neighbor Policy. A huge
labor strike against United Fruit in 1934 helped lay the foundation for
social reform, beginning with the presidency of Rafael Angel Calderón between 1940 and 1944.

COSTA RICA AND THE UNITED STATES DURING THE COLD WAR

Calderón's social reforms—an advanced labor code, a social security system, and a program of government-assisted housing—antagonized many
of his initial supporters but didn't seem to bother Washington until the
beginning of the Cold War. In a top-secret CIA report in 1948, Costa Rica
was viewed by the Washington intelligence community as the country in
Central America with the most likely potential for communist revolution.

Calderón's wartime alliance of convenience with the communists caused great concern and division within Costa Rica. In an effort to capture the presidency again in 1948, Calderón was defeated by a coalition of the traditional coffee oligarchy and young reformist social democrats. However, the Calderón-controlled Congress nullified the election, sparking a revolt led by José Figueres. Figueres was an anticommunist social democrat who accused Calderón in 1942 of turning Costa Rica over to the "Reds." Known affectionately as Don Pepe, he and his insurgents founded the Junta of the Second Republic and governed until November 1949.

The Rise of José Figueres

After serving as head of government during the period of junta rule, Figueres helped found the social democratic National Liberation Party and later served two terms as Costa Rica's elected president (1953–1958 and 1970–1974). The alleged irregularities in the 1948 elections provided the incentive for Figueres's insurrectionary army to remove Calderón from power. With economic and military assistance from the United States and Nicaragua's anticommunist dictator, Anastasio Somoza, Figueres's forces prevailed after a week of heavy fighting and thousands of casualties. Worried about "communist control" in San José, the United States informed Figueres that its military forces were ready in the Panama Canal Zone if needed to head off a leftist victory.

While in office between 1948 and 1949, Figueres carried out a number of surprising reforms in which his government disbanded the army, nationalized the banking system, taxed the very wealthy, extended full political rights to women and blacks, and announced a foreign policy of neutrality. During his presidency of 1953–1958, Figueres befriended Vice-President Richard Nixon and CIA director Allen Dulles. His anticommunism and pro-Americanism motivated him to support the CIA-supported overthrow of Jacobo Arbenz in Guatemala in 1954, Kennedy's Alliance for Progress, the Bay of Pigs invasion, and the overthrow of Dominican dictator Rafael Trujillo.

Although he was not president at the time, Don Pepe was on intimate terms with some of Kennedy's White House advisors such as Adolf A. Berle Jr. President-elect Kennedy appointed Berle to head a task force on Latin America in 1960 that recommended a program that was later incorporated into the Alliance for Progress. Berle's task force consulted with some of the leading democrats in Latin America, including Figueres, before making its recommendations. Its advocacy of a "Democratic International," an international movement to finance and provide direction for democratic movements in other countries, was rejected by the Kennedy administration, but it accurately reflected Berle's philosophy of inter-American relations and democratic governance.

His presidency during 1970–1974 overlapped with the Nixon administration but was tainted by his relationship with American fugitive Robert L. Vesco, who fled to Costa Rica after being criminally charged with stealing $224 million from his investment company and making large illegal campaign contributions to President Nixon. President Figueres's protection of Vesco damaged his presidency, but the scandal did not prevent his party from succeeding itself in 1974. He was instrumental throughout his career in helping the CIA fund the noncommunist left throughout Latin America and the Caribbean. In dealing with Nicaragua and other right-wing dictatorships, Figures helped create the Caribbean Legion, a loose alliance of forces dedicated to removing dictators, and he supported opposition efforts (including the Sandinistas) to topple Anastasio Somoza. By the time of his death in 1990, Costa Rica had embarked on a developmental path that would ultimately dismantle many of the reforms that made Don Pepe the modern father of Costa Rica.

Costa Rica versus the Reagan Administration

The Reagan administration's anti-Sandinista policy eventually carried over into Costa Rica, where a Southern Front was set up under Edén Pastora with financial assistance from the Central Intelligence Agency. National Security Council (NSC) staff member Oliver North, in charge of the U.S. Contra resupply operation, arranged to have an airstrip built in northern Costa Rica in 1985 that was used to provide weapons for those fighting against Nicaragua. Costa Rica's economic problems, and its concern about the influx of Nicaraguans into Costa Rican cities, contributed to its willingness to be pressured to accept large amounts of U.S. financial assistance in return for strengthening its modest security forces to confront mounting terrorist actions. The more hardline faction within the Reagan administration pressured Costa Rica to join the battle against Nicaragua despite its reluctance in being drawn into the Contra war, growing concerns about damage to Costa Rican democracy, its neutrality, and the national pride associated with its demilitarized society. The Costa Rican foreign minister at the time put the dilemma rather bluntly by saying, "We desperately needed United States aid to deal with an economic crisis. In order to get that aid we decided to play ball with the United States on the issue of the contras."[3] Costa Rica received large amounts of economic and military assistance. It received over $1 billion in economic aid during the Reagan years, and during a three-year span (1982–1985) it received almost four times as much military assistance from the United States as it had in the past 40 years combined. The United States appointed hardline ambassadors to convince Costa Rican leaders of the magnitude of the Nicaraguan threat and the importance of building up its security forces. One such ambassador

"Whoops, Sorry About That!"

was Curtin Winsor, known for his anti-Sandinista views, arrogance, and desire to involve himself in Costa Rica's internal affairs.

Worried about growing terrorist incidents in Costa Rica and protests against his subservience to Washington's Nicaragua policy, President Luis Alberto Monge tried to balance these forces by publicly committing Costa Rica to neutrality in the conflict with Nicaragua; but by 1985 this approach became untenable. The public anger increased after the United States began sending Green Berets to Costa Rica to provide counterinsurgency training to its security forces. Convinced that Monge was sacrificing Costa Rica's sovereignty, antimilitarism, and its democratic institutions, Costa Ricans replaced him in 1986 by electing Oscar Arias president. He relieved the tension by charting a different foreign policy course, one that refused to allow U.S.-backed Contra forces to use Costa Rican territory (including Oliver North's airstrip), putting in motion a high-profile campaign to bring peace to the region and publicly challenging Washington's strategy for dealing with the Central American crisis. President Arias was helped in his peace efforts by the Iran Contra affair in 1986 and the international condemnation of the United States for its blatant contempt for Costa Rica's sovereignty and democratic institutions. Although President Arias often muted his public criticism of Reagan's attitude toward the peace process and the dangers of the Southern Front strategy, he once told Reagan that "We want to be an intelligent friend, not a stupid ally."[4] Despite President's Reagan's opposition to President Arias and his assertion that his peace proposal was "fatally flawed," the Costa Rican president won the Nobel Peace Prize in 1987 for devising a plan to end the conflict and bring peace to the region.

COSTA RICA AND THE UNITED STATES AFTER THE COLD WAR

In general, U.S.–Costa Rican relations have been favorable since the end of the Cold War. After the dismantling of the Contras, the Sandinista electoral defeat in 1990, and the election of Rafael Calderón Fournier of the Social Christian Party, the United States and Costa Rica have returned to more cordial relations and a dramatic decline in U.S. economic assistance. After assuming office, Calderón announced that he was going to be a strong supporter and great friend of Washington's policy in Central America. As its neighbors have wrestled with demilitarization and democratization, economic reconstruction, and expanding trade and exports, Costa Rica has emphasized foreign economic relations, including reforms to make World Bank and International Monetary Fund lending more attractive.

U.S.–Costa Rican relations were strained during the Bush administration after Republican senator Jesse Helms arranged for Congress to withhold $10 million in Agency for International Development (AID) funds because he claimed that Costa Rica was not making sufficient progress in compensating U.S. citizens for property seized to create a national park (including the Santa Elena airstrip used for Contra resupply by the United States). To add further pressure on Costa Rica, President Bush managed to block Inter-American Development Bank development loans worth hundreds of millions of dollars.

Son of Figueres

José María Figueres, son of three-time president José Figueres, became president in 1994, promising to uphold his father's legacy of statist economic development. However, once in office he changed course by embracing free market economics and downsizing the welfare state. This has not made Figueres a popular figure in Costa Rica. In his effort to dismantle the European-style welfare state, he has become Costa Rica's most unpopular president in recent times. Facing accusations that he is betraying the socialist principles of his father and their party, Figueres has also experienced urban riots and deadly disturbances caused by his austerity plans.

The United States closed its AID office in Costa Rica in 1996, claiming it is no longer a developing country, and many of the money doctors advising Figueres argue that the economic reduction was long overdue after building up a foreign debt and receiving over $1 billion in aid from the United States in the previous decade.

Costa Rica versus Chiquita: Banana Wars in the 1990s

In 1993 the European Union (EU) adopted a banana policy that favored imports from former colonies in Africa and the Caribbean. Instead of taking a stance in favor of free trade, the United States tried to keep out of the feud until Colombia and Costa Rica persuaded the EU to allow a small quota of their bananas into the market. After Chiquita Brands International complained to the U.S. trade office claiming discrimination, the United States joined the banana war and it eventually worked its way into the 1996 presidential campaign. In a display of arrogance toward Costa Rica and Colombia, and at the risk of undermining democracy and worsening the drug trade, Republican presidential candidate Bob Dole—with close ties to Chiquita chief Carl Linder—raised the banana issue in Congress so that economic sanctions would be applied to Latin America's two major banana producers, Ecuador and Costa Rica. Dole finally gave up his banana crusade after the press revealed his ties to Linder and Chiquita Brands; trade sanctions were not imposed, but the episode demonstrated a willingness on the part of the United States to trample on two Latin American economies for the sake of partisan politics in the United States.

CONCLUSION

U.S. involvement in Costa Rica illustrates several things about policy-making in Washington. First, asymmetries in power leave small countries like Costa Rica with little autonomy when it comes to formulating an independent foreign policy. Second, with more than 100 years of almost uninterrupted democratic rule, Costa Rica's history is devoid of U.S. intervention, the Monroe Doctrine, and chronic anti-Americanism and animosity. If there is a lesson in the Costa Rican case, it may be that democratic institutions grow best from within, not from promotional efforts by policymakers in Washington. Finally, it is important to point out that while small countries can defy the United States on some occasions—for example, under the enlightened leadership of Oscar Arias—trade patterns, leverage over international lending agencies, and economic assistance still leave Costa Rica highly dependent on the United States.

NOTES

1. Paul J. Dosal, *Doing Business with Dictators: A Political History of United Fruit in Guatemala, 1899–1944* (Wilmington, DE: Scholarly Resources, 1993), p. 55.

2. Quoted in Mark Edelman and Joanne Kenan, eds., *The Costa Rica Reader* (New York: Grove Weidenfeld, 1989), p. 67.

3. Dario Moreno, *The Struggle for Peace in Central America* (Gainesville: University of Florida Press, 1994), p. 82.

4. Quoted in Dario Moreno, *U.S. Policy in Central America* (Miami: Florida International Press, 1990), p. 132.

SUGGESTED READINGS

Edelman, Mark, and Joanne Kenan, eds. *The Costa Rica Reader*. New York: Grove Weidenfeld, 1989.

Longley, Kyle. *The Sparrow and the Hawk: Costa Rica and the United States during the Rise of José Figueres*. Tuscaloosa: University of Alabama Press, 1997.

Stewart, Watt. *Keith of Costa Rica: A Biographic Study of Minor Cooper Keith*. Albuquerque: University of New Mexico Press, 1974.

8

Cuba

TIMELINE OF U.S. RELATIONS WITH CUBA

1848–1851	Narciso López organizes filibustering expeditions
1895	Cuba's second war of independence begins
1898	Battleship *Maine* explodes in Havana harbor; United States declares war on Spain
1899–1902	U.S. military occupation
1902	Platt Amendment is attached to Cuban constitution
May 20, 1902	Cuban independence from Spain is achieved
1906–1909	U.S. military occupation
1912	U.S. military intervention
1917–1922	U.S. military intervention
1924	Gerardo Machado is elected president
1933	U.S. ambassador Sumner Welles is dispatched to remove Machado
	Sergeants Revolt leads to rise of Fulgencio Batista
	Dr. Ramón Grau becomes president
1934	President Grau is driven into exile
	Platt Amendment is abrogated
1940	Fulgencio Batista is elected president
1944–1952	Carnival of graft characterizes administrations of Grau and Prío
1952	Batista seizes power in military coup
1953	Revolution begins with Castro's attack on Moncada army barracks

1955	Castro organizes M-26-7 (26th of July Movement) in Mexico
1959	Castro's revolution sends Batista into exile
1960	United States imposes trade embargo; assassination plots begin
1961	Diplomatic relations are severed
	Bay of Pigs invasion
1962	Cuban Missile Crisis
	Organization of American States (OAS) expells Cuba's government for its communist ideology
1964	OAS votes its economic sanctions against Castro's government
1967	Ché Guevara captured and executed in Bolivia
1974	OAS votes to lift mandatory economic sanctions
1977	Diplomatic interest sections are established
1980	Mariel boatlift
1981	Cuban American National Foundation is created
1983	U.S. military captures and arrests Cubans during invasion of Grenada
1985	Radio Martí begins broadcasting
1990	Soviet Union begins to withdraw subsidies
	T.V. Martí begins "broadcasting"
1992	Cuban Democracy Act is enacted
1994	Immigration-control agreement is signed
1996	Helms-Burton bill is enacted
1997	Jorge Más Canosa dies
1998	CIA's secret report on bungled Bay of Pigs invasion is uncovered and published

INTRODUCTION

Since the early 1800s, U.S.-Cuban relations have been characterized by a convergence of interests that have been pivotal to the development of both countries. After recognizing the strategic and economic importance of Cuba to its own early development, the United States often treated it as if it owned the island and was responsible for its fate, long before the island ceased to be a possession of Spain. Cuba's history has been a continual struggle to achieve control over its own national destiny, establish a legitimate government, and solve the problem of dependency on sugar and tobacco. Cuban leaders reasoned that the island's successful future would require both a strong sense of nationalism and a powerful and tightly controlled government.

After the Spanish-American War in 1898, Cuba's fate was determined by the United States through a variety of measures. These included the controversial Platt Amendment and favorable treaties signed by compliant governments. Cubans, frustrated because they lacked full independence, often attributed their failures to the constant meddling and penetration by the United States. After Spanish control ended, they came to resent American domination of their sugar plantations and public utilities; Cubans despised the presence of North American mobsters who worked hand-in-glove with greedy dictators who ran the legal casinos and converted the island into a tourist haven for gambling and other vices. Throughout the Yankee years, Cubans were treated as "children" who required civilized guidance to develop the proper culture, economy, and political system. From Washington's perspective the military interventions, lengthy occupations, economic control, and diplomatic manipulation were both necessary and proper for Cuba *and* the United States.

Since the revolution, Cuba and the United States have been what former U.S. diplomat Wayne Smith calls the "closest of enemies."[1] The failure to normalize relations over a span of four decades is a complex tale of poor judgment and missed opportunities in both Washington and Havana. There are similarities in the way Spanish pride resisted Cuban demands for independence in the nineteenth century, and the determination of the United States to resist all forms of compromise with the Castro regime, no matter what the costs. In any case, what has been done by the United States in trying to eliminate Castro from Cuba far exceeds the level of hostility (in the absence of war) directed at any other Latin American country for the sole purpose of changing its political behavior and leadership. Moreover, the animosity of eight U.S. presidents has often been counterproductive, serving to enhance Castro's legitimacy while undermining U.S. relations with long-standing allies in Canada, Europe, Latin America, and the Caribbean.

CUBA AND THE UNITED STATES IN THE NINETEENTH CENTURY

Cuba and the Independence of Latin America

Cuba remained a colony of Spain for almost 400 years, longer than any of its territorial possessions in the Americas. As South American liberators such as Simón Bolívar succeeded in driving Spanish rule out of the Western Hemisphere, the United States came to realize that revolutions close to its shores could pose threats to its security and economic interests. In the case of Cuba, John Quincy Adams felt that it better served the United States as a weak part of the Spanish Empire until the time came for it to tumble naturally into the grip of the United States (the so-called ripe fruit theory). Instead of having the legitimate right to rebel and become independent of

"It's Those Latin Commies We Can't Stand"

Spain, Cubans faced a different political fate due to the question of slavery and U.S. perceptions of security. Secretary of State Henry Clay (1825–1829) expressed the commonly held view that if Cuba became independent, its freed slaves would stimulate an insurrection among slaves in the United States. Cuban plantation owners favored Cuba's annexation by the United States as a way to sever ties with Spain, while at the same time retaining the necessary state powers to repress possible slave revolts. In any case, by thwarting Cuban independence the United States damaged its reputation as a supporter of freedom and self-determination in the Americas.

Cuba and the Monroe Doctrine

President Monroe's message of 1823 emerged from the concern of possible territorial plans among major European powers. Napoleon's deeds in Spain forced the United States to rethink its Cuba policy at a time when its capacity to challenge Europe was limited. However, in the 1820s U.S.-Cuban policy remained wedded to the cautious approach of Secretary of State Adams, who adhered to his ripe fruit (*la fruta madura*) theory—a clumsy and questionable set of assumptions, but the best that Washington had at the time. When the South American liberator Simón Bolívar considered freeing Cuba and Puerto Rico from Spanish control in 1823, Adams told him to stay out, arguing that Cuba could only belong to the United States. With Spain firmly in control of Cuba, the Monroe Doctrine had little to do with nineteenth-century U.S. policy toward the island.

Manifest Destiny and the Age of the Filibusters

By the 1840s the United States had shed the defensiveness of the Monroe Doctrine in favor of its own territorial expansion. Guided by the concept of Manifest Destiny, the United States engaged in a war with Mexico and at the same time tried to wrestle Cuba from Spain. Manifest Destiny grew out of the belief that U.S. territorial expansion would occur because of certain unique characteristics of the American people, particularly the sense of obligation to extend its civilization to those less fortunate, and a strong conviction in the positive features of the country's "democratic" political institutions.

In the 1850s, thousands of adventurers launched expeditions from the United States against Cuba, Ecuador, Honduras, Mexico, and Nicaragua. Three presidents—James K. Polk, Franklin Pierce, and James Buchanan—made attempts to buy Cuba from Spain, but all efforts ended in failure. The private mercenaries who ventured south violated U.S. and international law, but their expeditions captured the attention and support of many citizens in the United States. Motivated by Manifest Destiny and the expansion of slavery, they often created foreign relations headaches for the United States. With each effort to acquire Cuba by the United States in the 1850s, Spain refused to relinquish its Caribbean territory from the remains of its dying empire.

One of the most tenacious adventures who operated outside the law and against the wishes of U.S. presidents was Narciso López. A Venezuelan-born Cuban aristocrat, López led three aborted invasions of Cuba between 1849 and 1851, backed by Southerners committed to the expansion of slavery into new territory. His expeditions were aimed at liberating Cuba from Spanish control and then annexing the island to the United States, but the Spanish were too powerful to defeat in this way. Although López was captured and killed by the Spanish in 1851, his filibustering activities set the stage for future anti-Spanish uprisings among Cubans. As part of Manifest Destiny and the expansion of slavery, filibustering served to intensify sectional forces in the United States that eventually led to civil war. Presidents Zachary Taylor and Franklin Pierce tried to discourage these adventurers, but the power of private interests won out. Others worried that continual efforts to free Cuba from the Spanish Empire might lead to a slave uprising, independence, and a "second Haiti," even in a so-called controlled revolution. The failure of the López expeditions and the abolition of slavery in the United States dampened the desire of Cuban slave-holders to establish permanent relations with their northern neighbor.

After the U.S. Civil War, Cuba fell under the increasing control of American business interests as tariff policies created a "quota system" by which Cuban sugar was guaranteed a certain percentage of the American market. The devastation wrought by the Ten Years' War (1868–1878), Cuba's first struggle for independence that ended in failure, allowed the United States to gain a greater economic foothold in Cuba as many planters had to foreclose on land investments. By the time of the Spanish-American War in 1898, Cuba accounted for 75 percent of all Latin America's exports to the United States, and more than half of all Latin America's imports from the United States.

CUBA AND THE UNITED STATES IN THE TWENTIETH CENTURY

The Spanish-American War

Cuba's second war of independence began in 1895, but the odds of victory were in Spain's favor: 200,000 Spanish soldiers squared off against 4,000 Cuban guerrillas. President Cleveland at first tried to avoid getting entangled with Spain over its colonial possession, worried that if Spain should lose, then the United States—with $50 million in investments on the island—would have to take charge of Cuba. The fact that José Martí, the major force behind the push for complete independence, was killed in the first few months of the war did not help the rebel efforts; for three years the war dragged on with a vicious brutality but with no end in sight.

After the sinking of the battleship *Maine* in Havana harbor in 1898, cries from Americans to seize Cuba increased dramatically, especially with the yellow journalism (reporting designed to stir up war fever) spewed forth by William Randolph Hearst and other newspaper owners. The United States soon found itself at war with Spain despite the fact that President McKinley received a message of conciliation from the Spanish shortly before the war proclamation. In his war message, McKinley made no mention of Cuban independence or the recognition of any Cuban provisional government. The United States wanted the world to believe that it was intervening in Cuba to stop the war, whereas the real purpose was to ensure U.S. control over the island.

The war had a marked impact on the United States and helped to boost the popularity of Theodore Roosevelt. Afterwards, he once acknowledged: "It wasn't much of a war, but it was the best war we had." John Hay, U.S. ambassador to Britain, called it a "splendid little war" because U.S. forces won a swift and decisive victory, suffered relatively few deaths, and acquired a host of new overseas territories. Although just 385 Americans died in battle, 2,061 succumbed to tropical diseases—malaria, yellow fever, and dysentery—and 1,662 were wounded. Spain and the United States signed the Treaty of Paris that ended the war in 1898 but left the U.S. Army as an occupying force. The Spanish loss freed Cuba and ceded Guam, Puerto Rico, and the Philippines to the United States, a victory that contributed to more military and political muscle–flexing in the Caribbean region. Convinced that Cuba would eventually request annexation to the United States, American military officers tried to reshape Cuban institutions to resemble those in the United States.

The Platt Amendment and the Years of Yankee Paternalism

Cubans finally achieved their independence in 1902, but only after being forced to accept the Platt Amendment, a clause in the Cuban constitution that gave the United States the right to intervene for the preservation of Cuban independence and stability. Named after Republican senator Orville Platt of Connecticut, but the brainchild of Elihu Root, the Platt Amendment also gave the United States control over Cuban foreign policy and provided the legal basis for the acquisition of Guantánamo Bay. In many ways the Platt Amendment was a compromise between annexation and complete independence, a device by which the United States was allowed to continue the role of protector without having to put an occupation force on the island. The Platt Amendment gave rise to a 30-year period of paternalistic control over the island and a bitter animosity on the part of Cubans toward the way in which the island was manipulated for U.S. economic and political gain.

From the early part of the twentieth century, the United States developed a variety of ways to control Cuban political and economic life. First, the Platt Amendment, as part of the Cuban Constitution, provided a legal means for U.S. intervention from 1902 to 1934. Second, the United States created the Cuban army to protect its own economic and security interests. Third, the Monroe Doctrine provided the justification for further political meddling and supervision of fiscal and other budgetary matters. There were times when the United States maintained its control over Cuba by appointing its own citizens to govern Cuba. Until the Castro government took power in the late 1950s, U.S. ambassadors and political advisors were often more powerful than any elected president of Cuba. United Fruit and other companies dominated sugar production and owned vast amounts of the best land in eastern Cuba, and other American companies had tight control over the rest of the economy, including oil refining, rubber, chemicals, and banking.

Sumner Welles, Fulgencio Batista, and the Good
Neighbor Policy

The most critical year in U.S.-Cuban relations before 1959 was 1933. The convulsion that gripped Cuba for almost a year was a reaction by a younger generation against earlier revolutionaries who were seen to have "sold out" by accepting American paternalism and foreign economic control over the island. The 1933 revolution was a hostile reaction to the deep penetration of Cuba by the United States and decades of corrupt government. Although it failed, it had a dramatic impact on the future of Cuban politics and the future role of the United States in Cuba.

In July 1933, President Roosevelt sent Ambassador Sumner Welles to Cuba to oversee the removal of Gerardo Machado, a dictator whose brutal repression threatened American economic and security interests. The chaotic events of the summer of 1933 soon led to the removal of Machado and the formation of a new government under Dr. Ramón Grau San Martín, a favorite of the university students who had participated in the revolt. However, Ambassador Welles opposed Grau on the basis of his socialist reforms and eventually helped to drive him into exile by early 1934. Welles opposed diplomatic recognition and made repeated requests for U.S. military intervention, but President Roosevelt and Secretary of State Cordell Hull refused to intervene, citing previous pledges of nonintervention and the unwarranted claims of the American ambassador. Nevertheless, Grau's inability to gain recognition from the United States and political pressures from within contributed to his removal. From this point until 1959, Cuba was ruled by either Fulgencio Batista or a succession of elected governments that often presided over a carnival of graft and domestic violence. A new treaty with the United States eliminated the odious Platt Amendment, a boon to Batista's legitimacy as a ruler of Cuba. According to Louis Pérez Jr., "The abrogation of the Platt Amendment helped Batista to assume the mantle of defender of national sovereignty and protector of national honor," a political asset that no Cuban politician had ever acquired.[2] He governed from behind the scenes until 1940, then was elected to a four-year term of office.

THE UNITED STATES AND CUBA DURING
THE COLD WAR

During World War II, Batista aligned Cuba with the United States and the Soviet Union in the fight against Hitler's aggression in Europe. After his term of office ended in 1944, he returned to military life while two civilian presidencies (1944–1952) governed Cuba, often with close ties to organized crime figures in the United States. Realizing he could not win the 1952 presidential election, Batista carried out a military coup that brought

Cuba's weak democratic system to an end. The Cuban dictator ruled by terror and favoritism but was considered a "friendly dictator" by the United States in the Cold War struggle against communism in the Caribbean. Batista's collaboration with organized crime figures, mostly in drugs and prostitution, helped to strengthen the dictatorship. Meyer Lansky—the chief mob boss in Havana—is reported to have deposited more than $3 million in Batista's Swiss bank accounts, and the dictator's total wealth was estimated at somewhere between $100 and $300 million.

The United States and the Politics of Insurrection

On July 26, 1953, Fidel Castro and 125 followers attacked the Moncada Army Barracks in Santiago, a large city in eastern Cuba, hoping to spark enough resistance against Batista to drive him from power. After a series of tactical blunders the revolutionaries were defeated, and later most were hunted and killed by Batista's secret police. Although Fidel Castro survived, he was sentenced to 15 years on the Isle of Pines and immediately started plans for the next revolt. After serving a year and a half in jail Castro was released from prison and left for Mexico, where he met the Argentine revolutionary Ernesto "Ché" Guevara. Together they created the 26th of July Movement (M-26-7)—the organizational and philosophical basis for the insurrection designed to topple Batista. When Ché Guevara arrived in Guatemala in 1954, he was clearly anti-American and an admirer of revolutions, but not a communist. After witnessing the U.S.-directed coup against the elected government of Jacobo Arbenz, Ché turned toward communist ideology. During the early years of the Cuban revolution, he became the principal architect of Cuba's break with the United States and its military and economic alignment with the Soviets.

In November 1956 Castro, Ché, and 80 other revolutionaries left Mexico on a leaky second-hand yacht called the *Granma* (later to become the name of Cuba's Communist Party newspaper). Stormy seas delayed the arrival of the craft, the uprising that was to coincide with the arrival fizzled, and when the seasick revolutionaries arrived they were captured and most were killed by Batista's troops. The dozen or so survivors escaped into the Sierra Maestra mountains, where they set up their Rebel Army and began to plan the revolution.

During the next few years the revolutionaries attracted more followers among small farmers or campesinos, set up schools and hospitals in the countryside, and established an informal government as a structure with a manifesto for change in a Cuba without Batista. To publicize their efforts, the M-26-7 established Radio Rebelde, campaigned for a democratic Cuba, and brought Herbert Matthews, a reporter from the *New York Times*, to their mountain hideaway to put out their own counter-propaganda against Batista's claims that he had demolished the guerrillas. During the guerrilla campaigns the United States increased its military supplies to Batista. Castro deeply resented this support and appealed to the United States to terminate military assistance, but to no avail. However, in late 1958 Washington did finally cut off aid to Batista and tolerated arms being smuggled to Castro from the United States. Shortly after midnight on New Year's Eve, 1958, with guerrilla forces advancing on Havana and his own army defecting, Batista fled Cuba for the Dominican Republic with most of the Cuban treasury in his baggage. After Batista's escape, the United States tried to establish a "provisional government" excluding the guerrillas, but Castro's revolutionary charisma prevailed, leaving the United States with little choice but to deal with Castro. As people in Havana rejoiced at the overthrow of Batista, Castro and his guerrilla forces left Santiago for a victory sweep of the island ending in Havana on January 8, 1959. Chants of "Fidel, Fidel!" and "Cuba sí, Yanqui no" could be heard from the huge crowds that lined the streets on their arrival. Castro's guerrilla strategy would soon become the theme of the revolution, and his charisma the basis of legitimacy for the regime that emerged to change and govern Cuba.

The Cuban Revolution and the United States

The triumph of Castro's armed insurrection came as a surprise to many Cubans who were the beneficiaries of decades of U.S. domination. Few understood Castro's real intentions, and the Eisenhower administration at first adopted an optimistic but cautious approach to Cuba. Although the United States had managed to reach an accommodation with other Latin American revolutions, it seemed unlikely that a revolution could adjust to or alter the closely intertwined relationship with the United States. Havana resembled an American city in the 1950s, and the children of wealthy Cubans were often sent to school in the United States. The sugar industry was highly mechanized and was the beneficiary of railroads and roads built with the technical assistance of the United States. However, the apparent well-being in Cuba also consisted of shocking disparities in wealth between city and countryside, and between races; whites were far better off than Afro-Cubans and others of mixed race. Cubans of all classes reacted negatively to the corruption, graft, oppression, and inequality that had been fostered by Batista and his collaborators. Cuban youth who made up the Castro generation lived in a society of alienated intellectuals, corrupt politicians, and rampant violence; thousands of Cubans were murdered—mostly city youths accused of burning sugar fields and bombing electrical installations. Castro's revolution was the result of a long tradition of struggle reaching back to the nineteenth century, and its intellectual roots stemmed largely from earlier revolutionary leaders—Antonio Maceo and José Martí—heroes of the nineteenth-century struggle for independence, not Karl Marx and V. I. Lenin.

The Politics of Hostility, 1959–1968

Coming at the height of the Cold War, the Cuban revolution had a dramatic impact on the United States and inter-American relations. The United States was not prepared to acknowledge or accept the authenticity of Cuban grievances or their demands for self-determination. As soon as the Cubans aligned themselves with the Soviet Union, Washington was convinced that this consolidation of revolutionary strategy was part of a unified plan for world revolution. The large number of exiles who fled to Miami were convinced that Castro was nothing more than "Batista with a beard," or a committed Marxist-Leninist determined to rule in a ruthless fashion with the support of the Soviet Union. In their view, Castro had betrayed the Revolution.

Those who discredited this Cold War theory of the Cuban Revolution claimed that the United States had "pushed" Cuba into the hands of the Soviets. Castro's political ideology was more in the moralist and nationalist tradition of José Martí—removing the evils of crime, corruption, unemployment, disease, and U.S. imperialism—than a rigid Marxist-Leninist belief system. Further, to carry out a successful revolution in the shadows of the United States, Castro had no choice but to reduce the ... nly entrenched U.S. companies. In the place of a feeble capit ... e radical renovationists installed a socialist system to deal v ... - onomic and social problems and reforms, an impossibility i ... n had been left in place. In brief, Fidel Castro used socialism ... e resistance of powerful interests—national and internationa ... t against the revolutionary reforms in housing, agrarian, ... commercial areas. Many in the revolutionary elite had been v ... the Moncada attack and remembered the way the Unit ... thwarted the 1933 revolution and the brutal effort to rid ... Jacobo Arbenz in 1954; and they wanted to avoid a costly these events.

Cuba's seizure of American companies and citizens' prope. ... :d the most hostile U.S. response to revolutionary change in Lat ... an history. The fact that U.S. citizens owned over 3 million a ... ral property at the time of the revolution (with an estimated value of $1.2 million) complicated the relationship with the United States. Between 1959 and 1960, the new government seized U.S.-owned cattle and sugar property, two oil refineries, three banks, numerous manufacturing entities, public utilities, and hotels. A Foreign Claims Settlement Commission in the United States estimated that the Cuban government seized U.S. property totaling $3.3 billion out of 3,806 claims. Actual appraisals of the amount were half that of the claims, but U.S. losses in Cuba probably exceeded $1 billion and were far greater than those that occurred with other revolutions in Latin America. (Despite these apparent losses and claims, it is important to note that large multinational corporations—United Fruit and Hershey Chocolate—were able to write off their Cuban losses when filing their income tax returns, an advantage not enjoyed by the various small holders who lost property.) Cuban compensation for the seizure of U.S. property was problematic from the beginning, but Eisenhower's cut-off of the sugar quota and his authorization of an anti-Castro paramilitary force in early 1960 left Castro with little or no inducement to compromise on property settlements.

Castro's first goal was to consolidate power after the removal of Batista and his many supporters who remained on the island. Castro declared himself the prime minister, and Ché Guevara was appointed head of the National Bank. Batista's supporters were jailed, tried, sentenced, and publicly executed, a move that had highly negative consequences in the United States. The public trials and executions of Batista's followers shocked Americans who found it difficult to understand the violent forces that often come with a social revolution. Castro's postponement of free elections and his willingness to collaborate with the Cuban communists began to concern U.S. policymakers caught up in the anticommunist psychology of the Cold War. In Cuba an agrarian law was passed, property that belonged to U.S. companies was nationalized, and efforts were made to redistribute wealth. The revolutionary laws called for means of compensation, but the offer was unacceptable to American companies. After the middle and upper classes lost their privileges and homes, a large exodus of Cubans fled to Miami.

Bay of Pigs Invasion

By early 1960 the Eisenhower administration had decided it could no longer remain tolerant of Castro and his brand of anti-American nationalism because it threatened U.S. leadership in the hemisphere and endangered U.S. investments in the region. Convinced that it would be impossible to get along with Castro, Eisenhower's Latin American advisors decided it was necessary to undermine the Cuban Revolution. By January 1960, high-ranking members of the Eisenhower administration were calling for the overthrow of Castro in the same way Arbenz had been removed in Guatemala in 1954. U.S. hostility toward Cuba proved to be counterproductive, because Castro moved sharply to the left in both domestic and foreign policies after he discovered that the Eisenhower administration wanted to destroy his revolution.

The United States now faced the task of assessing Castro's character within the context of the Cold War. Was Fidel Castro a communist? Was he a Soviet agent under Moscow's domination that somehow threatened the security of the United States? Fidel Castro visited the United States in April 1959 and spent an afternoon discussing the revolution with Vice-President Richard Nixon. Nixon concluded that Castro was "incredibly naive about communism" and eventually came to believe that Castro was a communist. Nixon's memo from that encounter would become the genesis of the Bay of Pigs invasion two years later. For many in the Eisenhower administration, Castro's presence in Cuba was a grave challenge to the Monroe Doctrine. As Castro's links to the Soviet Union became more firm, U.S. policymakers began increasingly to refer to the Monroe Doctrine in the press and in Congress as the primary justification for some kind of hostile action against Cuba. In legislative debate on June 30, 1960, Congressman Mendel Rivers (D-SC) lashed out against Castro by invoking the Monroe Doctrine and asserting a formula of revenge:

> We should issue a proclamation telling him [Fidel Castro] what this Nation proposes to do if he keeps on blackmailing and vilifying our President and our people and taking property without due process of law. We should assert the Monroe Doctrine. We should threaten Castro with blockade. We should, if necessary, and, if conditions demand it, occupy Cuba.[3]

In March 1960, Eisenhower set in motion plans that would culminate in the disastrous Bay of Pigs invasion one year later. Eisenhower's top aides apparently ignored public opinion polls indicating an overwhelming degree of support for Fidel Castro. Nevertheless, with CIA successes in Guatemala and Iran in mind, the effort went forward despite erroneous assumptions and faulty planning. Political pressures to "do something" about Castro increased as he took over more and more U.S. property and the Soviets appeared to be creating a Russian colony near the U.S. mainland. When the United States eliminated Cuba's sugar quota, thereby wiping out the U.S. market, Castro retaliated by nationalizing American-owned industrial and agrarian enterprises, as well as banks. Shortly thereafter, Soviet premier Nikita Khrushchev called a press conference and announced the death of the Monroe Doctrine; the United States was furious, and demands for military intervention increased.

Meanwhile, Cuba became an issue in the 1960 presidential election. John F. Kennedy attacked the Eisenhower administration for its failure to remove Castro and stated that as president he would support the use of armed Cuban forces in exile to overthrow Fidel Castro. Kennedy's position was quite popular at the time, and he agreed to implement the CIA plan to forcefully overthrow Castro once he was in office. Using the successful overthrow of President Arbenz in Guatemala as a model, the Central Intelligence Agency trained and equipped 1,500 exile mercenaries to overthrow Castro in April 1961 (see Chapter 13). However, the invasion at the Bay of Pigs was a disaster for the Kennedy administration, as Castro managed to defeat the invaders in a series of lopsided battles that lasted only 72 hours. Most were taken prisoner and later released after the United

States traded $50 million in medicines for their return. The Bay of Pigs failure produced repeated charges from Republicans that Kennedy had failed to defend the Monroe Doctrine, and it further confirmed Khrushchev's claim that the Doctrine had died a natural death. In a spirit of vengeful retaliation, President Kennedy spent the remainder of his presidency trying to remove Castro from power by means of secret assassination attempts, a tightened trade embargo, and orchestrating the removal of Cuba's "Marxist-Leninist" government from the Organization of American States.

In one of the most secret documents of the Cold War, until its release under the Freedom of Information Act to the National Security Archive in 1998, the Central Intelligence Agency produced a brutally honest self-criticism that exposed its bungled efforts to end Castro's rule with a small exile brigade in 1961. The 150-page report, written by the CIA's inspector general Lyman Kirkpatrick in 1961, depicts the secret operation as "ludicrous or tragic or both" and states that among the officers chosen to carry out the operation, "very few spoke Spanish or had Latin American background knowledge."[4]

Assassination Attempts on Fidel Castro

Shortly after the Bay of Pigs disaster, the Kennedy administration decided that it would do whatever it took to get rid of Castro, including assassination. Although assassination of a foreign leader was not illegal at the time, the task of eliminating him required that the U.S. president be shielded from any guilt, utmost secrecy be maintained, and the murder attempt itself require the use of CIA assets that could hire the "hit squad" to do the dirty work. President Kennedy was wary of using the CIA against Castro after the Bay of Pigs, so he gave the job to Attorney General Robert Kennedy, then in charge of "Operation Mongoose," a covert effort to disrupt the Cuban economy and build unrest on the island in hopes of toppling Castro. Robert Kennedy used a private investigator from Las Vegas on the CIA payroll to hire Mafia boss Sam Giancana for the hit on Fidel. The murder-for-hire project was launched in May 1962. In a strange twist of events, while the CIA set $150,000 as payment for the successful assassination of Castro, the Mafia connection (according to recent documents) emphatically stated that it wanted no payment and would do the job for free. The fact that Castro survived more than a dozen assassination attempts by the CIA and that President Kennedy was later killed by an assassin has generated conspiracy theories that Kennedy's death was an act of revenge in retaliation for the plots against Castro's life. Following congressional investigations into these activities in the mid-1970s, President Ford issued an executive order in 1976 outlawing assassination as an instrument of American foreign policy.

The Cuban Missile Crisis

After the Bay of Pigs fiasco, Castro grew more fearful of a military effort by the United States to remove him from power. The Kennedy administration continued its efforts to rid the Caribbean of Castro by endorsing a range of covert efforts. General Maxwell Taylor, chairman of the Joint Chiefs of Staff, noted in a secret document in 1962 that a successful plan to overthrow Castro would ultimately require U.S. military action. The Soviets, anxious to close their missile gap with the United States, proposed a secret plan to ship over half their nuclear arsenal to Cuba, but with Cuban approval. In order to counter a direct invasion by the United States, Castro welcomed the missile-deployment plan of Premier Khrushchev.

The crisis began once the United States discovered the missile sites on the island and was forced to develop a response, one that ran the risk of a nuclear confrontation. After several meetings with his top advisors, Kennedy decided to confront the Soviets with a quarantine that would stop all incoming ships bearing Soviet missiles and then demand the removal of all existing missiles on the island. In a forceful but somber address to the nation, President Kennedy made no mention of the Monroe Doctrine but described the nature of the Soviet-Cuban maneuver as a deliberate violation of the Rio Pact of 1947 and the traditions and agreements binding the nations of the Western Hemisphere. By the time of the missile crisis, Cuban participation in the OAS had already been suspended by an Organ of Consultation meeting in Uruguay in January 1962 (additional collective sanctions were applied against Cuba by the OAS in 1964 and 1967).

But the origin of the missile crisis lay in the Bay of Pigs invasion and the ongoing efforts to destroy Castro and his regime. It is now clear to most analysts that had there been no CIA-backed invasion, no assassination plots, no military invasion plans, and no diplomatic and economic efforts to isolate and destroy Castro, Nikita Khrushchev would never have decided to move (nor would Castro have approved of moving) his nuclear missiles into the Caribbean less than 100 miles from the United States. The nuclear crisis was averted when Khrushchev agreed to withdraw his missile force from Cuba in exchange for a U.S. pledge not to invade Cuba and to remove its missiles in Turkey. The exchange of missiles in Turkey (earlier rejected by President Kennedy and his advisors) for missiles in Cuba was agreed to in a secret deal worked out in late October 1962 by Attorney General Robert Kennedy and Soviet ambassador Anatoly Dobrynin. Kennedy's important symbolic concession—the secret deal on the missiles—did not become public until the late 1980s.

Angry over the Soviet decision to back down and its largely ignoring the Cubans during the exchange of demands, Castro could claim some degree of victory with the U.S. pledge not to invade his island, although the CIA stepped up efforts to sabotage the revolution and revitalized its assassination efforts. After the Soviet-American agreement to remove the missiles, Kennedy was criticized by those who cited the Monroe Doctrine as evidence that he had betrayed the sacred message of President Monroe and suffered a grievous defeat. He resented the way his critics used the Monroe Doctrine to justify partisan sniping at his administration and was prepared to take his flag waving critics head-on in a speech he planned to deliver in Dallas, Texas, on the day of his assassination. According to Louis A. Pérez, "The worst nightmares of Thomas Jefferson and John Quincy Adams—that a potentially hostile European power would insert itself in Cuba and menace U.S. interests—seemed to have come to pass."[5] The "lessons" of the Cuban missile crisis are still being debated, but the confrontation was clearly the closest the Soviet Union and the United States ever came to the brink of nuclear war.

Cuba and the United States: From Nixon to Reagan

With his Revolution more secure after the Cuban missile crisis, Castro proceeded to further consolidate his power and pursue his radical reforms and programs. The fact that the Cuban opposition (both on the island and in the United States) believed that Washington would eventually "take care" of Castro served to diminish the ardor of revolt among those who longed for another counter-revolution. The Cuban Communist Party was established in 1965, and in the following year Castro proclaimed that the Andes would become the Sierra Maestra of South America. After a visit to the Congo in 1965, Ché Guevara left for Bolivia where he hoped to create the conditions for the spread of revolution in Latin America. He failed again, but this time he was killed in 1967 by Bolivian Rangers trained and equipped by the CIA (see Chapter 3). In the following year Castro endorsed the Soviet invasion of Czechoslovakia. At this point he directed his energies inward, trying to diversify the economy through industrialization, but found he still had to rely on sugar for national wealth. Repression increased during the 1960s, when many Cubans were jailed as socially unacceptable dissidents. Neighborhood watch groups called Committees for the Defense of the Revolution were established to root out counter-revolutionaries at the local level. After a series of skyjackings to Cuba from the United States during the Vietnam War, the Nixon administration signed a treaty with Castro to block such events.

In 1975 the OAS lifted its sanctions against Cuba, and many Latin American countries reestablished diplomatic and trade relations with Cuba. With large Soviet subsidies, Cuba advanced economically and socially, adding further legitimacy to the goals of the revolution. In an effort to align himself with Black Power movements in Africa and the Caribbean (including the large Afro-Cuban population), Castro sent thousands of soldiers to Angola

"You're Taking the Caribbean Too Seriously, Mr. President"

in 1975 to help it win independence from South Africa. Thereafter he sent sorely needed technical and medical help, and then repeated this gesture in Ethiopia. In 1979 Castro hosted the annual conference of the nonaligned movement; befriended left-leaning governments in Jamaica, Grenada, and Nicaragua; and supported the Soviet invasion of Afghanistan. In an effort to open up a dialogue with Cuba, President Carter established an "interest section" in Havana to deal with diplomatic matters and relaxed travel restrictions on Americans interested in visiting the island.

At the start of the 1980s, Cuba stood out as a symbol of Latin American independence from U.S. imperialism, but the quality of life began to worsen. As productivity decreased and health care and education deteriorated, Castro blamed the troubles on the "workers who do not work and the students who do not study," although Cuba's Soviet-style political system was also considered a culprit. After 10,000 disaffected Cubans took refuge in the Peruvian Embassy in Havana in April 1980, Castro approved the exodus of over 125,000 Cubans from all parts of the island in what became known as the Mariel Boatlift.

By the time Ronald Reagan came to Washington in 1981, a new source of domestic power over U.S.-Cuban relations was beginning to take shape. Modeled after the powerful pro-Israel lobby, wealthy Cuban exiles founded the Cuban American National Foundation (CANF) with headquarters in Miami and Washington and then formed the Free Cuba political action committee for fundraising and influencing key members of Congress. Since 1980 the Cuba lobby has poured more than $4.4 million into the U.S. political system in an effort to dictate Cuba policy. It pressured Congress to create both Radio and T.V. Martí at considerable expense to the American taxpayers and was instrumental in drawing up the legislation for both the Cuban Democracy Act (1992) and the Helms-Burton Act (1996).

Until his death in 1997, Jorge Más Canosa, a Miami multi-millionaire and veteran of the Bay of Pigs debacle, was another factor in the success of CANF. Beginning with the Reagan administration, Más enjoyed ready access to the White House, often through relatives of U.S. presidents living in south Florida. He was a vociferous critic of the Miami *Herald*, attacked the voices in favor of dialogue as communist sympathizers, and sued a number of people for speaking out against him and CANF. Opposed by all U.S. allies in North America and Europe, and frequently condemned in the United Nations, the U.S. trade embargo against Cuba continues to generate political controversy and demonstrate amazing staying power.

The Desovietization of Cuba

The collapse of the Soviet Union in 1990 dealt a devastating blow to Cuba through the withdrawal of vast amounts of assistance. The United States rejoiced, and many Cuban exiles predicted that Castro's Caribbean dictatorship would also fall. Cuba lost billions in economic aid and military assistance when the Soviets left, leaving the economy paralyzed. It now had to sell its sugar at fair market prices, and with over 500 Soviet-sponsored industrial projects left unfinished, Cuba came to a standstill. Sacrifices became so extreme that horse-drawn buggies were put back in service. A million Chinese bicycles were imported and the people were ordered to start pedaling. In order to get the economy moving again and subdue growing discontent, Castro made compromises in his revolutionary ideology. In 1991 he eased travel restrictions abroad, released many political prisoners, and granted economic autonomy to farmers. In 1993 he legalized the use of the American dollar and allowed people to go into business for themselves. Through increases in Canadian and European investment, mainly in a booming tourist industry, Cuba has been able to withstand the loss of Soviet subsidies and the continued efforts of the United States to internationalize the embargo against the island nation.

Bill Clinton and Cuba

The Clinton administration inherited a number of problems from its predecessor in dealing with Cuba, including domestic demands for tightening the economic noose around Castro and curtailing the flow of illegal immigrants from the island. The immigration crisis of 1994 was in part the result of the desovietization in Eastern Europe and the tightening of the U.S. trade embargo. The crisis for the Clinton administration was triggered in July 1994 when 30,000 Cubans tried to sail to Florida in rickety boats and makeshift rafts. Recognizing the seriousness of uncontrolled migration, the United States and Cuba agreed to develop measures to halt the flow of "boat people." The agreement ending Washington's policy of granting refugee status to virtually all Cubans rescued at sea now requires the United States to return any refugees caught in boats, and it establishes at least 20,000 immigrant visas to Cubans each year. Cuba, in return, has pledged not to harass or persecute the returnees and to allow U.S. officials to monitor their well-being. Nevertheless a Cuban court in 1997 sentenced six Cubans to long prison terms for trying to flee to Florida in a stolen tugboat. Since the agreement went into effect, more than 500 Cubans have been returned by the United States, including dozens of baseball players.

Cuban-U.S. relations have also worsened with the passage of the Helms-Burton Act of 1996, which aims to punish the Castro regime by allowing Cuban Americans to use U.S. courts to settle claims over property seized in Cuba at the time of the Revolution (that are now being used by non-Cuban companies). The passage of this punitive measure—largely the result of domestic politics in the United States and the shooting down of several civilian aircraft from Miami close to Cuban waters in 1996—which was designed to hasten democracy in Cuba and the demise of Fidel Castro, has all but ended the chances of a compromise with Cuba as long as Fidel is alive. In a move to soothe his international allies, President Clinton continues to issue six-month waivers that delay the full implementation of Helms-Burton, in hopes of swaying American allies to join the hardline anti-Castro bandwagon started by Senator Jesse Helms and Representative Dan Burton. The tone and legal intent of Helms-Burton have alienated virtually every trading partner the United States has, and the bill is now facing a series of counterproposals by Canada and the European Union designed to blunt the impact of current U.S. policy toward Cuba.

Pope John Paul II's January 1998 visit to Cuba and his criticism of the U.S. trade embargo as "morally unethical" unleashed a number of changes in Washington, Miami, and Havana. With the idea of limited trade and aid for Cuba gaining bipartisan respectability, the Clinton administration announced in March 1998 that it would loosen restrictions on travel and humanitarian aid. The death of Jorge Más Canosa—the Cuba lobby's legendary leader—has diminished the exile community's influence over Cuba policy and produced a growing disillusionment with the futility of economic sanctions. Inside Cuba, the Pope's trip served to embolden the Roman Catholic Church and the hopes of dissident groups calling for greater freedom and protection of human rights, a sign that greater change may be on the horizon.

CONCLUSION

With over 40 years of hostility toward Castro and the Cuban Revolution, there appears to be little reason to expect a change in current policy until Castro dies. Castro sometimes hints that he may step down if the United States lifts the economic blockade, but this issue is virtually dead in policy terms. Castro has told some of his followers that "I am a revolutionary, and revolutionaries do not retire," a sign he wants to remain in power as long as he is alive. In any case, until the spirits of Monroe are finally exorcized from the corridors of power in Washington, or Fidel Castro dies, the prospects for meaningful dialogue and cooperation seem remote. The tangled web of U.S.-Cuban relations is part of a sad and painful history—one that few political leaders seem to be able to understand, much less try to change—of two nations in close geographical proximity but with strongly divergent views of political life and social change.

NOTES

1. Wayne S. Smith, *The Closest of Enemies: A Personal and Diplomatic History of the Castro Years* (New York: W. W. Norton, 1987).

2. Louis A. Pérez Jr., *Cuba: Between Reform and Revolution* (New York: Oxford University Press, 1995), p. 279.

3. *Congressional Record*, 86th Congress, 2nd Session (June 30, 1960), vol. 106, Part II, p. 15228.

4. Tim Weiner, "C.I.A. Bares Its Bungling in Report on Bay of Pigs Invasion," *New York Times* (February 22, 1998), p. A6.

5. Louis A. Pérez Jr., "Cuba," in Bruce W. Jentleson and Thomas G. Paterson, eds., *Encyclopedia of U.S. Foreign Relations*, vol. 1 (New York: Oxford University Press, 1977), p. 384.

SUGGESTED READINGS

Benjamin, Jules R. *The United States and the Origins of the Cuban Revolution.* Princeton, NJ: Princeton University Press, 1990.

Kaplowitz, Donna Rich. *Anatomy of a Failed Embargo: U.S. Sanctions against Cuba.* Boulder, CO: Lynne Rienner, 1998.

Mazaar, Michael J. *Semper Fidel: America and Cuba, 1776–1988.* Baltimore, MD: Nautical and Aviation Publishing, 1988.

Paterson, Thomas G. *Contesting Castro: The United States and the Triumph of the Cuban Revolution.* New York: Oxford University Press, 1994.

Pérez, Louis A., Jr. *Cuba and the United States: Ties of Singular Intimacy*. Athens: University of Georgia Press, 1990.

Welch, David A. *Politics of Illusion: The Bay of Pigs Invasion Reexamined*. Boulder, CO: Lynne Rienner, 1997.

9

Dominican Republic

TIMELINE OF U.S. RELATIONS WITH THE DOMINICAN REPUBLIC

1821	Dominican independence from Spain is achieved
1821–1844	Haiti rules Dominican Republic
1844	Dominican independence from Haiti is achieved
1861–1865	Spain annexes Dominican Republic
1866	United States recognizes Dominican Republic
1869	President Báez tries to annex Dominican Republic to United States
1883	U.S. diplomatic relations are established
1892	San Domingo Improvement Company acquires control over customhouses
1899	General Heureaux is assassinated; U.S. economic interests are threatened
1904	Roosevelt Corollary to Monroe Doctrine
1905	Receivership is established
1912	U.S. military intervention
1916–1924	U.S. military occupation
1917	Dominican National Guard is established
1930	Rafael L. Trujillo arranges election as president and then establishes dictatorial power
1937	Trujillo orders massacre of Haitians
1941	U.S. customs receivership is terminated
1956	Trujillo orders kidnapping-murder of critic Jesús Galíndez

1961	Trujillo is assassinated with U.S. assistance
1962	Juan Bosch wins presidency; is ousted by military coup in 1963
1965	U.S. invasion of Dominican Republic
1966–1978	Joaquín Balaguer rules Dominican Republic with U.S. backing
1978	Guzmán Fernández is elected president with U.S. and OAS electoral supervision
1982	Salvador Jorge Blanco is elected president
1986	Balaguer is reelected president
1990	Balaguer is reelected amid charges of election irregularities
1994	Clinton administration helps negotiate "Pact for Democracy"
1996	Leonel Fernández Reyna is elected president

INTRODUCTION

Although it is small, the Dominican Republic has often been at the center of major U.S. policies—the Monroe Doctrine, dollar diplomacy, military intervention and occupation, support for friendly dictators, and democracy promotion efforts—toward Latin America and the Caribbean. Occupying the eastern two-thirds of the island of Hispaniola, the Dominican Republic has had a difficult relationship with its close island-neighbor (Haiti) and has been plagued by foreign intervention, dictatorship, political instability, and corruption throughout much of its history. Foreign intervention drained its wealth and chronic political turmoil undermined its ability to develop stable and legitimate rule. Between 1844 and 1930 the Dominican Republic experienced 50 different presidents (a new president once every 1.7 years) and 30 revolutions.

Throughout the Dominican Republic's turbulent history since independence, the United States has played a major role in its economic and political life. During the nineteenth century the United States recognized the importance of the island because of its harbors and location near vital sea lanes; later, the value of the Dominican Republic stemmed from its resources, mainly its commercial empire and its raw materials. During the twentieth century the United States struggled to solve the Dominican Republic's ongoing difficulties with financial and political matters. Often the Monroe Doctrine served as a convenient cloak for sending either money doctors (financial advisors) or Marines to stabilize a chaotic economic or political situation and to forestall any attempt on the part of extra-hemispheric powers to acquire the island. Dominican political instability and financial insolvency were the pretext for the 1904 Roosevelt Corollary to the Monroe Doctrine. The United States intervened and occupied the Dominican Republic on two occasions—1916-1924, and 1965-1966—and treated the tyrant Rafael Trujillo as a "friendly dictator" during the early part of the

Cold War. With its security interests in the Caribbean of less concern, the United States has spent the last two decades expanding trade, promoting democracy, and attempting to manage the flow of legal and undocumented Dominicans who have come to the United States.

THE DOMINICAN REPUBLIC AND THE UNITED STATES IN THE NINETEENTH CENTURY

The United States and Dominican Independence

Dominican independence was complicated by foreign control and the fact that it shared part of Hispaniola ("Little Spain"), the name given the island by Columbus in 1492. Without gold, silver, or obedient Indian labor, the number of Europeans on the island was never very large. Pirates and *filibusteros* (private mercenaries and adventurers) fought over Hispaniola (today made up of Haiti and the Dominican Republic) until France took over in 1795 and developed the western half into a booming sugar/slave economy. The harsh treatment of sugar workers contributed to the rebellion led by Toussaint L'Ouverture and the eventual establishment of Haiti in 1804, Latin America's first independent nation. Haiti included the present territory of the Dominican Republic from 1821 to 1844. The 1970 film *Burn* (*Quemada* in Spanish) featuring Marlon Brando dramatized the violent history of Hispaniola. In depicting the meddling by foreign powers, bribery and corruption, the savagery of colonial wars, and the popularity of former slaves as honest and effective leaders, *Burn* conveyed the difficulties of effective rule after independence.

Annexation and Reannexation

From the 1820s to the end of the U.S. Civil War, U.S. relations with most of Latin America were distant and sporadic, and many "violations" of the Monroe Doctrine were allowed to occur. During the 1860s Spanish moves to reannex the Dominican Republic were carried out while Washington struggled with its own problems of slavery and secession. Secretary of State William H. Seward wrote to President Lincoln suggesting that he warn Spain of its violation of the Monroe Doctrine—and have Congress declare war against it, if necessary—but there was little the president could do in the midst of the U.S. Civil War. After Seward's memo was leaked to the press, many European governments were furious and then sided with the Confederacy throughout the conflict. The Dominicans resented President Pedro Santana's voluntary efforts to restore Spanish sovereignty and were soon organizing to regain their independence.

The departure of the Spaniards in 1865 left the Dominican Republic divided and deeply in debt. This time General Buenaventura Báez, fearing another invasion of Dominican exiles in Haiti, sought annexation by the United States in 1869. President Ulysses S. Grant's motives for seeking annexation of the Dominican Republic centered on its strategic location and the Samaná Bay harbor, and as a place to settle ex-slaves. He was backed by Seward, who favored U.S. expansion into the Caribbean to advance commercial influence and as a means of spreading democracy. The black diplomat Frederick Douglass was sent to the Dominican Republic in 1871 to investigate the possibilities of annexation and later served as chargé d'affaires for the Dominican Republic from 1889 to 1891. If Grant had not faced corruption scandals in his administration and the forceful opposition of Republican Charles Sumner, chairman of the Senate Foreign Relations Committee, the Dominican Republic might have become territory of the United States in the 1870s. By obstructing bills and appointments favored by President Grant, Sumner managed to squash U.S. efforts to annex the Dominican Republic, but his unpleasant manner led to his removal as chairman of the Foreign Relations Committee in 1871.

The Ulises Heureaux Dictatorship

During the dictatorship of General Ulises Heureaux (1882–1889), the United States invested heavily in the sugar economy, helping to transform the island from its historical dependence on European markets and sources of credit. Throughout the 1880s and 1890s the United States negotiated reciprocity treaties, and a private company—the New York–based San Domingo Improvement Company—took charge of Dominican custom house offices to improve the collection of taxes or duties. When Heureaux was assassinated in 1899 the Dominican Republic faced a staggering debt, and this left custom houses vulnerable to foreign takeover and control. By the turn of the century the Dominican economy was clearly dominated by the United States, but European investors often demanded that their governments force the indebted Dominicans to repay or face the possibility of a forceful takeover of their custom revenues.

THE DOMINICAN REPUBLIC AND THE UNITED STATES IN THE TWENTIETH CENTURY

The Roosevelt Corollary and Financial Receiverships

Events in the Dominican Republic forced the Theodore Roosevelt administration to formulate a response to the growing threat of European challenges in the Caribbean. President Roosevelt feared that incompetent governments in the Caribbean region might provoke European imperialism in violation of the Monroe Doctrine. Citing the insolvency of the Dominican Republic, Roosevelt decided to incorporate a strategic interest within the rhetoric of international, humanitarian responsibility. In his annual message to Congress in 1904, President Roosevelt reinterpreted the Monroe Doctrine to make the United States the international policeman and prime debt-collecting agency in the Western Hemisphere (Roosevelt Corollary):

> If a nation shows that it knows how to act with reasonable efficiency and decency in social and political matters; if it keeps order and pays its obligations, it need fear no interference from the United States. Chronic wrongdoing, or an impotence which results in a general loosening of the ties of civilized society, may in America, as elsewhere, ultimately require intervention by some civilized nation, and in the Western Hemisphere the adherence of the United States to the Monroe Doctrine may force the United States, however reluctantly, in flagrant cases of such wrongdoing or impotence, to the exercise of an international police power. . . . It is a mere truism to say that every nation, whether in America or anywhere else, which desires to maintain its freedom, its independence, must ultimately realize that the right of such independence cannot be separated from the responsibility of making good use of it.[1]

Roosevelt's speech completely changed the meaning of the Monroe Doctrine by transforming its original negative and passive character into a more positive and active policy toward Latin America. Although some Latin American nations welcomed President Monroe's message as a form of protection from European intervention, the Roosevelt Corollary soon gave way to resentment and conflict with the United States. Although it made no direct reference to the Dominican Republic, the implications of President Roosevelt's "amendment" to the Monroe Doctrine were readily apparent to the small republics of the Caribbean region. As Emilio Betances argues, "None of these republics behaved in the manner Roosevelt prescribed, and therefore all were potential candidates for direct U.S. intervention."[2]

Roosevelt's interpretation of the Monroe Doctrine brought forth a new Latin American policy, one that combined the "big stick"—threats of a tough policy—with chronic intervention. When presidential warnings and admonitions failed to produce the desired effect, however, U.S. military intervention followed, along with financial protectorates and rhetorical justifications based on the need to foster democracy and political stability. This in turn produced widespread resentment and hostility in Latin America until it was finally repudiated by President Hoover starting in the late 1920s. The Roosevelt Corollary paved the way for gunboat diplomacy— the use of limited naval force as a supplement to diplomacy and an alternative to war—in dealing with Caribbean and Central American states from 1904 until the ending of such activity by Franklin D. Roosevelt's Good Neighbor Policy, which was formally announced in 1933.

Money Doctoring and Foreign Control

Dominican dictatorships developed the habit of taking out large loans with European and U.S. bankers. By 1904 the Dominican Republic was on the verge of bankruptcy due to a foreign debt that had grown to $32 million, with national revenues nowhere near the capability of repaying the debt. To solve this problem the United States imposed customs receiverships, formal arrangements between governments in which U.S. officials would take over Dominican custom houses and administer the collection of revenues for the sole purpose of paying creditors. These customs receiverships produced financial solvency, but they failed to bring political stability and eliminate revolutions.

The United States was motivated by the need to impose order so that extra-hemispheric powers would have no excuse for using military force to collect overdue debts. Money doctoring and financial restructuring became commonplace in Cuba, Panama, the Dominican Republic, Haiti, and Nicaragua, where protectorates were created under treaties conceding the right of U.S. intervention. According to Paul Drake, "From the 1890s through the 1920s, every Latin American country except Argentina and Brazil contracted U.S. financial consultants, and before World War II, Latin America had brought in more U.S. technocrats than any other world area."[3] By exporting economic/financial expertise through private agents rather than through government officials, Washington could more easily defuse anti-interventionist criticism at home and abroad.

The Dominican Republic was one of the first Caribbean "patients" to receive treatment for financial mismanagement and economic chaos. Jacob Hollander, an economist from Johns Hopkins University, devised a plan in 1905–1907 by which Dominican customs collections would be administered by a U.S. *receiver* appointed by the secretary of state but paid by the Dominican government. Hollander's advice opened the door for "dollar diplomacy," the cornerstone of William Howard Taft's foreign policy beginning in 1908. The U.S. Congress passed the Dominican Convention in 1907, a legally binding financial agreement that lasted until 1941. Through the use of money doctors and financial arrangements that constituted a sort of "colonialism-by-contract," the United States had invented a new tool for furthering its hegemony in the Caribbean region. U.S. financial and political interference eventually led to armed intervention and occupation in 1916.

U.S. Occupation of the Dominican Republic, 1916–1924

With German influence spreading to Haiti, and World War I under way, the Wilson administration began to realize the need to stabilize the Dominican Republic through military occupation. After the Dominican Congress impeached President Juan Isidro Jiménez in 1916—setting off a new wave of internal rebellion—U.S. forces landed to restore order but soon were authorized to proclaim military rule. Military occupation lasted until 1924, but the consequences of U.S. military occupation were enormous and were felt throughout the twentieth century. The Marines carried out extensive public works programs—establishing roads, schools, sanitation systems, public health, agriculture, and communications—financed by U.S. private-sector investors rather than the U.S. government. Many of these programs were of benefit to U.S.-owned sugar plantations, some of which experienced tremendous expansion during the eight-year occupation. As an occupation force the United States helped to popularize baseball, but fairly rigid attitudes toward racial discrimination undermined what had been a more flexible pattern of black-white relations on the island. Despite many beneficial effects of the occupation, Dominican opposition to and resentment of U.S. control did not decrease.

Given the history of political violence and instability in the Dominican Republic, the most urgent priority of the occupation was to establish "law and order" throughout the countryside. This was directed mostly at rebels (the Americans called them bandits) who resisted U.S. authority as infringement on their sovereignty. To achieve this goal, the United States created a constabulary force in 1917 called the Dominican National Guard. The constabulary—under U.S. guidance and control—worked together with the U.S. Marines to put down guerrilla uprisings, protect U.S.-owned sugar plantations, and oversee constitutional self-government. Upper ranks of the Guard were reserved for North Americans; Dominican recruits were from the lower middle class. These recruits often used the military as a means of upward mobility in Dominican society. Rafael L. Trujillo was one of the early recruits who joined the Guard in 1919, rose to the top of its ranks, and then used the Guard as a source of dictatorial control for more than 30 years. "The most powerful illustration of the tragic consequences of [U.S.] occupation, however unintended, was to be the emergence of the brutal Trujillo dictatorship."[4]

The election of President Warren Harding in 1921 became a watershed in U.S. Latin American policy as it reflected the American public's rejection of military intervention and the broad moralistic objectives of his predecessor, Woodrow Wilson. In his efforts to foster good will to improve commercial relations with Latin America, Harding arranged for the transfer of U.S. supervision of American troops from the Department of the Navy to the Department of State, the part of the executive branch that was more likely to terminate military occupations. Although Harding's presidency was brief (1921–1923), his administration was instrumental in bringing U.S. military occupation of the Dominican Republic to a close in 1924. Harding's tone of conciliation in foreign policy—settling claims with Mexico, Colombia, and Cuba—helped set the stage for the Good Neighbor

Policy, a commitment to nonintervention, and the policy overhaul of the Monroe Doctrine in the late 1920s.

The Trujillo Era, 1930–1961

From Trujillo's power base in the Dominican National Guard (by 1928 Trujillo was chief of staff and commander of the armed forces) he conspired in 1930 to take over the government from incumbent President Horacio Vásquez just three months before scheduled elections. Once in power, Trujillo ruled the Dominican Republic with an iron hand, convinced that as long as he pursued policies of economic modernization he could get away with extreme coercion of any opposition and little tolerance of dissent. Recognizing the power of the United States in the Caribbean, Trujillo managed to cultivate close diplomatic and political relations until the last few years of his dictatorship. In return for his unwavering support of the United States, Trujillo's dictatorship was given money, weapons, and moral support. U.S. presidents accepted Trujillo because he provided political stability, was strongly anticommunist, and served as a better alternative to revolution.

There were episodes, however, in which the United States expressed displeasure with Trujillo's harsh rule and withdrew its support in protest. For example, in October 1937 Trujillo ordered the massacre of thousands of Haitians (mostly illegal immigrants)—working out of squatter camps in the border provinces—out of fear that the country was becoming Haitianized (that is, African and black). To protest this genocidal action, President Roosevelt temporarily withdrew U.S. support and organized a commission to negotiate a settlement. In the wake of the international outcry over his slaughter of Haitians, Trujillo spent millions on propaganda to improve his political image. He admitted Jewish immigrants fleeing Nazi Germany, and anti-Franco Republicans from the Spanish Civil War. His all-out cooperation with the United States during World War II also helped improve his reputation. The genocide committed against Haitians in 1937 was soon forgotten once the United States entered the war in 1941.

One of the hemisphere's major anticommunists, Trujillo became a master of political manipulation in the United States by playing on the fears of policymakers haunted by the ghosts of President Monroe. If the repressive methods of his dictatorship brought stability, provided support for the United States against its foes in international organizations such as the United Nations, and kept a Castro-backed communist regime from coming to power, then General Trujillo could be tolerated. By hiring expensive public relations firms and lobbyists, and by contributing large amounts of money to members of the U.S. Congress, Trujillo was able to portray himself as a close ally of the United States and cleverly mask the tyrannical aspects of his regime. During Eisenhower's second term as president, Trujillo had 20 agents—registered with the Justice Department as representatives of the Dominican Republic—lobbying on his behalf in Washington. Franklin D. Roosevelt's law firm represented the Dominican Republic until its client's image as a tyrant was impossible to cover up through legal and public relations tactics. Documented estimates indicate that Trujillo spent $1 million lobbying in the United States in 1956.[5] He showered key members of Congress with gifts, lavish vacations in the Dominican Republic, and large campaign donations at election time. Thus, Trujillo gained the necessary international support where it counted the most.

The vocal minority in the U.S. Congress who supported Trujillo as a "friendly dictator" did so on the basis of his pro-Americanism, his anticommunism, and the purported material accomplishments of his regime. Speaking on the floor of the Senate in 1960, Senator Richard Russell (D-GA) defended Trujillo by saying that "if we must have a dictatorship, Trujillo has been about as liberal a dictator as a country could have."[6] The fact that Trujillo often invoked anticommunism to justify mass deportations, torture, and executions apparently did not bother Washington during the early years of the Cold War.

Trujillo's economic policies were clearly designed to bring about national prosperity and his own personal gain. By the time of his assassination in 1961, Trujillo is estimated to have amassed a fortune worth more than $500 million, mostly the result of widespread corruption and monopolistic control over the Dominican economy. Once in power, Trujillo developed a network of monopolies over basic commodities and industrial enterprises, using the power of the state to eliminate domestic and foreign competition and enrich himself, family, and friends. For Trujillo, the government was a profitable means of personal enrichment rather than an instrument of public service.

United States and the Dominican Republic during World War II

After the United States entered the war in late 1941, the importance of building a Caribbean defense system became paramount. The main geographic security concerns centered on protecting (1) the Panama Canal, (2) the Natal region of Brazil because it seemed vulnerable to a German invasion, and (3) the vital shipping lanes of the Caribbean Sea, Gulf of Mexico, and Atlantic Ocean. The importance of the Dominican Republic centered on its strategic position on the eastern approaches to the Caribbean and its role as a source of foodstuffs and raw materials (such as bauxite) imported by the United States.

In the name of national security, the United States and the Trujillo regime developed numerous strategies for mutual cooperation. For example, Trujillo received Export-Import Bank loans for arms purchases and the construction of military bases and harbors. When the Lend-Lease Act (Roosevelt's program of supplying war matériel to his allies) ended legal restrictions on supplying arms to Latin America in May 1941, the Dominican Republic acted quickly to become eligible for arms transfers. Trujillo and Secretary of State Cordell Hull signed the Trujillo-Hull Treaty in 1941; it restored Dominican sovereignty over its financial affairs by abolishing the administration of customs receiverships (U.S. agents in charge of customs receipts who exercised tremendous authority). Trujillo used this as the basis of a huge propaganda campaign designed to portray himself as "father of national financial independence."

The value of cooperation for defense and national security did not sit well with those who disagreed with Trujillo's dictatorial practices and the casual attitude of Washington toward them. At times the wartime goal of destroying dictatorial regimes in the name of democracy clashed with the support of friendly dictators in Latin America such as Trujillo. The United States became more critical of Trujillo's autocratic rule after the war by refusing to furnish arms and ammunition, but this "punishment" did not last long.

THE DOMINICAN REPUBLIC AND THE UNITED STATES DURING THE COLD WAR

The Problem of Mutual Security

Postwar hemispheric security rested primarily on the provisions of the 1947 Rio Treaty (a collective security pact) signed by 21 hemispheric states (it entered into force in 1948) and numerous bilateral military conventions. The most important of these was the Mutual Security Act of 1951 (passed in response to the start of the Korean War), designed to facilitate both the standardization of arms throughout the hemisphere and closer U.S.–Latin American military cooperation. Until Trujillo's assassination in 1961, the Dominican Republic received considerable amounts of military supplies from the United States. The establishment of military missions caused hundreds of Dominican officers to come to U.S. military schools for advanced training.

One of the beneficiaries of the program was Rafael Leonidas (Ramfis) Trujillo Jr., the dictator's playboy son. After failing a military course at Fort Leavenworth, Kansas, in 1958, Ramfis reportedly spent his time in Hollywood showering movie actresses with lavish gifts. The comic-opera nature of the Ramfis affair led to a number of rhetorical fights over the nature of the U.S. military aid program in the Dominican Republic. While Dominican senators accused the United States of hostility and lack of respect for the country's military cooperation, opponents of Trujillo in Washington tried to cut off aid to the dictator. Senator Wayne Morse (D-OR) "deplored a military program of the United States for the benefit of dictators in South America [sic] such as Trujillo."[7] Throughout President Eisenhower's second term, U.S.-Dominican relations deteriorated as Trujillo's actions became less and less acceptable to the United States.

The Fall of the Trujillo Dictatorship

Rafael Trujillo's propaganda machine could not whitewash the events that eventually led to his downfall in 1961. Between 1958 and 1961 the United States began to reevaluate its policy toward Latin America in the aftermath of the CIA-engineered overthrow of the Arbenz regime in Guatemala in 1954 and Vice-President Nixon's "good will" tour of Latin America in 1958 (see Chapters 13 and 25). On his return, Nixon's recommendations on how to deal with dictators without sowing the seeds of communist subversion started a process of policy review in Washington. However, until Castro's revolution toppled Batista in 1959, the United States was unwilling to seriously oppose Latin American dictators.

In the meantime, Trujillo continued to attack his opponents with all the force he could muster. In 1956 he arranged to have Jesús Galíndez—a refugee from Spain and an outspoken critic of the Trujillo dictatorship— kidnapped off the streets of New York and returned to the Dominican Republic, where he was tortured and killed. Surprisingly, this produced only mild protest from the State Department, since it claimed that the missile-tracking station on the island was "vital" to U.S. security needs in the Caribbean. After Dominican patriots invaded the Dominican Republic with the support of Castro and Venezuela's democratic president, Rómulo Betancourt, and were immediately defeated by Trujillo's forces, a brutal wave of torture and murder spread across the Dominican Republic. In retaliation Trujillo plotted to assassinate Betancourt for his anti-Trujillo efforts, but Betancourt survived the detonated bomb. This led to the imposition of economic sanctions by the Organization of American States.

Rather than an ally against communism, Trujillo was now seen as a negative catalyst for the possible spread of communism after the defeat of Batista and the success of Fidel Castro in Cuba. Policymakers in Washington further reasoned that if Trujillo was suddenly overthrown, there would most certainly be a political vacuum filled by a Castro-backed communist government. If this happened, then Haiti would follow and there would soon be a line of communist governments (a Caribbean domino theory) stretched throughout the Caribbean, threatening the Panama Canal and vital sea lanes.

In late 1960 the United States moved from a position of trying to persuade Trujillo to leave peacefully, followed by some kind of a moderate successor regime, to a covert plan to support and arm conspirators to overthrow the aging tyrant. With the backing of the Central Intelligence

Agency, a small band of Dominican conspirators assassinated Trujillo on May 30, 1961. When they were unable to mobilize the anti-Trujillo forces into a position of governmental control, the political situation deteriorated rapidly while Trujillo's agents and relatives tortured and killed scores of suspects. While Joaquín Balaguer served as the nominal chief executive, and Trujillo's son (Ramfis) struggled to maintain the old regime, it became apparent that the Trujillo era was over. By late 1961, following a show of U.S. naval force and threats, Ramfis and most of the Trujillo clan had fled the island and Balaguer had gone into exile.

In the following year Juan Bosch, a poet and lifelong opponent of Trujillo, was elected president in the country's first free democratic election (he was inaugurated in 1963). Once in power, his populist government programs and tolerance of leftist and progressive organizations angered traditional elites and the United States. To remedy this situation, some U.S. military advisors in the Dominican Republic conspired with key members of the Dominican military and recommended the overthrow of Bosch, which occurred after he was in power for only seven months. However, President Kennedy, on hearing of the anti-Bosch coup, withdrew the U.S. ambassador and suspended economic aid.

The Johnson Doctrine

The framework for U.S. policy during the period from 1960 to the Dominican revolt in 1965 was spelled out by President Kennedy's famous remark after the death of Trujillo: "There are three possibilities . . . in descending order of preference: a decent democratic regime, a continuation of the Trujillo regime, or a Castro regime. We ought to aim at the first but we really can't renounce the second until we are sure we can avoid the third."[8] U.S. policymakers paid close attention to developments in the Dominican Republic, fearful of another Castro-type socialist dictatorship aligned with the Soviet Union. President Kennedy was strongly opposed to the establishment of a second Cuba in the Caribbean, and his advisors tried to create the conditions that would prevent such an outcome. The regime that replaced Juan Bosch consisted of a conservative junta headed by Donald Reid Cabral (who enjoyed the backing of the Johnson administration) and William Tapley Bennett (U.S. ambassador in Santo Domingo). In April 1965 a countercoup took place when a faction of the armed forces mobilized to reestablish Bosch as the constitutionally elected president. After several days of intense conflict and an emerging civil war, President Johnson ordered 500 U.S. Marines into the Dominican Republic to protect American lives and property there.

Johnson's rhetorical justification changed as he introduced more troops under what became known as the Johnson Doctrine: "The American nations cannot, must not, and will not permit the establishment of another communist government in the Western Hemisphere." Within one month the United States had more than 20,000 troops in Santo Domingo to bring order and stability to the country. Convinced that heavy use of military force was the solution to defeating communist insurgents, President Johnson later used the same strategy in Vietnam through the large-scale use of American combat forces. According to Gaddis Smith, "A persistent theme of latter-day Monroeism was that by keeping the hemisphere secure, and not having to erect defenses on 'our own doorstep,' the United States could deploy forces all over the world."[9] In any case, the Dominican crisis and the U.S. response reminded some of the tendency of Washington policymakers to rely on oversimplifications and outdated myths and policies such as the Monroe Doctrine in formulating policy toward the Caribbean.

Despite widespread criticism of the invasion, the United States managed to pressure the OAS for approval after the fact, transforming the unilateral military action by the United States into the Organization's first Inter-American Peace Force under the command of a Brazilian general. With some careful political engineering, the United States managed to steer the Dominican Republic in a noncommunist direction in the aftermath of the 1965 invasion. The June 1966 presidential elections were designed to make sure that the candidate favored by the United States won. In a style reminiscent of Dominican caudillos (or quasi-military dictators) of the past, Balaguer continued to win elections and dominate national politics until 1996.

THE DOMINICAN REPUBLIC AND THE UNITED STATES AFTER THE COLD WAR

The End of the Caudillos

With the backing of the armed forces, Balaguer managed to rule by blending traditional elements of *caudillismo* with misguided economic policies that were designed to spur growth, but instead they produced high inflation and monetary chaos. His efforts to privatize the economy and decentralize the state produced little success. Long-time political boss and protégé of Rafael Trujillo, Balaguer ruled the Dominican Republic for 22 of the 30 years between 1966 and 1996. His authoritarian and personal style of rule received backing from Washington due in large part to the earlier fear of a communist takeover and the fear of Juan Bosch, perennial candidate of the Dominican Liberation Party (PLD). In the 1996 presidential election, Leonel Fernández of the PLD won through a modern, progressive, and pro-American campaign. A product of the U.S. educational system—he had spent 10 years in public schools in New York—Fernández represented a new force in Dominican politics. With Balaguer gone from the presidential palace, the Dominican Republic now faces the daunting task of developing a representative model of democracy while at the same time extricating itself from the aged caudillo who still influences Dominican politics.

Democracy, Corruption, and Human Rights

The United States has long assumed the role of promoter and protector of democracy in the Dominican Republic. It has exercised this external role by means of military intervention and/or occupation, economic sanctions, diplomatic recognition and other forms of political pressure, and military assistance. More recently the United States has served as an observer and verifier of Dominican elections along with the Organization of American States (OAS). Between 1978 and 1996 the United States intervened to ensure that democratic procedures prevailed during Dominican elections. The Carter administration urged the Balaguer administration in 1978 to carry out an honest vote and protect human rights or risk losing U.S. economic aid. The Dominican Revolutionary Party (PRD) governments of Antonio Guzmán and Salvador Jorge Blanco (1978–1986) struggled to maintain a semblance of democratic rule and independence from the United States while faced with riots, violence, and pressure from the International Monetary Fund (IMF) to end government subsidies and privatize the economy. When Balaguer returned to office in 1986 after eight years of PRD government and ruled until 1996, he was often accused of human rights violations and electoral fraud. The May 1994 election was observed by a large U.S. delegation sponsored by the National Endowment for Democracy (NED) and a team from the OAS, but again charges of fraud undermined the legitimacy of the democratic process. The two elections of 1996 were fought without the two old political protagonists—Balaguer and Bosch, now both in their late eighties—and the Dominican Liberation Party (PLD) candidate Leonel Fernández won the runoff with a bare 51 percent of the vote. However, large numbers of international observers were present to ensure the integrity of the democratic process.

The Clinton administration, after the Aristide debacle in Haiti (see Chapter 15), helped to negotiate a compromise between the government and opposition in 1994. Called the "Pact for Democracy," the compromise involved changes in the rules of the Dominican political game. These included prohibitions against successive reelection of the president; the requirement of an absolute majority to become president, even if it meant a second-round runoff; and, in recognition of widespread fraud in the 1994 elections, the extension of Balaguer's "illegitimate" regime for only two years instead of four. Although the Pact smacked of intervention by the United States in Dominican politics, Balaguer saw it as a face-saving way to exit from presidential power while at the same time continuing his influence via legislative control.

If Joaquín Balaguer's departure from Dominican politics after seven terms has finally come to pass, then it could possibly mark the end of another era of autocrats, leaders who cared little about whether elections were free, fair, or competitive. Establishing and consolidating democracy in the Dominican Republic after the dictatorships of Trujillo and Balaguer, reaching back to the 1930s, will not be easy given the fact that the authoritarian aspects of the political system are still very much intact. After Balaguer left office in 1996 he became the target of three lawsuits accusing him of misappropriating $740 million in government funds and ordering the deaths of two opponents. These accusations of illegal enrichment and the killing of two journalists who tried to expose Balaguer's corruption and arbitrary rule in the 1970s may ultimately prove to be false; however, the accusations have put current president Leonel Fernández in a quandary as to how best to carry out the moral and ethical revolution he promised during his campaign.

CONCLUSION

Despite a history of dependency on the United States, and numerous failed efforts to bring political stability and economic viability to the Dominican Republic, democratic rule has become more firmly established, in part due to the influence of the United States and the determined efforts of Dominicans to overcome the legacy of domestic tyrants—Santana, Báez, Heureaux, and Trujillo—from the nineteenth century. The fact that the Dominican Republic has been greatly influenced by foreign powers and international organizations throughout its history has helped produce growing feelings of nationalism and the need for greater independence among its people. Yet the United States continues to influence Dominican politics, producing tensions between those who would like greater control over their national destiny and those who fear the dangers of a policy of "benign neglect" on the part of the United States.

Despite the efforts of Dominican leaders to disconnect from the United States and reach out to the rest of the world, trade patterns, investment interest, and migration flows require that Dominicans remain within the orbit of the United States. The transformation of the Dominican economy over the past few decades has led to the creation of a service economy dependent on tourism, export manufacturing, and mining, with considerably less activity in sugar-related agribusiness. Dominican drug traffickers—working the transshipment of drugs from Colombia—transport an estimated one-third of the total volume of cocaine into the United States every year, mostly for distribution on the East Coast. As one of the leading sources of garment exports (due in large part to cheap labor) to the United States, the Dominican Republic cannot afford to jeopardize its new position in the Caribbean as a center of business and economic opportunity. Despite its troubled past, the Dominican Republic may finally emerge as a successful case of democratic consolidation and trade diversification with less dependence on the United States, but this is not likely to take place for quite some time.

NOTES

1. Quoted in A. H. Lewis, *A Compilation of the Messages and Speeches of Theodore Roosevelt*, vol. 2 (Washington, DC: Bureau of National Literature and Art, 1906), p. 857.

2. Emilio Betances, *State and Society in the Dominican Republic* (Boulder, CO: Westview Press, 1995), p. 78.

3. Paul W. Drake, ed., *Money Doctors, Foreign Debts, and Economic Reforms in Latin America from the 1890s to the Present* (Wilmington, DE: Scholarly Resources Books, 1994), p. xxvii.

4. Jonathan Hartlyn, "The Dominican Republic: Legacy of Intermittent Engagement," in Abraham F. Lowenthal, ed., *Exporting Democracy: The United States and Latin America* (Baltimore, MD: Johns Hopkins University Press, 1991), p. 61.

5. G. Pope Atkins and Larman C. Wilson, *The Dominican Republic and the United States: From Imperialism to Transnationalism* (Athens: University of Georgia Press, 1998), pp. 89–90.

6. Quoted in Robert D. Crassweller, *Trujillo: The Life and Times of a Caribbean Dictator* (New York: Macmillan, 1956), p. 326.

7. Quoted in G. Pope Atkins and Larman C. Wilson, *The United States and the Trujillo Regime* (New Brunswick, NJ: Rutgers University Press, 1972), p. 89.

8. Quoted in Jerome Slater, *Intervention and Negotiation: The United States and the Dominican Intervention* (New York: Harper and Row, 1970), p. 9.

9. Gaddis Smith, *The Last Years of the Monroe Doctrine: 1945–1993* (New York: Hill and Wang, 1994), p. 129.

SUGGESTED READINGS

Atkins, G. Pope, and Larman C. Wilson. *The Dominican Republic and the United States: From Imperialism to Transnationalism*. Athens: University of Georgia Press, 1998.

Betances, Emilio. *State and Society in the Dominican Republic*. Boulder, CO: Westview Press, 1995.

Hartlyn, Jonathan. "The Dominican Republic: Legacy of Intermittent Engagement." In Abraham F. Lowenthal, ed., *Exporting Democracy: The United States and Latin America*. Baltimore, MD: Johns Hopkins University Press, 1991.

Moya Pons, Frank. *The Dominican Republic: A National History*. New Rochelle, NY: Hispaniola Books, 1995.

10

Ecuador

TIMELINE OF U.S. RELATIONS WITH ECUADOR

1822–1830	Ecuador is a province of the independent republic of Gran Colombia
1830	Ecuador becomes an independent republic
1848	U.S. diplomatic relations are established
1855	President Franklin Pierce encourages exploration of guano as fertilizer
1897	Archer Harman receives contract to build railroad from Guayaquil to Quito
1926–1927	U.S. money doctors visit Ecuador
1939–1940	United States is allowed to build air bases on the Galápagos Islands and on the Pacific coast
1941	Border war between Peru and Ecuador
1942	Ecuador reluctantly agrees to Rio Protocol
1948–1952	Galo Plaza Lasso serves as elected president
1950–1962	Political stability follows in wake of banana export boom
1951	Beginning of tuna wars
1952	United States and Ecuador sign military assistance agreement
1952–1956	José María Velasco Ibarra serves as elected president
1960	Anti-U.S. demonstrations follow election of Velasco Ibarra
1967	Texaco-Gulf consortium signs oil exploration agreement
1968	Velasco Ibarra is elected to fifth term; tuna wars intensify
1970s	Texaco-Gulf consortium invests heavily in petroleum industry
1972	The military overthrows Velasco Ibarra
1972–1979	Two moderate military governments rule

1973	Ecuador joins Organization of Petroleum Exporting Countries (OPEC)
1974	Third UN Law of the Sea Conference reaches consensus for 12-mile territorial sea limit and 200-mile economic zone
1981–1984	Osvaldo Hurtado serves as elected president
1984–1988	León Febres-Cordero serves as elected president
1988–1992	Rodrigo Borja serves as elected president
1992	Ecuador withdraws from OPEC
1992–1996	Sixto Durán-Ballén serves as elected president
1995	Ecuador and Peru fight war over boundary
1996	Abdalá Bucaram is elected president
1997	Bucaram is removed from office because of "mental incompetence"
1998	Ecuador and Peru sign a peace treaty whereby Ecuador relinquishes its claim to disputed territory in return for permanent access to Amazon

INTRODUCTION

Located on the northwestern coast of South America between Colombia and Peru, Ecuador is the second smallest nation in South America with geographical diversity that has posed formidable obstacles to its economic and political development. Four geographically distinct regions—*sierra, costa, oriente*, and the Galápagos Islands—constitute present-day Ecuador, although its national territory has been nibbled away since independence in 1830. In seven border conflicts with Colombia, Peru, and Brazil dating back to the 1830s, Ecuador lost 61 percent of its total land area but still claims sovereignty over its lost territories.

The history of U.S. involvement in Ecuador has been closely associated with border disputes, trade and commerce, fishing rights, and perceived security needs related to the nearby Panama Canal and drug trafficking in the Andes region. Ecuadoran dictators have been masters of the art of manipulating U.S. policy for the purpose of obtaining economic assistance (and concealing their own harsh methods of rule) by either exaggerating the danger of foreign plans for aquiring strategically located territory or waving the "red" flag of communism. U.S.-Ecuadoran relations were influenced throughout the twentieth century by Ecuador's chronic political instability and the absence of democratic institutions. From independence until 1979, both elected governments and nonelected military regimes averaged less than two years in duration, making the formulation of U.S. policy a frustrating and difficult process.

ECUADOR AND THE UNITED STATES DURING THE
NINETEENTH CENTURY

The United States and Ecuadoran Independence

During the colonial period, Ecuador was a backwater area dominated by Lima, Peru, and later Bogotá, Colombia. It lacked the mineral wealth of its neighbors and offered no site for an interoceanic canal. When independence occurred in 1822, Ecuador was incorporated (along with Colombia and Venezuela) into the multinational merger known as the Confederation of Gran Colombia. Simón Bolívar became president of the Republic of Gran Colombia and pushed for cooperation among these newly independent states as a way to protect them from foreign intervention.

Bolívar was ambivalent about the role of the United States in the early development of Latin America. Although he admired the government of the United States for its republican institutions, his emphasis on unity led him to endorse a strong, conservative republic for Latin America run by an intellectual elite. Bolívar was suspicious of the growing power of the United States and saw only U.S. self-interest in the Monroe Doctrine of 1823. The two U.S. delegates who were to attend his Panama Congress in 1826 were late in departing—Congress debated for four months about the danger of foreign entanglements and economic interests in the region—and one died en route and the other arrived after the conference was over. Despite Bolívar's stature and influence, the Panama Congress ended with disappointing results and "the Liberator" soon lost interest in creating an American federation. Bolívar's rule became more dictatorial, and this contributed to the demise of Gran Colombia in 1830, the year of his death.

Ecuador became an independent republic in 1830, but political life soon degenerated into intense rivalries between Liberals and Conservatives, and foreign relations consisted of trying to maintain the integrity of its borders with Brazil, Colombia, and Peru in the Amazon region. Since its independence in 1830, Ecuador has gone to war five times with its neighbors over competing claims to its eastern territory. These border conflicts have given rise to Ecuadoran nationalism and a rather politicized military establishment. The United States has often served as a broker in some of the multinational efforts to end the bloodshed but in most cases has historically sided with Peru. Conservative military dictators continued to rule Ecuador until the 1895 revolution that brought Liberal president General Eloy Alfaro to power.

Ecuador and the Monroe Doctrine

The issues that gave rise to the Monroe Doctrine provided Ecuador the opportunity to appeal to the United States for protection on several occasions during the nineteenth century. While in exile in Europe after 1845, Ecuador's first president, Juan José Flores, tried to raise an army for the reconquest of Ecuador, favoring a monarchy under the guidance of a Spanish prince. Ecuador's president appealed to the Polk administration for military assistance under the Monroe Doctrine, but Flores ran into pressure from several South American countries and opposition abroad that squelched his plan. The Flores fiasco led to the convening of an American Congress in Lima, Peru, in 1847, where the participants passed a resolution reaffirming the noncolonization principle and denying the right of European powers to intervene in the Americas. The idea of a French protectorate over Ecuador was considered in the 1850s after it experienced the effects of Manifest Destiny and the filibustering activities operating out of southern parts of the United States. Former president Flores's great scheme failed, but it served to reawaken further interest in the Monroe Doctrine and the Bolivarian dream of a united South America. Flores continued to stir up trouble through his attempts to conquer southern Colombia until his death in 1865.

The Monroe Doctrine played a role in the war between Spain and four Andean countries in 1865 when Ecuador joined Peru (Spain had never recognized Peru's independence), Bolivia, and Chile in an alliance to prevent Spain from trying to reconquer part of its former territory. United against Spain, the Andean countries requested U.S. intervention in defense of the Monroe Doctrine. Secretary of State William Seward rejected the plea for direct intervention, arguing that Spain had abandoned its desire for territorial conquest. Nevertheless, Seward worried that if the conflict could not be settled under U.S. auspices, a "super alliance" against the Spanish could be used against the United States at some future date. The war marked a significant development in U.S.-Andean relations since it amounted to the first explicit request for direct U.S. intervention in internal Andean affairs. After policymakers in Washington helped to end the hostilities with an armistice signed in 1871, the Andean nations assumed that the United States was preparing to function as a peacekeeper in South America. Realizing that Monroe's words hardly constituted a binding commitment, Ecuador saw little need to appeal to Washington for protection after the U.S. Civil War.

Guanopreneurs and the Expansion of Empire

A number of entrepreneurs and adventurers, with strong backing from the U.S. government, played a major role in expanding the involvement of the United States in South America between 1856 and 1902. Beginning in the 1840s, the U.S. government became interested in acquiring cheap fertilizer made from guano, the dried excrement of sea birds. Pressured by southern farmers—faced with soils depleted by overintensive cultivation of cotton and tobacco—the Fillmore and Pierce administrations tried to gain access to guano islands off the coasts of Peru and Ecuador. Congress passed the Guano Act in 1854 that enabled a U.S. citizen to apply for government protection after demonstrating continual possession of a guano island, no matter what its size. With the backing of the president of the United States and U.S. army and naval forces to protect their discoveries and claims, the American guanopreneurs received individual assistance that has no parallel in the history of the United States. Foremost among the guanopreneurs were Alfred G. Benson and James W. Jennett, both energetic explorers but with little integrity in how they obtained or sold their U.S.-backed islands.

The United States became interested in the Galápagos Islands, located roughly 600 miles west of the port city of Guayaquil, believing at first that the islands contained vast amounts of guano. During the 1850s a U.S. ship captain made a deal to exploit the fertilizer with an Ecuadoran who held the rights to the islands. Once the secret deal became public knowledge, tremendous opposition developed in Ecuador. The United States was accused of trying to create a protectorate over the islands and eventually seize them outright. The Galápagos proved to be a poor source of guano, and eventually the United States lost interest in exercising control over them. The great guano rush continued throughout the western coast of South America and the Caribbean, but it declined rapidly in the late nineteenth century.

A "Yankee" President in the Age of Liberalism

The installation of Liberal Eloy Alfaro as president (1895–1901; 1906–1911) in 1895 marked a dramatic shift in political and economic power from Quito (the center of Conservatism) to Guayaquil on the coast that would last until the 1940s. Alfaro pushed ahead with economic modernization, building railroads and communication lines and encouraging foreign investment. One of his highest priorities was to join with North American capitalists to build a railroad between Quito and Guayaquil. He contracted with Archer Harman—a railroad engineer from Virginia—to form a company that would raise $17.5 million for the railroad project. Harman's close ties to Alfaro and the railroad angered Ecuadoran Conservatives for what they claimed was a sellout to Yankee capitalists. By the time Harman completed the railroad in 1908, he was considered the most powerful man in Ecuador and a key figure in advancing U.S.-Ecuadoran relations. Unwilling to give up power, Alfaro was lynched by a once-adoring Quito mob in January 1912.

ECUADOR AND THE UNITED STATES DURING THE EARLY TWENTIETH CENTURY

By the early twentieth century, Ecuadoran dictators and other incumbents were well versed in skillfully playing on American official and public ignorance to sustain themselves in office. For example, Ecuadoran politicians knew that U.S. policymakers wanted the Galápagos Islands as a place for naval bases. By spouting a steady stream of exaggerated tales of German and French intrigues to seize the islands, Ecuadoran officials were able to gain significant political and economic advantages. This strategy was particularly useful during times of international conflict (World Wars I and II) when the United States worried about hemispheric security.

As the Panama Canal neared completion, U.S. interest in the Galápagos Islands increased because many in Washington feared this strategic area might fall into the hands of another major power, thus making the new canal more difficult to protect. In order to further U.S. security interests, the United States began to negotiate with President Alfaro for a 99-year lease and a payment of $15 million to Ecuador to be spent cleaning up Guayaquil and putting its economic house in order. Alfaro welcomed a U.S. presence because payments for use of the islands would provide Ecuador (and members of his administration) with additional sources of revenue. However, when Secretary of State Philander C. Knox insisted on full and complete sovereignty over the islands during the duration of the lease, Alfaro resisted. Once the Ecuadorans learned of the negotiations, there was public outrage against Alfaro for considering the sale of national territory for private gain. Eventually he called off the negotiations. Ecuador is a good example of the obstacles Washington faced "in trying to conduct relations with a country perennially on the brink of war with one of its neighbors and a country where out-of-power politicians had already learned how to derive advantage from charging incumbents with complicity with nefarious Yankee capitalists."[1] The desirability and consequences of foreign capital continued through World War I, when Ecuadoran politicians found it easier to turn to the awakening masses for support, blaming the local oligarchy and foreign capitalists on their sorry plight.

During the 1920s policymakers in Washington decided that national security considerations in South America could be achieved by supporting American businessmen, rather than by following the Caribbean policy of relying on the U.S. Marines. Washington diplomats thought that using economic missionaries to preach and practice the capitalist ethic would foster a middle class, instill democratic practices, and eliminate political instability. In Ecuador, the depressed economy and the inability to pay off foreign debts dampened foreign investment until after World War II. As a result, the negative reaction to U.S. economic penetration that was so common elsewhere in Latin America did not become an important part of Ecuadoran domestic politics.

Money Doctors and Demagogues

The collapse of the cacao (the bean from which chocolate is made) market in the 1920s sent the Ecuadoran economy into a tailspin, compounded politically by the increasing power of working-class organizations and the military. One of the solutions to Latin America's economic problems was the foreign financial advisor, often sent on specific missions to sort out financial problems and satisfy foreign lenders that foreign debts were being paid on time. The most successful money doctor was Dr. Edwin W. Kemmerer of Princeton University, a sort of one-man International Monetary Fund (IMF) who came to Ecuador in 1926–1927 with free-market policy prescriptions. Armed with a bundle of suggestions including the adoption of the gold standard and the creation of central banks, Kemmerer set the stage for the dramatic increase in foreign investment that lasted until the onset of the Great Depression, when loan defaults and dictatorships returned to the region.

Ecuador and the Good Neighbor Policy

President Franklin D. Roosevelt's Good Neighbor Policy—withdrawing Marines, removing the last evidence of the protectorate era, and accepting the important principle of nonintervention—had little impact on Ecuador and the other Andean countries. The collapse of the cacao boom in the 1920s was compounded by the dramatic shrinkage of world markets during the 1930s. As political turmoil increased, Ecuador struggled to free itself of its difficulties by shifting from the golden cacao seed to bananas while restricting imports to protect infant industries. The Good Neighbor era also coincided with the rise of José María Velasco Ibarra, a fiery demagogue (a political leader using dramatic speech that often includes popular prejudices and false assertions), who mesmerized the masses with speeches on behalf of the "shoeless ones" (but his populist rhetoric was designed to appeal to just about everyone). So convinced of the power of his personalism and lofty ideals, he often said "Give me a balcony and I will govern." Velasco proved to be a durable caudillo and opportunist; he was elected president five times (1933, 1944, 1952, 1960, and 1968) but was overthrown four times by the Ecuadoran military. Ecuador's political situation did not improve after the overthrow of Velasco in 1934, as 14 different chief executives came and went over a 10-year period.

Ecuador and World War II

The United States found a "friendly dictator" in Ecuador during the war years who proved to be extremely cooperative, allowing Washington to build a naval base on the Galápagos Islands and an airbase on the Ecuadoran mainland. President Carlos Alberto Arroyo del Río managed to stay in power throughout most of the war despite his unpopular methods of ruling and a disastrous 1941 war with Peru in which Ecuador lost some 200,000 square kilometers of territory in its Amazon region. Arroyo was not prepared for the Peruvian attack that came in July 1941, despite the mounting tensions over the unsettled boundary with Peru and repeated warnings of a possible outbreak of large-scale hostilities. Peru—with an army that outnumbered Ecuador's by three to one—pushed northward and occupied a vast tract of land occupied by Ecuador. Peru's occupation ended in 1942 when the two nations signed the Rio Protocol (the informal name of the agreement) and Ecuador renounced its claim to territory then in the hands of the more powerful Peruvian military. The United States, Argentina, Chile, and Brazil were instrumental in establishing the terms of the agreement in which Ecuador relinquished most of the "Amazonian Triangle" to Peru. After the Rio Protocol was signed, and ratified by a bare plurality of the Ecuadoran legislature, the Ecuadoran government regretted having become a party to the protocol, claiming it had acted under pressure from the United States and did not plan to accept the revised frontier. Arroyo was accused of failing to "defend the national honor," which was the charge of opposition forces—civilian and military—who removed him from power in 1944 and put the populist Velasco back in the presidency for a second time.

ECUADOR AND THE UNITED STATES DURING THE COLD WAR

Ecuador's Banana Industry

The production of bananas started much later in Ecuador than in Central America and the Caribbean. The production and marketing of bananas in Ecuador began when the United Fruit Company purchased an old cacao plantation in 1933, but the Depression years were not good for the banana business. Later, thanks to supply constraints in the other banana-producing regions due to disease and natural disasters, Ecuador replaced Costa Rica and Honduras and became the leading world banana exporter in 1951. The banana boom lasted until 1983 and helped underwrite an unprecedented 15-year period of political stability. Foreign producers of bananas like the United Fruit Company played a minor role in Ecuador's banana boom, in contrast to its monopolistic control in Honduras and Guatemala. The company's activities were confined mostly to marketing instead of the production of bananas, and its banana exports rarely exceeded 20 percent of Ecuador's total.

Ecuador and the U.S. Military

After World War II the United States forged closer ties to Ecuador's military in an effort to coordinate military/intelligence efforts against the perceived influence of Cuba and the Soviet Union. Ecuador's armed forces are the product of assistance from the United States and Europe, both in terms of professional training and in the acquisition of arms and equipment. Ecuador received considerable amounts of U.S. military surpluses at reduced prices, including light naval vessels and other equipment. Ecuadoran officers have been trained at the School of the Americas (during the time it was located in Panama and later when it was moved to Ft. Benning, Georgia) and in various military installations in the United States. In most cases the military assistance was designed to preempt relations with other extra-hemispheric powers and promote internal stability as a bulwark against communism. The majority of Ecuadoran officers opposed communism, believing the ideology to be antithetical to everything the military stands for. As narcotrafficking increased early in the 1970s, U.S. troops traveled to Ecuador to engage in joint "civic action" programs to fight the drug war in the Andes.

Tuna Wars and Territorial Claims to the Sea

After losing its outlet to the Amazon River through border conflicts with Peru, Ecuador attempted to extend its territorial rights to include sole control over the natural resources and territorial sea within 200 miles of its coastline. Ecuador joined with Chile and Peru in 1952 to formalize a 200-mile maritime zone to protect its national fishing interests in the Pacific Ocean. On the basis of this claim, a lengthy political and legal conflict started with the United States and other maritime powers over territorial claims and fishing rights. The United States particularly objected to the 200-mile claim to protect tuna and other fish, arguing in terms of traditional international law that the area beyond the 3-mile territorial sea was considered the *high seas* and therefore open to all. The enforcement of these claimed "rights" to regulate tuna fishing resulted in a series of tuna wars after Ecuador and Peru seized and fined U.S. private tuna boats during the 1950s and 1960s. The United States opposed these claims and decided to simply reimburse fishing boat captains whose boats—and catch—were captured and fined. The conflict was temporarily resolved in 1963 when the Kennedy administration negotiated a secret agreement with the ruling military junta in which the U.S. tuna fleet was allowed to fish in the disputed territory without penalties. However, once the secret arrangement with Ecuador's military government was discovered several years later, public and official outrage erupted and the military was accused of a traitorous act.

The tuna wars intensified with the election of José María Velasco Ibarra for his fifth term in 1968. Between 1968 and 1971 Ecuador continued to seize U.S. fishing boats, which led to the suspension of military aid and arms sales to Ecuador. In retaliation, President Velasco terminated the U.S. military assistance program and the tuna wars continued. The conflicts over fishing rights reached their pinnacle in 1971 when Ecuador seized 51 U.S. tuna boats and assessed over $2.4 million in fines and fees. The folly and irony of the wars over fishing rights can be seen in the fact that (1) the fines were paid by the U.S. government through reimbursements, (2) the Ecuadoran navy—made up mostly of antiquated vessels sold or given to Ecuador by the United States—got to keep 70 percent of all fines paid, and (3) the majority of Ecuador's fishing fleet and tuna plants were already owned by U.S. companies. The tuna wars passed into history in the 1980s after the United States accepted the 200-mile economic zone, one of several approved at the Third United Nations Conference on the Law of the Sea, 1973–1982.

Ecuador and the Alliance for Progress

After the election of Galo Plaza Lasso (1948–1952), an era of cordiality developed in U.S.-Ecuadoran relations that continued through the Eisenhower years. However, in 1960 Velasco Ibarra returned to the presidency (his third term) with a campaign that emphasized the negative qualities of his pro–North American opponent, Galo Plaza. Unable to govern with any degree of stability, Velasco decided to turn to the communists and openly sympathized with Castro's Cuba, hoping the United States would increase the price it was willing to pay for his Cold War friendship. This strategy backfired on Velasco since the Ecuadoran military became concerned over the communist issue and staged a coup that toppled the president in late 1961. An extraordinarily gifted orator, Velasco's campaign charisma was never matched by his abilities as an administrator. His vice-president, Carlos Julio Arosemena, a prominent Guayaquil banker, then took over. But he embarrassed his country with his frequent drinking bouts and favorable comments on the Cuban Revolution, provoking the military to strike again. After the military assumed full control and applauded the reformist principles of the Alliance for Progress as an antidote to communist revolution, the junta gained speedy recognition from Washington as well as $84.5 million in aid and assistance during the three years it remained in power.

When Alliance for Progress funds dried up in the late 1960s, the military returned the presidency to civilian control under President Otto Arosemena Gómez. Arosemena reversed the cordiality of the military junta by refusing to endorse the Charter of the Alliance for Progress at Punta del Este, further angering the United States. As income from banana exports declined, Ecuador experienced an oil boom that attracted U.S. companies, such as Gulf and Texaco. Both played a major role in developing the petroleum industry, which by the 1970s was Ecuador's leading exporter. Ecuador joined the Organization of Petroleum Exporting Countries (OPEC) in 1972 but left the organization in 1992 due to the high costs of membership and the dramatic drop in oil prices. Velasco Ibarra was elected to his fifth (and final) term of office in 1968, but he mistakenly believed that oil prosperity would carry him through a full term without military removal.

León Febres Cordero and the Americanization of Ecuador

During the presidency of León Febres Cordero (1984–1988), a conservative businessman from Guayaquil, Ecuador again developed close ties with the United States. In what some called an experiment in "Andean Thatcherism," Febres tried to build a "special" relationship with the United States by breaking diplomatic relations with Nicaragua; shrinking the size of the state and promising prompt debt repayment in order to enhance good relations with international financial institutions; permitting the presence of U.S. military forces in Ecuador; and agreeing wholeheartedly with Reagan's narcoterrorism rhetoric and strategy. President Febres also invited back the U.S.-based Summer Institute of Linguistics, a Christian missionary group engaged in translating the Bible into Indian languages and widely accused of having links to the CIA.

Convinced that he could solve Ecuador's problems with an aggressive neoliberal economic strategy and the support of the Reagan administration, Febres became increasingly authoritarian in trying to force his reforms through a weakly constituted democratic system. The collapse in the price of petroleum in 1986 destroyed any cushion Febres enjoyed to implement his reforms, and a deep economic and political crisis soon gripped the country. With declining petroleum prices and charges of corruption, political ineptitude, and constitutional violations, Febres was kidnapped by forces loyal to a dismissed military figure, Frank Vargas Pazzos, and held for 11 hours until he agreed to grant an amnesty for Vargas and his release from detention for inciting an earlier military rebellion. After an earthquake struck the eastern oil region in 1987, disrupting the oil pipeline, Febres was forced to forego his economic plan and focus on post-earthquake reconstruction. He was severely criticized by Ecuadoran nationalists who felt that his acceptance of some 6,000 U.S. troops to help with post-earthquake reconstruction efforts in the Amazon region was a serious affront to national sovereignty. This joint military effort with the United States, known as Operation Blazing Trails, also reawakened old fears that the United States was again seeking a military training base in Ecuador to fight the drug war in the Andes. Nevertheless, Febres completed his term in 1988, and Ecuador managed to survive four years of authoritarian populism, a deep economic recession, and the continual threat of another military coup.

ECUADOR AND THE UNITED STATES AFTER THE COLD WAR

Ecuador and the War on Drugs

When compared with the other Andean nations such as Colombia, Peru, and Bolivia, Ecuador is a relative "island of peace" in the battle against drugs. For example, 1990 estimates of coca leaf production in Ecuador amounted to only 170 metric tons, as compared to 196,900 in Peru and 81,000 in Bolivia.[2] Within the Andean region Ecuador serves as a transit country for drugs moving northward from Peru and Bolivia, a location for money laundering, and an important spot for U.S. drug interdiction efforts. Ecuador's fragile political system is highly vulnerable to the influence of narco-trafficking, but its politicians have been the most willing to follow the U.S. anti-drug strategy—control, repression, and militarization—designed by the State Department and controlled by U.S. government agencies. It is a strategy that has been criticized for its harmful effects on Andean societies, including the diversion of needed resources to the military, human rights abuses, and negative reactions directed at the United States. Moreover, the war on drugs has been costly to both the United States and the Andean countries, which are caught between the huge demand in the United States and the increasing power of well-organized drug mafias operating throughout the Americas.

Peru-Ecuador Border Conflict of 1995

Peruvian troops invaded Ecuador in early 1995, and sporadic fighting continued for weeks before an emergency meeting of the Organization of American States (OAS) arranged for mutual negotiations that helped resolve the differences. The guarantor nations of the 1941 Rio Protocol (including the United States) became the basis for negotiations, but it was several months before troops were withdrawn from the contested area. The short, undeclared war (the actual fighting lasted a little over one month) was a costly affair with over 300 casualties and an expenditure of an estimated $500 million between both nations. The high cost and intensity of the war surprised Washington and raised questions in the Clinton administration about its democracy promotion rhetoric, particularly the popular theory that "democracies do not go to war against one another." After arguing over border claims since colonial times, Ecuador and Peru signed an agreement in January 1998, with May 30, 1998, as a target date for a peace treaty where Ecuador will give up its claim to the disputed land in return for permanent access to the Amazon River. With the help of the leaders of Argentina, Brazil, Chile, and the United States, both nations signed the treaty because they realized that trade and economic growth are more important than nationalist politics and war. After years of tension and war, the willingness of each party to accede to the existing peacekeeping machinery is encouraging.

The Perils of Ecuadoran Populism

Despite the end of the Cold War and chronic political instability, Ecuador's political system continued on its shaky democratic path that began in 1979. After seeking the presidency for years, the former mayor of Guayaquil, Abdalá Bucaram, won the presidency in July 1996 using ferocious attacks on the "oligarchy" and offering the masses a "government for the poor." During his flamboyant campaign, Bucaram would sometimes sing with a Uruguayan rock band and frequently referred to himself as "El Loco," or the crazy one. Before long Bucaram, the son of Lebanese immigrants, came to resemble a Hollywood caricature of a populist president. His time as mayor of Guayaquil earned his administration the nickname of "Ali Abdalá and the 40 thieves."

After becoming president, Bucaram stepped back from his populist campaign and adopted economic measures to reduce the protective role of the state. His new economic policies produced painful increases in the cost of telephones, cooking gas, gasoline, and electricity that were made worse by rampant corruption and favoritism. After being bombarded with complaints about bribery and extortion by U.S. businesses in Ecuador, the U.S. ambassador to Ecuador, Leslie Alexander, warned in January 1997 about the pervasive corruption gripping the country. The public might have put up with the corruption—Bucaram's stock in trade—but his austerity measures led to a general strike and days of angry protest that led the Ecuadoran Congress to remove him on charges of "mental incompetence" in February 1997. After just six months in office, Bucaram and his political cronies were reported to have made off with at least $80 million, according to charges made by a corruption commission appointed by Fabián Alarcón, the head of the legislature who succeeded Bucaram. With bags of cash in hand Bucaram left for Panama, where he remains in self-imposed exile. He claims that he is still president and that his removal for "mental incompetence" was an illegal coup by Congress and the military. While the 1997 episode to remove Bucaram seemed comic opera in its response to a constitutional crisis, the outcome did not require either military intervention from the United States or a coup led by Ecuadoran forces.

CONCLUSION

U.S.-Ecuadoran relations have experienced periods of friendship and cordiality along with times of tension. Although the nation was never a high priority for U.S. policymakers, the United States has targeted Ecuador because of its economic (agro-exports such as cacao and bananas, tuna fishing, foreign investment, and petroleum) and security interests (protecting the passages to the Panama Canal, fighting the drug war, and assisting with Ecuador's internal political turmoil and ceaseless border conflicts with its neighbors). The historic involvement of the United States in Ecuadoran affairs has been a source of irritation and belligerent nationalism. Yet at the same time Ecuador's politicians have often made opportunistic use of U.S. involvement to increase their popular political support at home and divert attention away from corruption, repression of opposition groups, and the negative economic effects of inefficient administrations, a mainstay of Ecuadoran politics. Since World War II, Ecuador has put more emphasis on inter-American organizations for the peaceful settlement of controversies than relying on Washington's mediation efforts.

NOTES

1. Frederick B. Pike, *The United States and the Andean Republics: Peru, Bolivia, and Ecuador* (Cambridge, MA: Harvard University Press, 1977), p. 167.
2. Peter H. Smith, ed., *Drug Policy in the Americas* (Boulder, CO: Westview Press, 1992), p. 8.

SUGGESTED READINGS

Hey, Jeanne A.K. *Theories of Dependent Foreign Policy and the Case of Ecuador in the 1980s.* Athens, Ohio: Ohio University Center for International Studies, 1995.

Schodt, David W. *Ecuador: An Andean Enigma.* Boulder, CO: Westview Press, 1987.

Scholes, Walter V., and Marie V. Scholes. "The United States and Ecuador, 1909–1913." *The Americas*, Vol. 19, No. 3 (1963), pp. 276–290.

Skaggs, Jimmy M. *The Great Guano Rush: Entrepreneurs and American Overseas Expansion.* New York: St. Martin's Press, 1994.

Smith, Peter H., ed. *Drug Policy in the Americas.* Boulder, CO: Westview Press, 1992.

11

El Salvador

TIMELINE OF U.S. RELATIONS WITH EL SALVADOR

1821	Salvadoran independence from Spain is achieved
1823	El Salvador requests annexation with United States
1838	Central American unity ends
1863	U.S. diplomatic relations are established
1931–1944	Maximiliano Hernández Martínez rules as dictator
1932	Peasant uprising leads to massacre of 30,000 civilians by government troops
1944	President Hernández Martínez resigns from office
1963	Central American Defense Council (CONDECA) is established
1969	Soccer War
1979	Reformist military officers take power
1980	Civilian progressives resign from junta; Archbishop Oscar Romero is assassinated
	José Napoleon Duarte assumes control of junta and later replaces Colonel Majano as president
	Farabundo Martí National Liberation Front is established
1981	Fifty-five U.S. military advisors travel to El Salvador
1983	El Salvador ranks as third largest recipient of U.S. aid
1984	Kissinger Commission Report calls for increased aid to El Salvador
	Duarte's election ends longest period of uninterrupted military rule in Latin America

1987	Frente Farabundo Martí de Liberación Nacional (FMLN) attacks major military base, killing two Americans, including a CIA agent and a military advisor
1989	Alfredo Cristiani is elected president
	FMLN launches major offensive
1990	UN creates Observer Group in El Salvador (ONUSAL) to assist with peacemaking efforts
1992	UN and ARENA government sign peace accord
1993	UN-appointed Truth Commission is established
	Clinton administration suspends military aid
1994	Armando Calderón Sol is elected president
1997	FMLN wins in local and parliamentary elections
1998	Members of National guard convicted of killing U.S. nuns in 1980 admit from prison they only acted on orders from above

INTRODUCTION

Since the early nineteenth century, El Salvador has suffered from chronic internal strife, long periods of military rule—often in alliance with a small oligarchy of wealthy coffee growers—and a 12-year span of intense U.S. involvement in a civil war beginning in 1979. Before peace could be attained in the 1990s, the bloody conflict left 75,000 people dead, crippled the nation, caused over one million Salvadorans to leave their country, and drew the United States into one of its longest Cold War paramilitary and military assistance efforts. Washington invested close to $6 billion to support military-dominated governments fearful that another revolutionary Nicaragua would emerge if several moderate and pro-Cuban groups came to power. Until a peace agreement was reached between the government and leftist insurgents in 1991, arrogance and miscalculation characterized American policymakers who deliberately turned a blind eye to the use of state-sanctioned terrorism against Marxist guerrillas, their supporters, and suspected sympathizers.

El Salvador is the smallest mainland country in Latin America and the only Central American country without a port on the Caribbean coast. Thus, it has no easy access to the major markets in the United States and Europe. With the highest population density of any country in the Americas, El Salvador has had to face demands for land ownership, resistance from wealthy European-descended whites, and border wars with its neighbors, Guatemala and Honduras. Racism against Indians and lower-class mestizos (people of Indian-Spanish ancestry) has been used by the ruling families to maintain an obedient labor force and control the hunger for land. A common strategy of the country's ruling elites has been to allow the killing of Indians; from the 1930s on, "Indian equals communist" was used to justify the suppression of demands for land reform and social justice. El Salvador was the site of the first communist uprising in the Americas in 1932, but the response from the government troops (and the private armies of the landowners) was a slaughter (*la matanza*) of close to 30,000 peasants—4 percent of the population at the time.

Throughout the twentieth century El Salvador has been ruled by a military-oligarchical alliance with an intense dislike of social movements in favor of reform. Extremely wealthy landholders and traders known as "the oligarchy" or "the 14 families" (the actual number is closer to 200) and the military have controlled economic and political life. From 1931 until 1986, El Salvador experienced the longest period of uninterrupted military rule anywhere in Latin America. During the Cold War the United States was instrumental in forming an alliance with the Salvadoran military designed to protect the Central American region against communism and, after 1980, the chance to "win" a military victory in the wake of the defeat in Vietnam and the failure to prevent the Nicaraguan revolution.

EL SALVADOR AND THE UNITED STATES DURING THE NINETEENTH CENTURY

The United States and Salvadoran Independence

At the time of independence in 1821, El Salvador was part of the Spanish colonial province of Guatemala, which also included Nicaragua, Honduras, and Costa Rica. Once the yoke of Spanish colonialism was gone, some of the Central American states decided to join the Empire of Mexico. El Salvador's resistance was so strong that Mexico felt it had to incorporate El Salvador by force of arms. However, the fall of Emperor Agustín de Iturbide came before the plan could be fully implemented, and the five Central American states were once more left in a kind of political limbo. To remedy this unstable situation, El Salvador passed an act annexing itself to the United States and sent several representatives to negotiate with the Monroe administration on the proposal, but the request was denied and El Salvador soon became part of the United Provinces of Central America in 1823. The Central American federation proved unworkable—political factions clashed both within each province and across provincial boundaries—and it ended in 1838. After the disintegration of the federation, El Salvador was ruled by a string of harsh civilian or military dictatorships that kept a tight lid on social protest and any form of rebellion.

International competition for building railroads and a future canal in Central America inevitably brought clashes between the United States and the British after 1850. After signing the Clayton-Bulwer Treaty, the United States sent Ephraim G. Squier, a journalist and diplomat from New York, to Central America to discuss American efforts to build railroads and the possibility of an interoceanic canal in Nicaragua (see Chapter 19). In a note of concern to El Salvador's minister of foreign relations, Squier stated that some form of political consolidation among the Central American states would be necessary against the encroachments of foreign and unfriendly governments. About the same time the Nicaraguan minister to London asked the U.S. minister whether El Salvador, Honduras, and Nicaragua might be admitted to the Union, or if this was not possible, then they would accept some form of protection from foreign intervention. President Franklin Pierce turned down the request, but El Salvador and some of its neighbors apparently felt that annexation to the United States was preferable to any purported protection from extra-hemispheric powers offered by the Monroe Doctrine.

EL SALVADOR AND THE UNITED STATES DURING THE EARLY TWENTIETH CENTURY

By the early twentieth century the United States had created a system of "protectorates," or client states, in Central America. European rivals gradually retreated, leaving Central America under the thumb of the United States. In response, Central American governments found it convenient to accept U.S. dominance while seeking concessions that would serve their needs. Throughout the twentieth century this strategy of accommodation strengthened elite resistance to social and political change, and it increased the level of U.S. supervision and assistance once a revolution had started.

The United States, Central American Conflicts, and World War I

Between 1890 and World War I the Central American republics quarreled constantly, often provoking military intervention and financial meddling by the United States. In what came to be known as the Roosevelt Corollary to the Monroe Doctrine, the United States assumed greater responsibility for unilateral peacemaking and conflict resolution. In 1906, El Salvador revived simmering conflicts by lending its support to rebels in neighboring Guatemala seeking to overthrow the pro-U.S. regime of Manuel Estrada Cabrera. After Estrada defeated the rebels and threatened retaliation, Honduras offered its assistance to El Salvador. In an effort to resolve the dispute, the United States persuaded Mexico and Costa Rica to jointly sponsor peace talks aboard a U.S. vessel. At first the five republics signed an agreement to end hostilities and refrain from aiding rebels seeking to overthrow other governments, but the agreements were short-lived and cross-border hostilities continued. In the following year the United States and Mexico invited the warring parties to a conference in Washington in

"Well, Look Who's Back — Mr. International Law and Order!"

order to develop some mechanisms that would reduce the regional hostilities. The Washington conference accepted the Tobar Doctrine of not recognizing unconstitutional governments and created the Central American Court of Justice; however, when the court rendered verdicts in 1912 and 1916 that challenged the legality of U.S. intervention in—and agreements with—Nicaragua, the United States ignored the decision. After it became evident that it was impossible to enforce the actions of the court, it ceased to exist in 1918. (The United States responded similarly to a World Court decision against it in 1985, after CIA-directed agents had secretly mined several of Nicaragua's major harbors.)

After decades of U.S. intervention in the Caribbean area, efforts by Washington to create a united American front against the Central powers during World War I failed. El Salvador, along with Argentina, Chile, Colombia, Mexico, Paraguay, and Venezuela, maintained neutrality toward the war effort and diplomatic relations toward Germany. Despite the inability to achieve hemispheric solidarity, World War I removed all potential threats to U.S. strategic and political dominance in Central America. "So complete was U.S. dominance after World War I," according to John Coatsworth, "that the cost-conscious Republican administrations controlling the White House from 1921 to 1933 became increasingly anxious to end the U.S. occupations of Nicaragua, Haiti, and the Dominican Republic."[1]

Washington also faced opposition to its interventionism by anti-imperialists in the United States weary of "dollar diplomacy" and military occupation. Sandino's rebellion against U.S. forces in Nicaragua challenged the hegemony of the United States and paved the way for the Good Neighbor Policy, beginning with the Warren G. Harding administration in the 1920s.

Peasant Massacres and the Rise of the Salvadoran Military

The Great Depression brought a sharp reduction in coffee prices to El Salvador and worsened social tensions, despite the completion of an important railroad connecting El Salvador with Guatemala. After a coup d'état led by a handful of young officers removed the regime of Arturo Araujo in late 1931, the military named Vice-President Maximiliano Hernández Martínez to succeed him. The United States suspended diplomatic relations, citing earlier guidelines for recognizing extra-constitutional governments. Salvadorans interpreted this as another form of Yankee imperialism, and relations were not resumed until the beginning of Roosevelt's Good Neighbor Policy in 1933.

In January 1932 a peasant revolt erupted in El Salvador that was quickly repressed. The government blamed the young Communist Party of El Salvador, which had participated in the revolt under the leadership of Augustín Farabundo Martí, as the source of every atrocity that occurred. Martí was a leftist known for his radical activities, influenced by his readings in socialist and Marxist-Leninist thought. He joined the forces of Augusto César Sandino, who was fighting U.S. forces in Nicaragua, and followed Sandino into exile in Mexico in 1929. The two men separated over ideological differences—Sandino was more interested in national independence and moral regeneration than in Martí's idea of a social revolution—and Martí returned to El Salavador in 1930, where he was jailed for his labor organizing and propaganda activities among the peasants (see Chapter 19). Having concluded that Martínez was not interested in allowing the Communist Party of El Salvador (PCS) to participate in elections or hold office through legal means, Martí called for simultaneous uprisings against the government.

The insurrection was unorganized and poorly coordinated and was met with a swift and bloody response. After several captured towns were taken by security forces, the massacre (*la matanza*) started. "Anyone in Indian dress, anyone running from the security forces was fair game. When the carnage was over 30,000 people were dead."[2] Martí and several students were tried by a military tribunal and then shot. The bloody revolt, and the involvement of communists, made the other Central American governments and their upper classes quake with fear of a possible contagion effect. In the aftermath of the massacre, General Martínez had no trouble justifying the righteousness of his course of action by telling critics that "It is a greater crime to kill an ant than a man, for when a man dies he becomes reincarnated, while an ant dies forever."[3] General Martínez rejected the services of the Special Service Squadron, American warships waiting offshore to assist "native governments" with the unpleasant task of keeping order. The 1932 revolt set back the leftist cause in El Salvador for decades, but it offered lessons for future revolutionaries. The Salvadoran military's success in putting down a communist revolt bolstered its reputation among the coffee oligarchy, and from 1932 onward it played a major role in the nation's political life.

EL SALVADOR AND THE UNITED STATES DURING THE COLD WAR

El Salvador and the Overthrow of Arbenz in Guatemala

After the fall of Guatemalan dictator Jorge Ubico in 1944, Guatemala became a refuge for Salvadoran communists committed to the reform efforts initiated by Juan José Arévalo and Jacobo Arbenz. By 1953 things had reversed, with conservative Guatemalan exiles residing in El Salvador rather than subjecting themselves to a "communist" regime nextdoor. In 1950, Major Oscar Osorio, a young military officer, won carefully orchestrated elections in El Salvador and then proceeded to implement a "revolution" in which he enacted mild reforms. At first sympathetic to Arbenz, in 1952 Osorio launched an anticommunist crusade and began to repress the Salvadoran labor movement. As Guatemala battled with the United States during the final months before the CIA-backed invasion against Arbenz in 1954, President Osorio remained aloof, apparently content to watch the ugly spectacle from the sidelines rather than spare his country the humiliation that Honduras had to endure (see Chapter 13). Arbenz's Guatemala was not a threat to El Salvador because of the communist influence in his government; the danger posed by his agrarian reform rested in its power as a propaganda weapon against the wealth of the oligarchy and U.S. investors.

The United States and the Salvadoran Military

During the 1930s the United States began to solidify its relationship with Latin American military officers by providing military equipment, training courses, and the standardization of equipment along U.S. lines. This arrangement made it possible for U.S. military planners to influence military doctrine and American foreign policy. After World War II the United States attempted to fit Latin America into its anticommunist orientation by courting the military at the expense of human rights and democracy. The State

Department's expert on Soviet Affairs, George Kennan, helped to outline the contours of the Cold War Latin American policy of the United States by indicating that it was not shameful to use harsh methods to repress communists because they were essentially traitors and Latin American democratic governments often too weak to resist the "virus" of communism.

To build Latin American armed forces under closer U.S. supervision, Congress passed the Military Defense Assistance Act (MDA) in 1951. Funding increased and counterinsurgency warfare training expanded at the Panama Canal Zone's School of the Americas. During the 1950s and 1960s, U.S. policy toward Central America became increasingly militarized and allied with the Central Intelligence Agency. After the Cuban revolution, the Kennedy administration sent a vastly increased number of military advisors, police-training missions, and CIA agents to Central America. Officers from throughout Central America formed friendships with U.S. military figures and shared intelligence information on suspected subversives. The Kennedy administration also tried to improve the image of military establishments that had acquired reputations for coup-making, corruption, and human rights violations by having the military engage in civic action programs.

In 1963 the Central American Defense Council (CONDECA) was created to formalize military cooperation among the high commands of El Salvador, Guatemala, Honduras, and Nicaragua; Panama and Costa Rica did not become members. The heavy hand of the Pentagon was evident in CONDECA's joint military maneuvers against a potential invasion from the Caribbean and its emphasis on creating a military bulwark against communism and threats from insurgents and guerrillas. CONDECA's promise as a regional organization was severely undermined by the 1969 Soccer War in which U.S.-trained soldiers and officers from El Salvador and Honduras engaged in fighting each other, not defending their countries against a communist assault. CONDECA sank into remission until Honduran General Álvarez took the initiative to revive the organization in the early 1980s as a mechanism to set in motion a joint invasion of Nicaragua.

Hundreds of U.S. Army soldiers, mostly Green Berets, served as military advisors in El Salvador beginning in the 1980s, lasting until a 1992 peace accord was signed by leftist guerrillas and the government. According to the U.S. Army, 22 Americans died helping the Salvadoran army fight Marxist insurgents and other opponents of the regime during the civil war. Because the United States armed and financed the army, whose human rights abuses resulted in many Salvadorans going into exile, few of them were able to obtain the refugee status granted to Cubans, Vietnamese, Kuwaitis, and others at various times during the Cold War.

El Salvador and the Alliance for Progress

El Salvador became the pride of Kennedy's (and later Johnson's) Alliance for Progress; it received more Alliance aid than any other Central American country between 1961 and 1965. U.S. support for military strongmen in El Salvador seemed to be the best antidote to communist threats and controversial reforms. With military force used to provide political peace, U.S. investment in El Salvador increased significantly during the 1960s, contributing to one of the highest economic growth rates (12 percent) in the mid-1960s. At first the Salvadoran oligarchs hated the Alliance, calling it a socialist experiment inspired by communists. Later, wealthy Salvadorans learned to turn Alliance for Progress funding into healthy profits and keep control of the new industries generating the wealth. The efforts to diversify its export base had disastrous results for El Salvador, as land under cultivation for food decreased while land used for coffee cultivation increased. By the time of the Soccer War in 1969, hundreds of thousands of Salvadorans had fled to Honduras in search of land, food, and work (see Chapter 16).

Human Rights and the Carter Administration

When Jimmy Carter became president in 1977 he significantly altered the direction of Central American policy by supporting the pursuit of human rights. In an attempt to distance his administration from the more repressive elements in El Salvador, Carter viewed the coup by reformist military officers in late 1979 as a key event that figured well for an improved relationship. Carter was not always successful in his human rights efforts, but he seemed serious in his rhetoric and made determined efforts to integrate human rights into the normal conduct of American foreign policy. Nevertheless, Carter's human rights policies provoked considerable controversy in Washington and throughout Latin America. The former governor of California, Ronald Reagan, and congressional critics argued that Carter's human rights policy in Central America was a misguided sacrifice of real U.S. interests in the region. Once he was elected president, Ronald Reagan embarked on an aggressive public campaign to reverse Carter's human rights efforts.

El Salvador and the Reagan Administration

El Salvador became the public focus of the battle over human rights policy in the 1980s with the U.S. Congress as the central battleground. When asked on *Meet the Press* in March 1981 if he thought leftist guerrillas in El Salvador were in control of or being dominated by communists, Secretary of State Alexander Haig Jr. answered: "There's no question about

"I'd Like to Demonstrate the Advantages of a Free Market Economy . . ."

that. . . . the command and control of communications . . . has been implanted in El Salvador, which manipulates the rebel activity, it is centralized *outside* of El Salvador."[4] As the human rights situation in Central America worsened, the legislative battle resulted in a legal requirement that the president certify human rights progress in El Salvador prior to the release of U.S. assistance. The Reagan administration countered by ignoring the facts of massive human rights violations in El Salvador in its certifications, and by fighting to weaken any further legislation. Despite the strains in applying international human rights standards to Central America, by the end of the Reagan administration there remained considerable bipartisan support in Congress—and from the general public—of the importance of human rights to American foreign policy. In a report from the Arms Control and Foreign Policy Caucus entitled "Bankrolling Failure" in late 1987, Congress concluded that the military solution to the civil war the Reagan administration was pursuing was both unsuccessful and unworkable. The U.S. media struggled to expose the lies and deceptions about El Salvador from an administration determined to define El Salvador in terms of a simple East-West struggle, but press reports often had little effect in reversing policy.

While the goal of the Carter administration had been to snuff the life out of the Monroe Doctrine, the Reagan administration retrieved the Doctrine from the diplomatic closet and tried to apply it to El Salvador in an effort to score a victory against the guerrilla insurgency of the Frente Farabundo Martí de Liberación Nacional (FMLN) and its allied groups. In offering huge amounts of military and economic assistance to El Salvador, a harsh and repressive regime fighting a leftist insurgency with support from governments outside the hemisphere, the Reagan administration applied the Kennan Corollary to the Monroe Doctrine and paid little attention to the absence of democracy and gross human rights violations. Robert E. White, appointed U.S. ambassador to El Salvador by the Carter administration as a symbol of the importance of human rights, was openly critical of the Salvadoran government and its allied death squads. However, 10 days after Reagan's inauguration White was fired for not following the new party line. Other diplomatic holdovers from the Carter years suffered the same fate, frequently being pressured to leave careers in the Foreign Service for expressing doubts about Reagan's Central American policy.

According to some of President Reagan's supporters, the Monroe Doctrine justifed the president's war in Central America. In 1981, former president Richard Nixon invoked the Monroe Doctrine to support U.S. military action in El Salvador. Senator Steven Symms of Idaho proprosed a joint resolution in Congress that reinstituted the Monroe Doctrine by asserting its authority to protect the Western Hemisphere from Marxism-Leninism. It passed both houses of Congress by overwhelming majorities in 1982. One year later, conservative Howard Philips asserted that any attempt to negotiate with "Communists" in the Western Hemisphere constituted a violation of the Monroe Doctrine.

El Salvador and the Kissinger Commission Report

After a quick fact-finding trip to Central America in 1983, the bipartisan Kissinger Commission found the brutality of civil war in El Salvador beyond belief: government-associated death squads had killed at least 1,300 people during the previous year without any murder convictions. When the Commission issued its report on Central America in 1984, revolutions were considered to be the result of hostile outside forces—Cuba backed by the Soviet Union working through Nicaragua—and El Salvador was considered to be one of the victims of this strategy. Therefore, the Commission recommended significantly increased levels of military aid and counterinsurgency capabilities for the Salvadoran government. Although the Commission recommended that increased military aid should be contingent on demonstrated progress toward free elections and termination of the activities of the death squads, during the Reagan administration not a single military officer was convicted for the tens of thousands of death-squad murders and other crimes. In the case of El Salvador, Washington "unwittingly hastened the death of the Monroe Doctrine by associating it with torture, death squads, and the very denial of democratic ideals that the original doctrine honored and vowed to protect."[5] Eventually Presidents Reagan and Bush put pressure on the Salvadoran government to give up its repressive tactics and disregard for human rights, and they encouraged the United Nations to take an active role in negotiating a peaceful solution to a conflict that had been so costly and misunderstood.

Major Blowtorch and the Death Squads

Between 1979 and 1985, almost 40,000 people were murdered by right-wing death squads in El Salvador. The most notorious symbol of Salvador's death squads during this period was Roberto d'Aubuisson, a former military figure known as "Major Blowtorch" because of his zeal as a torturer during the time he headed the National Guard's intelligence office. D'Aubuisson was the product of Salvadoran military academies and a "Hall of Fame" graduate of the U.S. Army School of the Americas in Panama, in each case receiving instruction from U.S. military officers in Cold War doctrine. A cunning and charismatic figure, d'Aubuisson became the leader of the Salvadoran death squads—an alliance between far-right military officers and the oligarchy—until his death in 1992. Documents that were uncovered in the early 1980s indicate he ordered the assassination of Archbishop Oscar Arnulfo Romero in March 1980 and had a hand in the rape and murder of three American nuns and a lay worker, and the murders of two American land reform advisors and the head of Salvador's land reform program. To the disbelief of many critics, the Reagan administration claimed not to be able to determine who was behind the killings even though d'Aubuisson often used national television to denounce teachers, students, union organizers, and politicians as communists. Within a matter of days their mutilated bodies would be discovered in one of El Salvador's many killing fields. He denied the existence (and coverup) of the massacre of the villagers of El Mozote, carried out by the elite U.S.-trained Atlacatl Battalion in 1981.

Although the U.S. Embassy in San Salvador and top officials in the Reagan administration had clear evidence of d'Aubuisson's involvement in death squad activities, no overt move was made to curb the death squads or cut off U.S. assistance. D'Aubuisson thrived because top officials in Washington feared a communist takeover in El Salvador and were willing to look the other way as long as "communists" were being killed. The responsibility for this misguided policy of Cold War indifference to violence and terrorism began with President Reagan and included William Casey, Judge William Clark, Alexander Haig Jr., George Bush, Jeanne Kirkpatrick, Jesse Helms and his congressional staff, and Lt. Col. Oliver North. The carnage that was left in El Salvador as a result of the civil war was as much an American tragedy as it was a reflection of a society torn by past patterns of injustice and oligarchic domination.

EL SALVADOR AND THE UNITED STATES AFTER THE COLD WAR

As the last U.S. president during the Cold War, George Bush recognized the importance of human rights in foreign policy, especially in places like El Salvador. Convinced that the United States was no longer threatened by Soviet-Cuban proxies in El Salvador, Bush increased pressure on El Salvador to improve its human rights record, particularly after the events of late 1989 that contributed to the assassination by death squad of six Jesuit priests. To begin the search for peace, President Alfredo Cristiani was pressured to negotiate with the FMLN rebels; after a period of tension and prodding, a peace agreement was reached between the ARENA (Alianza Republicana Nacionalista) government and the FMLN in December 1991. This promised to put an end to Salvador's long war.

The Agony of Demilitarization, Accountability, and Democratization

Under United Nations supervision, the Salvadoran government struggled to reduce the size of its bloated armed forces and the FMLN rebels made strides in disbanding its forces so as to reconstitute itself as an opposition political party. Efforts to bring to justice the perpetrators of the thousands of murders and other human rights violations of the past decade were less successful. In 1993 a UN Truth Commission report condemned top military and government officials (70 percent of the human rights violations and killings were found to have been committed by government forces) for a good part of the brutal war, and by implication the policies of the Reagan administration that had strengthened and sustained them over a 10-year period. Five years after the long civil war, and after more than $670 million in U.S. assistance to rebuild the country, many jobless former combatants have turned to drug trafficking and other criminal activity as a means of economic survival. In 1998 all four of the Salvadoran national guardsmen convicted of killing the U.S. nuns in 1980 admitted from prison that they acted only after receiving orders from their superiors. Although the Truth Commission found that two National Guard officers had organized a coverup of military complicity in the killing, both men have been granted residence in the United States and currently live in Florida. The U.S. State Department continues to maintain that the killers acted on their own and is apparently unable to explain the circumstances under which the two Salvadoran generals were allowed the right of residence in the United States.

El Salvador has made a remarkable transition from destruction and disarray during the 1980s to peaceful efforts at economic integration and political reconciliation. With peace and trade liberalization in the air, El Salvador's economy has been growing at an average annual rate of 6 percent. With the help of consultant Michael Porter, a Harvard professor of economics, El Salvador is engaged in reforms designed to deregulate and attract foreign investment, and other economic innovations. To reach the global market, El Salvador's new economy has spawned sweat shops (factories that rely on young and cheap workers) that contribute to an overworked and underpaid labor force. Efforts to humanize some of the recent economic reforms have led to significant political gains by the leftist FMLN, now a legal political party. In 1997 it won San Salvador's municipal elections and now represents over half of El Salvador's urban dwellers.

CONCLUSION

U.S. involvement in El Salvador has often been the result of domestic crises that were perceived as requiring military intervention or other forms of assistance. Despite its small size and vulnerability, El Salvador was never occupied by U.S. military forces and was largely ignored by Washington until 1960. Nevertheless, today the United States is the dominant external power in El Salvador even though at times it has been unsuccessful in preventing the emergence of social and political forces hostile to its interests. The United States failed to obtain the military defeat of the Salvadoran guerrillas, despite the expenditure of vast amounts of resources on the U.S.-backed Salvadoran armed forces. The recent peace agreement reached with the assistance of the United Nations and the OAS would have been next to impossible during the Cold War. By the end of the Cold War, the United States had little choice but to accept the former guerrillas as a legitimate political force and welcome the role of international organizations to reach a peaceful solution. Unfortunately, to reach this point Washington had to spend over $6 billion and administer 10 years of misguided policymaking in a failed effort to defeat the Salvadoran guerrilla forces.

NOTES

1. John H. Coatsworth, *Central America and the United States: The Clients and the Colossus* (New York: Twayne Publishers, 1994), p. 39.

2. Tommie Sue Montgomery, *Revolution in El Salvador: Origins and Evolution* (Boulder, CO: Westview Press, 1982), p. 52.

3. Quoted in Lester D. Langley, *Central America: The Real Stakes* (Chicago: Dorsey Press, 1985), p. 68.

4. Secretary of State Alexander Haig Jr., "Interview on Meet the Press" (March 29, 1981), emphasis added. The U.S. Department of State published the interview as part of its public affairs service (*Current Policy*, No. 271).

5. Gaddis Smith, *The Last Years of the Monroe Doctrine, 1945–1993* (New York: Hill and Wang, 1994), p. 71.

SUGGESTED READINGS

Anderson, Thomas P. *Matanza: El Salvador's Communist Revolt of 1932*. Lincoln: University of Nebraska Press, 1971.

Bonner, Raymond. *Weakness and Deceit: U.S. Policy and El Salvador*. New York: Times Books, 1984.

Byrne, Hugh. *El Salvador's Civil War: A Study of Revolution*. Boulder, CO: Lynne Rienner, 1996.

Conroy, Michael E., Douglas L. Murray, and Peter M. Rosset. *A Cautionary Tale: Failed U.S. Development Policy in Central America*. Boulder, CO: Lynne Rienner, 1996.

Danner, Mark. *The Massacre at El Mozote: A Parable of the Cold War*. New York: Vintage, 1994.

Montgomery, Tommie Sue. *Revolution in El Salvador: Origins and Evolution*. Boulder, CO: Westview Press, 1982.

12

Grenada

TIMELINE OF U.S. RELATIONS WITH GRENADA

1877	Grenada becomes a Crown Colony
1950	Eric Gairy organizes poor agricultural laborers and a political party
1950–1979	Gairy dominates Grenadian politics
1973	New Jewel Movement (NJM) is founded by Maurice Bishop and Kendrik Radix
1974	Grenada achieves independence from Britain
1979	Prime Minister Gairy is removed in bloodless coup
1979–1983	Revolutionary Government of Maurice Bishop introduces socialist programs
1979	Diplomatic relations are established between Grenada and Cuba
1981	Concern arises over "communist" expansion in Grenada
1983	Bishop is removed in a coup, then is assassinated
	U.S. military forces invade Grenada
1984	Pro-U.S. leader wins first postrevolutionary election
1985	U.S. troops leave Grenada; economic aid is terminated in 1986
1996	Grenada opposes U.S. proposal to construct a military base on the island

INTRODUCTION

Until its independence from Britain in 1974, Grenada—the southernmost of the Windward Islands in the West Indies—was of little interest to the United States. It served as a colony of France until the end of the eighteenth century and then experienced a long period of British rule. Despite its small size, limited resources, and emotional and economic dependence on other nations, Grenada did have geostrategic importance for Britain and France as they quarreled for possession of the island. As one of the least developed microstates in the Caribbean Basin, Grenada struggled with an agriculturally based economy that was dependent on the export of sugar, bananas, cacao, and nutmeg. Slavery was the institution that best served the colonies, and it was responsible for the large African influence in the Caribbean.

Although the United States relied on its European allies to maintain security in their Caribbean colonies up through World War II, the advent of the Cold War and British efforts to disengage with dignity from the Caribbean territories heightened Washington's concern in the region. After a bloodless coup removed the corrupt and mismanaged government of Eric Gairy in 1979 and replaced it with a revolutionary one with a socialist orientation, U.S. interest in Grenada expanded dramatically. With the establishment of a People's Revolutionary Government (PRG) under the leadership of Maurice Bishop, the United States—first under President Carter and then under President Reagan—became concerned about Grenada's radical foreign policy, which included close ties with several communist countries. Although the Carter administration was concerned about the revolution in Grenada, it only applied economic and political pressure on the new government. After several years of tension and bitterness over the threat of Bishop's revolution in Grenada, the Reagan administration used military force to overthrow the People's Revolutionary Government in 1983, a move that some people in Washington felt reflected the spirit of the Monroe Doctrine. After the U.S. invasion, Washington quickly forgot Grenada after producing a pro-U.S. leader backed with large amounts of economic assistance. The United States now had little to fear that Grenada would serve as an outpost of some extra-hemispheric power, help to spread revolution throughout the region as another Cuba, or upset the strategic balance between the United States and the Soviet Union.

GRENADA DURING THE NINETEENTH CENTURY

During the nineteenth century Grenada remained a colony of European powers, first by the French (until 1763) and then by over 200 years of British colonial rule. The colonial experience resulted in the importation of African slaves and European culture; this eventually led to numerous rebellions and insurrections that required military power to crush. The French and British engaged in a tug-of-war with Grenada until it was restored to British control in 1783. Under the British, slavery increased and efforts were made to suppress the Roman Catholic faith introduced earlier by the French. As the condition of Grenadian slaves worsened toward the end of the eighteenth century, rebellions increased and soon became slave insurrections. The most serious occurred in 1795 when Julien Fedon, a Grenadian mulatto, led a slave insurrection in hopes of restoring French rule. It took the British 15 months to end the revolt, but foreign domination continued to influence economic and political life on the island.

When slavery was abolished in 1838—largely the result of economic competition from larger sugar producers in the Caribbean—Grenada's plantation owners shifted from sugar production to spices, particularly nutmeg and cacao. European domination throughout the Caribbean in the nineteenth century set the stage for the revolutionary upheavals that became more frequent in the twentieth century. By the time Grenada became a Crown Colony of the British in 1877, commercial activities had created a native bourgeoisie that opposed the domination of the island's economic and political life by the British Crown and local plantocracy, or ruling planter class.

Anglo-American Relations and the Monroe Doctrine

When Spain's King Ferdinand VII suggested in 1823 that the major European powers help restore his throne and American colonies, both the United States and Britain became alarmed. In a prelude to the Monroe Doctrine, British foreign secretary George Canning suggested a joint Anglo-American statement that Spanish American territories were closed to future colonization. Although President Monroe was impressed with the proposal, John Quincy Adams, his secretary of state, opposed the offer, claiming that America's best interests lay in a *unilateral* pronouncement of the legitimacy of Latin American independence. Monroe's message to Congress in late 1823 rejected Canning's overture, but it contained important implications for Anglo-American relations throughout the rest of the nineteenth century. Monroe's warning to European monarchies was enforceable only by the British navy; the United States would have to wait until the 1890s to put teeth into the Monroe Doctrine. By 1901 the British had signed several treaties with the United States that in effect conceded naval and military supremacy to Washington in Central America and the Caribbean.

GRENADA AND THE UNITED STATES DURING THE EARLY TWENTIETH CENTURY

After the Spanish-American War in 1898 and the creation of Panama in 1903, commercial and security interests in the Caribbean became more important to the United States. To consolidate its power in the Spanish- and French-speaking Caribbean after 1900, the United States established protectorates, intervened and occupied several countries, and applied diplomatic nonrecognition and other forms of coercion to protect its interests. To help protect the Panama Canal's Atlantic approaches, the United States purchased the Danish Virgin Islands in 1914, and during the 1930s the Franklin D. Roosevelt administration considered annexing the English-speaking British colonies in the Lesser Antilles. In the Anglo-American agreement of 1940, the United States traded 50 warships to the Royal Navy for the construction and operation of a string of U.S. Air Force bases from the Bahamas to Trinidad and British Guiana. In addition to the strategic value of the British Caribbean, substantial amounts of war-related raw materials such as oil and bauxite constituted other reasons to control shipping lanes from Venezuela to the United States. After World War II, the United States relied on its European allies to maintain security in their colonies. The one exception was British Guiana (which became independent as Guyana in 1966). In 1964 there was Anglo-American collaboration to remove the Marxist regime of Cheddi Jagan, followed by electoral manipulation to ensure the accession to power of Forbes Burnham, a more suitable ally for Washington during the Cold War and the rising tensions in the Caribbean in the aftermath of the Cuban revolution (see Chapter 14).

GRENADA AND THE UNITED STATES DURING THE COLD WAR

The Rise of Power of Eric Gairy

Grenada's transition from colony to island self-rule is rooted in labor politics and the charisma of Eric Gairy, who dominated the political scene through his organization and leadership of poor agricultural workers. Born into a poor family in 1922, Gairy developed populist ideas and programs through observing the conflicts between the extreme poverty of poor workers and the wealth of economic and political elites on the island. In 1950 he organized the Grenada Manual and Metal Worker's Union (GMMWU) and founded the Grenada United Labour Party (GULP) in an effort to mobilize agricultural laborers. By leading violent strikes and demonstrations, Gairy was able to wring wage concessions from wealthy landowners and soon became a key figure in achieving independence from the British.

Although he positioned himself as a champion of the dispossessed, Gairy soon gravitated toward enriching himself and ruling in a corrupt and authoritarian manner. Prior to independence Gairy was repeatedly censured for "squandermania" (misappropriating public funds), condemned for using his security forces to murder and brutalize his opposition, and criticized for his generally incompetent administration. Furthermore, he humiliated Grenadians by claiming that God had anointed him to rule and by giving lectures at the United Nations and other international organizations about the need for psychic research and the investigation of flying saucers.

After becoming Grenada's first prime minister on achieving independence in 1974, Eric Gairy became even more repressive and autocratic, generating further opposition on the island and general condemnation throughout the Caribbean. However, since Gairy's government was pro-Western in its foreign policy, the United States ignored the human rights abuses and absence of democracy in Grenada. According to Gaddis Smith, "He proclaimed his anti-Communism, caused no trouble for the United States, and admired the Pinochet regime in Chile."[1]

The greatest challenge to Gairyism came from Maurice Bishop and Kendrik Radix after they founded the New Jewel Movement (NJM)—a leftist party with a large membership base—in 1973 to counter the Gairy dictatorship. Bishop, 22 years younger than Gairy, was a gifted politician who clashed with Gairy's security forces and competed for the same working-class constituents. Trained in law in England, Bishop soon impressed Grenadians with his ability to articulate the needs and concerns of the average person. Bishop was elected to the Grenadian parliament in 1976 and became the prime mover in the opposition to put an end to the Gairy dictatorship.

The Grenadian Revolution, 1979–1983

Problems with Grenada's agriculturally based economy and the corrupt and repressive nature of Gairy's government served as the catalyst for the nearly bloodless coup that toppled the Gairy regime. On March 13, 1979, while Prime Minister Gairy was on a visit to New York City, members of the New Jewel Movement seized power, suspended the independence constitution, and established a People's Revolutionary Government (PRG) under the leadership of Maurice Bishop and his deputy prime minister, Bernard Coard, a self-proclaimed Marxist. A joyous crowd sang in celebration of the end of Gairy: "Freedom come, Gairy go, Gairy gone with UFO." Although the new government assured everyone of its moderate and constitutional goals, the coup that brought the PRG government to power was the first unconstitutional change of government in the English-speaking Caribbean and produced unprecedented tensions throughout the region.

The Carter administration recognized the Bishop government despite its socialist orientation and the fact that it had overthrown an elected government. However, shortly after securing recognition the PRG shifted to a more radical foreign policy that included diplomatic and economic ties with the Soviet Union, other Eastern bloc countries, and Castro's Cuba. Growing military relations with Cuba brought a message of concern from the American ambassador, Frank Ortiz, but this backfired when Prime Minister Bishop publicly denounced the United States for meddling in Grenada's affairs. A few days later Bishop criticized U.S. efforts to dictate Grenadian foreign relations, and he went on to say "We are not in anybody's back yard," an effort to defuse the symbolism of the Monroe Doctrine that portrayed the United States as the "natural protector" of the hemisphere. Rather than confront the PRG head on, the Carter administration decided to assist the democratic governments in the Caribbean region in matters concerning economic development and regional security, while at the same time withholding aid and rejecting overtures for better relations from the Bishop administration.

After Ronald Reagan became president in 1981, Bishop's Grenada became a outcast state to U.S. policymakers, part of the growing perception of communist expansion in the Caribbean. Tensions increased with the knowledge that Grenada had brought in Cuban military advisors and that Cuban construction crews were building a long runway at the international airport, ostensibly to assist the local economy by expanding the tourist trade. The Reagan administration exerted added pressure on the island by refusing to accept the credentials of the country's ambassador to the United States and deliberately excluded Grenada and Nicaragua from economic assistance programs such as the Caribbean Basin Initiative (CBI), a preferential trade program with political overtones. Prime Minister Bishop charged the United States with intentions of invading his island, and President Reagan countered with additional anticommunist charges. On a trip to Barbados in 1982 Reagan declared that Grenada had teamed up with Cuba, the Soviet Union, and Nicaragua to "spread the virus" of international communism among its Caribbean neighbors. In a March 1983 speech announcing the Strategic Defense Initiative, President Reagan linked the construction of the Point Salines airport's new runway to the security of the United States, claiming (with no evidence) that it was intended to enhance global military goals of the Soviet Union and Cuba.

Operation Urgent Fury

Tensions continued to mount inside Grenada as the PRG government continued down its revolutionary path. By late 1983 a split in the Central Committee of the PRG resulted in the arrest and imprisonment of Prime Minister Bishop and his closest followers, followed by their execution and a declaration of martial law by the hardline faction. The execution of Bishop and his supporters prompted discussion among the United States and some members of the Organization of East Caribbean States (OECS) regarding the possibility of a military operation in Grenada. In a meeting of the heads of government of OECS members on October 21, 1983, it was agreed that a package of economic and political sanctions be applied to Grenada's newly formed Revolutionary Military Council (RMC) and that a request (encouraged by policymakers in Washington) be made to the United States to intervene in order to establish law and order.

In the meantime, at the National Security Council in Washington the newly appointed Latin American specialist, Constantine Menges, soon recognized how the turmoil on the island could serve as a pretext for a U.S. military invasion together with a small force from the nearby islands in the eastern Caribbean. Four days after the OECS meeting of October 21, the Reagan administration orchestrated Operation Urgent Fury with the landing of 6,000 troops (including 300 from the Commonwealth Caribbean force) in Grenada to liberate the people of Grenada, safeguard U.S. citizens (mostly American medical students), and demonstrate general American resolve after the humiliating deaths of over 200 U.S. Marines in Lebanon a few days earlier.

President Reagan justified the U.S. action in terms of protecting "innocent lives," ending the "chaos," and restoring "law, order, and democratic institutions" in Grenada. Although Grenada was a member of the British Commonwealth and had a governor general who served as representative of the Crown, the United States did not consult the British government in advance of the invasion, an omission that produced a sharp rebuke from Margaret Thatcher. The action provoked great controversy, especially among the Latin American states, because they argued that the Organization of American States (OAS), not the OECS, was the appropriate regional body to handle the crisis and the United States was not a member of the latter. The United States countered this criticism by arguing that the OECS was a subregional organization under the OAS and therefore an appropriate vehicle for dealing with turmoil on the island. The international reaction to the invasion was mostly negative, but the American public approved of Reagan's action because they perceived it as quick, relatively inexpensive, and decisive.

The U.S. military invasion was definitely *not* a well-executed effort to remove a Marxist government from the Caribbean, and a post-invasion army investigation under Lt. Col. Norman Schwartzkopf revealed and admitted such. For example, it took almost a week to rescue the 1,000 U.S. citizens, defeat the Cuban and Grenadian forces, and restore order. The invasion cost $75 million. The casualty figures included 18 Americans (mostly from friendly fire), 45 Grenadians, and 29 Cubans. Despite the loss of life and the rebuke from international organizations such as the United Nations, the Reagan administration viewed the intervention as an important triumph over hostile forces and a military success for the United States in the aftermath of the Vietnam debacle. Legal arguments that demonstrated U.S. actions violated the nonintervention principle of the OAS charter, the alienation of Latin American allies, and the invalidity of claims that Grenada was being readied for a major Soviet bloc military base—all mattered little to the Reagan administration when an important Cold War victory (one of the few produced by force) could be declared.

The invasion of Grenada in 1983 marked the first time the United States had intervened military in an English-speaking Caribbean country, and it was the first U.S. military intervention in the Caribbean since the Dominican crisis of 1965. Reagan's invasion grew out of rising tensions with the Soviet Union and the nettlesome Nicaraguans, who were the target of a variety of U.S. counter-revolutionary efforts to eliminate the Sandinistas. It was designed in large part to send a warning to Cuba's Fidel Castro (and indirectly the Soviet Union) to stay out of the Caribbean. Reagan could now claim a military victory, something no American president had been able to do since President Johnson invaded the Dominican Republic to prevent a "second Cuba" in 1965. Although not invoked in name, the Monroe Doctrine remained very much alive in 1983; by defeating the tiny Grenadian forces and expelling a small contingent of Cuban workers extending an airport runway, the Reagan administration had defused a perceived strategic threat and brought life to the Monroe Doctrine. In his memoirs, Reagan wrote that "I probably never felt better during my presidency than I did that day."[2]

GRENADA AND THE UNITED STATES AFTER THE COLD WAR

U.S. troops were withdrawn from Grenada by mid-December 1983, and new elections were held in the following year. To ensure the election of a pro-U.S. leader, the CIA spent $675,000 and the Reagan administration promised the new government $48 million in economic assistance. Herbert Blaize, representing the New National Party (NNP), was elected prime minister and soon developed a close friendship with the Reagan administration. Until his death in 1989 Blaize carried out reprisals against former backers of the Bishop regime (although he commuted the death sentences of the major conspirators), expanded tourism into the country's major industry (with the completion of the Point Salines airport), and received large amounts of U.S. economic assistance. After perceived threats to Grenada's security subsided, the Reagan administration terminated its economic assistance in 1986. Nicolas Brathwaithe followed Blaize as prime minister after another election in 1990, and his government made efforts to reconcile the major divisions in Grenadian society that were left over from the Gairy era and the revolution between 1979 and 1983. Grenada's importance to the United States surfaced again in 1996 when the Clinton administration proposed sending a detachment of Marines to Grenada to build a small military base so that the Grenada Coast Guard would be in a stronger position to combat hemispheric drug trafficking. Memories of the 1983 intervention and small-island nationalism combined to generate serious objections on grounds of national sovereignty that caught the United States by surprise.

CONCLUSION

The history of U.S. involvement in Grenada has been minimal and sporadic. Content to let European allies deal with the island's internal economic and political struggles, the United States could easily ignore the island since it posed no threat to its security or access to important raw materials. However, when Grenada embarked on a revolutionary path that included close ties with Cuba, Sandinista Nicaragua, and the Soviet Union, U.S. displeasure escalated. The U.S. invasion of Grenada was a major event in the annals of foreign policy, both for the United States and Grenada. It was significant for the United States because it was the first direct military intervention after the Vietnam War, and the outcome had a valuable demonstration effect for other leftist governments in the Western Hemisphere that the Reagan administration disliked. It proved to be a valuable confirmation of the administration's resolve to use force when ideologically necessary, and it contributed to Reagan's winning the 1984 presidential election. The assassination of Prime Minister Bishop and the violent termination of the PRG government at the hands of U.S. military forces was a humbling experience for newly independent Grenada. A large number of Grenadians welcomed the invasion, calling it a "rescue mission." Although Operation Urgent Fury launched a new centrist government under de facto U.S. control, Grenada still faced the difficult task of political reconstruction and economic self-sufficiency. With the Cold War over, Grenada must refocus its political agenda on global issues by means of its historical and economic ties to Europe, and as a member of the Organization of American States and other international organizations.

NOTES

1. Gaddis Smith, *The Last Years of the Monroe Doctrine: 1945–1993* (New York: Hill and Wang, 1994), p. 179.
2. Ronald Reagan, *An American Life* (New York: Simon and Schuster, 1990), p. 457.

SUGGESTED READINGS

Beck, Robert. *The Grenada Invasion: Politics, Law, and Foreign Policy*. Boulder, CO: Westview Press, 1993.
Burrowes, Reynold A. *Revolution and Rescue in Grenada*. Westport, CT: Greenwood Press, 1988.
Heine, Jorge, ed. *A Revolution Aborted: The Lessons of Grenada*. Pittsburgh: University of Pittsburgh Press, 1990.
Schoenahals, Kai, and Richard Melanson. *Revolution and Intervention in Grenada*. Boulder, CO: Westview Press, 1985.

13

Guatemala

TIMELINE OF U.S. RELATIONS WITH GUATEMALA

1821	Guatemala declares independence from Spain
1823–1838	Guatemala becomes part of Central American Federation
1850	Clayton-Bulwer Treaty is signed between United States and Britain
1856–1858	William Walker's filibustering activities affect Guatemala
1871–1885	Justo Rufino Barrios rules Guatemala
1880s	Cornelius Logan proposes Guatemalan protectorate over Central America
1897–1920	Manuel Estrada Cabrera rules Guatemala
1899	United Fruit Company is founded
1929	United Fruit merges with Cuyamel
1930–1944	Jorge Ubico rules Guatemala
1944	Ubico is removed from power
1945	Juan José Arévalo is elected president
1950	Jacobo Arbenz is elected president
1952	Operation Fortune attempts to remove Arbenz
1954	Operation Success overthrows Arbenz; the military takes control
1957	Carlos Castillo Armas is assassinated
1960	Guatemala becomes a staging area for Bay of Pigs invasion
	Beginning of 36 years of guerrilla-military warfare
1967	Right-wing death squads begin operation
1969	U.S. embassy personnel are killed in guerrilla attack
1977	President Carter suspends military aid to Guatemala

1980	Ronald Reagan is elected U.S. president
1982	General Efraín Ríos Montt is overthrown in military coup
1986	Democracy returns with election of Vinicio Cerezo
1996	Guatemalan government and guerrilla forces sign peace accord
1997	CIA admits it has records of Guatemala intervention but declassifies less than 1 percent
1998	Bishop Juan Gerardi is murdered after publishing report on human rights violations committed in Guatemala's 36-year war

INTRODUCTION

Located between Honduras and Mexico, Guatemala is the largest of the Central American republics. It has a significant agricultural economy that has generated intense internal struggles and external conflicts since independence from Spain. From the turn of the century multinational fruit companies, working with corrupt Guatemalan dictators, have complicated the relationship between Guatemala and the United States. Armed with negative stereotypes—and little knowledge of Guatemala—policymakers in Washington have tried to manage a society consisting of rebel groups, democratic reformers, a powerful military, conservative landed elites, and foreign interlopers, particularly during times of global and regional turmoil.

The United States rarely used its own military to protect its interests in Guatemala, unlike in other Central American countries. Since Guatemala's independence, the United States has intervened militarily on only one occasion—in 1920—to protect the diplomatic corps and other American interests during a period of civil war. Diplomatic and other forms of U.S. intervention in Guatemala have been sufficient to protect economic and security interests, aided and abetted by what Paul Dosal calls "a corrupt cadre of caudillos who were more interested in personal aggrandizement than in national development."[1] The U.S.-backed overthrow of President Jacobo Arbenz in 1954 marked the end of the Guatemalan revolution begun under Juan José Arévalo 10 years earlier, but its future impact on the rest of Latin America and the United States was profound. It contributed to the radicalization of Ché Guevara, Castro's revolution against Batista in Cuba, the Alliance for Progress, and the Bay of Pigs invasion; and it initiated over 30 years of military-dominated governments, human rights violations, and hundreds of thousands of civilian deaths. The Guatemalan affair during the Eisenhower years was a serious blow to Franklin D. Roosevelt's Good Neighbor Policy and the legitimacy of using international organizations for the peaceful settlement of disputes in the hemisphere. The methods used to remove Arbenz undermined the pledge of nonintervention in the Organization of American States (OAS) charter signed in 1948, and they signaled the use of the OAS by the United States as an anticommunist alliance during the Cold War.

GUATEMALA AND THE UNITED STATES IN THE NINETEENTH CENTURY

The major U.S. concerns in Central America during the nineteenth century were encouraging trade, coping with massive British naval power, and securing an efficient transit route across the isthmus. However, by the 1890s the United States embarked on a burst of extra-continental imperialism, sponsored by such leaders as Theodore Roosevelt, Henry Cabot Lodge, and naval philosopher and strategist Alfred T. Mahan. With the success of the Spanish-American War in 1898, the desire to acquire and control a transisthmian canal led the United States to take Panama from Colombia in 1903, and then to oversee events in Central America. Nicaragua and Panama were the prime locations of U.S. strategic concern, but other countries such as Guatemala were considered close enough to warrant protection from potentially encroaching foreign powers.

The United States and Guatemalan Independence

Guatemala achieved its independence from Spain in 1821 but elected to join the Mexican empire of Agustín de Iturbide in the following year in hopes of securing more stability and prosperity. This option did not work out. When Iturbide's empire collapsed in 1823, the five Central American states created the United Provinces of Central America (Central American Federation) with Guatemala City as the seat of the federal government. Power struggles soon emerged between Liberals and Conservatives over a variety of issues, including land ownership and foreign investment, that led to civil war. This early experiment in unity—modeled after that of the United States—collapsed in 1838, and thereafter Guatemala assumed the status of an independent nation that was nevertheless heavily dependent on British loans and a growing debt. After 1838 Guatemala was ruled by ruthless dictators who received the backing of outside powers—first Britain, and then the United States. The stormy debates and bloody internal strife generated by Liberals and Conservatives in Guatemala continued throughout the nineteenth century and well into the next. From 1838 to 1944, Guatemala was ruled largely by four powerful dictators (José Rafael Carrera, 1838–1865; Justo Rufino Barrios, 1871–1885; Manuel Estrada Cabrera, 1897–1920; and Jorge Ubico Castañeda, 1930–1944) who used the state to improve the economy while encouraging foreign investment. To assist local entrepreneurs, Guatemala's dictators also mobilized cheap Indian labor for the coffee aristocracy by passing forced-labor, debt-servitude, and stiff vagrancy laws. Carrera tyrannized Guatemala in the name of conservatism and the Catholic faith, and with British backing he conducted three wars against neighboring El Salvador, which was backed by American interests.

After independence, Central Americans were generally divided in their attitudes toward U.S. involvement in Guatemala. Conservatives avoided close contact with the United States, fearing that the relationship would infringe on their economic and political power. The other political faction, usually the Liberals, generally favored intimate ties with the United States, arguing that the Monroe Doctrine and the advanced U.S. society would protect them and help in the process of modernization. When the Liberals dominated Guatemala in the late nineteenth century, they made important concessions to private banana and transportation companies from the United States.

Guatemala and the Monroe Doctrine

The first test of U.S. intentions to invoke the Monroe Doctrine to shield Central America from European (mainly British) expansion came in 1835 when Juan Galindo—a Briton who took up Guatemalan citizenship so he could acquire a million-acre tract in the Petén region and Belize—traveled to Washington to try to convince President Andrew Jackson to invoke the Monroe Doctrine after the British had established control over Belize (then British Honduras) in what came to be part of the Miskito Kingdom. Claiming that the British encroachment at Belize was a threat to North American security, Galindo told the Jackson administration that the policy of the United States should be to prevent European settlement in the Americas. However, President Jackson had recently acquiesced to Britain's reoccupation of the Falkland Islands, and he perceived no visible threat to the Monroe Doctrine by the British actions in Central America.

The Monroe Doctrine also came into play during the last two decades of the nineteenth century. During the jingoism (extreme patriotism) of the 1880s Cornelius A. Logan, U.S. minister to Central America, proposed to President Barrios a protectorate over all of Central America under the Guatemalan's leadership. Logan's plan would not only reinvigorate the Monroe Doctrine but also pave the way for the construction of a canal under U.S. control. Barrios liked the plan, pledged cooperation, and sent a special envoy to Washington to formalize the arrangement, but it was turned down by President Rutherford B. Hayes. During the dictatorship of Estrada Cabrera (1897–1920), foreign-bond debt contributed to U.S. efforts to reform Guatemalan fiscal management in the name of the Monroe Doctrine. In 1905, U.S. minister Leslie Combs proposed a financial trusteeship in Guatemala to prevent another European violation of the Monroe Doctrine. At first Estrada Cabrera balked at the plan, calling it an infringement on Guatemalan sovereignty; but after the British threatened to use force against Guatemala in 1913, Estrada Cabrera capitulated and settled the financial mess. Secretary of State William Jennings Bryan feared that if he invoked the Monroe Doctrine against British claims, the United States would be supporting an extremely unpopular dictator. "There was no outcry in the United States over the alleged British violation of the Monroe Doctrine, because in this case Estrada Cabrera was even more unpopular than British interference in the Western Hemisphere."[2] The United States didn't need the Monroe Doctrine to deal with Guatemala between 1920 and 1950 since its interests were well protected by powerful fruit companies working hand-in-glove with Guatemalan dictators.

The Clayton-Bulwer Treaty

After the Mexican War in 1848, U.S. foreign policy shifted to where the British had extended their control over the eastern coast of Central America, known as the Miskito Kingdom. British encroachment prompted negotiations with the United States that culminated in the 1850 Clayton-Bulwer Treaty, one of the most controversial—and far-reaching—in U.S. history until it was nullified by the second Hay-Pauncefote Treaty in 1901 (see Chapter 20). The treaty was negotiated by John M. Clayton, secretary of state, and British special negotiator Sir Henry Bulwer, to settle Anglo-American difficulties in Central America. The urgent domestic crisis in the United States and the Whig Party's policy of compromise with the British helped produce the treaty, which provided for *joint* control over any future transisthmian canal in Central America. After Clayton returned to the Senate, he was attacked by the Young America faction of the Democratic Party for signing a treaty that violated the Monroe Doctrine by permitting the British to "colonize" a part of Central America. By conceding valuable rights to the British in Central America, the Clayton-Bulwer Treaty proved to be a disaster for the Whigs by contributing to a sweeping Democratic victory in 1852 and their disappearance from the electoral map of the United States. Beginning as an anti-Andrew Jackson movement in the 1830s, the Whig Party produced four presidents—William H. Harrison, John Tyler, Zachary Taylor, and Millard Fillmore—between 1841 and 1857, but eventually self-destructed over the slavery issue. President Taylor was a military hero from the Mexican War and a strong proponent of Manifest Destiny and expansionism.

In Central America, the Clayton-Bulwer arrangement was symbolic of the frustration of trying to gain some advantage by maneuvering one power against another, only to discover later that the United States and Britain would withdraw to their own countries and then arrive at some mutually beneficial arrangements. Despite the criticisms of the Clayton-Bulwer Treaty in the United States, the fact that Britain recognized the increasing influence of the United States in the isthmus, and the legitimacy of its claims to build a future canal, proved immensely valuable for American imperialists.

Guatemala and William Walker

Under President Carerra's harsh rule in the 1850s, Guatemala became involved in Central American efforts to fight against William Walker. Walker was part of a group of nineteenth-century North American filibusters who planned and launched private military invasions of Latin America and the Caribbean in an effort to expand slave territory and satisfy personal dreams of wealth and glory. Walker's audacious maneuver to conquer and Americanize Nicaragua helped to mobilize and unify Central American elites against the foreign intervention. Guatemala and Costa Rica provided most of the troops and did most of the fighting, while U.S. and British naval forces aided in the capture of Walker in 1857–1858. Walker returned to the United States to a hero's welcome, regrouped, and carried out two more expeditions before he was captured again and executed by the Hondurans (see Chapters 7, 16, and 19).

Guatemala and the U.S. Civil War

U.S. diplomats expected that Guatemala would be a focal point of North-South competition in Central America because of its size, wealth, and traditional leadership role in Central America. Elisha O. Crosby, U.S. minister to Guatemala between 1861 and 1864, worked to improve relations between the two countries by undermining Confederate efforts to obtain advantages in the country. He criticized Walker's filibustering activities, expressed regret that previous ministers to Guatemala had been Southerners interested in the extension of slavery, and won some Union sympathizers. He failed, however, in his efforts to establish a colony of emancipated blacks in Guatemala because of strong resistance to such an idea.

Conservative governments in Guatemala expressed ambivalent views toward the United States during its secessionist struggle. Guatemala rejected Union objectives—forced unification versus the right of the South to secede—but it also expressed sympathy for the Union because of Southern support for filibustering and territorial expansionism. Guatemala also used the U.S. Civil War to express its opposition to the Monroe Doctrine and Manifest Destiny. For example, Guatemalan minister Antonio José Irisarri told Secretary of State William H. Seward that he resented the Monroe Doctrine because it placed "all Hispanic American states in the sad position of minors submitted to the tutelage of a foreign tutor who governs us as he best sees fit."[3] In criticizing expansionism Irisarri argued that the United

States, during the past several decades, had robbed the Latin American states of their sovereignty, territory, and independence.

Tyranny and Bananas: The Rise of Manuel Estrada Cabrera

The foundations for Guatemala's vast banana empire were laid during the period of Liberal reform beginning in the 1870s, with modernization programs that served the interests of the coffee aristocracy. At the heart of this effort was railroad construction, but it required vast amounts of capital and technology, something Guatemalans were unable or unwilling to provide. The banana industry, in its formative years, was linked to foreign capital and liberal concessions from a string of dictators who ruled Guatemala. Out of the fruit growing of the 1880s and early 1890s would emerge the United Fruit Company (UFC) of Boston—the most important private enterprise in the history of Guatemala and Central America—formed in 1899 from the combination of 20 existing fruit and steamship companies.

The prime mover in creating the United Fruit Company was Minor Cooper Keith, a railroad builder and entrepreneur from Brooklyn, New York. Keith was a master at developing the economic and political infrastructure to move bananas from plantation to market in the most profitable way (see Chapter 7). United Fruit began its first banana production in Guatemala in 1908 and soon monopolized the railroads and banana business, with the help of "friendly dictators." As historian Paul Dosal points out, "United Fruit discovered that it was much more profitable to do business with a dictator than a democratic president."[4] Between 1898 and 1944, Guatemalan dictators provided large parcels of land, freedom from government regulation, and generous concessions that included extremely low taxes.

GUATEMALA AND THE UNITED STATES IN THE TWENTIETH CENTURY

U.S. economic and political leverage over Guatemala was well under way by the dawn of the twentieth century, based in large part on three large companies that monopolized banana production, land ownership, transportation, and electrical facilities. The United Fruit Company (UFC) eventually monopolized banana production and became Guatemala's largest landowner. By 1950 it controlled (directly or indirectly) close to 40,000 jobs in Guatemala, and its investments in the country were valued at $60 million. UFC cultivated 85 percent of the tropical lowlands suitable for banana production, although this was only a small fraction of its total land holdings. International Railways of Central America (IRCA), a subsidiary of United Fruit, owned nearly every mile of railroad track in Guatemala.

Electric Bond and Share (EBS) controlled 100 percent of Guatemala's electrical facilities. For close to five decades, UFC was a colossus built around political power, generous concessions, and large privileges. United Fruit also had a bevy of friends and supporters in Washington that helped to solidify its ability to perpetuate its power. From the beginning of the twentieth century, United Fruit was *the* major player in the Guatemalan economy. After UFC merged with Cuyamel Fruit Company in 1929, Samuel Zemurray replaced Minor C. Keith as the driving force behind United Fruit Company in Guatemala (see Chapter 16).

The United States and Ubico: Prelude to Revolution

After the death of Estrada Cabrera in 1920, Guatemala experienced a brief democratic interlude and then more undemocratic governments before the 14-year dictatorship of Jorge Ubico (1930–1944). Ubico seemed like a reliable and friendly dictator; he had worked closely with the Rockefeller Foundation and catered to the United Fruit Company. The son of a politician and wealthy coffee planter, Ubico worked his way to the top during the Estrada Cabrera dictatorship by displaying organizational skills in the military and local politics. Good at resolving political crises and restoring order, Ubico soon became a favorite of the Liberal oligarchy and the United States. After winning a fraudulent election in 1931, Ubico ruled Guatemala until 1944. An admirer of Napoleon, Ubico surrounded himself with busts and paintings of the great French general. His method of imposing a strict political order on Guatemala spared the local oligarchy and foreign companies from the demands of popular democratic forces. Severe distortion in landownership—98 percent of all cultivated land was owned by 142 people—formed the basis of reformist efforts to reverse this pattern between 1945 and 1954. Washington seemed pleased when General Ubico was overthrown in 1944, but it remained in doubt concerning the motives of the revolutionaries led by Juan José Arevalo, Jacobo Arbenz, and Jorge Toriello.

GUATEMALA AND THE UNITED STATES DURING THE COLD WAR

During World War II the United States stationed thousands of troops in Guatemala to defend the distant Panama Canal and various economic interests. Dictator Ubico helped to counter Nazi and German influences in Guatemala. After World War II the United States continued to focus its attention on economic and security concerns, but with a heightened interest in containing Soviet-inspired communism. The Monroe Doctrine was applied regionally to contain the expansion of Soviet influence since policymakers in Washington believed that Latin America was a prime target for Soviet military strategists.

Democratic Reform in Guatemala

The downfall of Ubico and unsuccessful efforts to continue the old regime fed the opposition forces led by disgruntled military officers—Jacobo Arbenz and Francisco Arana—and civilians who demanded national elections and a democratic revolution. The junta government (known as the "October Revolution") scheduled elections, won easily by Juan José Arévalo in 1945, and set out to make the capitalist system more responsive to the needs of the downtrodden. The young Guatemalans who helped topple Ubico were mostly doctors, lawyers, teachers, and students who sought to rid the nation of its dictatorial past. During his six years in office (1945–1951), Arévalo opened up the political system by respecting freedom of speech and press and allowing political parties to form and compete for office. Labor unions were encouraged and given favorable treatment by the government, and the large Indian population received numerous benefits from the new government. Arévalo's domestic reforms produced both excitement and confusion as nationalist and anti-imperialist forces pushed him to radically alter the wealth and power of the United Fruit Company. Many of his supporters believed that UFC—controlled by U.S. stockholders, and the beneficiary of lucrative contracts with prior dictators—exploited Guatemala for the benefit of foreigners. Although they were not interpreted as such, Arévalo's reforms were modeled in many ways after Roosevelt's New Deal.

As Arévalo's left-of-center policies gained support among the workers and dispossessed, the Guatemalan elite and middle class became concerned about the nature of the new society that was being put in place. Although Arévalo was opposed to communism, his critics labeled him and his supporters "communists" and conspired to bring about his downfall. The United States, confused about the nationalist character of Arévalo's politics, felt that the disparity of wealth and land ownership in Guatemala made the country ripe for communist expansion in the hemisphere. Washington's concern with Guatemalan communism continued after Jacobo Arbenz succeeded Arévalo in March 1951.

To protect U.S. business interests in Guatemala, the Truman administration appointed Richard C. Patterson Jr. as ambassador in 1948. Patterson's anticommunism and blustering manner undermined U.S.-Guatemalan relations and eventually led to his recall to Washington. He continued to speak out concerning what he considered the communist dangers in Guatemala. In his speeches around the United States, he devised the "duck test" as a practical method of detecting whether a certain individual is a communist or not.[5] Patterson's interference in Guatemala—although never explicitly authorized by the Department of State—contributed to the radicalization of Guatemalan politics under Arévalo, the polarization of domestic politics, and increasing U.S. hostility.

Once Arbenz was elected in 1950, Guatemalan politics moved further to the left by promoting agrarian reform, courting the Communist Party, and stubbornly defying the United States. As he amplified his revolutionary program, Arbenz weakened his ties to the Guatemalan military and betrayed the hopes of the Truman administration for Guatemala. His gradual radicalization moved him closer to the leaders of the fledgling Communist Party and others on the left (including his Salvadoran wife). Although he was interested in communist ideas, Arbenz could not formally be called a communist and Guatemala never became a Soviet beachhead, but many in Washington thought it was close enough to raise major security concerns for the United States. At the heart of Arbenz's revolutionary program was agrarian reform. This would ultimately require a confrontation with the Guatemalan elite, United Fruit Company, and policymakers in Washington. The Cold War crisis that developed in Guatemala under Arbenz culminated in the first of the many CIA covert schemes to rid the hemisphere of leftist governments.

The Kennan Corollary to the Monroe Doctrine

In March 1950 George Kennan, a Soviet specialist in the State Department, and famous as principal author of the Cold War doctrine of containment, argued that defense of the Monroe Doctrine required that the United States support authoritarian forms of rule to counter the communist menace. After a brief visit to Latin America, Kennan advanced what Gaddis Smith calls the Kennan Corollary to the Monroe Doctrine:

> We cannot be too dogmatic about the methods by which local communists can be dealt with . . . where the concepts and traditions of popular government are too weak to absorb successfully the intensity of communist attack, then we must concede that *harsh measures of government repression* may be . . . the only alternative to further communist success.[6]

The first application of the Kennan Corollary occurred in Guatemala in 1954 when the United States assisted in the removal of Jacobo ("Red Jacobo," as he was known in Washington) Arbenz and his replacement with Carlos Castillo Armas, a military leader who implanted a regime advocated by Kennan. Since Kennan's long memorandum on U.S. Latin American policy was classified "secret" until it was uncovered in the 1980s, it is impossible to know precisely what impact it had on official thinking. Nevertheless, it did offer the Monroe Doctrine as a justification for supporting repressive governments.

Policymakers in Washington had a sense of worldwide danger during the years of the Cold War, but rarely was Latin America considered on its own terms. Invariably the region was viewed in terms of global strategy by the men who crafted U.S. Latin American policy. The foreign policy and national security officials in Washington were well informed on leaders and events outside the hemisphere, but not in Latin America. Few cared about Latin America enough to live there or acquire a rudimentary knowledge of Spanish or Portuguese. Moreover, when officials in Washington did direct their attention to Latin America, their views were often arrogant, prejudiced, and condescending. John Foster Dulles, for example, thought he had figured out how best to deal with Latin Americans: "You have to pat them a little bit and make them think you are fond of them."[7] Dulles knew very little about Latin America—except for brief stints as a corporate lawyer for U.S. companies in Guatemala—and had no interest in inter-American issues unless they surfaced as a side issue in his global crusade against communism. He was a firm believer in friendly dictators because he reasoned they were more dependable than other kinds of leaders. Dulles believed that any form of Soviet intervention would jeopardize the principles of the Monroe Doctrine, undermine the global policy of containment, and possibly precipitate a nuclear war.

Operation Fortune: Conspiracy Number One against Arbenz

On a private trip to the United States in 1952, Nicaraguan dictator Anastasio Somoza praised the United States as the champion of democracy (something sorely lacking at home) and passed a covert scheme to the Truman administration in which the CIA and United Fruit would join him in a clandestine effort to rid Guatemala of Arbenz. The plot, code-named Operation Fortune, would arm (with the help of United Fruit freighters) an exile army headed by Somoza's protegé, Colonel Carlos Castillo Armas, and other officers in the Guatemalan army. The State Department was kept in the dark while the plan unfolded, but once it learned of the arms shipment in late 1952, several officials notified Secretary of State Acheson, who told Truman. At that, the plot was quickly terminated. However, as Arbenz pressed ahead with his land reform programs in 1953, Washington became more worried about communist influence inside Guatemala. Recently declassified government documents from the 1950s indicate that the CIA compiled an "elimination list," using information on "top flight Communists" gathered by the Guatemalan military that were to be used in preparation for the coup against Arbenz and its aftermath. The CIA director at the time was Walter Bedell Smith, an aggressive anticommunist with a deep suspicion of Marxist philosophy and a hatred of the Soviet Union and any form of socialism in the United States, but he was sorely misinformed about the situation in Guatemala.

Operation Success and the Overthrow of Arbenz

The decision to draw the line against communist expansion in Guatemala was known in the Eisenhower administration as Operation Success. The events that contributed to the covert efforts of the Central Intelligence Agency to remove the constitutionally elected Jacobo Arbenz centered on his domestic and foreign policies, and on perceptions of his threat in Washington. In 1953, after some viewed the Arbenz regime as posing a communist danger, cries rang out in Washington for a recognition of the applicability of the Monroe Doctrine to deal with Guatemala. The strategic thinking of Dulles, Eisenhower, and the CIA connected perceptions of communist influence in Guatemala with the security of the Panama Canal. After it was discovered that Soviet arms were being shipped to Guatemala in 1954, Dulles and others claimed that they were to be used to sabotage the Panama Canal.

The expropriation of United Fruit lands in Guatemala by the Arbenz government in 1952–1953 forced company officials to devise a strategy that would somehow reverse the agrarian reform decree. At one point United Fruit's public relations counsel, Edward Bernays, suggested to Sam Zemurray (the owner of United Fruit) that a prominent lawyer be hired to write to the Senate Foreign Relations Committee condemning expropriation, find a democratic Latin American leader to publicly condemn the property expropriation, and pressure the president of the United States to issue a statement expressing the dangers of expropriation based on the Monroe Doctrine. Bernay's suggestions were rejected, but he continued his assault on Arbenz by arranging "fact-finding" trips to Guatemala for reporters from leading newspapers and magazines to convince them that communism had indeed taken control under the Arbenz regime. John Clements, a supporter of Joseph McCarthy's anticommunist campaign and part of a Washington public relations firm, was contracted to produce reports on the extent of communist influence in Guatemala. The reports produced by Clements Associates were filled with inaccuracies and innuendo but were frequently cited by officials in Washington to demonstrate the penetration of Guatemala by communists.

To add further fuel to the overthrow plan, several members of the Eisenhower administration had close links to the United Fruit Company. Both Dulles brothers came to Washington from Sullivan and Cromwell, the New York law firm that handled United Fruit's account. Other policymakers at the time had connections with United Fruit, including John M. Cabot (assistant secretary of state for inter-American affairs), Henry Cabot Lodge

(U.S. ambassador to the United Nations), Sinclair Weeks (secretary of commerce), Robert Hill (U.S. ambassador to Costa Rica), John McCloy (an advisor), and Ann Whitman (Eisenhower's personal secretary). Friends of United Fruit seemed to make up a significant part of the upper echelon of the Eisenhower administration. When he retired from government service in 1955, Walter Bedell Smith took a job with the United Fruit Company.

Despite the close connections between United Fruit and the Eisenhower administration, there is still controversy over Washington's motives for overthrowing Arbenz. Was Operation Success designed to restore United Fruit's banana business after the devastating agrarian reform law, or was it a result of the dangers posed by the rising influence of communism in Guatemala? In a recent evaluation of the disposal of Arbenz, Piero Gleijeses argues that the deciding factor was not United Fruit's bananas but the perception that a communist takeover of Guatemala was a real threat to its neighbors and an "intolerable challenge" to the security of the United States. "In the heart of the American sphere of influence, in an upstart banana republic, there stood—proud, defiant—a president whose procommunist sympathies were obvious, a president and his communist friends were successful. . . . It was an intolerable challenge to America's sense of self-respect. Fortuny [Guatemala's foreign minister] was right when he said, 'They would have overthrown us even if we had grown no bananas.' "[8] Once the "Red Jacobo" was gone from Guatemala, President Eisenhower boasted of having assisted Guatemala in liberating itself from communism, a theme that would recur in U.S.–Latin American relations throughout the Cold War. The successful overthrow of Arbenz induced a sense of euphoria concerning the ease with which the regime collapsed, and it led to repetition of mistakes in dealing with future revolutionaries in Latin America.

The Washington intelligence and security bureaucrats who participated in the operation—Allen Dulles, Richard E. Bissell, E. Howard Hunt (later, of Bay of Pigs and Watergate fame), David Phillips, J. C. King, Adolf Berle, and Thomas Mann—were proud of the role they had played in the victory against Arbenz and were anxious to repeat it. Shortly after Arbenz's resignation, Secretary of State Dulles told the American people that "the intrusion of Soviet despotism was . . . a direct challenge to the Monroe Doctrine" and elimination of this "menace" in Central America marked "a new and glorious chapter to the already great tradition of the American states."[9] Operation Success became the standard for "quick-fix" covert intervention within the CIA's Latin American division, but revolutionary upheavals in Central America did not cease. In the process of watching the revolutionary events unfold in Nicaragua and El Salvador after 1979, one State Department official lamented, "What we'd give to have an Arbenz now. We are going to have to invent one, but all the candidates are dead."[10] Between 1954 and 1990, over one hundred thousand Guatemalans were killed, and at least fifty thousand disappeared, by military-dominated governments intent on preserving the fruits of their victory over Arbenz and his followers.

Post-Coup Guatemala: Counterrevolution and Counterinsurgency

Following the overthrow of Arbenz, Guatemala experienced government-directed counterrevolution and brutal military counterinsurgency. Castillo Armas became the first in a line of Guatemalan presidents—all supported by the United States—who ruled by terrorism and repression in the name of anticommunism. Castillo Armas reversed most of the reforms of the Arévalo-Arbenz era but did not live to see the final results of his efforts. He was assassinated in 1957 inside the National Palace by one of his former bodyguards. While the military ruled the country, a number of guerrilla groups formed to oppose the injustices imposed by repressive and violent governments in Guatemala City. The use of guerrilla warfare and Marxist-Leninist ideology by these groups prompted the United States to increase military aid to the Guatemalan armed forces, in addition to $50 million in Alliance for Progress funds during the early 1960s.

U.S.-Guatemalan relations improved with the election of Miguel Ydígoras Fuentes (1958–1963) because he cooperated with the Eisenhower administration by allowing Cuban exiles to train in Guatemala in preparation for the Bay of Pigs invasion (see Chapter 8). When the army revolted against Ydígoras in late 1960, he tried to counter the revolt by filling a transport plane with Cubans (then involved in training to overthrow Castro) to fight his own army. The revolt was halted on orders from the U.S. ambassador, a signal of Ydígoras's ineptitude and dependence on the United States. When he allowed former president Arévalo to campaign for the 1963 presidential elections, he was overthrown by the military.

The United States and the Guatemalan Military

Beginning in the early years of the Cold War, the United States decided that to secure the Western Hemisphere from an external attack it would provide military assistance and training to Central America. To build Latin American armies under U.S. direction, a carrot-and-stick approach was put into effect through the Military Defense Assistance Act (MDA) beginning in 1951. Protecting the hemisphere against external attack, not fighting internal insurgencies mounted by guerrilla armies, was the primary focus. However, as small bands of guerrilla forces emerged in the early 1960s, the United States shifted its military assistance to providing equipment and training in counterinsurgency warfare.

After the rebellion against Ydígoras Fuentes in 1960, and after some officers joined the guerrillas in the countryside, Guatemala became a testing ground for Washington's counterinsurgency warfare strategy. President Johnson provided $17 million in new military equipment and assistance, while the Guatemalan government allowed the Green Berets from Fort Bragg, North Carolina, to enter the country in 1967. During the 1960s and 1970s violence and repression escalated to defeat the guerrillas, but the battle for Guatemala soon reached a stalemate in which neither side was capable of defeating the other. In the late 1960s guerrilla violence moved to urban areas, where attacks resulted in the deaths of the American ambassador and the head of the U.S. military mission, among others.

After the removal of Arbenz, Guatemalan military officers received advanced training at the Panama Canal Zone's Army School of the Americas. Until the end of the Cold War the School of the Americas (critics call it the School for Dictators)—located at Ft. Benning, Georgia, since 1984—was shrouded in mystery and free of scrutiny despite having trained over 60,000 military soldiers and officers from 21 Latin American countries. The Pentagon released training manuals from the School of the Americas in 1996; these manuals recommend interrogation techniques such as torture, execution, blackmail, and the arrest of relatives of those being questioned. Efforts to shut down the School of the Americas by Representative Joseph Kennedy, and others, have failed despite the long roster of graduates who have returned home to become military dictators, death squad operators, and armed silencers of democratic discourse.

Two Guatemalan military officers—Colonel Julio Alpírez and General Héctor Gramajo—are graduates of the School of the Americas and are accused of torture and assassination of Guatemalan and American citizens living in Guatemala. Colonel Alpírez—a paid agent of the CIA—was implicated in the torture and deaths of U.S. citizen Michael Devine, and Efraín Bámaca Velásquez, the Guatemalan guerrilla leader who was married to American lawyer Jennifer Harbury. General Gramajo was Guatemalan defense minister during the 1980s and known for the scorched-earth campaigns against rural villages in which thousands of peasants were killed by the army. The U.S. Department of Defense continues to defend the education and training of foreign militaries *and civilians* as a critical part of engendering national security and promoting democracy throughout the hemisphere.

Guatemala and Human Rights: From Jimmy Carter to Ronald Reagan

By the end of the 1970s, Guatemala had earned its reputation as one of the hemisphere's worst violators of human rights. The Carter administration responded by terminating all military aid in an effort to improve the deteriorating human rights situation. In response, Guatemala's military government turned to Israel, Taiwan, and South Africa for weaponry and to Argentina's military dictatorship for further assistance. Although U.S.-Guatemalan relations were strained between 1977 and 1983, U.S. economic aid continued to flow, as did a steady stream of Guatemalans who emigrated to the United States for their own peace and security. After four chilly years of relations under the Carter administration, the election of Ronald Reagan brought cheers from the Guatemalan right.

The Reagan foreign policy team was sympathetic to the Guatemalan military government, led by General Lucas García, who in 1980 was engaged in a "dirty war" against four major guerrilla groups. Recognizing the importance of having Washington's support, Lucas García gave $500,000 to Reagan's 1980 presidential campaign. In return, Mario Sandoval Alarcón—known as the "Godfather" of Guatemalan death squads—was a guest at Reagan's first inaugural celebration in Washington. As army brutalities increased in 1980, Guatemala's civilian vice-president resigned in protest, claiming "There are no political prisoners in Guatemala, just political assassinations."[11] However, Reagan administration officials saw Guatemala as a victim of Cuban-Soviet aggression and potentially the final domino in Central America, possibly opening the door to the communist domination of Mexico. To defeat the rebels in Guatemala, hardliners in Washington wanted to reestablish U.S. military assistance as part of U.S. democracy promotion efforts. However, Guatemala was too far from anything resembling democracy to stretch the term that far, so the Reagan administration decided not to censure the Guatemalan military over human rights issues. Instead, it engaged it in dialogue while sympathizing with its battle against an insurgency.

After a fraudulent election and another military coup in 1982, retired general Efraín Ríos Montt assumed the presidency and declared a state of siege to pursue "communist subversives." A born-again evangelical, Ríos Montt at first gained the support of the Reagan administration, including U.S. ambassador Frederic C. Chapin. President Reagan claimed that Ríos Montt was given a "bum rap" by human rights groups and that he was taking care of problems left over from his predecessor. Guatemala's Pentecostal president delivered a televised homily to the nation every Sunday in which he stressed his "three-finger" campaign—*No robo, no miento, y no abuso* (I will not rob, lie, or abuse authority)—in an effort to maintain cordial relations with Washington. More important to Washington, however, was using Guatemala to fight its counterrevolutionary war against Sandinista Nicaragua. As one of the implementers of Reagan's war against Nicaragua, Oliver North courted the Guatemalan military and was directly involved in circumventing the 1977 congressional ban on military aid to Guatemala.

Guatemala and the Return of Civilian Rule

In 1985, Christian Democrat Mario Vinicio Cerezo Arévalo became Guatemala's first elected civilian in 16 years (he assumed office in 1986). Despite the fact that he wore a revolver to his inauguration, Cerezo offered the possibility of some improvement in the human rights situation; however, despite winning two-thirds of the popular vote, he admitted he could not control the military or the death squads that had tried on several occasions to assassinate him. The United States provided support through several agencies for what it called "democracy strengthening" to aid in the transition process. Cerezo's foreign policy of "active neutrality," in which he stressed peaceful solutions to the larger regional conflict, found favor among congressional Democrats in Washington, but it bothered the Reagan administration. However, President Cerezo found it difficult to resist U.S. pressure to conform to its position on the Central American crisis and reject support for his anti-guerrilla campaign. In May 1987 he requested that U.S. pilots ferry Guatemalan troops into rural areas controlled by Guatemala's main guerrilla organization, the Guatemalan National Revolutionary Union (UNRG). The Reagan administration continued its close ties to the Guatemalan military, providing assistance to defeat the Marxist-Leninist guerrillas in the countryside throughout the 1980s despite human rights abuses and opposition in Washington.

GUATEMALA AND THE UNITED STATES AFTER THE COLD WAR

The Bush administration recognized the importance of moving Central America off the U.S. foreign policy agenda, and it made a number of gestures in that direction. It was helped by the success of the Central American peace process, the defeat of the Sandinistas in a February 1990 election in Nicaragua, the collapse of the Soviet Union, and the end of the Cold War. Despite several coup attempts against Cerezo, civilian Jorge Serrano Elias was elected president in a runoff election in 1991. With peace talks already under way (under the aegis of the United Nations) aimed at ending Guatemala's long-running civil war, President Serrano faced the difficult task of continuing the negotiations while balancing opposing forces, including the powerful military. When peace talks broke down in 1993, followed by mass demonstrations, Serrano reacted by conducting a "self-coup," dissolving the congress and the supreme court. The reaction by the Clinton administration and the Organization of American States (OAS) was swift and punitive. Clinton condemned the antidemocratic maneuver, suspended economic and military assistance, and joined the OAS in threatening broader economic sanctions. Serrano was forced from office less than a month later and was replaced by Ramiro de León Carpio, a respected leader known for his support of human rights and democracy.

After 36 years of bloody civil war, a UN-brokered peace accord signed in December 1996 offered a means of healing the horrors of the past. President Alvaro Arzú was given high marks for the speed with which he ended the conflict and called for reducing the size and power of the Guatemalan army. While critics assailed the sweeping amnesty law that would exempt both soldiers and guerrillas from prosecution for killings, kidnappings, and acts of torture, Guatemalans threw red carnations on the tomb of Jacobo Arbenz and shouted "Long live the Guatemalan martyrs!" The Clinton administration praised the accord, promised $260 million in U.S. aid, and called for more foreign investment. However, CIA involvement in Guatemala since the overthrow of President Arbenz in 1954, and the continuing power of the Guatemalan army, have complicated the march toward peace and justice. The 1998 murder of Bishop Juan Gerardi after releasing a four-volume report on human rights violations during Guatemala's 36-year war brought a disturbing sense of déjà vu to Guatemalans and others in the region.

Much of what has happened in Guatemala since the overthrow of Arbenz remains shrouded in deceptions, lies, and coverups. Some of the horrific behavior of the Guatemalan military and CIA involvement became the focus of world attention due to several hunger strikes and protests by Jennifer Harbury, an American lawyer whose husband, guerrilla leader Efraín Bámaca Velásquez, was murdered by the Guatemalan military. Evidence presented by Congressman Robert Torricelli and State Department official Richard Nuccio revealed close CIA links to the Bámaca case and others. Believing that Congress ought to know of CIA involvement in the killings in Guatemala, both Torricelli and Nuccio made the mistake of placing conscience over secrecy and misconduct. Richard Nuccio was vilified by the CIA and some members of Congress, eventually losing his security clearance and terminating his State Department career.

CONCLUSION

The paradox of U.S. involvement in Guatemala centers on the fact that despite substantial economic interests, and at times perceived security interests that jeopardized the Monroe Doctrine, the United States never deployed its troops to Guatemala for either short or long periods. The ease with which multinational fruit companies were allowed to do business with "friendly dictators" provided the necessary stability and protection of economic interests that the United States desired in Central America. Although far from the Panama Canal, the United States still worried about the possibility of a foreign power taking over Guatemala and then threatening Mexico, its northern neighbor. While the formula worked until the beginning of the Cold War, the U.S. response to revolutionary change during the 1950s not only contributed to hundreds of thousands of civilian deaths at the hands of brutal military governments and leftist guerrillas, but also did tremendous damage to the Latin American policy of the United States. Today, U.S. government documents concerning the sordid affair are still considered too "sensitive" to be made public. Those at the CIA in charge of declassifying information insist that releasing more documents would seriously damage intelligence collection activities in places such as Guatemala.

NOTES

1. Paul J. Dosal, *Doing Business with Dictators: A Political History of United Fruit in Guatemala, 1899–1944* (Wilmington, DE: Scholarly Resources, 1993), p. 230.

2. Thomas M. Leonard, *Central America and the United States: The Search for Stability* (Athens: University of Georgia Press, 1991), p. 68.

3. Quoted in Thomas D. Schoonover, *The United States in Central America, 1860–1911: Episodes of Social Imperialism and Imperial Rivalry in the World System* (Durham, NC: Duke University Press, 1991), p. 19.

4. Dosal, *Doing Business with Dictators*, p. 3.

5. Speaking to a Rotary Club audience in 1950, Patterson explained his method of determining whether a Guatemalan was a communist or not: "Many times it is impossible to prove legally that a certain individual is a communist, but for cases of this sort I recommend a practical method of detection—the 'duck test.' The duck test works this way: suppose you see a bird walking around in a farm yard. This bird wears no label that says, 'duck.' But the bird certainly looks like a duck. Also, he goes to the pond and you notice that he swims like a duck. Then he opens his beak and quacks like a duck. Well, by this time you have probably reached the conclusion that the bird is a duck, whether he's wearing a label or not." See Richard H. Immerman, *The CIA in Guatemala: The Foreign Policy of Intervention* (Austin: University of Texas Press, 1982), p. 102.

6. Gaddis Smith, "Monroe Doctrine," in Bruce W. Jentelson and Thomas G. Paterson, eds., *The Encyclopedia of U.S. Foreign Relations*, vol. 3 (New York: Oxford University Press, 1997), p. 164 (emphasis added).

7. Quoted in Gaddis Smith, *The Last Years of the Monroe Doctrine, 1945–1993* (New York: Hill and Wang, 1994), p. 67.

8. Piero Gleijeses, *Shattered Hope: The Guatemalan Revolution and the United States, 1944–1954* (Princeton, NJ: Princeton University Press, 1991), pp. 365–366.

9. Quoted in Cole Blasier, *The Hovering Giant: U.S. Responses to Revolutionary Change in Latin America 1910–1985*, rev. ed. (Pittsburgh, PA: University of Pittsburgh Press, 1985), pp. 171–172.

10. Quoted in Immerman, *The CIA in Guatemala*, p. 197.

11. Quoted in Walter LaFeber, *Inevitable Revolutions: The United States in Central America*, 2nd ed. (New York: W. W. Norton, 1993), p. 259.

SUGGESTED READINGS

Black, George. *The Good Neighbor: How the United States Wrote the History of Central America and the Caribbean*. New York: Pantheon Books, 1988.

Dosal, Paul J. *Doing Business with Dictators: A Political History of United Fruit in Guatemala, 1899–1944*. Wilmington, DE: Scholarly Resources, 1993.

Gleijeses, Piero. *Shattered Hope: The Guatemalan Revolution and the United States, 1944–1954*. Princeton, NJ: Princeton University Press, 1991.

Immerman, Richard H. *The CIA in Guatemala: The Foreign Policy of Intervention*. Austin: University of Texas Press, 1982.

Schlesinger, Stephen, and Stephen Kinzer. *Bitter Fruit: The Untold Story of the American Coup in Guatemala*. New York: Doubleday, 1983.

14

Guyana

TIMELINE OF U.S. RELATIONS WITH GUYANA

1803	British control is established
1834	Slavery is abolished
1899	Paris settlement ends border dispute with Venezuela
1928	British Guiana becomes a Crown Colony
1947	Janet Rosenberg Jagan's U.S. citizenship is revoked
1950	Dr. Cheddi Jagan, Forbes Burnham, and others form the People's Progressive Party (PPP)
1953	Dr. Cheddi Jagan is elected chief minister
	Jagan is imprisoned by the British
1961	Jagan becomes Guyana's first prime minister after the colony is granted self-government
1964	Jagan is overthrown following CIA destabilization campaign
1964–1966	United States pressures Britain to delay Guyana's independence
1966	Guyana becomes independent
1966–1992	People's National Congress (PNC) dominates Guyanese politics
1978	Jonestown massacre
1985	Forbes Burnham dies while in office
1992	Cheddi Jagan is elected president
1997	Cheddi Jagan dies; his widow becomes prime minister
	Janet Rosenberg Jagan is elected president

INTRODUCTION

Guyana (British Guiana until independence in 1966), although the only English-speaking country in South America, is usually considered part of the English-speaking Caribbean due to its history and culture. Colonized by the Dutch and British, its history is marked by economic dependency, racial and radical politics, and considerable instability. Guyana figured three times in the history of the Monroe Doctrine, reaching back to 1895, and became a security concern for the British and the United States during the Cold War. It produced two leading (and contentious) political figures—Cheddi Jagan and Forbes Burnham—who dominated Guyanese politics from the 1950s to the 1980s, although their brand of socialism and ties to Cuba and the Soviet bloc raised concerns in Washington about the intentions of nonhemispheric powers in the Americas. Guyana gained unwanted notoriety in 1978 when People's Temple messiah Rev. Jim Jones orchestrated the suicide-murder of over 800 followers, claiming CIA efforts to destroy his religious mission.

BRITISH GUIANA AND THE UNITED STATES IN THE NINETEENTH CENTURY

Following the independence of Latin America from Spain, Great Britain remained the paramount power in the Western Hemisphere. Its chief interest was in capitalist expansion in the region rather than acquiring more territory. Although the British did seize the Falkland/Malvinas Islands in 1833, the rest of its possessions in the hemisphere—British Guiana, British Honduras (Belize), and certain Caribbean islands—had been obtained before Latin American independence. Anticipating further U.S. expansion after the war with Mexico, the British established the Miskito Kingdom, a protectorate along the Caribbean coast of Nicaragua in the 1840s, provoking a challenge to U.S. strategic and commercial interests in Central America. To avoid a war with the British over control of Central America, Secretary of State John M. Clayton negotiated the Clayton-Bulwer Treaty of 1850 to settle Anglo-American conflicts in Central America. The treaty provided for joint control of a future transisthmian canal, thereby allowing the British to maintain their influence in the region. Representing Delaware in the U.S. Senate in 1853, Clayton was criticized by members of the Democratic Party for signing a treaty that violated the Monroe Doctrine by permitting a permanent British influence in the region.

With the possession of bases, treaties, and fishing rights in Latin America, the British were able to dominate the sea lanes of the region and protect and maintain favorable trade activity. By forestalling the spread of U.S. power, maintaining influence over any future isthmian canal, and controlling trade flows, Britain was the dominant power in Latin America and the Caribbean until the 1890s. The period in inter-American relations between 1870 and 1895 was relatively tranquil, and the Monroe Doctrine went into a sort of diplomatic remission. The British navy protected the Caribbean area from incursions by other European nations, while the United States concentrated on developments at home. However, the Aluminum Company of America (ALCOA) began production in British Guiana in 1888, and by 1925 it had acquired monopoly control over available bauxite deposits. Events in 1895 would usher in a new Latin American policy with the U.S. reaction to an old dispute between Great Britain and Venezuela over the proper boundary between Venezuela and British Guiana (see Chapter 25). By the time the dust had settled in 1899, the United States had pumped considerably more vigor into the Monroe Doctrine, assumed the role of an imperial power, and by awarding Great Britain most of the originally con-tested territory, perpetuated a border dispute that would last well into the twentieth century. When independence finally came to Guyana in 1966, the new government faced the difficulty of having to devote considerable en-ergy to legal and physical defense of its national territory. For example, Guyana was not allowed to join the Organization of American States until the 1980s due to its boundary dispute with Venezuela.

BRITISH GUIANA, THE UNITED STATES, AND THE EARLY TWENTIETH CENTURY

The United States emerged from the Spanish-American War of 1898 as unquestionably the major power in the Caribbean region. By the 1930s the United States had surpassed Great Britain as the main source of foreign investment in the Caribbean. In the name of peace, stability, and demo-cratic rule the United States intervened militarily in the Caribbean and Cen-tral America 33 times between 1898 and 1926. This intense involvement and concern were justified by U.S. policymakers in several ways. First, the building of the Panama Canal required the protection of vital strategic interests in the Caribbean Basin area. Second, the region needed protection against any further European encroachments, especially on the part of the predatory Germans. Third, to challenge the traditional economic domi-nance of Great Britain in the region, the United States decided it was im-portant to make the Caribbean a privileged zone for investment and exports.

Between the two world wars, tensions brought on by increased foreign investment, intra-regional migration, and emphasis on raw material exports resulted in social protest movements in the mid-1930s (exacerbated by the Great Depression) followed by anticolonial rebellions throughout the English-speaking Caribbean. The political struggles of the 1930s forced the British to consider ways to allow greater self-government in the region, leading to independence in subsequent decades. With emphasis on agricultural and mineral exports (mainly bauxite and manganese) controlled largely by four foreign corporations, Guyana's economy was devoid of economic diversity and mostly of little benefit to the Guyanese.

GUYANA, THE UNITED STATES, AND THE COLD WAR

Soon after the end of World War II, Guyana became embroiled in the intense ideological aspects of the Cold War at the same time that demands for democracy and independence from the British were increasing. The United States became involved in the drama of independence in Guyana during the 1950s and 1960s, largely due to the perceived ideological and security threats posed by its two dominant leaders, Cheddi Jagan and Forbes Burnham.

Cheddi Jagan and the United States

The elections that occurred in the final years of British colonialism in Guyana involved two political parties: Cheddi Jagan's PPP (People's Progressive Party) and Forbes Burnham's PNC (People's National Congress). Dr. Cheddi Jagan, a dentist by training, helped lead Guyana to independence and was one of the Caribbean's most contentious political leaders for 50 years until his death in 1997. Born in 1918 on a sugar plantation where his father worked as the foreman of a work crew, the young Cheddi was exposed early to poverty and exploitation. Later he enrolled at Howard University in Washington, D.C., and in 1943 he graduated from the Northwestern University Dental School in Chicago, where he met his future wife, Janet Rosenberg, a student nurse active in left-wing politics.

On returning to Guyana in the late 1940s, he juggled his dental practice with labor organizing among agricultural workers. He and his wife founded the People's Progressive Party together with Forbes Burnham, a black lawyer, in 1950. With a new constitution providing for universal suffrage and increased home rule, Jagan was elected chief minister in 1953 at the age of 35. Worried about his Marxist ideology and program for radical social and economic reforms, the British government (under Winston Churchill, serving his last term as prime minister) declared a state of emergency, suspended the constitution, and landed troops and warships to depose him, claiming he and the PPP were completely under the control of a communist clique. After leading a civil disobedience campaign against British rule (modeled after Gandhi's strategy in India earlier), Jagan was arrested and jailed for six months. These events produced a split in the PPP, with Burnham leaving the party to later found the People's National Congress (PNC).

Jagan continued to win elections on a socialist and pro-independence platform that had the unwavering support of the Indian majority. Seven months after John F. Kennedy was inaugurated as president, Jagan and his PPP won a majority of seats in the lower house of parliament but only narrowly defeated Forbes Burnham in the popular vote. Shortly after the election, Jagan announced that he would seek economic assistance from the United States and Britain but would also accept aid from the Soviet Union. On his visit to the United States, Jagan refused to deny he was a communist, said nothing critical about the Soviet Union, and praised socialism as the appropriate economic system for Guyana. In his meeting with Kennedy he requested about $40 million in aid, a huge sum at the time, but Washington refused to give him a firm commitment on economic assistance. After Jagan's return to Guyana from Washington, the Central Intelligence Agency undertook a destabilization campaign against him.

Over the next two years Jagan faced labor unrest, sabotage, and disinformation efforts that led to race riots between East Indians and blacks that left over 100 dead. As an alternative to Jagan the United States shifted its support to Burnham, calling him a member of the noncommunist left, and prodded the British to delay Guyana's independence until a more pro-U.S. political figure could be found. One of Kennedy's top Latin American advisors—Arthur Schlesinger—counseled that Burnham would cause the United States far fewer problems than Jagan. The process of shifting power from the more radical Jagan to the more compliant Burnham involved using the AFL-CIO Institute for Free Labor Development, working in conjunction with the CIA, to stir up strikes, cripple the economy, and heighten political and racial tensions. Kennedy's main concern was that a communist takeover in Guyana could defeat his reelection bid in 1964. The Kennedy administration even solicited support from Canada, given its large mining operations in British Guiana, claiming the country was lurching toward a communist or Castro-type regime, but little in the way of Canadian help appeared forthcoming. Although Jagan's party led the voting in the 1964 elections, Forbes Burnham formed a coalition government to prevent Jagan's reelection. With Washington's support, Guyana became fully independent on May 26, 1966, under a coalition government headed by Prime Minister Forbes Burnham.

Cheddi Jagan would have to fight for his principles as part of the parliamentary opposition until the PPP won the 1992 elections. Once Burnham was safely in power, he used wire taps and physical surveillance to follow and intimidate his political opponents, winning one rigged election after another until his death in 1985. Despite the use of electoral fraud and a somewhat independent foreign policy, Burnham enjoyed Washington's support throughout his time in office. By 1992, with Guyana near economic collapse as a result of years of misrule and corruption, Jagan returned from years in the political wilderness by winning 54 percent of the vote in the national election. However, once back in power (this time as president due to earlier constitutional changes), Jagan proved to be less ideological and more restrained than in the past. To spur development he joined hands with the International Monetary Fund (IMF) and the Inter-American Development Bank (IDB), courted foreign investment, and encouraged private investment. By the time of Jagan's last term in office the Cold War had ended, and relations with the Clinton administration remained cordial until his death in 1997.[1] Despite years of turmoil with the United States during the Cold War, Cheddi Jagan will be remembered for his advocacy of Guyana's downtrodden Indian majority, his views as a staunch nationalist, and his role as one of the major forces in bringing independence to the Commonwealth Caribbean in the 1960s.

The Jonestown Murder-Suicide

U.S. relations with Caribbean and Latin American countries have been influenced by U.S. foreign missionary activity designed to promote the Christian gospel, but many missionaries engaged in activities that extended far beyond their immediate religious concerns. While the mainline Protestant churches have reduced their missionary activity in the Caribbean in recent years, others—Fundamentalist, Pentecostal, and Mormon churches—have substantially increased their foreign missionary activity. Foreign missionaries from the Assemblies of God and the Southern Baptist Convention have gone to Guyana to spread the gospel since the 1950s. In 1974 the Reverend Jim Jones founded the People's Temple of the Disciples of Christ in Guyana's tropical rain forest. Under a lease of the land granted by the Guyanese government in 1976, Jonestown expanded with followers of the charismatic Rev. Jones until the temple included close to 900 members by 1978. All members of the People's Temple died in a mass suicide and murder episode in 1978 after the self-declared messiah—Jim Jones—told his followers that CIA-directed Guyanese soldiers were advancing on the compound to torture, murder, and castrate them. Jonestown has since been abandoned.

CONCLUSION

Guyana not only suffered as a slave colony for centuries and didn't achieve independence from the British until the mid-1960s, but it had to endure the enmity of the United States throughout the Cold War. The type of leadership that emerged to forge an independence movement coincided with the revolutionary changes taking place in the 1960s that posed constant strains on U.S. relations with the Third World. With Cheddi Jagan—a Marxist-Leninist of the pro-Soviet mold and a close ally of Fidel Castro—the United States was fortunate that it did not have to face a "second Cuba" on the mainland of South America. Washington never had to send in the Marines or invoke the Monroe Doctrine, but the thinking and rhetoric of Presidents Eisenhower, Kennedy, and Johnson concerning Guyana were infused with Monroeism during the height of the Cold War. While some of the current economic restructuring has been successful in improving the country's infrastructure, and Guyana has become a more respected member of the international community, the flight of managerial, technical, and professional talent to the United States and Europe does not bode well for the future of the former British colony in northwestern South America.

NOTE

1. One week after Cheddi Jagan died, his American-born Marxist wife, Janet Rosenberg Jagan, was sworn in as president by the Guyanese parliament. In December 1997, after 54 years of battling the British and American governments, the American-born grandmother was elected president of Guyana. During the Cold War she was stripped of her American citizenship because of her Marxist views.

SUGGESTED READINGS

Latin American Bureau (LAB). *Guyana: Fraudulent Revolution*. London: LAB, 1984.

Richardson, Bonham C. *The Caribbean in the Wider World, 1492–1992*. New York: Cambridge University Press, 1993.

Sunshine, Catherine A. *The Caribbean: Survival, Struggle, and Sovereignty*. Boston: South End Press, 1986.

Tardanico, Richard, ed. *Crises in the Caribbean Basin*. Beverly Hills, CA: Sage Publications, 1988.

Thomas, Clive Y. *The Poor and Powerless: Economic Policy and Change in the Caribbean*. New York: Monthly Review Press, 1988.

Watson, Hilbourne A., ed. *The Caribbean in the Global Political Economy*. Boulder, CO: Lynne Rienner, 1993.

15

Haiti

TIMELINE OF U.S. RELATIONS WITH HAITI

1804	Haitian independence from France is achieved
1844	Dominican Republic gains independence from Haiti
1862	United States recognizes Haiti
1914	U.S. Marine intervention
1915	More U.S. Marines arrive
1916	Marine occupation is legalized with treaty (ends in 1934)
1919–1920	Caco wars
1937	Trujillo orders massacre of Haitian workers
1957	François Duvalier is "elected" president
1963	President Kennedy terminates most U.S. assistance
1971	François Duvalier dies; his son, Jean-Claude, takes power
1985	Father Jean-Bertrand Aristide criticizes dictatorship
1986	Duvalier is overthrown
1988	Leslie Manigat is elected president
	Manigat is overthrown by the military
1990	Aristide wins first free and democratic election
1991	Aristide is overthrown by the military
1992	Organization of American States (OAS)–arranged Washington agreement is signed but ignored
	President Bush announces new refugee policy
1993	UN-arranged Governor's Island agreement is signed

1994	UN Security Council approves U.S. plan for intervention
	U.S. troops (building up to 23,000) land unopposed in Haiti
	President Aristide resumes power
1995	U.S. troops are replaced by 6,000-member UN force
	René Préval is elected president (inaugurated in 1996)
1996	U.S. combat troops are withdrawn, but 250 U.S. troops remain for civic action projects
1997	President Clinton seeks extension of UN peacekeeping forces
1998	Chronic political instability paralyzes Haitian "democracy" with political infighting and cutoff of foreign aid
	UN peacekeeping mission continues while hundreds of U.S. troops remain in Haiti to build roads and bridges, renovate schools, and provide medical treatment to slum dwellers

INTRODUCTION

Haiti shares the mountainous Caribbean island of Hispaniola with the Dominican Republic; the product of a long period of French colonialism, it has the distinction of being the oldest independent black nation in the world. Since separating from France in 1804, Haiti has suffered from severe poverty, chronic rebellions, racial tensions, and environmental devastation. Brutal dictators, many of whom espoused racial hatred, flourished from the early years of independence. When wars erupted in Europe or revolutions broke out in the Caribbean, policymakers in both Haiti and Washington worried about foreign intervention and ways of protecting economic and security interests on the island. From 1915 to 1934, U.S. Marines ruled Haiti, the longest period of U.S. military occupation in Latin America.

Haiti's relations with the United States have evolved from a history of distrust and conflict, due in part to its racial makeup, geographical proximity, and vulnerability to foreign intrusion. The values of political pluralism and economic freedom never took root in Haiti, despite repeated efforts of the United States to implant its own institutions and beliefs among Haitians through intervention and military occupation. Profound cultural and ethnic differences seem to have prevented the United States from gaining an adequate understanding of a country consisting of blacks and mulattoes who speak only Créole or French, not American English. Without a viable government and economy, Haiti has had to rely on economic, military, and humanitarian assistance from the United States and international organizations.

THE UNITED STATES AND HAITI DURING THE
NINETEENTH CENTURY

The United States and Haitian Independence

Officially, the United States remained neutral during the Haitian revolution (1791–1803) that eventually achieved independence from France; however, the Haitian rebels were covertly supplied by the United States. Masters of guerrilla warfare, the Haitians—along with the decimating effects of yellow fever on French forces—eventually forced France to withdraw from Saint-Domingue (Haiti's former name) in 1802. The French loss of Saint-Domingue caused Napoleon Bonaparte to sell the Louisiana Territory to the United States, a $15 million transaction known as the Louisiana Purchase. Haiti proclaimed the independence of the island colony on January 1, 1804, the first new nation in Latin America. Jean-Jacques Dessalines, a radical black, became Haiti's new leader and tried to emulate the French government by stressing equality and better understanding between blacks and mulattoes.

Haitians faced enormous difficulties after independence as the military leaders who defeated the French assumed power in the aftermath of a long and destructive war. The French left a population that was 95 percent illiterate and lacking experience in self-government. Racial hostility—black against white, and mulatto against black—continued after independence, as practically all whites were driven off the island. Effective governing was made more difficult by the fact that other nations refused to recognize Haiti until decades after its independence. The French delayed recognition until 1825, and the United States did not recognize Haiti until 1862, almost 60 years after independence. To complicate matters further, Haiti was forced to share the island of Hispaniola with Santo Domingo (later the Dominican Republic), a former Spanish colony with a different language, culture, and religion.

Haiti and the Monroe Doctrine

Haiti was independent for almost two decades by the time President Monroe delivered his message to Congress that later became known as the Monroe Doctrine. Since the Monroe Doctrine was combined with the question of diplomatic recognition, Haiti was excluded from the protective umbrella of American foreign policy. After the end of the U.S. Civil War, Haitian rulers made unsuccessful efforts to appeal to the United States on behalf of the Monroe Doctrine. The United States applied the Monroe Doctrine to Haiti in the 1880s after suspecting that President Étienne Solomon was interested in transferring Môle St. Nicolas—a well-protected and highly prized harbor—to either the French or British, but there was no evidence that Haiti planned such a transaction or that either country would have accepted it. In 1922, Secretary of State Robert Lansing told a Senate committee investigating the U.S. military occupation of Haiti that one reason for the occupation was to prevent any foreign power from gaining a foothold in the Americas, in "flagrant defiance of the Monroe Doctrine."[1]

The U.S. Civil War and the Recognition of Haiti

Until the outbreak of civil war in 1861, Washington feared that recognizing Haiti would lead to slave revolts in the United States, inspired by the vision of freedom and independence available to former slaves on the island. Spanish reannexation of the Dominican Republic in 1861 and the outbreak of civil war in the United States contributed to President Lincoln's decision to recognize Haiti (see Chapter 9). Faced with the possibility of Spanish aggression against Haiti, President Fabre Geffrard appealed to President Lincoln for formal recognition in 1861. Influenced by Senator Charles Sumner, a staunch abolitionist, President Lincoln requested congressional approval for U.S. recognition of Haiti in his annual message in late 1861. Domestic politics also played a role in Lincoln's decision to recognize Haiti. The president believed that the best solution to the "Negro problem" in the United States was to ship them to other countries where presumably they would be better treated, and Haiti seemed like one of the logical choices. After Congress approved recognition in 1862 it appropriated $600,000 to settle American blacks in Haiti and elsewhere, but the project faltered due to the opposition (and hostility) of American blacks to colonization and the lack of support within the Haitian government. From the end of the U.S. Civil War in 1865 to the American military occupation in 1915, Washington paid little attention to Haiti, with the exception of Môle St. Nicolas as a naval base in the Caribbean. President Benjamin Harrison appointed Frederick Douglass as minister to Haiti in an effort to force Haiti to give up the valuable harbor, but the effort failed through diplomatic bungling and the U.S. public's opposition to the use of force.

THE UNITED STATES AND HAITI DURING THE EARLY TWENTIETH CENTURY

The desire to build an interoceanic canal across Central America and the removal of Spain from the Caribbean in the aftermath of the Spanish-American War in 1898 brought renewed attention to the region. Concerned that Haiti's chronic poverty and political turbulence might lead to extra-hemispheric intervention, President William Howard Taft (1909–1913) convinced the Haitian government to accept a major loan and other concessions in 1910. Taft reasoned that the loan would bring economic and political stability to Haiti and allow the United States to eliminate any security threats in its "backyard." However, the stabilizing strategy failed, and several years later President Woodrow Wilson (1913–1921) sent marines to Haiti to restore order and constitutional rule.

U.S. Military Occupation of Haiti, 1915–1934

The U.S. military occupation of Haiti began at a time when widespread violence, anarchy, and threats to foreigners' lives and property threatened the Caribbean. Following the brutal murder of Haitian president Vibrun Guillaume Sam in 1915, President Woodrow Wilson sent troops to Haiti in an effort to correct the deteriorating political situation. President Wilson's intervention decision coincided with the opening of the Panama Canal in 1914, the establishment of other protectorates throughout the Caribbean, and the threat of French and German intervention in Haiti during World War I.

Although the Haitian government "invited" U.S. intervention, the United States used its power to establish a formal protectorate—similar to the Platt Amendment in Cuba—that included direct control of the Haitian government and control over its finances. President Wilson favored the idea of a protectorate, and the U.S. Marine occupation was "legalized" with the Haitian-American Treaty of 1916. The occupation regime proved costly to the United States, generating anti-American hostility without improving Haiti's underdeveloped economy and its authoritarian and violent political system. "The Haitian protectorate was unprecedented in its duration [1915–1934], the racism that characterized U.S. behavior in the black republic, and the brutality associated with pacification efforts."[2]

The policies implemented by the occupying U.S. Marines were not popular and contributed to a major revolt in 1919–1920. Marine occupation revived forced labor, enacted press censorship and curfews, removed restrictions on land ownership by foreigners, and introduced racial segregation. The local economy failed to improve, and Haitians resented the conditions imposed by military force. Rear Admiral William B. Caperton, head of the U.S. military forces, tried to "fix" Haiti by disarming all presidential candidates and disbanding the *cacos*, or peasant mercenaries who served as private armies for the regional strongmen dominating Haitian politics. In a counterinsurgency campaign called the Caco wars, U.S. military forces—and the so-called Gendarmerie d'Haïti—defeated the guerrillas with ruthless success. A major turning point in the war against Haitian peasants was the Marine capture and execution of Caco leader Charlemagne Péralte in late 1919. In a scene much like that of the death of Ché Guevara in Bolivia in 1967, the Marines photographed Péralte's body on a plank as if he had been crucified, and then buried the rebel leader in concrete to deter future use of the corpse for ceremonial purposes. However, Péralte's photo only confirmed his martyrdom status as a patriot who gave his life to remove foreign control of his homeland.

After the pacification campaign, rumors about the most flagrant offenses filtered back to Washington, where Republicans used the peasant war in Haiti to discredit the Democrats. After a Senate investigation in 1921—calling for an end to human rights abuses and improved administration—a high commissioner in charge of a shadow government was appointed. The task of administering Haiti went to John B. Russell of Georgia, a Marine officer with service during the early years of the occupation, who many in Washington believed would provide the needed discipline and good government for the unruly Haitians. Beginning in 1922, General Russell teamed up with Haitian president Louis Borno to operate a "two-headed dictatorship" that lasted for eight years. The balance sheet for the occupation reveals a series of costly public works projects and the elimination of yaws (a debilitating eye disease) and malaria-breeding mosquitoes, but at the price of Haiti's sovereignty and national dignity. The rosy reports released by Marine officers eventually clashed with more critical reports on the occupation, leading to a process of Haitianization of civil, military, and police functions and Marine withdrawal in August 1934. The occupation left behind a professional armed force with modern weapons—the Gendarmerie, later called the Garde d'Haïti—to staff and operate a national guard. The United States intended the Garde to have no role in governance, but its acceptance of a strictly professional ethic was only superficial. With the Marines gone, Haiti celebrated its second independence day, this time after 20 years of U.S. military occupation. U.S.-Haitian relations improved considerably after 1930, thanks to two "good neighbor" diplomats, Dr. Dana G. Munro (1930–1932) and Norman Armour (1932–1934). They followed General Russell, an insensitive and autocratic high commissioner who made up half of the "two-headed dictatorship" during the 1920s.

Haiti and the Good Neighbor Period, 1930–1946

The United States resumed normal relations with Haiti after the termination of the occupation while the Haitian army assumed a major role in the political arena, and Haitian presidents—Sténio Vincent (1930–1941) and Élie Lescot (1941–1946)—adopted a more conciliatory policy toward the United States. The Hoover and Roosevelt administrations accepted former leaders who were bitter opponents during the occupation, a gesture that influenced both Vincent and Lescot. Haiti enjoyed relative stability between 1930 and 1946, despite economic distress and racial tension and hostility with the Dominican Republic over the integrity of national borders. During the 1930s the United States became Haiti's principal foreign trade partner and banker.

The Vincent administration had to face high levels of unemployment among peasants, made worse by the expulsion of Haitian workers from Cuba and the declining value of coffee and tropical fruit exports. After thousands of Haitians crossed the border in search of employment on plantations in the Dominican Republic, Dominican dictator Rafael Trujillo ordered their massacre in 1937, a move that some speculate was based on a perceived opportunity to divert attention from his domestic difficulties. Vincent's agreement to negotiate directly with Trujillo to settle the matter undermined his support at home, and there were several coup attempts on his increasingly dictatorial government. Opposition in Washington to Vincent's desire to run for a third term contributed to his decision to name his ambassador to the United States, Élie Lescot, as his successor in 1941. Lescot turned out to be more pro-American than Vincent, declared war on the Axis powers after Pearl Harbor, and allowed the United States to oversee Haitian politics and attend to Haitian problems. The United States initiated agricultural programs in 1941 and provided economic assistance in 1944, the only country to maintain a resident aid mission in Haiti.

President Lescot's pro-American administration, black-mulatto tension over administrative appointments, and the desire for economic and social reforms led to his removal in a bloodless coup in 1946, supported by Dominican dictator Trujillo. President Dumarsais Estimé (1946–1950) replaced Lescot and planned a "Revolution of 1946," through which he attempted to reduce mulatto influence by increasing black power in the government. This effort stimulated further problems and contributed to his overthrow in 1950. Haiti remained unstable until François Duvalier, a key figure in public health campaigns during Estimé's administration, came to power in 1957 with Haitian military support.

THE UNITED STATES AND HAITI DURING THE COLD WAR

During the first decade of the Cold War, Haitian leaders followed Washington's lead in foreign affairs, with the exception of the pro-Trujillo policies of the Truman and Eisenhower administrations. The United States seemed to benefit from the mutual hostility between the Dominican Republic and Haiti because Trujillo helped restrain the unruly Haitians, and Trujillo could be more easily disciplined by Washington if it so desired. At the same time, the Haitian military was viewed as a source of badly needed domestic law and order; with the Rio Pact (1947), a mutual security alliance, the United States had some protection against extra-hemispheric intervention. After the outbreak of the Korean War, Haiti agreed to the Mutual Security Act of 1951 (replaced by the Foreign Assistance Act of 1961) to become the beneficiary of economic and military assistance from the United States. The rift between blacks and mulattoes, and growing civil-military conflict, set the stage for 30 years of Duvalier family dictatorship.

François ("Papa Doc") Duvalier (1957–1971)

François ("Papa Doc") Duvalier was a *noir* (black) who earned a medical degree and got involved in public health campaigns against yaws (a contagious tropical eye disease caused by a parasite) and malaria. He received his medical training in Haiti, worked with the U.S. Army Medical Corps, and studied public health at the University of Michigan in 1944 while on a year-long fellowship program. His ideas about race and politics evolved from his medical studies and public health campaigns. Duvalier's opposition to mulatto rule was manifested in his belief in black nationalism and *négritude*, a political movement stressing African roots and voodoo. His political outlook was shaped by the U.S. occupation, Rafael Trujillo's massacre of Haitians in 1937, mulatto control of economic and political life, and army intervention in national politics. After a year of political instability and civil war in 1956, Duvalier was elected president in 1957 with military support.

Papa Doc's dictatorship rested on his anticommunism, the ruthless suppression of all opposition through a secret police apparatus called the Tonton Macoutes, and the use of voodoo theology and black nationalism to appeal to Haiti's impoverished majority. Duvalier's Tonton Macoutes ("bogeymen" in Créole) arrested, attacked, terrorized, and murdered members of the press and broadcasters. The army was neutralized through the purging of disloyal and potentially disloyal members. By appointing the Tonton Macoutes to positions of authority, Duvalier created a patronage machine that was personally loyal and responsible to him. "What was unique about Duvalier's rule," according to Larman Wilson, "was that he controlled everything and almost everyone by making them responsible to him—loyalty was more important than competence."[3] It was "government by franchise" whereby the dictator and his family and closest advisors got a financial slice of all government enterprises. Duvalier also "blackened" the government by replacing whites and mulattoes; however, since he only "promoted" blacks already existing within the government, the country as a whole did not benefit from his *négritude*.

Duvalier's blatant human rights violations were ignored in Washington as U.S. presidents were typically all too willing to aid and support anticommunist dictatorships. The United States tolerated Duvalier for the first several years because of the 1959 Cuban Revolution and Cuba's geographical proximity to Haiti, but eventually was embarrassed by the brutality of the dictatorship and its misappropriation of aid money. After President John F. Kennedy ended most U.S. assistance to Haiti in 1963, Duvalier renounced all aid from Washington, refusing to accept the strict accounting procedures required for aid renewals. As a result, Haiti did not participate in the Alliance for Progress. The Johnson administration was ashamed of Haiti's human rights violation but did send military aid to Haiti because of its strategic location near Castro's Cuba. Confident that he had gained the acceptance of Washington, Papa Doc declared himself "President for Life" in 1964. Duvalier's anticommunism convinced President Nixon of the strategic importance of Haiti, and economic aid was restored in 1970. In failing health, Duvalier named his 19-year-old son, Jean-Claude "Baby Doc" Duvalier, as his successor in 1971.

Jean-Claude ("Baby Doc") Duvalier (1971–1986)

Jean-Claude Duvalier (1971–1986), an unsuccessful law student and playboy, became "President for Life" after his father's death. For the first several years Jean-Claude Duvalier's title was in name only, as a Papa Doc–appointed council of state made all the decisions, designed to ensure that Duvalierism did not die with the dictator. Baby Doc's mother, and his father's principal advisors, remained the power behind the throne until 1972. To consolidate his power Duvalier announced an "economic revolution," one that included some reductions in political repression and some genuine economic incentives designed to improve Haitian-U.S. relations and put an end to Haiti's isolation in the Western Hemisphere. Baby Doc's modest efforts to modify the more repressive aspects of the family tyranny and improve opportunities for U.S. corporate investment gave Washington a rationale for renewed economic and military support for the regime. Between 1972 and 1981 Haiti received $584 million in development assistance from the United States and other donor countries. During President Reagan's first term he provided virtually unqualified support for any dictator who was staunchly anticommunist; however, during his second term he began to shift away from repressive dictators such as Duvalier and General Pinochet in Chile.

Duvalier's downfall began in 1980 when he married mulatto Michèle Bennett, daughter of a wealthy exporter-importer. Although Baby Doc envisioned that his biracial marriage would unite Haiti's ruling class and put an end to the chronic racial and political strife, his marriage had the opposite effect. It enraged many anti-mulatto blacks (including the Duvalierists), since they perceived the marriage as an indication that the old mulatto elite was regaining power. After the marriage the Duvalier-Bennett family fortunes improved substantially, including Bennett family involvement in illicit drug trafficking. Michèle Bennett's spending sprees in Paris and lavish lifestyle caused a national revulsion, leading to riots and demonstrations beginning in 1984.

In 1985, two years after the papal visit to Haiti, Father Jean-Bertrand Aristide criticized the larcenous dictatorship and called for drastic change.

The United States urged Jean-Claude's resignation, threatening to withhold assistance after serious food riots of 1985. As the political turmoil and human rights situation continued to deteriorate in 1986, the Reagan administration postponed a $26 million aid package to Haiti. Unable to pacify the country, and without the guarantee of U.S. support, Duvalier and his family, and a few close advisors, were airlifted into exile in France on a U.S. cargo plane in early 1986. As most Haitians celebrated Baby Doc's abdication and the end of Duvalierism, an army-dominated government replaced the family dynasty and continued the politics of repression. The most ruthless members of the secret police were lynched, and the symbols of the Duvalier dictatorship were destroyed.

The devastating effects of 30 years of Duvalierism left Haiti under the thumb of the United States and the Haitian military, a risky combination that made the task of economic and political reconstruction problematic. Having been trained and supplied by the United States, the Haitian military displayed no interest in democratization or economic reform. During the last two decades of the Duvalier regime, Haiti lost 40 percent of its remaining forests and vegetation, an ecological disaster brought about by (1) poor farmers who chopped down trees for charcoal, and (2) the dictatorship's faulty reasoning that clearing forests would eliminate sanctuaries for anti-government guerrillas.

Duvalierism without Duvalier

The army-dominated Conseil National de Gouvernement (CNG) became the provisional government of Haiti after the demise of the Duvaliers in 1986. Henri Namphy, a U.S. Army–trained general, became Haitian chief of state after coaxing from the U.S. embassy. The United States resumed foreign assistance programs and substantially increased grant money to Haiti. The CNG attempted to restore order in Haiti by policing protests and maintaining curfews, but many saw this type of government as nothing more than "Duvalierism without Duvalier," a dismal future indeed. The Duvalier dictatorship left a more politicized and participatory nation, one that would be much more difficult to govern than at any time in the twentieth century.

The reforms that Haitians demanded in post-Duvalier Haiti included a popularly elected civilian government and some form of legal accountability for crimes committed by the followers of the Duvaliers. Under domestic and international pressure to move Haiti toward democracy, General Namphy scheduled presidential elections for November 1987, and the CNG unenthusiastically began prosecuting Duvalierists thought to have committed crimes during the dark days of the dictatorship. President Reagan withheld nonhumanitarian assistance when the army-dominated government suspended the election in the midst of widespread terrorism caused by Du-

valierists. The presidential election was rescheduled for January 1988, but the turnout was scant, and Leslie Manigat assumed the presidency with little legitimacy, having colluded with the CNG for the presidency. When he defied the CNG six months later, Manigat was removed and army juntas and repeated military coups continued to dominate Haitian politics with support from the United States, particularly military assistance.

HAITI AND THE UNITED STATES DURING THE POST–COLD WAR ERA

The Rise and Fall of Father Aristide

President George Bush (1989–1993) inherited the Haitian problem from the Reagan years and continued to use carrot-and-stick policies in a futile effort to steer Haiti in a more stable and democratic direction. The December 1990 presidential election that brought Jean-Bertrand Aristide—former priest and professed enemy of Duvalierism—to power was carefully supervised by the United States. Aristide, campaigning as a foe of Duvalierism and foreign meddling and as a champion of the impoverished majority, won the election with over 70 percent of the vote. He also dished out severe criticism of the United States for its long-time support of the Duvalier dynasty. Tensions increased as Aristide tried to put redistribution policies in effect, hampering his ability to rule. In the midst of continuing political turmoil, General Raoul Cédras conducted a military coup in September 1991 that removed Aristide from power. Many of Aristide's supporters were slain in the coup, thousands of Haitians fled the island in rickety boats for the United States, and Father Aristide narrowly escaped death to begin a life of exile, hoping someday to finish his elected term of office.

The Haitian military under General Cédras soon assumed its traditional role as defender of the status quo with no intention of ending repression or promoting democracy. In a feeble effort to return Haiti to democracy, the Bush administration imposed trade sanctions on Haiti and supported mediation efforts (and trade sanctions) of the Organization of American States. These efforts had little impact on the military government, as the human rights abuses continued, drug smuggling increased, and tens of thousands of Haitian refugees tried to flee the island only to be intercepted by the U.S. Coast Guard and forcibly repatriated to Haiti. Although Bill Clinton criticized Bush's Haiti policy as being insensitive to the plight of Haitians and the lack of democracy, he did not reverse the policies he criticized after taking office in 1993. The administrations's harsh treatment of Haitian refugees—in contrast to the welcome mat for Cubans leaving Castro's Cuba—on the grounds that they were economic, rather than political, refugees gained little support in the U.S. public and elsewhere.

Return of Aristide and the Politics of Intervention

After Jean-Bertrand Aristide began his residence-in-exile in the Georgetown section of Washington, D.C., the Clinton administration soon faced one of its major foreign policy dilemmas. Using the Organization of American States and the United Nations, the Clinton administration spent almost two years trying to negotiate the removal of the Haitian military and the return of the democratically elected Aristide. In a reversal of political roles in the United States, liberals such as Senator Edward M. Kennedy and Reverend Jesse Jackson advocated military intervention, whereas conservatives such as Senator Robert Dole spoke out against military involvement. Several agreements were signed (the Washington Agreement in 1992 and the Governor's Island Agreement in 1993), but on each occasion the diplomatic arrangements failed.

The frustration of failed agreements and economic and arms embargoes led the United Nations Security Council to approve the use of multilateral force to attempt a last-ditch effort to return Aristide. On September 15, 1994, President Clinton, buffeted by critics who accused him of conducting a weak and vacillating foreign policy, declared his intention to invade Haiti unless the generals stepped down. The following day, a last-minute mission by former president Jimmy Carter brokered a deal whereby the military junta would leave Haiti so that President Aristide could return to Port-au-Prince. On September 19, 1994, U.S. troops landed in Haiti (building to 23,000) with virtually no opposition, and on the following day multinational forces arrived from other countries. Aristide returned to power a month later and resumed the presidency in November 1994. With the sanctions lifted, Haiti faced the daunting task of national reconstruction, including efforts to redesign the government to improve the economic situation and prevent a return of the military and the Duvalierists. U.S. forces focused on creating the Interim Public Security Force, and its troops began to withdraw before the end of 1994. During the following year, the UN Mission in Haiti (UNMIH) replaced many of the U.S. troops. President Aristide faced the impossible task of pleasing the United States and international donors and lenders while fulfilling his populist promises to his followers.

Democracy and Its Discontents

According to the Governor's Island Agreement, Aristide pledged not to run for a second term as president and to permit presidential elections to take place on schedule. Although Washington shifted to a more pro-Aristide policy, it put pressure on Aristide to follow conservative economic policies and cooperate with international lenders. Haitians remained frustrated and disappointed with Aristide's government, and relations with the United States did not improve. While many were willing to acknowledge the U.S. contribution to the restoration of an elected government and stability, they disagreed with the methods employed by Washington to rehabilitate the country.

Despite this dissatisfaction and sporadic violence, the pro-government electoral alliance, Plate-forme Politique Lavalas (PPL), and its presidential candidate, René Préval, were victorious in the 1995 elections. In that same year the Haitian National Police Force replaced the Interim Public Security Force and the United Nations withdrew more of its forces, leaving 1,300 international troops in Haiti. Préval improved Haitian-Dominican relations and denounced tax evasion and corruption, but instability and dependence on foreign assistance made his political survival tenuous.[4] By 1998 political infighting had so paralyzed Haitian democracy that the country was left without a prime minister and deprived of large amounts of foreign aid. The UN peacekeeping mission remained in place while hundreds of U.S. troops worked to help rebuild the country.

CONCLUSION

Haiti and the United States both emerged from anticolonial rebellions in the eighteenth century, but their developmental paths produced some striking differences as each faced the challenge of ending slavery and establishing republicanism, democracy, and economic development. Haiti's importance to the United States varied according to how it affected U.S. interests. During the nineteenth century, the United States paid little attention to Haiti until the U.S. Civil War. After the Spanish-American War in 1898, the security value of Haiti increased as the United States established protectorates throughout the Caribbean and constructed the Panama Canal. The long period of U.S. military occupation preceding the Good Neighbor Policy helped to create the foundation for future military governments and the 30-year Duvalier dictatorship during the Cold War. After the Cold War, the Bush and Clinton administrations found it impossible to ignore Haiti due to its volatile government and the continual threat from refugees and drugs, and the almost impossible task of promoting democracy and protecting human rights.

NOTES

1. Quoted in Rayford W. Logan, *Haiti and the Dominican Republic* (New York: Oxford University Press, 1968), p. 125.

2. Brenda Gayle Plummer, *Haiti and the United States: The Psychological Moment* (Athens: University of Georgia Press, 1992), p. 101.

3. Larman C. Wilson, "François Duvalier," in Barbara A. Tenenbaum, editor-in-chief, *Encyclopedia of Latin American History and Culture*, vol. 2 (New York: Scribner and Sons, 1996), p. 423.

4. While President Aristide opposed privatization and resisted it and other advice of the International Monetary Fund (IMF) and World Bank, Préval agreed to privatization and other requirements since his government desperately needed funds to rule.

SUGGESTED READINGS

Bellegarde-Smith, Patrick. *Haiti: The Breached Citadel*. Boulder, CO: Westview Press, 1990.

Logan, Rayford W. *Haiti and the Dominican Republic*. New York: Oxford University Press, 1968.

Plummer, Brenda Gayle. *Haiti and the United States: The Psychological Moment*. Athens: University of Georgia Press, 1992.

Wilson, Larman C. "François Duvalier." In Barbara A. Tenenbaum, editor-in-chief. *Encyclopedia of Latin American History and Culture*, vol. 2. New York: Scribner and Sons, 1996.

16

Honduras

TIMELINE OF U.S. RELATIONS WITH HONDURAS

1821	Honduran independence from Spain is declared
1858	U.S. diplomatic relations are established
1899	First banana concession is granted
	United Fruit Company is founded
1907	Sam Zemurray founds Cuyamel Fruit Company
1910–1911	Lee Christmas revolution
1929	United Fruit buys Cuyamel Fruit Company for $32 million
1932–1948	General Tiburcio Carías Andino rules as dictator
1954	Military assistance agreement is signed
1969	Soccer War
1975	Bananagate scandal
1980–1991	Honduras receives $1.2 billion from United States in exchange for acting as a base for the United States to carry out anti-Communist crusade in Central America
1981	Roberto Suazo Córdoba is elected president
	Contra operation begins
1986	Iran Contra affair reveals depth of U.S. involvement in Honduras
1990–1994	Rafael Leonardo Callejas serves as elected president
1990	Contras are disbanded
1994–1998	Carlos Roberto Reina serves as elected president
1995	*Baltimore Sun* publishes a series on the human rights abuses of Battalion 3–16

INTRODUCTION

U.S.-Honduran relations have been influenced more by developments in other parts of Central America and the world than by the debilitating tendencies that characterize Honduras: chronic political instability, frequent military takeovers, government inefficiency and corruption, and economic underdevelopment. The only Central American country bordering three countries—El Salvador, Guatemala, and Nicaragua—Honduras did not attract the same degree of political attention devoted to Nicaragua and Guatemala until the Cold War era. The United States sent military troops to Honduras at least 10 times between 1896 and 1925 to protect American lives and interests during periods of turmoil and revolution. One of the famous individuals who was instructed to enforce U.S. Central American policy during the period was Major General Smedley D. Butler, who confessed in 1935 (after retirement) that:

> I spent thirty-three years and four months in active service as a member of our country's most agile military force, the Marine Corps. I served in all the commissioned ranks from second lieutenant to major-general. And during that period I spent most of my time being a high-class muscle man for Big Business, for Wall Street and for the bankers. In short, I was a racketeer for capitalism. . . . I helped make Honduras "right" for American fruit companies in 1903.[1]

While serving the interests of banana companies, banks, and other foreign investors, Honduras also became one of the closest friends of the United States in responding to revolutionary "threats" deemed dangerous to U.S. security. On two major occasions—regarding Guatemala in 1954 and Nicaragua from 1979 to 1989—the United States used Honduras as a staging area to either remove or "destabilize" revolutionary governments. Unlike Nicaragua, Honduras never experienced extended periods of occupation or the status as a formal U.S. protectorate. Moreover, the virulent anti-Americanism that developed elsewhere never took hold in Honduras, making it prime territory for foreign manipulation and domination.

Honduras lacked rich volcanic soils and a large indigenous population to exploit as cheap labor, which hindered the development of a powerful landed elite. As a result, Honduras avoided the extremes of wealth and poverty, polarization, and revolutionary upheavals that have characterized its neighbors. Until the end of the nineteenth century, Honduras operated in isolation with a population mostly engaged in subsistence agriculture. To change this situation, the Honduran elite courted foreign investment by providing lucrative concessions to foreign investors. Two U.S. banana companies—United Fruit and Standard Fruit—soon dominated Honduras, often exercising as much, or more, power than the Honduran president. For the first half of the twentieth century, under the thumb of large private banana companies and corrupt rulers, Honduras fit the image of the quintessential "banana republic": economically dependent on foreign money and markets, coup-prone, corrupt, and economically backward. Hollywood movies and foreign authors often ridiculed the country and its people, fostering a deep sense of inferiority and dependency on the United States. Throughout the Cold War, Honduras was mostly ruled by military personnel trained and equipped by the United States.

HONDURAS AND THE UNITED STATES IN THE NINETEENTH CENTURY

Honduras declared its independence from Spain in 1821 as part of the Central American Federation. After the Federation collapsed in 1838, Honduras became an independent republic along with the rest of Central America. During the early decades of separation from Spain, Central Americans looked naturally to the United States for protection against Mexico, Great Britain, and the large nations to the south.

Honduras and the Monroe Doctrine

The Monroe Doctrine has not been a major factor in U.S.-Honduran relations even though Honduras was by no means immune from external involvement and colonizing efforts on its territory. During the first half of the nineteenth century, Britain established the colony of British Honduras in the Guatemalan territory of Belize and the Miskito Protectorate along the eastern coast of Nicaragua in order to protect mining, timber, and political interests. In 1838 the British seized the Bay Islands lying off the coast of Honduras and held them until 1860. When Honduras, El Salvador, and Nicaragua faced another invasion from Mexico in 1849, the Nicaraguan minister in London asked the U.S. minister whether they might be admitted to the Union. The United States refused in large part because Northerners feared that Southerners were interested in annexation of Central America for additional slave territory. When the filibustering expedition of William Walker seized the government of Nicaragua and received formal recognition from the Pierce administration in the 1850s, Honduras began to worry about the usefulness of the Monroe Doctrine to their sovereignty and independence. Each of these cases might have provoked a protest from Washington over violations of the noncolonization principle proclaimed in the doctrine, but the United States did not seem to care or interpret the violations as serious threats. Hondurans tended to reject the Monroe Doctrine because it was considered less a guarantee of independence than a menace to its very existence.

HONDURAS AND THE UNITED STATES IN THE EARLY TWENTIETH CENTURY

The Emergence of a Banana Republic

Banana plantations developed in the 1880s after railroads were constructed and oceangoing steamships made it possible to export perishable fruit with less chance of damage. By 1900 bananas were Honduras's most important export crop. The key figures in Honduras's banana business were the Vacarro brothers, Sicilian immigrants from New Orleans and founders of Standard Fruit Company, and Samuel ("Sam the Banana Man") Zemurray, founder of Cuyamel Fruit Company and a later director of United Fruit Company. With keen entrepreneurial skills, access to large funds of investment capital, and ties to Honduran dictators, these banana pioneers amassed huge fortunes during the first half of the twentieth century. Until his retirement as president of United Fruit in 1951, Sam Zemurray was the most powerful man in Central America, worth an estimated $30 million after more than 50 years in the banana business. With a local oligarchy lacking the necessary capital to develop an export economy, Honduran politicians provided generous concessions to foreign investors in order to attract sufficient funds to address the country's lack of development.

The first boatload of bananas from Honduras to New Orleans took place in 1899, which marked the beginning of U.S. interference and decades of political instability. Honduras's dynamic banana empire at first received support from the government, expecting the fruit companies to build a needed railroad that would link the northern coast with the mountainous interior but which never was built. Three banana companies—Standard Fruit, Cuyamel, and United Fruit—competed among themselves and with the Honduran government to see who could extract the best concessions. Soon the banana companies were engaged in electioneering and party politics, each seeking ways to outmaneuver the competition by catering to Honduran politicians. This meddling in Honduran politics included the financing of armed rebellions, bribery of government officials, and pressing the government to repeal unfavorable legislation. The banana companies developed a symbiotic relationship with the government of Honduras, based in large part on the need for favorable labor laws, land grants, and permission to build railroads and port facilities. Honduras needed the United States for its steamships to get the fruit to market before it spoiled, as well as the capital and the marketing expertise to succeed. To compensate for its weak economic position, Honduras taxed every stem of bananas exported and attempted to support local growers by encouraging competition and passing various forms of protective legislation.

After a peaceful and constitutional transfer of power in 1899, Honduran politics became more unstable and conflictual due to the power of the U.S.

banana companies and the greed of Honduran politicians. In 1903 General Manuel Bonilla seized power, after his predecessor tried to perpetuate himself in power, and soon proved to be a great friend of the banana companies. During his first term (1903–1907) Bonilla promoted internal improvements, settled several border disputes, and made generous concessions to the fledgling banana companies. However, his repressive treatment of the opposition ultimately led to his ouster in 1907 by militant Liberals led by General Miguel Dávila.

After a border conflict between Nicaragua and Honduras in 1907, President José Santos Zelaya invaded Honduras, occupied Tegucigalpa, and forced President Bonilla into exile aboard a U.S. warship. In an effort to reach a settlement among the disputants, the U.S. State Department allowed Washington S. Valentine, an American with extensive mining interests in Honduras, to mediate along with American diplomats. Known as the "King of Honduras" because of his dominance over oil and mining interests, Valentine was the obvious choice to be "our man in Honduras." However, to the shock and dismay of the U.S. State Department, Valentine suggested that the Nicaraguan leader be permitted to establish a military government in Honduras as a way of preventing further foreign interference. The United States refused Valentine's proposal and called for a Central American Peace Conference in 1907. The five Central American republics agreed to a provision for permanent neutrality of Honduras in any future conflict and several other agreements designed to stimulate constitutional government and stability.

Lee Christmas: Soldier of Fortune and Friend of Sam

U.S. plans to stabilize the Honduran financial system and promote political stability were interpreted by the "banana man" as a threat to his private interests in Honduras. In defiance of Washington in 1910, Zemurray befriended former president Manuel Bonilla, then in New Orleans after a failed invasion plan against President Dávila. Bonilla borrowed money from Zemurray, purchased a yacht and loaded it with arms, recruited a small army headed by soldier of fortune Lee Christmas and Colonel Guy "Machine Gun" Maloney, and then set sail for Honduras to overthrow the Dávila government in 1911. The Bonilla-Zemurray revolution, with Lee Christmas in command, proved easy and Tegucigalpa fell in a matter of hours without a fight. Within a short time Bonilla was restored to the presidency, ready to provide generous concessions to Zemurray. Christmas was rewarded with command of the Honduran army, and his lieutenant, "Machine Gun" Maloney, was given the task of subduing peasants whose land was needed to make good the concessions granted to Cuyamel Fruit. Not content to remain in Honduras, Christmas also provided revolutionary services in Nicaragua, El Salvador, and Guatemala, and he is credited with helping place five Central American presidents in power through revolution before he died in 1924. Although Washington was angry at Zemurray and United Fruit, it never took legal action against them even though the evidence strongly suggests a conspiracy to break U.S. neutrality laws and overthrow the Honduran government.

The Carías Dictatorship, 1932–1948

Tiburcio Carías Andino came to power through an election in 1932, but by using strong-arm methods of rule and constituent assemblies to extend his term of office he managed to rule Honduras longer than any individual in his country's history. Carías faced the negative effects of the Depression combined with a particularly bad economic situation throughout the 1930s. The banana industry was hit by a dramatic drop in exports caused by the Depression and a serious outbreak of plant diseases that threatened production after 1935. Carías strengthened his power over the country by expanding the military and pursuing conservative economic policies that pleased the banana companies. After three years in power, stressing the need for peace and internal order, Carías had solidified his dictatorship through propaganda and repression of opposition forces. Carías fit the mold of what Hollywood might call the perfect "banana republic" dictator. He was "six feet four, weighing 260 pounds, . . . eccentric, irascible, puritanical, and tyrannical. He carried a cane and wore a fedora, but his thick leather belt and cheap rough-cut boots bespoke his peasant origins."[2]

The 16-year dictatorship of Tiburcio Carías Andino brought an end to the banana company–backed civil wars and the possibility of greater political stability for Honduras. It was a rather vicious brand of authoritarianism with features that seemed particularly harsh on its political opponents. Until his young nephew convinced him otherwise, Carías banned baseball to prevent his enemies from using the bats as weapons against him. His was one of several Central American dictatorships during the 1930s and 1940s that seemed out of tune with President Franklin D. Roosevelt's Good Neighbor Policy. Having abandoned its interventionist practices in the 1930s, Washington would have to ignore the tyranny, electoral fraud, and constitutional maneuvering of the "friendly dictators" operating in Central America prior to World War II. Under Carías, peaceful demonstrators against the dictatorship were fired on by troops with intent to kill. His motto of dealing with the opposition became known as "round them up, throw them out, and bury them." He jailed hundreds of innocent people on charges of either being communists or aiding communism in some fashion. Despite continual efforts to topple his government, Carías remained in power until 1948, when he decided to yield to U.S. pressure to step aside after 16 years in power.

HONDURAS AND THE UNITED STATES DURING THE COLD WAR

The Honduran Military and U.S. Security

The Carías dictatorship helped to forge close ties between the armed forces of the United States and Honduras that extended throughout the Cold War. The beginning of a professional Honduran military dates from 1952, when the Francisco Morazán Military Academy was established with the assistance of the U.S. Army. After Honduras and the United States signed a Military Assistance Agreement in 1954, the power of the Honduran military increased with financial and technical assistance from Washington. The United States supplied modern equipment, provided advanced training to Honduran officers, and helped establish a network of military bases. Between 1949 and 1964 the United States trained 810 Honduran military officers at the U.S. Army School of the Americas in Panama. Honduras experienced its first Cold War military coup in 1956. In the following year a new constitution was written making the armed forces independent of the elected government and, thus, a powerful force in national political affairs. For the next 30 years the military—with U.S. backing—controlled Honduran politics despite efforts to promote democracy and human rights in the region.

Counterrevolution and Intervention in Guatemala

During the final years of the Jacobo Arbenz (1950–1954) government in Guatemala, exiles gathered around their leader—Colonel Carlos Castillo Armas—in Tegucigalpa, Honduras. A protegé of Somoza in Nicaragua, Castillo Armas aspired to be the "supreme savior" of Guatemala by garnering U.S. support to overthrow Arbenz (see Chapter 13). The plotters were given encouragement and material assistance by the United Fruit Company and various dictators in the region. President Eisenhower's plan to oust Arbenz—code-named Operation Success—called for the CIA to train and equip a small liberation army under a compliant leader to invade from Honduras. U.S. ambassador Whiting Willauer was given the task of prodding President Gálvez to keep the Honduran government in line. He also worked with other activist ambassadors in the region such as Tom Whelan (Nicaragua) and Jack Peurifoy (Guatemala). Both Willauer and Peurifoy knew little about the region, having never set foot in Central America before their arrival as ambassadors.

As the day of the invasion approached, security concerns were heightened by the arrival of Soviet-bloc weapons in Guatemala and a strike against United Fruit and Standard Fruit in Honduras among 40,000 workers. President Gálvez requested that two U.S. warships be stationed off the northern coast, ready to land if necessary, but plans for a Marine landing had already been set. Honduran officials blamed the strike on the communists and singled out Guatemala as the source of the labor conflict. Before the conflict was over Guatemala appealed to the United Nations to play a mediating role, but the United States, preferring the Organization of American States (where it could control the votes of any proceedings), was successful in getting the UN Security Council to defer to the OAS.

The events in 1954 that led to Arbenz's downfall in Guatemala, and the big 1954 strike action, were important for future U.S.-Honduran relations. For example, the strike convinced the government that it should sign a defense assistance agreement with the United States, but it did not provide base access or provisions to put large numbers of U.S. troops in Honduras. Later, during the Reagan administration, the agreement was amended to give the United States base rights that allowed for the later military buildup under the promise of almost perpetual joint military exercises.

Honduras and the Alliance for Progress

The Kennedy administration was supportive of Honduran president Ramón Villeda since he was perceived in Washington as an anticommunist, supportive of private initiatives, and a fan of the goals of the Alliance for Progress. To help modernize and expand the economy, Villeda brought Honduras into the Central American Common Market and proposed an agrarian reform law in 1962. The U.S. ambassador to Honduras, Charles Burrows, warned Villeda that he should delay the agrarian law legislation until it was approved by the State Department, while the U.S. military tried to dissuade the Honduran generals—fearful of Villeda's "communist" agrarian measures—from going forward with their coup. U.S. efforts to halt the military overthrow of Villeda in 1963 were unsuccessful, leaving the White House and State Department to wonder about the Pentagon's argument that training, equipment, security assistance, and personal relationships are vital to U.S. security because they provide the United States important leverage with their Latin American counterparts. By now, the frequency of military takeovers in Honduras had earned it the title of Tegucigolpe (a play on words: *Tegucigalpa* being the capital, and *golpe* meaning a coup d'état). Despite the coup, the new president—Oswaldo López Arellano—was soon recognized by Washington and economic assistance continued to flow. At his inaugural, the top corporate executives of United Fruit and Standard Fruit were given places of honor. The new military leaders proved inept at managing the economy, but this did not prevent continual military rule, and coups, over the next decade.

The *Fútbol* (Soccer) War of 1969

A brief war erupted between El Salvador and Honduras (July 14–18, 1969) after several violence-plagued soccer matches throughout June 1969. The real causes of the war were rooted in domestic problems in both countries, including the expulsion of thousands of Salvadoran peasants living illegally along the Honduran border, many for generations without title to the land. Many of the early Salvadoran immigrants had come from densely populated El Salvador in search of employment with the banana companies. Often the victims of harassment, Salvadorans living in Honduras were forced to return to El Salvador after Honduran president Oswaldo López Arellano decided to distribute government-owned lands to Honduran peasants. The massive exodus of Salvadorans to their homeland brought horrific tales of their treatment while in Honduras, which further inflamed tensions. With pressure mounting on Salvadoran president Fidel Sánchez Hernández from the military and conservative opponents of land reform, Sánchez Hernández severed diplomatic relations and ordered troops, and air force attacks, into Honduran territory.

By the time of the Soccer War, the Nixon administration had adopted a low-profile approach to Central America. The Alliance for Progress disappeared from presidential discourse, economic assistance was cut drastically, and one heard less frequent condemnation of the region's military rulers in Washington. As El Salvador and Honduras prepared for war, the embassies of the United States were kept in the dark. Meanwhile, two U.S. military officials—the Military Group Commander and Army Section Chief—actually directed much of the mobilization and attack planning for the Salvadorans, while informing U.S. officials in Tegucigalpa that there were absolutely no signs of military mobilization or increased readiness nextdoor in El Salvador. The astonishing deceit and duplicity of U.S. military officials led to an intelligence failure for the United States, contributing to a major foreign policy disaster (and bloody war) in Central America when a diplomatic solution offered possibilities of success. While there is no evidence that embassy officials in El Salvador and Honduras, State Department personnel in Washington, and even CIA operatives in the region were aware of the infraction, the fact that two senior U.S. military officers secretly sided with El Salvador in the war is a reflection of one of the primary flaws in the conduct of U.S. Central American policy.

After the conflict had subsided, both Honduras and El Salvador blamed the United States, although for different reasons. Since both countries violated the terms of their military agreements with the United States, Washington and the Organization of American States embargoed both countries. Nevertheless both Honduras and El Salvador found ways of placing the blame for the invasion elsewhere, particularly on the United States. The

Nixon administration was also criticized by some in Congress who blamed the United States for supplying the weapons that each country used to pursue the war effort.

The initial cease-fire—arranged by the Organization of American States and the United States—came quickly, but the war was brutal: "perhaps as many as two thousand people were killed, twice that number wounded, a hundred thousand refugees created, fifty million dollars lost, and the dream of Central American unity again shattered."[3] Although the fighting itself lasted only four days, the conflict dragged on until the two sides agreed to final peace terms in 1980. The war had a lasting impact on Central America as well as on the two desperately poor countries that fought the brief, and unnecessary, war. It left in its wake a simmering border dispute that disrupted relations, all but killed the Central American Common Market, and aggravated the impending social crisis that would erupt in El Salvador during the 1970s. The whole affair increased the militarization of each society and destroyed any real hope for peaceful political change. The Soccer War paved the way for nine years of military rule and the "purchase" of Honduras by the United States after the Nicaraguan revolution had brought an end to the Somoza dynasty.

The Bananagate Scandal

After a long period of stagnation in the price of bananas, a grower's cartel—the Union of Banana Exporting Countries (UPEB)—was established in 1974 with hopes of raising banana prices by charging an export tax of one dollar per 40 pound crate of bananas. The three U.S.-controlled companies all refused to negotiate a price-fixing plan with the UPEB and announced they would not pay the tax. In what became known as the Bananagate scandal, United Brands (formerly United Fruit) was discovered to have paid $1.25 million in bribes to officials in Honduras in exchange for a tax decrease. The revelation was made by the *Wall Street Journal* in early 1975 after Eli Black, president of United Brands, jumped to his death from his New York office window. After the "banana bribe" was discovered, political instability followed, President Oswaldo López was forced to resign, and the banana cartel collapsed. The banana companies resumed normal business practices after the scandal, and the new military government in the hands of General Juan Melgar Castro (1975–1978) pursued more conservative economic policies and did its best to avoid alienating the United States.

The Central American Crisis and the Militarization of Honduras

The principal architects of U.S.-Honduran relations between 1980 and 1985 were William Casey (CIA), Duane ("Dewey") Clarridge (CIA), and

Pentagon planners. The U.S. assistant secretary of state for inter-American affairs, Thomas Enders, played a secondary role, as did Jeanne Kirkpatrick. Ambassador John Negroponte, a Yale graduate and career diplomat but with little experience in Central America, worked with the Hondurans and put the plans of Casey and Clarridge in action. Both Casey and Clarridge had little respect for Congress and international law, and the fact that neither had served in Latin America or knew much about the region did not seem to be relevant, or necessary, to those in the Reagan administration. As part of the Core Group for Central America, Clarridge also worked with Oliver North and other members of the National Security Council (NSC) until 1984, when he was replaced by Alan D. Fiers Jr. Clarridge was the instigator of the CIA plan to mine Nicaraguan harbors, one of the most counterproductive projects he carried out while part of the Reagan team to destroy Sandinista Nicaragua, producing outrage on Capitol Hill (see Chapter 19). In the wake of the Iran Contra affair, Clarridge retired from the CIA in 1987 after being formally reprimanded by the agency for his role in the sordid affair. In November 1991 a federal grand jury indicted Clarridge on seven counts of perjury and false statements he made to congressional investigators and the Tower Commission, a presidential commission headed by former Senator John Tower that investigated the Iran Contra affair in 1987. However, Clarridge was spared a trial after President Bush pardoned him and five other Iran Contra defendants in December 1992.

The Contras emerged in 1978 when Argentine Army Intelligence Battalion 601 sent advisors to Central America to counter what was viewed as Carter's "soft on communism" Central American policy. The Argentine advisers worked with Somoza's National Guard to bolster his crumbling dictatorship but were not able to prevent his downfall. After the Sandinistas overthrew Somoza in 1979, the Argentine advisers began training Somoza's former guardsmen—the first Contras in Central America—to battle the government in Managua. Shortly thereafter Honduras became an important ally of the United States in responding to revolutionary change in Nicaragua, and the Argentines served as CIA surrogates in part to give the United States a measure of deniability.

The Honduran military was needed to serve as a base of operations for the U.S.-backed Contra war during the Reagan years. In March 1980, Honduran president Policarpo Paz García was told that the Pentagon had chosen Honduras to replace Nicaragua as a dependable pro-American country that would serve—bought and paid for by U.S. military and economic largesse—as a bulwark of anticommunism against revolutionary forces in Central America. General Gustavo Álvarez Martínez, head of the public security forces in Honduras, was the key liaison with Washington. He made several trips to the United States during which he met with Casey, Enders, and others and was the first to broach the Contra operation (already under

"What About the Iran-Contra Indictments, Mr. President?"

way with Argentine support) to CIA director Casey. Casey agreed and in doing so made the United States an instrument of Honduran military policy, not the reverse. Honduras was now ready to serve as a stationary battleship (often dubbed the USS *Honduras* by critics of the policy) for the Reagan administration's plan to remove the Sandinistas from Nicaragua and protect the Salvadoran government from the threat of leftist guerrillas.

Ambassador Negroponte teamed by up with General Gustavo Álvarez Martínez, head of the armed forces and a fervent anticommunist. Convinced he was fighting a holy war, Álvarez once said that "Everything you do to destroy a Marxist regime is moral."[4] Álvarez had attended officer training schools in Argentina and Peru and taken advanced courses in infantry and counterinsurgency training at Fort Benning, Georgia, and the U.S. Army School of the Americas in Panama. Despite his command of the Contra operations and his close ties to the CIA and U.S. military figures, Álvarez did not last through Reagan's first term in office; human rights abuses, corruption, and mistreatment of military colleagues forced his resignation in 1984.

The Contras were eventually disbanded as part of the Central American peace process in the late 1980s. After the Central American presidents requested the UN Security Council to create an Observer Group in 1989 (ONUCA—UN Observer Group in Central America) to assist with the dismantling of the Contra forces in Honduras, it joined with the Organization of American States (OAS) in disarming and escorting the Contras back to Nicaragua in 1989–1990. The repatriation of the Contras through the use of international forces was facilitated by the election of Nicaraguan president Violeta Barrios de Chamorro in 1990, the defeat of the Sandinistas, and the election of President George Bush, who was anxious to get Central America off the foreign policy agenda in Washington.

Death Squads and Guerrillas

Soon after the United States moved into Honduras to assume control of the Contra war, human rights violations began to escalate, particularly by those who made up Battalion 3–16, a Honduran military unit trained by the CIA and the FBI that engaged in a systematic program of disappearances and political murder from 1981 to 1984. General Gustavo Álvarez Martínez commanded the unit that targeted mainly leftist activists—students, teachers, unionists, and would-be guerrillas—who were captured and never seen ("disappeared") again, dead or alive. Although John Negroponte, U.S. ambassador in Honduras at the time, has denied the existence of death squads in Honduras on his watch, the Inter-American Court of Human Rights found Honduras responsible for these atrocities and ordered the government to pay damages to the relatives of the victims. A veil of secrecy surrounding the extent of CIA involvement in Honduras has prevented a full explanation of the U.S. government's role in Battalion 3–16. The Clinton administration has not seen fit to declassify the documents needed to illuminate what has become a shameful chapter in U.S.-Honduran relations.

HONDURAS AND THE UNITED STATES AFTER THE COLD WAR

Honduras is a prime example of how politically motivated cash transfers from Washington to fight the Cold War in Central America declined rapidly after the crisis ended in the early 1990s. With Honduras no longer needed as a safe haven for anti-Sandinista Contra guerrillas and a training base for Salvadoran soldiers and thousands of American troops, the big money that poured into Honduras disappeared, leaving in its wake bitterness and frustration. With the struggle against communism over, Washington had little use for the Honduran military, now viewed as a largely corrupt and expensive obstacle to the consolidation of democracy. Important social and economic programs were started with U.S. assistance, but most of the aid was either wasted or stolen by corrupt politicians or military officers. The sharp decline in U.S. assistance has made it easier for Honduran presidents to tackle necessary reforms, including reduction in size of the military, economic modernization, and eradication of corruption and government inefficiency. Nevertheless, these economic and military reforms have been the result of U.S. pressure, a sign that Honduras is still highly dependent on the United States.

CONCLUSION

Relations between the United States and Honduras continue to reflect the legacies of intervention, domination, dependency, and economic exploitation. The banana companies are not as powerful as they once were—bananas accounted for only 36 percent of export revenues in 1992—and the name United Fruit Company no longer exists, but Honduras still resembles a "banana republic" with limited sovereignty over its national territory. Chiquita Brands International (Chiquita controls 35 percent of world trade in bananas) with headquarters in Cincinnati, Ohio, still exercises considerable power over the outcome of agrarian conflicts. The Honduran military and the U.S. embassy continue to call the shots, regardless of who sits in the presidential palace in Tegucigalpa. Approximately 500 U.S. forces continue to operate out of Honduran bases, built during the height of the Cold War. In a public opinion poll published in 1996, Honduran respondents named the "U.S. ambassador" as the nation's most powerful man, outpolling President Carlos Roberto Reina (1994–1998) by eight percentage points. The ease with which the United States has been able to dominate Honduran society with large amounts of economic assistance and military aid (particularly in the 1980s) has often been counterproductive, leaving military authoritarianism, corruption, and mass poverty in its wake. Although the blame does not rest solely on the United States or the multinational fruit companies, U.S. policies and attitudes have often been of little overall benefit to Honduras, one of the Latin America's poorest countries.

NOTES

1. Quoted in Alison Acker, *Honduras: The Making of a Banana Republic* (Boston: South End Press, 1988), p. 21.
2. Ibid., p. 74.
3. Thomas P. Anderson, *The War of the Dispossessed: Honduras and El Salvador, 1969* (Lincoln: University of Nebraska Press, 1981), p. 1.
4. Quoted in Acker, *Honduras*, p. 115.

SUGGESTED READINGS

Acker, Alison. *Honduras: The Making of a Banana Republic*. Boston: South End Press, 1988.

Armony, Ariel C. *Argentina, The United States, and the Anti-Communist Crusade in Central America, 1977–1984.* Athens: Ohio University Press, 1997.

Euraque, Dario A. *Reinterpreting the Banana Republic: Region and State in Honduras, 1870–1972.* Chapel Hill: University of North Carolina Press, 1997.

Langley, Lester D., and Thomas Schoonover. *The Banana Men: American Mercenaries and Entreprenuers in Central America, 1880–1930.* Lexington: University Press of Kentucky, 1995.

Meyer, Harvey K., and Jessie H. Meyer. *Historical Dictionary of Honduras*, 2nd Edition. Metuchen, NJ: Scarecrow Press, 1994.

Peckenham, Nancy, and Annie Street, eds. *Honduras: Portrait of a Captive Nation.* New York: Praeger, 1985.

17

Jamaica

TIMELINE OF U.S. RELATIONS WITH JAMAICA

1838	Slavery is abolished
1890s	United Fruit Company begins banana production/export
1914	United Negro Improvement Association (UNIA) is established by Marcus Garvey
1916	Garvey moves UNIA to New York
1926	Garvey is sentenced to three years in a Georgia prison
1928	Garvey returns to Jamaica
	People's Political Party (PPP) is established
1930	Workingman and Labourers Association is formed
1938	Norman Manley founds People's National Party (PNP)
1939–1945	World War II; bauxite is discovered in Jamaica
1942	Alexander Bustamante founds Jamaica Labour Party (JLP)
1944	British allow limited self-government
1944–1952	Major U.S. aluminum companies begin operations
1958–1962	British create West Indies Federation
1962	Jamaica becomes independent
1972–1976	Michael Manley serves first term as prime minister
1974	Manley declares his government socialist
1976	Jamaica establishes the International Bauxite Association (IBA)
1980	Edward Seaga's Jamaica Labour Party (JLP) wins election
1989	Michael Manley returns as prime minister
1992	Manley resigns
1997	Manley dies at age 72

INTRODUCTION

Jamaica's relationship with the United States has been influenced by its size and strategic location in the northern Caribbean sea (particularly its proximity to Cuba), its long period as a colony of Great Britain (1655–1962), and a number of Jamaican black nationalists who have had a profound impact on the black population in the United States. When Jamaica finally achieved its independence in 1962, it possessed an economy that was structurally weak and dependent on the United States, Europe, and international financial institutions. The first prime minister, Alexander Bustamante, described Jamaica as pro-Western, anticommunist, and Christian, ready to align itself with the United States in the Cold War. The growing hostility between the United States and Cuba at the time of Jamaica's independence increased its importance during the Cold War.

U.S.-Jamaican relations remained friendly until the 1970s, when the Manley government decided to break out of the historical reliance on the United States and Britain. This shift contributed to his downfall in 1980, but a close alliance with the United States followed with the new conservative and anticommunist government headed by Edward Seaga. Despite the reelection of Michael Manley in 1989, and the continuation of People's National Party (PNP) rule into the 1990s, relations with the United States have remained cooperative and cordial.

JAMAICA AND THE UNITED STATES DURING THE NINETEENTH CENTURY

Until the abolishment of slavery in 1838, the British in Jamaica utilized slave labor imported from Africa and tried to maintain a monopoly on the production of sugar. However, the emancipation of slaves only worsened Jamaica's economic and social problems as the British struggled to maintain control over the island throughout the rest of the nineteenth century. Jamaica's sugar exports shifted to the United States after 1870, and by the mid-1880s the United Fruit Company had developed a banana business that in time rivaled the sugar industry. It was during this period that Jamaican-born Marcus M. Garvey took up the cause of the island's working poor, openly challenging racism, British colonialism, and foreign penetration of the economy.

JAMAICA AND THE UNITED STATES DURING THE EARLY TWENTIETH CENTURY

With the imposition of direct colonial rule under the Crown Colony arrangement, Jamaica entered a period of social protest and organization in which island labor organizers began to address the problems of poverty and exploitation of banana and sugar workers. Any form of political change was restrained by tight British control that forced middle-class elements of Haitian society—both black and brown—to seek change through nongovernmental agencies and labor organizations. After 200 years of British control, labor disturbances over wages and working conditions converged into two closely linked movements: black nationalism, and labor union organization.

Marcus M. Garvey: Black Nationalist and Labor Organizer

At the head of the early black nationalist protest movement was Marcus M. Garvey, a Jamaican of humble peasant origins who became outraged at the exploitation of black workers on the fruit plantations, railroads, and Panama Canal. One of the first black populists in the Americas, Garvey focused on racial solidarity, "Africa for Africans," and anticolonialism. His organizing skills on behalf of poor blacks had a profound impact on all Jamaicans and on the black population in the United States. In 1914 he established the United Negro Improvement Association (UNIA) to unite "all the Negro peoples of the world into a great body to establish a country and Government absolutely their own."[1] Unable to recruit better-off, educated blacks in Jamaica to his cause, Garvey left for New York in 1916, just in time to confront a growing tide of racial animosity and economic competition between blacks and whites. Working out of Harlem, Garvey built the UNIA into an organized force with an estimated two million members by 1925.

Garvey's success as an organizer of the poor and working classes was also his downfall. He was perceived as a threat to the white establishment in the United States and was sent to prison in Georgia on phony charges in 1926. After his release in 1928, he returned to Jamaica where his UNIA was attacked by powerful West Indians. His emphasis on the illegitimacy of British colonialism earned him the wrath of British administrators in Jamaica. The relentless attacks on Garvey and the devastating effects of the Great Depression on his organization took their toll on his health and resources. He continued to fight for his principles until his death in 1940, leaving behind the seeds of future struggles against colonialism and racism.

JAMAICA AND THE UNITED STATES DURING THE COLD WAR

The anticolonial struggles for independence in the Caribbean collided with the international events surrounding the end of World War II and the early decades of the Cold War. Despite the importance of the Caribbean during the war, the United States never challenged the European presence—

despite the availability of the Monroe Doctrine—or attempted to articulate a distinctly Caribbean policy that included Jamaica or the West Indies. It was only after European withdrawal from the area in the 1960s that the United States began in earnest to consider an authentic Caribbean policy. To give U.S. Caribbean policy legitimacy in the aftermath of the Vietnam War, emphasis was placed on foreign relations that reflected the independent role of Caribbean/Latin American nations in world affairs and respect for ideological diversity and types of economic organization. This revised outlook came to an end with a renewed emphasis on Caribbean security and anticommunism, beginning with the Reagan administration in 1981.

Decolonization and the Cold War

After World War II the United States began to play an increasingly important role in the Caribbean, anxious to replace its major European rival in the region. Under pressure from the United States and the growing power of Jamaicans clamoring for independence, the road to decolonization involved a combination of skills in the hands of labor-party leaders such as Alexander Bustamante, Norman Manley, and others throughout the Caribbean. As U.S. and Canadian aluminum multinationals moved into Jamaica in the early 1950s to mine the rich bauxite ore, an anti-imperial dimension was added to the independence struggle. When Fidel Castro came to power in 1959, only two Spanish-speaking countries (and one Créole–French) in the Caribbean were independent; but by 1983 the situation had changed dramatically, with the creation of 13 independent (English- and Dutch-speaking) Caribbean states.

The Failure of Federation and the End of British Colonialism

Commonwealth Caribbean independence evolved under the aegis of a British-imposed federation, which was supported by the growing labor movement. The West Indies Federation took shape in the late 1950s but collapsed as politicians from the larger islands—Jamaica and Trinidad—envisioned a political future based on national independence rather than some form of union. By 1961 Jamaica had pulled out of the Federation, claiming it would have to subsidize the smaller islands, and Trinidad followed shortly thereafter. Alexander Bustamante, a charismatic labor leader and founder of the Jamaica Labour Party (JLP), became Jamaica's first prime minister, following his party's success at the polls. Bustamante's pro–United States and pro–foreign investment policies pleased Washington in light of the difficulties the Kennedy administration faced in neighboring Cuba. Under Bustamante and two other prime ministers, the JLP dominated Jamaican politics until 1972. No longer a colony of Britain, Jamaica took an active role in international organizations and world affairs during the first two decades of independence. It has enjoyed full diplomatic relations with the United States since independence; taken an active role in the British Commonwealth of Nations; joined the Nonaligned Movement (a Third World movement founded in 1955 to deal with anticolonialism, neutrality toward the Cold War, and opposition to racism) and the Organization of American States (OAS); and helped create the Caribbean Community and Common Market (an organization of Caribbean states designed to coordinate foreign economic policy and achieve greater cooperation in economic and technical matters) in 1973.

The Rise of Michael Manley

Allegations of corruption within the JLP and growing tensions stemming from the black power movement that had produced serious riots on the island in 1968 paved the way for the election of People's National Party (PNP) candidate Michael Manley in 1972. The son of Norman Manley, the party's new leader declared his government's commitment to democratic socialism and a more independent foreign policy. His imposition of a heavy tax on foreign-owned bauxite companies, and later nationalization, contributed to animosity and a sharp reversal of policy from Washington. Under Manley's charismatic leadership, Jamaica's foreign policy shifted toward a Third World, nonaligned status, including membership in the Socialist International (a broad-based association of socialist labor unions and political parties) and friendly relations with Castro's Cuba and the Soviet bloc. In response the United States cut its traditional military relationship with Jamaica, eliminating training programs and other forms of assistance. Economic aid was reduced through declining levels of bilateral assistance and through pressure on multilateral lending agencies such as the International Monetary Fund and the World Bank. Allegations of CIA involvement in internal violence to disrupt the tourist industry were also made. Despite pressure from the United States, Jamaica maintained uninterrupted diplomatic or consular ties with Cuba until the election of Edward Seaga in 1980.

As Jamaica became more nationalist and Third World–oriented during the Manley years, the United States tried to reverse the trend with economic and diplomatic pressure and destabilization schemes. Jamaica frequently opposed the United States in the United Nations and the OAS with votes against Israel, and the U.S. trade embargo against Sandinista Nicaragua. Jamaica saw a promised aid package disappear after Prime Minister Manley came out publicly in favor of Cuban troops in Angola, in defiance of Secretary of State Henry Kissinger's request to remain neutral on the matter.

A pro-Manley group in New York, the Jamaican Progressive League

(JPL), raised money and tried to influence U.S. policy in favor of Jamaica during the Manley years. It was successful in improving U.S.-Jamaican relations while Jimmy Carter was president by working through UN ambassador Andrew Young to open up bauxite markets. In more recent times it has worked to improve U.S. immigration laws in favor of Jamaicans. The Carter administration launched a new Caribbean policy through multilateralism and a new emphasis on human rights, political and social pluralism, and a reduction in the flow of U.S. military equipment to the region. It was a rare interlude in U.S. policy toward the Caribbean until geopolitical and military concerns returned in 1979, a sobering reminder of the lingering effects of the Cold War.

Edward Seaga, Ronald Reagan, and the Caribbean Basin Initiative

The perception of a Cuban threat contributed to the electoral victory of Edward Seaga's anticommunist Jamaican Labour Party (JLP) in late 1980. Seaga's governing approach was to reverse the previous administration's policies by severing ties with Cuba, encouraging foreign investment, and cooperating with the IMF. Once Ronald Reagan was inaugurated in 1981, the Caribbean Basin was defined as having considerable strategic importance to the United States. In exchange for needed U.S. economic assistance, the Reagan administration demanded allegiance in its confrontational crusade against Cuba and leftist-oriented governments in Nicaragua, Grenada, and elsewhere in the region. Jamaica denounced the Grenada revolution under Maurice Bishop and supplied troops when the time came for the U.S.-led invasion of the island in late 1983.

In an effort to strengthen Caribbean economies against further insurgencies, civil wars, and pro-Cuban governments, President Reagan launched the Caribbean Basin Initiative (CBI)—a Seaga government proposal—in 1982 (approved by Congress in 1984). At the heart of the CBI was an emphasis on foreign private investment, combined with increased U.S. foreign assistance and preferential trade access to American markets. With Edward Seaga as prime minister, a conservative and pro-business leader, Jamaica was singled out as a Caribbean "showcase" to demonstrate the effectiveness of the CBI and the benefits of an alliance with Washington. Development assistance increased dramatically, in contrast to the drastic reductions during the Manley era. When it was originally proposed by President Reagan, the CBI was strongly endorsed by Canada, Mexico, and Venezuela, but they soon became critical when it was clear that its intent was *political*, to isolate and pressure the pro-Castro Sandinista government in Nicaragua. Although the CBI helped solidify support from Jamaica during the Reagan years, preferential market access did not solve other chronic economic problems, including U.S. restrictions on sugar quotas, textiles, and apparel, and the fears of being unable to enter, or compete with, Mexico after its inclusion in the North American Free Trade Agreement (NAFTA), a comprehensive agreement to set up a free trade area among Canada, Mexico, and the United States beginning in 1994.

U.S.-Jamaican Drug Trade

The power of drug trafficking operations tends to expand in the Caribbean as a result of the small operating budgets of governments to engage in counternarcotics activities and the vast resources available to private drug operations. The security of the state—against money laundering, crime, corruption, arms trafficking, the viability of the military, and threats to sovereignty—is a constant concern of government officials in Jamaica. Only marijuana is produced in the Caribbean, mainly in Jamaica, the Bahamas, Belize, and Guyana. The disparities in anti-drug capabilities has drawn the United States into drug-related security efforts in the Caribbean where most Caribbean countries have signed Mutual Legal Assistance Treaties (MLATs) with the United States. MLATs allow the United States to share intelligence, equipment, and interdiction efforts (shipboarding and overflight strategies) where such agreements exist. By the early 1990s Jamaica had become a major cocaine transshipment site for South American suppliers to the U.S. market. Although marijuana production has been illegal since 1913, crop expansion has increased dramatically since the mid-1960s (see Table 22.1). Jamaican gangs involved in drug trafficking, money laundering, and firearms operate in over 15 major cities in the United States, adding to the burden of local law enforcement efforts. An estimated 20 percent of the total amount of marijuana smuggled into the United States each year originates in Jamaica.

JAMAICA AND THE UNITED STATES AFTER THE COLD WAR

The end of the Cold War coincided with defeat of Edward Seaga's JLP and the return of Michael Manley in 1989. Seaga's conservative and pro-business economic policies and his anticommunism pleased Washington, but his efforts to court international financial institutions proved to be harmful for ordinary Jamaicans, particularly his slashes in health and social service expenditures. Manley promised not to repeat the errors of his earlier term in office and instead pursued orthodox free-market economic policies—privatization of state-owned enterprises, and relaxed restrictions on foreign investment—that won him praise from the Bush administration. Until ill health forced him to resign in 1992, Michael Manley continued to maintain he was a socialist, vowing never to give up his commitment to economic and racial justice. He died in Kingston, Jamaica, in 1997.

CONCLUSION

Although there are some similarities between U.S.-Jamaican relations and those in the Spanish- and French-speaking parts of the Caribbean, especially in the realm of large multinational fruit and mineral corporations, the general pattern throughout the twentieth century has been quite different. For example, the United States has never used the Monroe Doctrine in Jamaica as a justification for military force, and with British control over the region did not have to worry about defining its security on the basis of Jamaican stability and leadership. Since the British managed to supplant their form of parliamentary rule on Jamaica, the United States avoided the unpleasant task and questionable practice of teaching Jamaicans the arts of statecraft or legitimate rule. The negative consequences of supporting "friendly dictators" before and during the Cold War were avoided in Jamaica since none existed; nor was there any anti-Americanism that is often the consequence of that practice. Nevertheless the transference of racial politics from Jamaica to the United States and the island's ongoing dependency (in terms of security, bauxite, and countering drug trafficking) will no doubt continue to influence Jamaica's foreign policy and relationship with Washington.

NOTE

1. Quoted in Catherine A. Sunshine, *The Caribbean: Survival, Struggle and Sovereignty*, updated ed. (Washington, DC: Epica, 1994), p. 36.

SUGGESTED READINGS

Braveboy-Wagner, Jacqueline Anne. *The Caribbean in World Affairs: The Foreign Policies of the English-Speaking States*. Boulder, CO: Westview Press, 1989.

Griffith, Ivelaw L., and Betty N. Sedoc-Dahlberg, eds. *Democracy and Human Rights in the Caribbean*. Boulder, CO: Westview Press, 1997.

Heine, Jorge, and Leslie Manigat, eds. *The Caribbean and World Politics: Cross Currents and Cleavages*. New York: Holmes and Meier, 1988.

Manley, Michael. *Up the Down Escalator: Development and the International Economy—A Jamaican Case Study*. London: Andre Deutsch 1987.

Meditz, Sandra W., and Dennis M. Hanratty, eds. *Islands of the Commonwealth Caribbean: A Regional Study*. Washington, DC: The Division: Headquarters, Dept. of Army, 1989.

18

Mexico

TIMELINE OF U.S. RELATIONS WITH MEXICO

1821	Mexico becomes independent from Spain
1822	U.S. diplomatic relations are established
1836	Texas declares independence
1844	James K. Polk is elected president
1845	Polk Corollary to Monroe Doctrine
1846–1848	Mexican-American War
1848	Treaty of Guadalupe Hidalgo
1853	Gadsden Purchase
1862–1867	French occupy Mexico
1876–1910	Porfirio Díaz rules Mexico
1910	Porfirio Díaz is reelected president, sparking revolts
	Francisco Madero calls for political reforms
1911	Mexican Revolution begins; Díaz is overthrown and Madero assumes power
1912	Lodge Corollary to Monroe Doctrine
1913	Madero is assassinated; Victoriano Huerta becomes president of Mexico
	Woodrow Wilson is elected U.S. president
1914	U.S. troops occupy Vera Cruz
1916	Pancho Villa's army invades Columbus, New Mexico
1916–1919	President Wilson sends punitive military expeditions to Mexico
1923–1929	Plutarco Elías Calles serves as elected president
1923	Bucareli Agreements are signed

1927	Dwight Morrow becomes U.S. ambassador to Mexico
1929	One-party system of government is formed
1934–1940	Lázaro Cárdenas serves as elected president
1938	Mexico nationalizes oil industry
1942	*Bracero* program begins
1945–1960	Mexico embarks on industrialization programs
1946	Institutional Revolutionary Party (PRI) is established
1961	Mexico opposes Bay of Pigs invasion
1970–1976	Luis Echeverría serves as elected president
1976–1982	José López Portillo serves as elected president
1982	Mexican economy nears bankruptcy
1982–1988	Miguel de la Madrid serves as elected president
1983	Mexico joins Contadora Group
1988–1994	Carlos Salinas de Gortari serves as elected president
1992	North American Free Trade Agreement (NAFTA) is signed; is approved by U.S. Congress in the following year
1994	Zapatista revolt begins in opposition to NAFTA
1994–2000	Ernesto Zedillo serves as elected president
1996	Former president Salinas leaves Mexico for exile in Ireland
1997	President Clinton visits Mexico to discuss bilateral issues
	PRI loses control of lower house of Congress and mayor's job in Mexico City
1998	Mexico criticizes United States for Operation Casablanca, a sting operation in which 26 Mexican bankers are caught and charged with laundering drug funds

INTRODUCTION

The history of U.S. involvement in Mexico has been greatly influenced by a long land border that has intertwined the two nations in intense conflict as well as periodic collaboration on bilateral issues—trade, immigration, energy, and drugs—of importance to both governments. Historian Gaddis Smith argues that Mexico has had more impact on the United States than any other Latin American or Caribbean country because it is the "second-most-populous Latin American nation (after Brazil), the only country in the region with a land border with the United States, the only Latin American country with whom the United States has been formally at war, the source of millions of immigrants to the United States, more in the twentieth century than from any other country in the world, [and] the country with more social and economic ties to the United States than all the rest of Latin America."[1]

U.S. relations with Mexico have also been complicated by diplomatic blundering and ignorance, arrogance, racism, intervention, and economic dependency. Between 1836 and 1920 the United States intervened with military force at least 15 times to protect American interests. Since the Mexican Revolution (1910–1917), the United States has developed and used a variety of indirect and nonmilitary techniques for exerting and maintaining its influence. In dealing with the United States, Mexican leaders have struggled to retain a strong sense of nationhood despite the close proximity to the United States and the many negative experiences with the United States since independence. Although Mexican anti-Americanism has declined in recent years, it remains a part of Mexican national identity. Mexican schoolchildren visit the Museum of Intervention in Mexico City to view the displays portraying Mexico as the victim of foreign imperialists—American, French, British, and Spanish—since the time of independence. It is a sobering display of Mexico's feelings toward foreign involvement.

Mexico's relationship with the United States has also been influenced by authoritarian rule. Powerful dictators dominated Mexico during the nineteenth century, except for a brief period of democratic rule from 1867 to 1876. During the twentieth century, various forms of autocratic rule have been the norm—including seven decades after 1930 under the control of a revolutionary family and a dominant one-party governing structure. Under this arrangement Mexico has always held regular elections, but until recently only the candidates of the Institutional Revolutionary Party (PRI) would win. From the time of President Wilson's admonition to teach the Mexicans "to elect good men" in 1913, until the 1980s when "democracy promotion" became a catch-phrase in Washington, the United States did little or nothing to promote democracy in Mexico.

Mexico is now America's second largest trading partner, and both investment flows from the North and debt problems influence the bilateral relationship. The creation of a comprehensive free trade area among Canada, Mexico, and the United States, the North American Free Trade Agreement (NAFTA), and the international bailout of Mexico after the peso devaluation in 1995 demonstrated how closely tied Mexico is to the United States. No American president can afford to ignore Mexico, given its economic, cultural, and political impact on the United States. Mexico's proximity to the United States has conditioned patterns of immigration that have generated controversies over the presence of Mexicans—both legal and illegal—in the United States. However, when the United States faced labor shortages in times of war, it promoted controlled flows of Mexican workers to the United States. Moreover, U.S. business leaders have had few complaints about the value of Mexican labor.

MEXICO AND THE UNITED STATES IN THE NINETEENTH CENTURY

Mexico and the United States clashed repeatedly over boundaries and territorial control from the time of Mexican independence until the 1870s. As Mexico struggled to achieve control over its national territory, the United States pursued economic growth and territorial expansion, eventually fighting a major war with Mexico in the 1840s. Although victory over Mexico greatly increased the size of the United States, it also intensified the issue of slavery and contributed to the U.S. Civil War of 1861–1865. The Southern slave owners sponsored numerous private mercenary expeditions into Latin America to acquire new slave states, which in turn drew some Latin American countries into the growing conflict between the North and South. U.S.-Mexican relations were also undermined by incompetent diplomatic representatives from the United States. Many were arrogant, inept, and racist, fostering a bitter aspect to the bilateral relationship that lasted well into the next century.

The United States and Mexican Independence

Mexico's struggle for independence began in 1810, and by 1821 Spain's most prized possession in the Americas was lost. During their struggle against Spanish control, some Mexicans hoped for U.S. support and recognition while others remained apprehensive about U.S. desires to acquire Mexican territory. The United States recognized Mexico in 1822 while it was being ruled by Emperor Iturbide. Great Britain followed suit in 1826. These diplomatic actions gave international legitimacy to Mexico's new status. The first U.S. diplomatic contact with Mexico was through the special mission conducted by Joel R. Poinsett between 1823 and 1824, and later as U.S. minister in 1825. Poinsett's appointment proved to be ill advised since his undiplomatic efforts to counter British influence (by establishing anti-monarchical York Rite Masons, a secret branch of freemasons) were considered violations of Mexican sovereignty. In an angry protest, the Mexican government requested his recall in 1829. Poinsett introduced the poinsettia flower to the United States in what would later become his most memorable contribution while minister to Mexico.

Mexico and the Monroe Doctrine

Mexico figured prominently in the use and expansion of the Monroe Doctrine on two occasions that involved the United States—during the

Mexican War, and during Japanese attempts to buy Mexican land on the Baja Peninsula. President James K. Polk's desires for westward expansion under the banner of Manifest Destiny in the 1840s led to serious diplomatic tangles and, eventually, war with Mexico between 1846 and 1848. In his December 1845 message to Congress, Polk warned Europe against both forcible intervention and the use of diplomatic schemes in Texas or California for purposes of acquisition. Until 1845, U.S. references to the Monroe Doctrine seemed to stress the importance of keeping Europe out of the Western Hemisphere combined with U.S. adherence to the noninterference principle of the Monroe Doctrine.

After Polk's annexation of Texas in 1845, he declared that "the people of this continent alone have the right to decide their own destiny" and that if those constituting an independent state wished to unite themselves with the United States, "this will be a question for them and us to decide without any foreign interposition."[2] Shortly after this enlarged interpretation of the Monroe Doctrine, the United States annexed New Mexico and California. Polk went even further in his rather free interpretation of the Monroe Doctrine by urging the annexation of the Yucatán—after a formal request for transfer of sovereignty in exchange for assistance with a troublesome insurrection—claiming it was permissible for the United States to accept such an offer from a Latin American state, but unacceptable for a European nation to engage in such a transfer of territory. From this point on, Monroe's words of 1823 acquired the honorific designation "Doctrine" and a long history of corollaries and interpretations in inter-American relations.

The second incident occurred after the Spanish-American War and the U.S. acquisition of Hawaii and the Philippines. American anti-imperialists at the turn of the century questioned how the United States could deny Europeans the right to acquire colonies in the Western Hemisphere while it was doing the very same thing in other parts of the world. After Japanese business interests offered to buy land in Baja California in 1912, Senator Henry Cabot Lodge, chairman of the Senate Committee on Foreign Relations, introduced a resolution (the Lodge Corollary) proclaiming that:

> when any harbor or other place in the American continents is so situated that the occupation thereof for naval or military purposes might threaten the communications or the safety of the United States, the government of the United States could not see without grave concern the possession of such harbor or other place by any corporation or association which has such a relation to another government, not American, as to give that government practical power of control for naval or military purposes.[3]

The Lodge Corollary placed a veto on the transfer of private property between individuals (the land in Baja California was owned by Americans), extended Monroe's principles to corporations or associations under the control of a non-American government, made the Doctrine applicable to Asia, seriously infringed on Mexico's sovereignty, and generated considerable ill will in Latin America toward the United States.

The Mexican-American War, 1846–1848

Westward expansion under Manifest Destiny in the 1840s led to a war with Mexico, the only time war has been declared by the United States against a Latin American country. After the United States annexed Texas in 1845, President Polk's major objective was to acquire California, at the time a province of Mexico. Recognizing the weakness and political disorganization in Mexico, Polk provoked the war. Worried about British and French designs on Mexico, Polk at first tried to get Mexico to negotiate away its northwest territories, but Mexico refused. With strong currents of anti-Mexican racism growing in the United States, Polk increased the pressure on Mexico until a minor provocation gave him cause to declare war in 1846. After almost two years of military conflict, secret offers through special agents, and bitter disputes about the continuation of the war in the United States, Polk forced Mexico to accept his terms of acquisition of territory.

President Polk faced a hostile Congress and a frustrated public divided over the conduct of the war with Mexico. Many Whig Party members, abolitionists, peace advocates, and other critics called the war with Mexico a crime and an outrage and demanded that Polk withdraw all U.S. forces from Mexican territory. However, as the war dragged on, and after U.S. forces captured Mexico City, an "all-Mexico" movement in the United States urged annexation of all of Mexico in a burst of heightened imperialism. Polk resisted these demands as he tried to legitimize his more limited goals. At the height of the war, mostly European-Catholic immigrants deserted from the U.S. Army and formed the Saint Patrick's Battalion (Batallón de San Patricio). Alienated from American society and mistreated by the U.S. Army, the San Patricios realized that the battle with Mexico was not a war of liberty but a conquest against fellow Catholics such as themselves. Many were killed in action and some were executed—including the Battalion's leader, John Riley—by the U.S. Army as betrayers and deserters. The unit continued to function after the war with Mexico, although it was disbanded in 1848 and many of its surviving members stayed on in Mexico.

American troops left Mexico City in May 1848 after Mexico had ratified the Treaty of Guadalupe Hidalgo, which ceded to the United States 55 percent of Mexican territory (including present-day California, Arizona, New Mexico, Texas, and parts of Colorado, Nevada, and Utah). In return, the United States paid Mexico $15 million and assumed responsibility for

$3.5 million in claims against the Mexican government by U.S. citizens. The war cost the United States $100 million and 15,000 lives (1,733 were battle deaths; the others died of tropical diseases or simply disappeared), but many considered the price very low for what the United States had achieved: a vast amount of territory, valuable resources, and a continental power base stretching from the Atlantic to the Pacific Oceans. The extremely harsh terms of the treaty ending the war contributed to further tensions between the United States and Mexico that lingered for decades.

Mexico and the U.S. Civil War

Mexico became embroiled in the U.S. Civil War due to the foreign policy blunders of the Confederate states and French efforts to install a monarchy while President Abraham Lincoln was consumed by internal war. The Confederate government attempted to open relations with Mexico in 1861, sending John T. Pickett to negotiate a commercial treaty with President Benito Juárez. The Mexicans were angered by Pickett's blustering and insulting remarks and overt plans for southern expansionism. After failing to get the Mexicans to agree to a transparent scheme to return lost territories from the Mexican War in exchange for recognizing the Confederacy, Pickett was forced to leave Mexico in disgrace and was later condemned by Jefferson Davis, president of the Confederacy (1861–1865).

The French invasion and occupation of Mexico (1862–1867) was the most spectacular and dangerous challenge to the Monroe Doctrine yet encountered by the United States. Not only did it refocus attention on the clash of European and American systems, but it was a concerted effort to check the United States and all forms of republicanism in the Western Hemisphere. The French intervention in Mexico was originally sanctioned by Spain and Great Britain on the grounds that their nationals had just claims from economic damages arising out of the violence and chaos in Mexico at the time. The struggle to drive the French out of Mexico and uphold the Monroe Doctrine was carried out in Washington by Secretary of State Seward and Mexico's minister, Matías Romero, a young and energetic diplomat who lobbied Congress to invigorate Juárez's cause. While Seward spoke the language of the Monroe Doctrine throughout the Civil War, Romero resorted to a successful propaganda campaign on behalf of Mexico in U.S. newspapers and periodicals. The real victors in the conflict, of course, were the supporters of Juárez and Juárez himself, who fought a guerrilla war (one that included American soldiers of fortune, recruited by Mexican secret agents in the United States) against the French while maintaining vital links with the United States. Ironically, Mexico's efforts to solicit U.S. assistance to drive out the French resulted in the beginning of large-scale foreign investment in agriculture, mining, petroleum, and mail-steamship communication. Thus, the U.S. Civil War and the period of French intervention actually helped propel the further expansion of foreign investment in Mexico.

The Porfirian Dictatorship

General Porfirio Díaz seized power in 1876 and didn't relinquish it until he was toppled by revolutionary forces in 1911. U.S. relations with Mexico improved during this time as the earlier desire for physical conquest under Manifest Destiny was replaced by the pursuit of economic domination through expanded trade and investment. Díaz believed that Mexico's economic development required extensive foreign investment and a strong state, capable of stifling all opposition and protecting the nation's territorial sovereignty. In exchange for diplomatic recognition in 1878, Díaz changed Mexican law to allow greater foreign investment, mainly in railroads and mining. He then granted a railroad concession to Americans William J. Palmer and James Sullivan to build a railroad from Mexico City to Laredo and from Mexico City to Manzanillo.

With foreign investment now welcome in Mexico, U.S. capital and industrial surpluses extended into Mexico during the last two decades of the nineteenth century and continued to expand during the administrations of Theodore Roosevelt, William Howard Taft, and Woodrow Wilson. By 1911 the United States controlled almost 40 percent of foreign investment—mostly in railroads, mining, and real estate—in Mexico, a figure almost equal to that of all U.S. investment in Latin America. Although trade and investment generated a kind of "economic miracle" during the Porfirian era, many Mexicans resented U.S. ownership of Mexican land and economic resources. While foreign investment spurred economic growth, it also evoked a hostile nationalist reaction toward U.S. influence in Mexico. By the time of the Mexican Revolution, Mexico had become "the father of foreigners and the stepfather of Mexicans."[4]

Porfirio Díaz's early efforts to accommodate foreign investors and his willingness to subordinate Mexico to U.S. economic and political interests eventually gave way to a concerted defense of Mexican sovereignty and criticism of U.S. interventionism after 1895. In an 1896 speech attacking U.S. hegemonic pretensions contained in the Olney Corollary to the Monroe Doctrine (see Chapter 25), the Mexican dictator spelled out the Díaz Doctrine, a belief that one of the principles contained in the Monroe Doctrine—keeping Europe out of the Western Hemisphere—was a responsibility for all countries in the Americas, not just the United States. While one of the major goals of the Díaz dictatorship was to modernize Mexico, the difficult task of balancing the growing forces of nationalism and xenophobia with the expansionism and gunboat diplomacy of the United States eventually contributed to the outbreak of the Mexican Revolution and the demise of the aging dictator.

MEXICO AND THE UNITED STATES IN THE TWENTIETH CENTURY

The United States and the Mexican Revolution

The United States contributed to the conditions that brought about the Mexican Revolution, one of the most massive and violent civil wars of the twentieth century. Once the Mexicans initiated a coup d'état that toppled the old regime in 1911, the United States faced a major problem in trying to control the forces unleashed by 36 years of the Díaz dictatorship. The Mexican Revolution challenged two administrations—those of William Howard Taft and Woodrow Wilson—at a time when war loomed in Europe and revolutionary nationalists threatened U.S. investments, access to raw materials, and security related to the Panama Canal. With a long border with Mexico and a concern for stability, it was inevitable that the United States would meddle in Mexican affairs. The Revolution also attracted the interests of oil executives, journalists, photographers, and soldiers of fortune, many of whom benefitted from the turmoil inside Mexico and the frustrations that plagued policymakers in Washington.

President William Howard Taft (1909–1913)

President Taft continued many of the policies of his predecessor, stressing the importance of money and power as key ingredients in successful American foreign policy. Taft's strategy of using dollars (via market expansion and increased American investments) instead of war to promote order in Central America and the Caribbean became known as "dollar diplomacy." President Taft believed that if the United States could reorganize and control Latin American finances, it could eliminate the likely reason for foreign intervention. By the time Taft left office in 1913, Mexico was in turmoil and was threatening the security of the United States. Although Taft maintained a "hands-off" policy toward Mexico in the early stages of the efforts to rid Mexico of Porfirio Díaz, he later allowed Franciso Madero to arm and organize a revolt in San Antonio, Texas, and ordered the U.S. Army to form a "Maneuver Division" in 1911 in anticipation of a possible invasion of Mexico. Henry Lane Wilson was sent as U.S. ambassador to protect American business interests during the turmoil. Madero's attempt to launch his revolution against Díaz from the United States was a risky endeavor since it clearly violated U.S. neutrality laws; however, the Taft administration viewed Díaz as a political anachronism, and Madero was a popular figure in the United States.

Five months after Madero began his revolt, Porfirio Díaz resigned under pressure from the United States and the growing success of Madero's troops in the north. Although President Taft did not intervene to remove Díaz, he sent 20,000 troops to the Texas border and ordered U.S. warships to several Mexican ports. By the time Woodrow Wilson assumed the presidency in March 1913, Madero had been assassinated and his government replaced by a coup led by General Victoriano Huerta (a former Díaz general) with the encouragement of U.S. ambassador Henry Lane Wilson. Over time the revolution became more violent and the U.S. role in it more substantial. All evidence suggests that Henry Lane Wilson was actively involved in the conspiracy of Mexican forces to remove Madero, often acting against his instructions from Washington. Of course, Ambassador Wilson's actions violated Mexico's sovereignty, and his association with the fall of Madero seriously damaged U.S.-Mexican relations.

President Woodrow Wilson (1913–1921)

President Woodrow Wilson denounced dollar diplomacy and the misuse of the Monroe Doctrine, but in an effort to "moralize" American foreign policy he ultimately became one of the greatest interventionists of all American presidents. With a missionary zeal President Wilson—a former political science professor at Princeton University—tried to promote democracy and stability through a variety of diplomatic tools: nonrecognition of unconstitutional governments, special envoys sent to share Yankee wisdom, Pan-Americanism (a belief in close cooperation among the American states), electoralism (a belief in the value and necessity of democratic elections), the creation of more efficient and (presumably) nonpartisan police and military forces, the encouragement of private foreign loans, and threats of force. Wilson tried to make his nonrecognition doctrine more inclusive during 1914–1916 in what he called the Pan American Liberty Pact—a treaty arrangement in which signatories would agree to support only republican governments in the hemisphere—but it failed to gain much support due to Latin American fears of U.S. intervention.

When diplomacy failed, Wilson intervened with military force. Between 1913 and 1921 the United States intervened repeatedly in Latin America and the Caribbean. Wilson sent troops into Mexico three times between 1913 and 1918. After watching events unfold in Mexico, Wilson came to detest revolutions and viewed democracy and elections as a cure-all for the region. On assuming office he told the U.S. Congress "We are the friends of constitutional government in America; we are more than its friends, we are its champions," and "I am going to teach the South American republics to elect good men."[5] Wilson's "crusading moralism" in foreign policy was resented in Latin America and opposed by European powers such as Britain with virtually no interest in promoting democracy of any type.

President Wilson viewed the situation in Mexico with horror and dismay and refused to recognize the Huerta government. With little information to go on, he was buffeted by conflicting forces in the United States; American corporate interests wanted the United States to tolerate Huerta on the basis of his ability to provide stability and protect American investments while his advisers wanted tough measures. Wilson sent William Bayard Hale to Mexico to report on Huerta. Hale was part of a group of special agents, many of whom knew absolutely nothing about Mexico or revolutions, that the president would dispatch to Mexico. After his visit to Mexico in 1913 Hale recommended not recognizing the Huerta regime, a policy that was adopted by the president.

In dealing with Mexico, Woodrow Wilson thought he could act as his own secretary of state, thus avoiding expert authorities, and refused to admit that his policies had failed. Having little confidence in his own consuls, he came to rely on amateur diplomats and special agents who were responsible only to him or his inept secretary of state, William Jennings Bryan. In his analysis of the Tampico incident, a clash between Mexican and American troops, and the invasion and occupation of the Gulf of Mexico port city of Veracruz in 1914, Robert E. Quirk argues that:

Many of these agents did not speak Spanish and had never been to Mexico. John Lind, the former governor of Minnesota, for example, knew nothing of the Mexican situation, did not know the language, and was an implacable anti-Catholic. He was singularly unequipped to handle his mission. Yet he had been sent to Mexico by Wilson and Bryan to try to persuade Victoriano Huerta that he should resign the presidency and hold free elections.[6]

By sending ill-informed emissaries to advise and cajole Mexican revolutionary leaders, and by sending American troops onto Mexican soil—Veracruz in 1914, and a punitive expedition in northern Mexico to capture the elusive "bandit" Pancho Villa—Wilson left a legacy of animosity in U.S.-Mexican relations that lasted for generations. As Howard F. Cline points out, "Part of Wilson's difficulties were based on sheer ignorance and the naïve assumption that one man with a portable typewriter and self-righteousness could handle the innumerable details of foreign policy."[7] Ignorance and false assumptions among Monroe's ghosts in Washington would condemn the United States to repeating some of the mistakes made by Wilson's successors, particularly during the Cold War when dealing with Central America and the Caribbean.

By the time the violent phase of the Mexican Revolution had ended in 1917, nearly 10 percent of the population was dead (1.5 million) and a million people had fled into exile, mostly to the United States. Despite the end of the revolution in Mexico, the United States found it more difficult to operate unchallenged in Central America because of domestic opposition in the United States—people were tired of "dollar diplomacy" and repeated military intervention—and the lack of support for U.S. policies among other Latin American states. Angered by repeated U.S. intervention during the revolution, Mexico refused to cooperate with U.S. efforts to capture and subdue Nicaraguan rebel Augusto Sandino and, instead, sent him arms and money between 1926 and 1933. Argentina spearheaded diplomatic efforts on behalf of the principle of nonintervention throughout the 1920s and attracted a majority of the Latin American countries to the cause. Even the Central American leaders, often the most subservient to U.S. domination, began to protest Washington's actions. Mexicans continued to criticize the Monroe Doctrine during the 1920s and 1930s, and U.S. diplomats eventually learned the importance of ignoring the slogan in dealing with Mexico. Mexico and the Monroe Doctrine were rarely discussed at the same time by American officials after 1920.

U.S. Petroleum and the Bucareli Agreements

The network of railroads constructed with American expertise and capital during the Porfirian era, combined with the investments of British and American oil companies, helped Mexico become the world's third-largest petroleum producer by the time of the revolution. Oil was the only U.S. economic interest in Mexico that underwent a boom during the Mexican Revolution, due in large part to increased demand during World War I, the conversion of the world's naval fleets from coal to oil, and the beginnings of assembly-line production in the automobile industry. Those who participated in the Mexican petroleum industry between 1911 and 1921 were not deterred by the revolution, although some were enemies of the goals of the revolution. As W. Dirk Raat argues, "By the end of the decade [1920], the oil companies had financed the Mexican Revolution in the form of taxes, forced loans, and theft, and in return, North American companies had gained preeminence in the industry by having outmaneuvered their British competitors in Mexico . . . [and] several individuals made small fortunes."[8]

Of the American oilmen who left the United States and went to the petroleum-producing regions of Mexico, conspired against the revolutionaries, and made millions off of black gold (that is, oil), William F. Buckley (father of the well-known conservative author and editor of the same name) was the most notorious (see Chapter 25). He moved to Tampico, Mexico, in 1911 to open a law office with his two brothers and founded the Pantepec Petroleum Company of Tampico in 1915, but he was forced to withdraw from Mexico in 1917. He then formed the American Association of Mexico—a network of agents and informants to spy on alleged revolutionaries in the United States and Mexico—and aided the unfriendly Senate investigation into Mexican affairs by Albert Bacon Fall. Buckley opposed

President Venustiano Carranza on grounds that he had ties to Bolshevism and radical labor leaders, and President Álvaro Obregón as well when he replaced Carranza in 1920. He was sympathetic to President Harding's hardline policy toward Mexico but was forced to leave in 1922 after being expelled by the Mexican government.

The ideals of the Mexican Revolution were embodied in the 1917 Querétaro Constitution—the first socialist constitution in history—but some of its provisions became sources of friction with the United States that were not settled until the 1940s. Of chief concern to the United States was the interpretation and application of Article 27 of the Constitution, involving the nationalization of subsoil mineral and oil deposits. American oil companies, fearing they would be expropriated, applied strong pressure on Washington to oppose Mexican efforts to apply the constitutional provision retroactively. President Obregón repeated Carranza's promise that Article 27 would not be applied retroactively, but he refused to put it into treaty form. As a result the U.S. government refused to recognize Obregón until August 1923, when the diplomatic impasse was broken by the Bucareli Agreements.

The Bucareli Agreements—named after the site of the conference in Mexico City—amounted to a gentlemen's agreement between personal representatives of President Warren G. Harding and Mexican President Alvaro Obregón. It attempted to pacify the oil companies concerned about constitutional provisions concerning the ownership of subsoil mineral rights. The agreements modified the effects of Article 27 by establishing the doctrine of "positive acts"—an interpretation whereby Mexico recognized the legitimacy of oil concessions made prior to the 1917 Constitution if the owners had taken positive acts (such as drilling a well) to initiate oil production. The Bucareli Agreements paved the way for de jure recognition of the Mexican government by the United States and provided the basis for a long-term improvement in U.S.-Mexican relations. However, between 1923 and 1927 Mexican-U.S. relations worsened when Mexican governments enacted petroleum laws limiting the ownership of oil rights, contending that the Bucareli Agreements were binding only on the Obregón regime. As a result, business interests in the United states mounted a vigorous campaign to intervene in Mexico. It wasn't until President Calvin Coolidge appointed Dwight W. Morrow, a Wall Street financier, as ambassador to Mexico in late 1927 that relations improved. Morrow, a good diplomat with a *simpático* style, helped pave the way for a Good Neighbor Policy for Mexico.

The Good Neighbor Policy

The Morrow mission marked an important step in eliminating the interventionism in Mexican affairs during the first three decades of the twentieth century and set in motion diplomatic initiatives that reaped major dividends during the 1930s. Although the Good Neighbor Policy is associated with Franklin D. Roosevelt, the concept had been employed earlier by Elihu Root, Charles Evans Hughes, and President Herbert Hoover. In reviewing his Latin American policy, Hoover declared in 1930 that "As a result of these policies, carried on throughout my administration, the interventions which had been the source of so much bitterness and fear in Latin America were ended. We established a good will in Latin America and not hitherto known for many years, under the specific term 'Good Neighbor.' "[9] The origin of this new Latin American policy was the increasingly tense environment in inter-American relations caused by contrasting interpretations of the Monroe Doctrine and its various corollaries, years of U.S. military intervention and occupation, dollar diplomacy, and heavy-handed diplomacy. Beginning in the 1920s, Washington recognized the linkage between improving the image of the United States in Latin America and expanded opportunities for trade and investment. During the Roosevelt administration, nonintervention, reciprocity (a basic principle of international law and foreign policy based on equal rights and duties among states), and multilateralism (diplomacy that is open and includes a large number of states) became increasingly important as the possibility of war in Europe increased.

The most difficult test of the Good Neighbor Policy occurred in 1938 when Mexico decided to expropriate the properties of 16 foreign oil companies, including the powerful Standard Oil. The companies responded aggressively by establishing a boycott of Mexican oil and carrying out a vicious propaganda campaign in the United States through company-subsidized magazines. In hopes of convincing the Roosevelt administration to intervene and put a halt to the seizure of American oil companies, Mexicans were accused of being thieves, fascists, and Bolshevists. The campaign against President Lázaro Cárdenas failed when Roosevelt and his ambassador to Mexico, Josephus Daniels, resisted the pressure to intervene from aggrieved oil company owners, jingoistic or bellicose nationalists interested in an aggressive foreign policy, and Secretary of State Cordell Hull. Roosevelt did not want to see the Good Neighbor Policy "drown in Mexican oil" and realized that Mexico's strategic location was an important factor with war pending in Europe.

In contrast to earlier disputes over U.S. property rights, the United States did not contest the legality of the expropriation and ruled out both military intervention and economic reprisals. To settle the dispute the United States insisted that the owners of expropriated properties be compensated by the Mexican government, although negotiations dragged on until the Nazi threat to the hemisphere spurred a settlement agreement signed on November 19, 1941. In return for Mexico's agreeing to pay the oil companies $40 million for American-owned oil properties, the United States continued to purchase Mexican silver at world market prices, promised the extension of credits, and continued military assistance. The American attitude toward Mexico during the petroleum nationalization controversy, and the U.S. decision to adhere to the nonintervention pledges made during the Good Neighbor Policy, opened the way for Latin American collaboration with the United States during World War II and fostered cordial relations during the early stages of the Cold War.

The United States and Mexico during World War II

The outbreak of war in Europe and the end of the more radical phase of the Mexican Revolution with the election of Manuel Ávila Camacho in 1940 signaled the beginning of a new era in U.S.-Mexican cooperation that lasted for over three decades. After German submarines sank several Mexican tankers in the gulf of Mexico in 1942, Mexico declared war on the Axis powers, and the United States and Mexico became formal allies. This marked the first military alliance between the two nations, sealed a historic reconciliation, and set the stage for an era of good feelings throughout the war years. For the United States, Mexico represented a strategically important part of the Americas as well as an important source of raw materials and cheap labor. Wartime collaboration with the United States facilitated the influx of foreign capital to finance Mexican industrial development. Mexico and the United States developed joint defense arrangements during the war effort, although the United States provided the bulk of military assistance funds. U.S. aid helped Mexico to develop a modernized air force squadron of 300 men who were trained in the United States and later saw combat in the Philippines. To counter the shortage of labor in the United States throughout the war, President Roosevelt and Ávila Camacho established the Bracero Program in 1942 to allow Mexican agricultural workers to replace American workers who had been drafted into the war. This contract labor program continued until 1964. The United States and Mexico also collaborated during the war to eliminate subversive activity in Mexico, mainly through J. Edgar Hoover's Special Intelligence Service (SIS) and Radio Intelligence Division agents of the U.S. Federal Communications Commission. Wartime collaboration involving U.S. and Mexican secret police and security agencies continued after 1945, particularly in anti-drug efforts during the 1980s and 1990s.

MEXICO AND THE UNITED STATES DURING THE COLD WAR

Relative harmony prevailed in U.S.-Mexican relations during the Cold War, with Mexico emphasizing economic growth while Washington worried about combating communism, building an anticommunist alliance, and establishing stability along its southern border. To stimulate its own industrial production after the war, Mexico's government emphasized state-owned enterprises and economic regulation. Bilateral trade increased steadily during the Cold War, reaching nearly $5 billion in 1980 and accounting for more than 60 percent of Mexico's imports and exports. However, with Mexico's revolutionary heritage of strong nationalism and antipathy toward outside intervention, policy disputes in the hemisphere often injected a discordant note in U.S.-Mexican relations. For example, Mexico opposed U.S. intervention in Guatemala (1954), Cuba (1961), the Dominican Republic (1965), Chile (1970–1973), Grenada (1983), and Panama (1989), and U.S. policies in Central America during the 1980s. Mexico maintained diplomatic relations with Cuba and the Soviet Union during the Cold War and opposed the collective sanctions imposed on Cuba by the Organization of American States in 1964 at the urging of the Johnson administration. Mexico alienated the United States by extending aid to the beleaguered Sandinista government in Nicaragua, opposed the Contras, and recognized the Marxist FMLN guerrillas in El Salvador and their political party as legitimate political actors.

Mexico and the Soviet Union

The Soviet Union's interest in Mexico stemmed from its long border with the United States, its revolutionary heritage, certain economic advantages, and its tradition of one-party governments. Mexico was the first country in Latin America to recognize the new Soviet government in 1924; throughout the Cold War, Mexico maintained close and uninterrupted relations with the Soviet Union and Cuba despite repeated reprimands from Washington for what it considered a political heresy. The relative durability of Soviet-Mexican relations during the Cold War was closely associated with Mexico's sense of vulnerability to the United States. By maintaining access to great powers outside the hemisphere, Mexico felt that it could offset the historic domination and exploitation of its territory carried out by its northern neighbor. Interestingly, while Washington complained about Soviet influence in Latin America from the 1940s to the end of the Cold War, Mexico allowed the Soviet Embassy to operate significant intelligence operations against the United States and Latin American countries.

Paradoxically, the United States never found it necessary to invoke the Monroe Doctrine or intervene militarily in Mexico during the Cold War era, despite the presence of "alien" powers lurking to the south. President Eisenhower told a group of advisors in 1960 that if the Soviets ever took over the government of Mexico, the United States would have to declare war on its southern neighbor. Although in some cases the perceptions of U.S. policymakers have been real, in most cases the dynamics of the fundamental causes of revolutions, and the consequences of U.S. responses, have been poorly understood in Washington. As the Mexican Revolution demonstrates, domestic circumstances create the conditions that bring about revolutions, not arms, propaganda, and agitators from the Soviet Union.

From Cordial to Unfriendly Relations

From 1970 to 1982, with the help of new discoveries of petroleum and natural gas, Presidents Luis Echeverría and José López Portillo sought to reorient Mexico's domestic and international policies. To stimulate and regulate the Mexican economy, the government intervened more and expanded the number and size of state enterprises, but it incurred large debts that eventually led to a long and profound economic crisis during the 1980s after the price of petroleum dropped. The petroleum boom enhanced Mexico's role as a Third World leader in the 1970s, and the Mexican government sharply criticized American foreign policy.

After the dramatic drop in petroleum revenues, Mexico announced in 1982 that it could no longer service its foreign debt. It started a series of economic adjustment policies—deregulating the economy and privatizing state enterprises—that were accelerated after the election of Carlos Salinas de Gortari in 1988. President Salinas lowered tariff barriers—on the assumption that manufacturers would thereby become more efficient and competitive in the world market—liberalized rules governing foreign investment, and proposed a free trade agreement with the United States and Canada in 1991. This export-led industrialization of the Mexican economy brought on a flood of American products and investment in Mexico that some found to be an affront to Mexico nationalism and a sign of increasing dependency on the United States.

Mexico and the Central American Crisis

Mexico's severe economic plight in the early 1980s stirred a lot of alarmist talk in Washington, including statements about countries falling like "communist" dominoes and the possibility of a Castro-type revolution in Mexico. With little understanding of Mexico and events in Central America, the Reagan administration tried to demonstrate a connection between Mexico and the revolutionary turmoil under way in El Salvador and Nicaragua. By portraying Mexico as a "weak domino" subject to revolutionary forces from Cuba, Central America, and elsewhere, Reagan and conservative members of Congress hoped to gain support for a military solution to perceived security threats in the region.

Mexico joined the Contadora Group in 1983 along with Colombia, Panama, and Venezuela to push for negotiated settlements of the armed conflicts in Central America (see Chapter 19). While appearing to support the idea of a negotiated settlement, the Reagan administration was firmly opposed to such a solution since it would have accepted what Washington abhorred, namely, a revolutionary government in Nicaragua and the legitimacy of at least some of the demands of rebel groups in Guatemala and El Salvador. Although the Contadora peace process failed due to the opposition of the Reagan administration, it provided an experience in negotiations that set in motion the leadership of and motivation for a Central American–generated peace agreement in August 1987. In the end, President Reagan's struggle to stop revolutions in Central America helped drive millions of people to *el norte* (the United States) in an effort to escape the violence and destruction being carried out in the name of anticommunism.

The North American Free Trade Agreement and the Zapatista Revolt

The North American Free Trade Agreement (NAFTA) linking Mexico with the United States and Canada has brought renewed attention to the close ties between Mexico and the United States. The brainchild of President Carlos Salinas, NAFTA was first signed on October 7, 1992, ratified by the U.S. Congress in late 1993, and went into effect on January 1, 1994. It established an economic union whose combined gross national product (the total amount of goods and services produced, usually measured on a yearly basis) exceeded that of the European Union. At first there was little resistance to accepting NAFTA in Mexico since it promised more jobs and cheaper goods, but in the United States—with an economy 20 times larger than Mexico's—the general public disapproved of NAFTA; indeed, major currents of opposition came from organized labor and within the Democratic opposition in Congress. However, with the Clinton administration lobbying hard for its passage, and with Mexico spending millions on its own lobbying effort, NAFTA passed by a narrow margin. Many trade experts believe that eventually NAFTA will help the Mexican and American economies, but after three years in operation NAFTA's benefits have been minimal in the United States.

On the same day that NAFTA went into effect, 1,000 peasant soldiers of the Zapatista Army of National Liberation (EZLN) captured four towns in southern Mexico and held them for several days, claiming their revolt was in opposition to NAFTA and neglect of impoverished areas such as Chiapas by the PRI government. The EZLN revolt embarrassed the Mexican government while gaining sympathy due to well-organized publicity and propaganda efforts from its leadership, including the charismatic Rafael Sebastián Guillén Vicente, known as Sub-Comandante Marcos. The Mexican government responded with military force and has since contained the revolt in Chiapas. However, the use of the name of the revered hero of the revolution by Mexican peasants has helped to prolong the tension over government policies and economic development strategies such as NAFTA.

The 1997 massacre of 45 unarmed women and children in Acteal by paramilitary forces allegedly aligned with the PRI indicates the fragility of peace in Southern Mexico.

Drugs and Corruption

The cultivation of illicit drug crops and transshipment to the United States expanded greatly throughout Latin America after the economic tragedies of the 1980s. In Mexico, the flow of cocaine (along with opium and marijuana) to the United States created powerful drug cartels and increased involvement of the U.S. government in combating drug production and trafficking inside Mexico. Beginning with President Nixon's creation of the U.S. Drug Enforcement Agency (DEA) in the early 1970s, drug trafficking has become a sensitive issue for the United States and Mexico. By the 1990s the major locus for combating the drug trade was along the Mexican border, not in the Andean countries where most of the world's coca leaf is grown and processed into cocaine (see Chapter 22). Evidence of close ties between drug traffickers and Mexican law enforcement authorities has not helped diminish the inflow of drugs or improved Mexico's image in the United States.

The extent of drug-funded official corruption in Mexico in 1996–1997 has generated skepticism among U.S. legislators and anti-drug officials about Mexico's commitment to combat drug trafficking and related corruption. The arrest of three Mexican army officers in 1997 underscored how deeply the drug traffickers have penetrated Mexico's governmental institutions and the military. General Jesús Gutiérrez Rebollo—the head of Mexico's anti-drug agency—was arrested in 1997 for protecting drug traffickers while amassing $500 million between 1990 and 1996. Carlos Salinas's older brother, Raúl, has been in jail for two years on corruption and murder charges, which he continues to deny. In a successful 1998 undercover sting operation, U.S. Customs officials captured 26 Mexican bankers involved in the laundering of drug funds.

As Mexican drug gangs have grown into drug lords in their own right, they have eclipsed organized crime from Colombia as the major law enforcement threat to the United States. The expansion of Mexican drug-trafficking activities near the U.S. border has shifted the front line of the drug war from the Andean jungles of Colombia, Peru, and Bolivia to America's doorstep. Mexico's number one cocaine trafficker (until his death in 1997 while undergoing radical plastic surgery to mask his identity) was Amado Carillo Fuentes, commonly known as "Lord of the Skies" for his use of aging Boeing 727s to fly Colombian cocaine into Mexico for reexport to the United States. At one time Carillo Fuentes allegedly employed General Gutiérrez Rebollo, before he was arrested in February 1997.

Viva Democracy?

Throughout the Cold War era, government officials in Washington refrained from interfering in Mexican domestic politics and largely ignored violations of human rights and the undemocratic nature of Mexico's political system. However, the U.S. media and a growing number of nongovernmental organizations, disturbed with the trends in Mexico in the 1980s, began to focus more attention on the lack of democracy, the plight of Mexican labor along the border, drug trafficking, and immigration. As the quality of Mexican elections has improved since 1988—driven in part by domestic pressures for authentic reform—the PRI has had to endure greater challenges from the left and right to maintain its hold on power. In July 1997 the PRI lost its monopoly of power for the first time in 68 years, indicating further erosion of authoritarian rule south of the border. The election of Cuauhtémoc Cárdenas of the Democratic Revolutionary Party (PRD) to the mayor's job in Mexico City, and the loss of PRI control of the lower house of Congress, dealt a major blow to the country's ruling party. President Ernesto Zedillo is now the first Mexican leader since 1913 who does not have virtual control over the congressional branch.

With over $50 billion in American investments, $156 billion in bilateral trade, over 10 million American tourists who flock to Mexico each year, and some 350,000 Americans living in Mexico, the United States has good reason to worry about political turmoil and economic uncertainty. Moreover, many of the new lawmakers in Mexico are cool toward NAFTA and believe that PRI governments have been too pro-American in recent years. With multiple forces within and outside Mexico pushing in the direction of greater democracy, Mexico is likely to have a more competitive and complex form of government in the twenty-first century. The political adjustments that this will require will not come easily, neither for Mexico nor its "distant" neighbor, the United States.

CONCLUSION

Important legacies from a complex and difficult past continue to influence U.S.-Mexican relations. The loss of territory in the middle of the nineteenth century, followed by repeated U.S. interventions in Mexico's internal affairs, have strained bilateral relations until recently. With the increasing importance of trade and investment the United States and Mexico show signs of cultural integration, but problems still loom on the political front, particularly the nature of Mexico's political system in the aftermath of the Cold War. The fact that the two countries are so closely intertwined economically and socially has made use of the Monroe Doctrine as a justification for direct intervention costly and problematic. Large numbers of Mexican Americans residing in the United States have served an important role in both the Mexican and American economies through labor benefits and remittances. On issues such as drug trafficking and environmental degradation along the border, the United States has come to realize that cooperation with Mexico is not a luxury but a necessity.

NOTES

1. Gaddis Smith, *The Last Years of the Monroe Doctrine, 1945–1993* (New York: Hill and Wang, 1994), p. 225.

2. Quoted in Graham H. Stuart and James L. Tigner, *Latin America and the United States*, 6th ed. (Englewood Cliffs, NJ: Prentice-Hall, 1975), pp. 125–126.

3. Quoted in Federico G. Gil, *Latin American–United States Relations* (New York: Harcourt, Brace, Jovanovich, 1971), p. 72.

4. Frank Brandenburg, *The Making of Modern Mexico* (Englewood Cliffs, NJ: Prentice-Hall, 1964), p. 40.

5. Quoted in Paul W. Drake, "From Good Men to Good Neighbors, 1912–1932," in Abraham F. Lowenthal, ed., *Exporting Democracy: The United States and Latin America, Themes and Issues* (Baltimore, MD: Johns Hopkins University Press, 1991), p. 13.

6. Robert E. Quirk, *An Affair of Honor: Woodrow Wilson and the Occupation of Veracruz* (New York: W. W. Norton, 1962), p. 32.

7. Howard F. Cline, *The United States and Mexico* (New York: Atheneum, 1963), p. 162.

8. W. Dirk Raat, *Mexico and the United States: Ambivalent Vistas* (Athens: University of Georgia Press, 1993), p. 123.

9. Quoted in Bryce Wood, *The Making of the Good Neighbor Policy* (New York: W. W. Norton, 1961), p. 123.

SUGGESTED READINGS

Domínguez, Jorge I., and James A. McCann. *Democratizing Mexico: Public Opinion and Electoral Choices*. Baltimore, MD: Johns Hopkins University Press, 1996.

Eisenhower, John S. D. *So Far from God: The U.S. War with Mexico, 1846–1848*. New York: Random House, 1989.

Fuentes, Carlos. *A New Time For Mexico*. Berkeley: University of California Press, 1997.

Knight, Alan. *U.S.-Mexican Relations, 1910–1940: An Interpretation*. San Diego: Center for U.S.-Mexican Studies, University of California, 1987.

Oppenheimer, Andres. *Bordering on Chaos: Guerrillas, Stockbrokers, Politicians, and Mexico's Road to Prosperity*. Boston: Little, Brown, 1996.

19

Nicaragua

TIMELINE OF U.S. RELATIONS WITH NICARAGUA

1821	Nicaraguan independence from Spain is achieved
1850	Clayton-Bulwer Treaty is ratified
1851	U.S. diplomatic relations are established
1852	Cornelius Vanderbilt establishes transit company
1855–1857	William Walker declares himself Nicaraguan president
1860	Walker is killed by firing squad in Honduras
1893–1909	José Santos Zelaya serves as elected president
1910	U.S. Marines land in Bluefields
1911–1925	U.S. Marines occupy Nicaragua
1916	Bryan-Chamorro Treaty is ratified
1925	United States sponsors presidential elections; Marines withdraw
1926	U.S. Marines invade and lead effort to capture Augusto César Sandino
1933	President Hoover withdraws U.S. Marines after failing to capture Sandino
1934	Anastasio Somoza's army assassinates Sandino
1936	Somoza is installed as dictator; rules until 1956
1954	Somoza supports overthrow of Jacobo Arbenz in Guatemala
1956	Somoza is assassinated; son Luis Somoza assumes presidency
1961	Bay of Pigs invasion is launched from Nicaragua
	Sandinista National Liberation Front (FSLN) is founded
1967	Luis Somoza dies of heart attack; Tachito Somoza assumes power

1977	Jimmy Carter is elected U.S. president; emphasizes human rights
1978	Somoza orders assassination of Pedro Joaquín Chamorro
1979	Somoza is overthrown; Sandinista Revolution begins
1980	Somoza is assassinated in Asunción, Paraguay
1981	Ronald Reagan assumes U.S. presidency, with intentions of getting rid of the "Communist menace" in Nicaragua
	Contras are formed in opposition to Sandinista rule
1984	CIA mines Nicaraguan harbors
1986	Iran–Contra affair derails Reagan's Contra policy
1990	Violeta Barrios de Chamorro is elected president
1996	Daniel Ortega is defeated by conservative Arnoldo Alémán

INTRODUCTION

Since independence in 1821, Nicaraguans have rarely experienced a long period without the presence of U.S. troops and mercenaries. From the middle of the nineteenth century to the end of the Cold War, Nicaragua played a significant role in U.S. history because it was seen as a prime location for a transoceanic canal, and its revolutionary politics raised security and economic concerns during times of international conflict. Until Theodore Roosevelt arranged for the separation of Panama from Colombia in 1903, Nicaragua was the likely spot for an isthmian canal. With a river and lake system facilitating transit across the Central American isthmus, Nicaragua became a target for external intervention, great power conflict, and foreign adventurism. Between 1853 and 1933, U.S. armed forces intervened in Nicaragua 13 times; after 1911, the U.S. Marines occupied Nicaragua continuously for a period of 22 years. What differentiates Nicaragua from the rest of Latin America (even Cuba or Mexico) is the duration and intensity of U.S. control over its destiny.

The history of U.S. involvement in Nicaragua reflects well-intentioned efforts to achieve a better society, including the imposition of the trappings of democratic government and improved fiscal management. However, little attempt was made to consider the needs or interests of the Nicaraguan people, and inevitably the U.S. interest in promoting democracy contributed to some form of military intervention. For the past 90 years the United States has been a critical actor in Nicaragua's internal affairs, setting the terms of development assistance, foreign policy, and a national identity. Yet what is surprising about U.S. involvement in Nicaragua is how little the policymakers in Washington understood, or cared about, Nicaragua itself.

"Nicaragua Is Different!"

NICARAGUA AND THE UNITED STATES DURING THE NINETEENTH CENTURY

Nicaragua and the Monroe Doctrine

Nicaragua's independence from Spain came in two stages—the first when it attached itself to the Mexican Empire in 1821, and the second when it broke from Mexico in 1823 and joined the United Provinces of Central America. This arrangement lasted until 1838, when the federation collapsed. Partisan-regional hostilities and economic devastation plagued Nicaragua as it attempted to forge its own political identity during the nineteenth century. The Monroe Doctrine was dormant until the British captured San Juan del Norte in 1847, an important Caribbean port, eliciting a strong U.S. protest because it violated the noncolonization clause of the Monroe Doctrine. Washington's concern over British encroachments in Central America led to the signing (without consulting Nicaragua) of the Clayton-Bulwer Treaty of 1850 (see Chapter 13), which provided for joint U.S.-British control over any future canal. Later, top officials in Washington began demanding the termination of the Clayton-Bulwer Treaty and exclusive rights to build a canal in Nicaragua.

In 1869, President Ulysses S. Grant determined that an American-owned canal was essential to U.S. security and prosperity. He appointed an Interoceanic Canal Commission to study possible routes. The commission recommended Nicaragua, rather than Panama, and use of the San Juan River and Lake Nicaragua. The Monroe Doctrine made numerous appearances in U.S.-Nicaraguan relations over the next century, but Nicaragua never became a cause of the numerous corollaries appended to President Monroe's message.

A Yankee President for Nicaragua

During the 1850s Nicaragua played a major role in the expansionist movements in the United States. After the Mexican War and the subsequent discovery of gold in California, people from the East Coast streamed westward. However, until the completion of the transcontinental railroad in 1869, the most popular route was through Nicaragua via the San Juan River, Lake Nicaragua, and stage coaches to the Pacific coastal town of San Juan del Sur. Cornelius Vanderbilt and his associates soon obtained concessions from Nicaragua to establish a transit route across Nicaragua and by 1851 were operating a lucrative transit company linking New York with San Francisco. During this time Nicaragua was constantly embroiled in civil wars between Conservatives in Grenada and Liberals in León, a carryover from the colonial period that continued well into the twentieth century.

Into this volatile situation stepped William Walker, a native of Tennessee with degrees in law and medicine and a passionate advocate of Manifest Destiny, who teamed up with enemies of Vanderbilt, disgruntled Liberals from Nicaragua, and financial backers from New Orleans who wanted more slave territory. Walker invaded Nicaragua in 1855 with 57 other Americans and before long had captured Grenada and taken over the country. With the support of officials in Washington and proslavery Southerners, Walker had himself "elected" president of Nicaragua, the only time a U.S. citizen ruled as chief of state in Latin America. Only the United States recognized the fraudulent government. In search of a Central American empire, Walker legalized slavery, decreed English as the national language (he had no time, or need, to learn Spanish), decreed an anti-vagrancy law to ensure forced peasant labor for landowners, offered large land grants to attract more American troops, and pursued a general plan to Americanize Nicaragua.

To get rid of Walker, Central Americans united in a National War that resulted in expelling the "Yankee president" in 1857. Walker returned to Nicaragua three more times to pursue his dreams of wealth and empire, but he was eventually captured by British naval forces. They handed him over to the Hondurans, who ended his romantic filibustering activities before a firing squad in 1860. William Walker's agents in Washington stressed the importance of driving the British out of the region and upholding the principles of the Monroe Doctrine. Walker was endorsed by leaders within President Pierce's Democratic Party who were instrumental in convincing the president to recognize Walker's minister to the United States. The Walker episode left deep scars in U.S.-Nicaraguan relations. It discredited the United States throughout Central America and raised fears of losing sovereignty at the hands of Manifest Destiny or the Monroe Doctrine. When U.S. Marines began to intervene and occupy Nicaragua during the first three decades of the twentieth century, Nicaraguans were immediately reminded of the exploits of William Walker 50 years earlier, now considered the first U.S. "Marine" to intervene in their country.

Although filibusters failed, the episodes of William Walker and others had an important impact on the development of the Monroe Doctrine and U.S.–Central American relations. As numerous private mercenaries and soldiers of fortune attempted to extend American influence over Central America, the Monroe Doctrine assumed a new significance among policymakers in Washington. The excitement of Walker's exploits contributed to the frequent use of the doctrine in congressional debates and in the press. The efforts of the *filibusteros* to use repeated military expeditions (which were indirectly supported by American presidents) to achieve a tropical empire were of little benefit to those on the receiving end of U.S. aggression. Walker's band of mercenaries did not bring prosperity to the region and closed the transit route across the isthmus. The filibusters also contributed to the reinforcement of common stereotypes of Central Americans as inferior to Anglo-Saxon North Americans through the use of "greaser" and other words of disparagement which hastened the U.S. Civil War by attempting to spread slavery into Central America and the Caribbean. Whatever support there may have been for the Monroe Doctrine as a strategy against foreign interference during its first three decades of existence was erased by Walker's greed, arrogance, and racism in Nicaragua.

NICARAGUA AND THE UNITED STATES DURING THE TWENTIETH CENTURY

The Battle for a Canal Route

Republican Theodore Roosevelt set the tone for U.S. relations with Central America after becoming president in 1901. For Roosevelt and his advisors, there was no question whether a canal was needed to span the isthmus. The only questions that remained to be answered were where to build the canal—in Panama or Nicaragua—and how to nullify the Clayton-Bulwer Treaty of 1850 that called for the British to be included in any canal construction project. By the turn of the century, the British had all but conceded U.S. strategic superiority in the Western Hemisphere and agreed to replace the Clayton-Bulwer Treaty with the Hay-Pauncefote Treaty of 1901, giving the United States sole authority to proceed with a canal. In late 1901 the Walker Commission recommended the Nicaraguan route because it would cost less and involve a shorter distance than a canal through Panama.

At this point, two individuals—William Nelson Cromwell and Phillipe Bunau-Varilla—mounted a furious lobbying campaign on behalf of the former French company that had gone bankrupt trying to build the canal in Panama several decades earlier. Acting on behalf of the New Panama Canal Company, Cromwell made a $60,000 contribution to the Republican Party through Senator Mark Hanna of Ohio, a good friend of President McKinley's. A wizard at numbers and politics, Cromwell convinced the New Panama Canal Company, now in the hands of the Frenchman Bunau–Varilla, to lower its price and the Walker Commission switched its recommendation to Panama. In the meantime, under intense pressure from the pro-Nicaragua lobby, the House of Representatives passed the Hepburn Bill, which ordered that the canal be built in Nicaragua.

The debate now included the flamboyant Bunau-Varilla, who joined Cromwell to lobby for legislation that would put the canal in Panama. Within six months they had the votes to pass the Spooner amendment, instructing President Roosevelt to buy the Canal Company's claims for $40 million and start construction in Panama, provided he could obtain the necessary treaty from Colombia. Following a volcanic eruption in the Caribbean, Bunau-Varilla lobbied the Senate suggesting that Nicaragua could suffer the same fate, thereby weakening the argument for the Nicaraguan route. After the Nicaraguans denied publicly that volcanoes presented a problem in their country, Bunau-Varilla bought out the entire supply of Nicaraguan stamps (showing several volcanoes) in Washington and placed one on each senator's desk with the note: "Official testimony regarding volcanic activity in Nicaragua."[1] The Frenchman's ploy worked. Roosevelt's dramatic diplomacy shifted to Colombia, where more treaty work was needed before canal construction could begin. After the Colombians balked at the deal offered by Secretary of State John Hay in 1903, attention focused again on Nicaragua; but by this time it was too late to stop the powerful players—Roosevelt, Cromwell, and Bunau-Varilla—from securing the Panama route, regardless of the recalcitrant Colombians (see Chapter 6).

Although Nicaragua lost in the battle for an Atlantic-Pacific waterway, its importance to the United States did not end with the completion of the Panama Canal in 1914. The Panama decision shattered any hope Nicaragua might have had to possess a canal and contributed to events that influenced future U.S.-Nicaraguan relations. Nicaragua's dictator at the time, José Santos Zelaya, became a thorn in the side of the Roosevelt and Taft administrations by approaching the Japanese and Germans about a Nicaraguan canal that would compete with the U.S.-controlled canal in Panama. This action set in motion U.S. efforts to get rid of Zelaya, including collusion with Nicaraguan Conservatives and the landing of 400 U.S. Marines to protect the rebels. Zelaya was forced to leave, but his removal was the beginning of a political drama—including more intervention and Nicaraguan efforts to manipulate the United States for its own political and economic advantage—that continued for decades.

The Bryan-Chamorro Treaty of 1916

With the presence of U.S. Marines in Nicaragua after 1911, the United States was assured of a succession of governments in Managua that were compliant to its needs and demands. To solve a deteriorating financial situation, Nicaragua proposed to sell to the United States, for the sum of $3 million, exclusive rights to build a canal through its territory. Several years later the Bryan-Chamorro Treaty was signed (1914) and ratified (1916), giving the United States (1) exclusive and perpetual rights to build an interoceanic canal through Nicaragua; (2) 99-year leases of two small islands in the Caribbean; (3) rights to establish a naval base in Nicaraguan territory bordering on the Gulf of Fonseca; and (4) the option to renew both leases and access rights for another 99 years. In exchange for this generous arrangement, the United States would pay Nicaragua $3 million in gold to be applied to the reduction of its debt. The Wilson administration viewed the Bryan-Chamorro Treaty as the only practical solution to end the constant political turmoil, but it also served the purpose of deterring further European encroachments in the region. The Bryan-Chamorro Treaty turned out to be a short-term solution to what would eventually become a long-term problem: continual U.S. intervention. Obviously the United States did not need, or want, a second canal in Central America after spending $352 million to construct a canal through Panama. But the Bryan-Chamorro Treaty offered the United States a monopoly over isthmian transit and would virtually ensure U.S. strategic and economic dominance in the hemisphere.

Unfortunately, the canal-option agreement with Nicaragua proved to be one of the most disruptive and contentious issues in U.S.–Latin American relations at the time. It led to the collapse of the Central American International Court of Justice, contributed to the rise of the anti-imperialists and nationalist revolutionaries such as Augusto Sandino, and became a major factor in President Coolidge's decision to intervene in Nicaragua after failed elections and turmoil in 1925. Coolidge and his advisors also worried about what was erroneously perceived to be a "Bolshevik" threat from Mexico that might upset U.S. interests in Central America.

An "Election Doctor" for Nicaragua's Ailing Government

By 1922, Washington's attitude toward Latin America had changed from believing in the necessity of military intervention to stabilize governments and drive out foreign powers, to the belief that honest elections would pave the way for the withdrawal of U.S. military forces. To improve the Nicaraguan political system, at the urging of Washington, the Nicaraguan government contracted with Harold W. Dodds, a young political scientist, to come to Nicaragua and write a new electoral law. He arrived in 1922 with the intention of fixing Nicaragua's electoral and party system so that the State Department could retire the Marines from Nicaragua, leaving behind a U.S.-trained legation or embassy guard that would maintain order and supervise the elections to make sure they were fair.

The 1924 presidential election of Conservative Carlos Solórzano was fraudulent and grossly unfair, but the United States had little choice but to recognize him so that the Marines could be withdrawn. However, less than three months after the departure of the Marines, Solórzano was forced to leave office and Liberal-Conservative revolts broke out once again, requiring the redeployment of U.S. Marines to Nicaragua in 1925. Dr. Dodds's political medicine had obviously not worked, and U.S. Marines remained in Nicaragua to try to end the civil war. As more and more Marines landed, President Calvin Coolidge struggled to justify the U.S. intervention. At first he claimed that troops were needed to protect American lives and property; later he invoked national security considerations to protect the interoceanic canal rights that the United States had received from Nicaragua under the Bryan-Chamorro Treaty, and to halt Mexican efforts to foment disturbances in Nicaragua.

Augusto César Sandino and the Anti-Interventionist War

President Coolidge relied on diplomatic supervision and the U.S. Marines to solve Nicaragua's political problems. Although he was criticized at home for sending troops back into a country wracked by seemingly endless and internal bloody conflict, he was convinced that military power and the diplomatic wisdom of Henry L. Stimson could straighten out the situation in Nicaragua. After failing to stabilize the situation by backing a doomed minority government and promoting power-sharing, the United States poured more troops and naval forces into Nicaragua to protect U.S. interests. Before long Nicaragua was in chaos again and the United States was deeply involved in another Central American war. By 1928 U.S. naval vessels were in Nicaraguan ports, and more than 5,000 U.S. Marines were occupying the principal cities.

With the United States now caught in a political/military stalemate, Pres-

ident Coolidge sent Stimson to Nicaragua to mediate the conflict. By promising to supervise the next presidential elections and demanding that the
Nicaraguans organize a truly nonpartisan guard to exercise military and
police functions, Stimson was able to get both government and rebel forces
to end their hostilities, except for one lone holdout—Augusto César Sandino. Outmanned 5 to 1, Sandino's forces retreated to the mountains,
where they fought against the U.S. Marines for the next six years. Stimson
left Nicaragua shortly after his mediation efforts, not realizing he had
helped to start an anti-imperialist war of liberation to rid the country of a
U.S.-backed dictator and the conception of a revolution in Sandino's name
some 50 years later.

With his Defending Army of National Sovereignty, Augusto Sandino
launched a campaign against U.S. imperialism that resonated throughout
the twentieth century. The U.S. Marines searched in vain to find and capture Sandino and his rebel army, one of the few Nicaraguan efforts that
proved effective against U.S. domination in Central America at the time.
Using guerrilla tactics, Sandino and his ragtag army, under a red and black
flag emblazoned with "Liberty or Death," fought against the United States.
Sandino was a complex figure; his political ideology incorporated a range
of ideas that were frequently misunderstood or mythologized. Some of his
formative years were spent as an exile in Mexico, where he became an
admirer of the socialist dimensions of the Mexican Revolution. In his struggle against dictatorship and foreign domination in Nicaragua, Sandino considered himself a nationalist and anti-imperialist. At one point he
collaborated with Farabundo Martí, a rather well-known communist from
El Salvador. However, they differed over both goals and strategy. In one
meeting with Martí, Sandino explained to him that "our first task was to
defend and liberate the Nicaraguan people from the imperialist claw, by
expelling the dogs [Marines] and the Yankee companies from our soil; and
that the next step was to organize the workers."[2] Sandino succeeded with
the first task but was killed before he could tackle the second. A supporter
of Pan-American ideals such as a formal alliance of Latin American states,
Sandino often called for the abolition of the Monroe Doctrine as part of
his anti-imperialist message.

With Marine casualties mounting and the cost of the war escalating during the Depression, President Hoover caved in to domestic opposition to
the Nicaraguan war and withdrew the Marines in 1933. At this point the
responsibility of terminating Sandino's rebellion was left to the National
Guard, under the command of Anastasio "Tacho" Somoza García. Somoza
convinced Sandino and his weary army to surrender in 1934 and then, in
an act of treachery and betrayal, had Sandino, his brother, and two members of his armed guard assassinated. Although there is no evidence linking
American officials with Somoza for the murder of Sandino, it was widely

believed in Latin America that the United States was guilty—if only indi-rectly—in the affair. Once in power, Somoza made sure that Sandino's name was purged from all Nicaraguan textbooks.

The Somoza Dynasty

After the death of Sandino, power fell into the hands of National Guard commander Anastasio Somoza García, who used the Guard, his Partido Liberal Nacionalista (PLN), and U.S. assistance to rule Nicaragua until his assassination in 1956. Power then passed to his sons Luis (1956–1967) and Anastasio "Tachito" Somoza Debayle (1967–1979). The Somoza dynasty—in a little over four decades—came to own most of Nicaragua and accu-mulated a fortune to close to $600 million. Control of the National Guard became the major instrument of the dictatorship and the longevity of the Somoza family rule. "To dominate the Guard [a disciplined fighting and police force 3,000 strong] and its power would provide Somoza the means to overcome his lower-middle-class background and his history as a busi-ness failure, petty criminal, and sometime inspector of latrines."[3] The pa-triarch of the Somoza family, he was not content to remain the head of the Guard and in 1936 had himself "elected" president of Nicaragua. With these two positions in hand, Somoza operated a ruthless dictatorship char-acterized by corruption and greed, increased economic inequality, political manipulation, and friendship with the United States. Under his slogan of "Bucks for my friends, bullets for my enemies," Somoza murdered tens of thousands of Nicaraguans who impeded his rule, including peasants, work-ers, and students.

All three Somozas had studied in the United States (Luis at several uni-versities, and Anastasio Jr. at West Point), were fluent in English (including the special language of U.S. politicians), and displayed a fawning obedience to the needs of U.S. foreign policy. In 1939 the elder Somoza received an official invitation to visit President Franklin D. Roosevelt at the White House. In a much-disputed anecdote that has been repeated many times, Secretary of State Cordell Hull is alleged to have shown Roosevelt the list of visiting heads of states. On seeing the list, Roosevelt spotted Somoza's name and then asked Hull, "Isn't that man supposed to be a son of a bitch?" Secretary of State Hull fired back: "He sure is, but he is *our* son of a bitch!"[4] With Washington's seal of approval, Somoza returned to brag about how he was now the best friend of the United States in Latin Amer-ica. In exchange for his friendly treatment by the United States, Somoza named Managua's main street Avenida Roosevelt. During World War II, the United States poured millions of dollars of military aid into Nicaragua that expanded the power of the National Guard and made Somoza even richer. Nicaragua's armed forces benefited from hemispheric defense efforts during World War II with a U.S.-built naval station, ships, an air base, and troop training.

NICARAGUA AND THE UNITED STATES DURING THE COLD WAR

Somoza's dictatorship managed to survive the postwar elimination of dictatorships in neighboring El Salvador and Guatemala and growing hostility from the United States during the first few years of the Cold War. As the United States traded its nonintervention and prodemocratic principles for anticommunism beginning in the Truman administration, Somoza managed to notice the change, modify his style and rhetoric, and attempt to meet the needs of the United States during the Cold War. The United States turned down Somoza's offer to send troops to Korea, but the aging dictator offered the United States unflagging support in the Organization of American States (OAS) and the United Nations.

During the Eisenhower administration Somoza provided critical support for the 1954 CIA operation to overthrow Guatemalan President Jacobo Arbenz (see Chapter 13). He was rewarded handsomely with more aid, but most of it filtered down into the pockets of his own family and cronies, including the National Guard. When Somoza was gunned down by an assassin in 1956, President Eisenhower sent his personal physicians to Nicaragua to try to save the wounded dictator, but to no avail. Luis Somoza followed in his father's footsteps and allowed CIA-trained Cuban exiles to leave from Nicaragua in their effort to overthrow Castro at the Bay of Pigs in 1961. He was so excited about the prospects of Castro's demise that he came down to the docks at Puerto Cabezas and shouted to the departing invaders: "Bring me a couple of hairs from Castro's beard!"[5] Nicaragua benefited during the period of the Alliance for Progress by receiving increased amounts of economic and military assistance (in a U.S. effort to keep Nicaragua from becoming another Cuba). When Luis died in 1967 of a heart attack, Tachito assumed absolute power. To further seal Nicaragua's close relationship with Washington, he contributed $1 million to Richard Nixon's presidential election campaign.

The Somoza Lobby

The Somoza dictatorship would have ended earlier if it were not for Nicaragua's friends in Washington, carefully cultivated through a lobby network with direct access to the floors of Congress. Somoza's friends were known as the "dirty thirty," mostly conservative members of Congress who were willing to protect Nicaragua from cuts in American aid based on its human rights abuses and other offenses. Although there were anti-Somoza members of Congress and their staffs, they lacked the clout of the pro-Somoza lobby. As the insurrection against Somoza gained strength after 1975, Somoza used public relations/lobbying firms and friends in the U.S. Congress to improve his image in the United States. Somoza paid three public relations firms $250,000 yearly to provide him with a political facelift. He hired Washington lawyer William Cramer (a former congressman) and Fred Korth (a former secretary of the navy) to lobby against cuts in military and economic aid to Nicaragua. In Congress, Somoza courted old friends including Representatives John Murphy (a classmate of Somoza's in military preparatory school and a fellow graduate of the U.S. Military Academy at West Point); Charles Wilson of Texas, a blustering anticommunist; and George Hanson, Larry McDonald, Jesse Helms, and Robert Bauman. Somoza's defenders saw him as an anticommunist ally of the United States; to lose him would jeopardize U.S. interests in Nicaragua and elsewhere.

The Ghosts of Sandino and the Nicaraguan Revolution

The chronic repression under the Somoza dynasty eventually gave rise to a revolutionary coalition headed by the Sandinista National Liberation Front (FSLN). Founded in 1961 by Marxist-Leninists—Carlos Fonseca, Tomás Borge, and Silvio Mayorga—who had broken with the Communist Party, the FSLN struggled as a small guerrilla force until 1978, when it emerged as the major force in the anti-Somoza movement. The 1972 earthquake and a series of changes in the international environment accelerated the revolt against Somoza. When international relief funds were donated to Nicaragua after the earthquake, Somoza and his cronies walked off with the bounty while the rest of the nation grieved over the loss of life and the damage. Middle-class opposition was directed by newspaper editor Pedro Joaquín Chamorro, who organized a boycott of Somoza's staged elections. The revolt against dictator Somoza eventually became a popularly backed insurrection endorsed by the Catholic Church and other major sectors of Nicaraguan society.

After Jimmy Carter was elected president, the United States turned against Somoza by emphasizing the protection of human rights, leading to more defiance from the dictator and increased violence against the opposition. After Somoza ordered the assassination of Chamorro in 1978, the insurrection escalated with the FSLN serving as a unifying force, further broadening the opposition coalition. By the middle of 1978 Somoza had ordered his National Guard to bomb cities suspected of harboring insurrectionary forces, and the FSLN gained strength at the expense of the dictator's loss of authority and international support. With his country and his dictatorship in shambles, Somoza was forced to step down and leave Nicaragua in July 1979.

"Let's Go For It, We're On a Roll"

After he arrived in Miami, Florida, U.S. disagreements with the new government in Managua contributed to Somoza being denied exile in the United States. He soon fled to Paraguay, where he was protected by the dictator General Alfredo Stroessner until he was assassinated by Argentine leftists in 1980. The last Somoza left Nicaragua a bitter man, critical of the ingratitude of the United States for forcing his departure after years of his support for the United States during the Cold War. He called President Carter "Fidel Carter" for betraying Nicaragua and told U.S. representatives in Managua before packing his bags that "I helped them [Washington policymakers] for thirty years to fight communism. I'd like the American people to pay back the help we gave in the Cold War. The U.S. can't afford to lose a good partner. I am transitory but the reds are not."[6] During the long reign of the Somoza dynasty, Nicaragua became so closely identified with the United States that Somoza's removal at the hands of a bloody revolution was portrayed as the end of the National Guard and prior military rule. Unfortunately, the long nightmare of foreign involvement did not end with Somoza's departure.

By the time the Sandinista-led rebel coalition took power in 1979, the war to remove Somoza had resulted in 50,000 deaths (almost 2 percent of the population) and Nicaragua faced an estimated $1.5 billion in property

"We're Keeping Out of It — We Just Let Them Use the Back Yard for Training"

losses and huge foreign debt inherited from the dictatorship. Once in power, the Sandinista-led coalition drew its inspiration from the anti-imperialist stance of an earlier generation of Nicaraguans who had opposed U.S. intervention in Nicaragua. Despite the fact that several members of the collective leadership of the Sandinistas were Marxists or Marxist-oriented, the Nicaraguan revolution did not try to mimic the Cuban revolution under Fidel Castro. Government policies aimed for a redistribution of wealth and income along socialist lines, but the regime was hardly totalitarian in its political or economic orientation.

At War with Nicaragua

President Reagan's approach to events in Central America consisted of using U.S. economic and military assistance to "roll back" what he believed were communist advances in the region. Once U.S. military and economic assistance was terminated, the Sandinistas committed the Cold War "sin" of seeking support—hundreds of advisors and hundreds of millions of dollars in assistance—from the Soviet Union and Castro's Cuba. To restore U.S. predominance after the Carter years, the Reagan administration fo-

"Your Team Got a Player Named Martinez, From Nicaragua?"

cused on Nicaragua, where it hoped to subvert and eventually overthrow the Sandinista regime.

In an effort to bring down the Nicaraguan government, the Reagan administration organized and equipped a counterrevolutionary army called Contras, mostly Nicaraguan exiles operating out of neighboring Honduras. Many of the Contras were former National Guard personnel and political allies of the former dictator, financed (after Congress stopped funding) through secret appeals to foreign governments (mostly conservative authoritarian regimes) and wealthy private individuals in the United States. With assistance from the CIA, the National Security Council, and the White House, the Contras began a strategy of hit-and-run attacks on the Sandinista government. As the Reagan administration's war against the Sandinistas continued—with little in the way of military success on behalf of the Contras—opposition developed in Congress, the media, college campuses, and the general public. Once the Iran-Contra scandal (involving the selling of arms, at inflated prices, illegally to Iran to finance the counterrevolutionaries trying to defeat the Sandinistas in Nicaragua) became public in late 1986, and the Central American presidents mobilized efforts to end the war, the White House was doomed in its efforts to keep the battle going. In his determination to keep the Contras alive, Reagan gave 20 major speeches on the importance of Contra aid. Reagan's 1988 request for six months of additional funding was defeated by an eight-vote margin in Congress, reversing U.S. policy in Central America from military solutions to diplomatic solutions. Without U.S. assistance, the Contras were no more than a hollow fighting force with little chance of success.

Although the Contra war failed militarily, it inflicted great pain on Nicaragua, destroying sections of the nation's infrastructure and causing 30,000 deaths. The Contras became part of the peace process negotiations in 1988 and were finally disarmed and repatriated in 1990. The economic tragedy that remained after the war stimulated much of the domestic discontent in Nicaragua that led to the Sandinistas' defeat in the February 1990 elections. By subjecting themselves to democratic elections, the Sandinistas hoped to move forward with the important task of rebuilding war-torn Nicaragua without having to devote large sums to the anti-Contra effort.

NICARAGUA AND THE UNITED STATES AFTER THE COLD WAR

The surprising defeat of the FSLN's candidate, Daniel Ortega, in the 1990 presidential elections put an end to Nicaragua's revolutionary experiment and Sandinista rule. With the election of Violeta Barrios de Chamorro, leader of the United Nicaraguan Opposition (UNO), Nicaragua now entered the post–Cold War world, but the task of healing the wounds of two decades of internal war presented formidable challenges. As if things were not bad enough in Nicaragua, President Chamorro faced difficulties in obtaining assistance from the U.S. Congress, now in the hands of conservative Republicans, disruptions from former Contras, and further complications due to the FSLN's continuing control of the Nicaraguan army, police, and unions. As president she devoted her time to reversing the Sandinista revolution, pushing for national reconciliation, and struggling for ways to achieve economic recovery. However, during her six-year presidency she dueled with the Bush and Clinton administrations (and the conservative members of the U.S. Congress) over strings attached to foreign assistance promised to Nicaragua. Without a perceived security threat in Nicaragua, the United States seemed more interested in pressuring her to change certain government personnel and settling the claims of Nicaraguans who had emigrated to the United States, than in supporting her reconciliation policy.

In the 1996 presidential election, FSLN candidate Daniel Ortega tried to camouflage his revolutionary past while campaigning for the presidency again, but he was defeated handily by arch-conservative José Arnoldo Alemán, who considers himself the antithesis of everything the Sandinista revolution once stood for. On taking office President Alemán faced a litany of economic and political woes left over from ten years of revolution and six years of the Chamorro administration. In 1997 Nicaragua had 60 percent unemployment and the worst poverty in the Americas outside of Haiti. To change the situation inside Nicaragua, Alemán must still deal with a powerful Sandinista Front and large numbers of Nicaraguan Americans living in Miami who are demanding the return of more than 100,000 homes, farms, ranches, and businesses seized from supporters of the Somoza dictatorship.

CONCLUSION

Of all the countries in Central America, Nicaragua has suffered the most in the hands of Washington policymakers. Each of the periods of U.S. intervention proved to be counterproductive to U.S. interests and detrimental to the development of Nicaragua. The William Walker episode was extremely damaging to Nicaragua, and the decades of U.S. Marine occupation failed to establish democracy or stability there. Constant meddling spawned a revolutionary environment and the need for dictators and a National Guard to maintain political control in Nicaragua. The nation's misfortune of trying to carry out a socialist-style revolution during the presidency of Ronald Reagan proved damaging for both Nicaragua and the United States. It is ironic that a country so closely tied to the United States should have become the site of so much bloodshed and brutality. Although one can debate whether internal or external factors are the cause of revolutionary upheaval, there is no doubt that Nicaragua's close and subordinate relationship with the United States carries much of the blame in this case.

NOTES

1. Quoted in Walter LaFeber, *The Panama Canal: The Crisis in Historical Perspective*, expanded ed. (New York: Oxford University Press, 1979), p. 22.

2. Quoted in Donald C. Hodges, *Sandino's Communism: Spiritual Politics for the Twenty-First Century* (Austin: University of Texas Press, 1991), p. 73.

3. John A. Booth, *The End and the Beginning: The Nicaraguan Revolution* (Boulder, CO: Westview Press, 1982), p. 52.

4. Eduardo Crawley, *Dictators Never Die: A Portrait of Nicaragua and the Somozas* (New York: St. Martin's Press, 1979), pp. 98–99.

5. Quoted in Robert E. Quirk, *Fidel Castro* (New York: W. W. Norton, 1993), p. 370.

6. Quoted in Bernard Diederich, *Somoza and the Legacy of U.S. Involvement in Central America* (Maplewood, NJ: Waterfront Press, 1989), p. 266.

SUGGESTED READINGS

Berman, Karl. *Under the Big Stick: Nicaragua and the United States since 1848.* Boston: South End Press, 1986.

Findling, John E. *Close Neighbor, Distant Friends: United States–Central American Relations.* Westport, CT: Greenwood Press, 1987.

Gutman, Roy. *Banana Diplomacy: The Making of American Foreign Policy in Nicaragua, 1981–1987.* New York: Simon and Schuster, 1988.

Pardo-Maurer, R. *The Contras, 1980–1989: A Special Kind of Politics.* New York: Praeger, 1990.

Pastor, Robert A. *Condemned to Repetition: The United States and Nicaragua.* Princeton, NJ: Princeton University Press, 1988.

Prevost, Gary, and Harry E. Vanden, eds. *The Undermining of the Sandinista Revolution.* New York: St. Martin's Press, 1997.

Walker, Thomas W., ed. *Revolution and Counter-Revolution in Nicaragua.* Boulder, CO: Westview Press, 1991.

20

Panama

TIMELINE OF U.S. RELATIONS WITH PANAMA

1821	Panama declares independence from Spain, but as part of Gran Colombia
1846	Bidlack-Mallarino Treaty is signed (ratified in 1848)
1850	Clayton-Bulwer Treaty is ratified
1856–1903	Fourteen major interventions by U.S. forces
1898	Spanish-American War increases demand for canal
1899–1902	Pro-Nicaragua and pro-Panama route advocates battle in Washington
1901	Hay-Pauncefote Treaty is signed
1903	Hay-Herrán Treaty is signed but rejected by Colombian Senate
	Republic of Panama is established
	Hay-Bunau-Varilla Treaty is signed
1914	Panama Canal opens for transit
1934	United States agrees to modify 1903 treaty in favor of Panama
1946	U.S. Army School of the Americas is founded
1964	Anti-U.S. riots in Canal Zone
1967	President Robles is impeached over treaty negotiations
1968	Arnulfo Arias is elected president; is overthrown by Colonel Torrijos
1970	Colonel Noriega becomes head of military intelligence
1977	Carter-Torrijos treaties are signed; are ratified by one vote in U.S. Senate

1983	General Noriega becomes commander of Panamanian Defense Forces
1984–1986	Noriega assists United States in Contra campaign
1988	Noriega is indicted for drug trafficking
1989	United States invades Panama to capture Noriega
	Guillermo Endara is placed in power by the United States
1991–1992	Noriega is tried, convicted, and sent to a Miami prison
1994	Ernesto Pérez Balladares is elected president
1997	Multinational Drug Interdiction Center is proposed to coordinate anti-narcotics efforts from Howard Airforce Base after December 31, 1999
1998	Approval of counter-narcotics center delayed after President Pérez Balladares denounces written agreement as "an ill-conceived pile of paper"
2000	Panama assumes sovereignty over its national territory under Carter-Torrijos Treaties

INTRODUCTION

Panama's importance to the United States stems from its location as a land bridge between Central America and South America and its narrow width separating the Atlantic and Pacific Oceans. Instead of establishing independence at the time of separation from Spanish control in 1821, Panama's leaders joined the newly formed Confederation of Gran Colombia. As Colombia's northern province, Panama eventually became important as one of several sites for an interoceanic crossing in Central America. By the middle of the nineteenth century, French, British, and U.S. interests began to converge on a series of isthmian projects that would enhance national interests in the region. By the 1840s the French had acquired rights to build a railroad, a canal, or both in Panama. The British concentrated on routes in Costa Rica and Nicaragua, whereas the United States focused on building a passage for ships across the Isthmus of Tehuantepec in southern Mexico. However, it was not until Panama's independence in 1903 that the United States forged an alliance, allowing for the construction of a canal, to continue a project that had been started by the French in the 1880s.

The key to U.S.-Panamanian relations was a lopsided treaty signed in 1903 giving the United States rights that ultimately generated anger, violence, and resentment from Panamanians for the next three-quarters of a century. Under the treaty, the United States built and operated the Panama Canal—one of the marvels of transportation technology in the early twentieth century—but more than 30,000 people died building the canal, first under the French and later during the 10 years it took the United States to finish the canal. Panamanians got such an unfair deal in the 1903 treaty crafted by a Frenchman and a U.S. secretary of state that they spent years demanding concessions and modifications from Washington. President Carter finally replaced the old treaty with two new treaties that will eventually turn over full control of the canal to the Panamanians after December 31, 1999.

Panama is still important to the United States as a remnant of its need to control events in Latin America. Drug trafficking and money laundering in the 1970s and 1980s eventually led the Bush administration to mount an invasion of Panama to remove its military dictator, General Manuel A. Noriega, in 1989. Since that time the United States has been slowly extricating itself from both Panama and the operation of the Canal, in anticipation of the day in which the alliance, forced on Panama in 1903, comes to an end.

PANAMA AND THE UNITED STATES DURING THE NINETEENTH CENTURY

Panama and the Independence of Latin America

Panama's economic and strategic importance was recognized by the Spanish long before a railroad or canal was constructed across the isthmus. Although Panama did not become independent until 1903, it emerged from the tumultuous period of struggle for independence as an integral part of Colombia. Prior to Panama's separation from Spain, the United States expressed little interest in Panama; trade was almost nonexistent, and Panamanian leaders remained loyal to Spain. The Monroe administration recognized Colombia's independence (and indirectly, Panama's) in 1822 and sent diplomatic representatives who were instructed to emphasize free trade and U.S. involvement in any future interoceanic canal in Panama. Panamanians viewed the possibility of a ship canal through the isthmus as a savior for their economic difficulties, and they regarded independence as a prerequisite for achieving that goal.

As the United States expanded westward under the banner of Manifest Destiny during the nineteenth century, interest in an interoceanic crossing in Central America blossomed. By the 1850s, Panama and the United States were being drawn into an alliance that would last for another 150 years. U.S. expansionists faced numerous obstacles in Central America, not the least of which was British and French interest in building a transportation link. Recognizing the importance of gaining concessions and crossing rights in Panama, U.S. diplomat Benjamin Bidlack signed a treaty—the only alliance treaty signed by the United States in the nineteenth century—with Colombia's foreign minister, Manuel María Mallarino, in 1846 (ratified in the United States in 1848) giving the United States transit rights in Panama in exchange for U.S. promises to protect Colombia's sovereignty over Panama.

The Bidlack-Mallarino Treaty committed the United States to an interoceanic route through Panama with the right to intervene militarily to protect whatever transit facilities existed. In short order the United States had a strategic interest in Panama, the right to send U.S. troops to put down secessionist outbursts, and a huge stake in the political destiny of the Panamanians. Between 1848 and 1902, U.S. troops landed in Panama 13 times, often pitting U.S. forces against the local population. The Bidlack-Mallarino Treaty was somewhat nullified in 1850 when the United States and Britain signed the Clayton-Bulwer Treaty, which provided for joint control over any future canal. The Clayton-Bulwer Treaty was controversial in the United States and frustrating for Central Americans interested in playing off one power against another for economic gain. When the French entrepreneur Ferdinand-Marie de Lesseps started a French canal project in the Panamanian region of Colombia in the 1880s, the United States threatened war and invoked the Monroe Doctrine; but the French project failed due to tropical diseases and poor planning, including the plan to build a sea-level canal instead of following a lock-system design.

PANAMA AND THE UNITED STATES IN THE TWENTIETH CENTURY

The United States and the Diplomacy of the Panama Canal

U.S. interest in a transisthmian canal increased after 1898 when the USS *Oregon* had to go around Cape Horn to reach Cuba during the Spanish-American War. Under pressure from those who recognized the strategic value of a canal, the U.S. Congress established the Isthmian Canal Commission (ICC) in 1899. However, after it investigated possible canal routes, the ICC recommended that the canal be built in Nicaragua, not Panama. When Theodore Roosevelt, a longtime canal advocate, assumed the presidency in 1901, expectations increased that the complicated diplomatic knot preventing construction could be unraveled.

The first obstacle for the United States was to acquire treaty rights to build a canal either in Nicaragua or Panama. In 1902 the U.S. Congress passed the Hepburn Bill authorizing canal construction in Nicaragua, but it was later amended to allow the president to negotiate first with Colombia and, if this failed, with Nicaragua. To this end the United States and Colombia signed the Hay-Herrán Treaty in 1903. The agreement offered extremely favorable terms to the United States, but the Colombian Senate rejected it largely on the basis of the inadequate monetary incentives and intrusions on its national sovereignty.

The decision to build the Panama Canal was the most costly and strategic commitment of the United States in Latin America up to that time. With expanding trade and investments in the region, the construction of the Panama Canal increased concern about the region's stability. The diplomacy of building in Panama involved a complex set of foreign and domestic actors that required new leadership and initiatives by the United States. First, the United States had to confront the Clayton-Bulwer Treaty that called for a joint project with the British in the event a canal was to be constructed. Second, the Colombians displayed little interest in getting rid of their northern province, despite the fact that the Panamanians had long struggled to separate from Colombia.

The 1903 Treaty

After the United States helped create an independent Panama, the Roosevelt administration negotiated the Hay-Bunau-Varilla Treaty in November 1903. This was an extremely favorable arrangement giving the United States rights "in perpetuity" to a canal zone 10 miles wide and 40 miles long. The United States also acquired the right to intervene militarily to quell riots and maintain order and the right to take additional lands necessary for the canal's defense. Panama's part of the bargain included a payment of $10 million and an annual payment of $250,000. For the next 75 years the Hay-Bunau-Varilla Treaty, designed by a French adventurer-investor and a forceful U.S. secretary of state, defined the relationship between the United States and Panama. John Hay, secretary of state, could not have been more pleased with the favorable terms acquired by the United States. In a letter to Senator Spooner he confided that the new treaty was "very satisfactory, vastly advantageous to the United States, and we must confess, with what face we can muster, not so advantageous to Panama. . . . You and I know too well how many points there are in this treaty to which a Panamanian patriot could object."[1] Although Roosevelt faced criticism for his handling of both Panamanian secession and the terms of the treaty, he defied his critics by telling them it was for the good of mankind and the nations of the world.

The construction of the canal was an engineer's nightmare. The difficulties of excavation spawned a barrage of criticism of the expensive project. In a splash of bravado, President Roosevelt toured the isthmus in 1906, the first president to leave the country while in office, and returned to answer his critics. As completion neared, the nation began plans for a grand celebration of the project with praises for those who helped create one of the engineering marvels of the Western Hemisphere. Controversy continued to swirl around the 1903 revolution and the treaty. In speaking at the University of California in 1911, Theodore Roosevelt bragged that "If I had followed traditional conservative methods [i.e., constitutional procedures], the Canal debate would have been going on yet; but *I took the*

Canal Zone and let Congress debate, and while the debate goes on the Canal does also" (emphasis in the original).[2] The construction of the Panama Canal cost the United States $352 million (including the $10 million paid to Panama and $40 million paid to the French company) and 5,609 lives from disease and accidents. More than 30,000 people died before the canal was finished, first under the French in the nineteenth century and later during the 10 years that the United States spent constructing the canal. No single construction project in American history had cost as much in dollars and in human life. The Canal was a masterpiece of design and engineering, a relatively clean project in terms of graft and corruption, and the culmination of decades of phenomenal effort and human sacrifice.[3]

Panama and the United States between the Wars, 1914–1940

The opening of the Panama Canal in 1914 symbolized the rise of the United States to the status of a great power and the dominant power in the Caribbean. Paradoxically, the gunboat diplomacy that provided the United States its microstate in Panama did not carry over into further efforts to acquire more territory in Latin America. Between World Wars I and II, Panama was expected to serve the national interests of the United States. In reality, for the first three decades there were two Panamas living side by side: the Republic of Panama, and the Canal Zone—a mixed civilian-military compound under the control of the U.S. secretary of war.

The 1920s were troubled times for the United States and Panama as power over the canal came to reside in the hands of the governor of the Canal Zone administration. The governor—a senior officer in the Army Corps of Engineers—exercised dual authority, setting policy for both the republic and the operation of the canal. With a racially based economic reward system in operation in Panama—the white managers were on the lucrative gold roll, while West Indian blacks and Panamanians had to make do with the silver roll—strikes and protests were frequent. Panamanian presidents, angered over U.S. efforts to take over more and more Panamanian land and the feeling of being short-changed in a lopsided economic relationship, made constant demands for a new or revised treaty, but the United States refused. Nationalist politicians were outraged when a boundary dispute with Costa Rica led to a brief war after Costa Rican troops (assisted by the United Fruit Company) seized Pacific lands that had been in dispute for some time. After driving out the Costa Ricans, Panamanians were forced to return the land to Costa Rica with the help of U.S. Marines that landed in 1921. This interventionist response made Panamanians even more determined to do something about the unpopular 1903 treaty.

The Great Depression affected Panama through layoffs and the devaluation of the U.S. dollar, which greatly reduced the annual payment to Panama. Political turbulence increased as the economy declined and thousands of silver workers joined the ranks of the unemployed. In January 1931, Acción Comunal (a nationalist pressure group designed to reduce U.S. influence and gain more benefits for Panamanians) engineered a coup that placed one of its sympathizers in the presidency. The United States, in the atmosphere of the Good Neighbor Policy, refrained from taking part in the coup despite concerns over the possible damage to U.S. interests in the zone. In an effort to reduce the growing resentment against the United States and the Monroe Doctrine, Secretary of State Henry Stimson and others recognized that constant intervention in the internal affairs of small countries like Panama and others, along with lengthy periods of military control, was undermining U.S. influence in the region.

U.S.-Panamanian relations in the 1930s were marked by the emergence of new and aggressive leadership in Panama (untainted by the 1903 treaty) and new initiatives by the Roosevelt administration to improve U.S.–Latin American relations. At the heart of the relationship was the determination of Panamanian nationalists to modify the terms of the 1903 treaty. After the inauguration of Franklin D. Roosevelt in 1933, Panamanians took advantage of the changing atmosphere in Washington where the tenor of inter-American relations seemed to bode well for concessions on the seriously strained relationship. President Harmodio Arias made a surprise visit to President Roosevelt in late 1933 in hopes of convincing him of the urgency of altering the lopsided U.S.-Panamanian relationship. In the spirit of the Good Neighbor Policy, Roosevelt agreed to a few changes immediately and then arranged for negotiations to begin in an effort to modify the terms of the 1903 treaty.

The Arias-Roosevelt meetings eventually culminated in the formal treaty modifications that were signed in 1936. The 1936 treaty changed Panama's status as an appendage of the United States, but the concessions were hard fought between Zonians (American residents of the Panama Canal zone) and the U.S. War Department on one side, and the Department of State and the White House on the other. The War Department and the Zonians resisted most concessions on the grounds of security interests and the right to special privileges. The State Department and Roosevelt's White House favored the promotion of better relations by ceding in nonstrategic areas. The U.S. Senate finally ratified the new treaty in 1939, but it was not enthusiastic about giving way on the importance of U.S. strategic interests. As World War II loomed on the horizon, the concessions wrought in the revisions to the 1903 treaty added more fuel to the fires of Panamanian desires to achieve greater independence from the United States.

The Good Neighbor Policy paved the way for political changes inside Panama that had serious and lasting effects, particularly in government-opposition party relations and the use of the National Police (Policía Nacional) to rig elections and undermine opposition forces. In pledging to adhere to the new principle of nonintervention in the internal affairs of the Latin American countries, the United States would no longer send troops to supervise elections or preach the virtues of democracy. For Panama, this change meant increasing use of the National Police by elected politicians to gain and retain power, even if it meant intimidation and violence. Eventually the militarization of Panamanian society came to haunt those who had forcibly separated Panama from Colombia in the name of the Monroe Doctrine and imperial grandeur.

Panama and the United States during World War II

World War II brought Panama to world attention through its importance as a critical link in both the Allied defense strategy and the naval empire of the United States in the Caribbean. Two of Panama's presidents during the war years—Arnulfo Arias and Ricardo Adolfo de la Guardia—projected different views of how best to deal with the United States in times of war, since the protection of the canal was of vital interest to both countries. Until his overthrow in 1941, Arias's intensely nationalist position and attitude toward the war in Europe worried the United States. By demanding high payments for lands leased for military bases, keeping Panama neutral, and maintaining his association with pro-Axis individuals in Italy and Germany, Arias angered policymakers in Washington. Once he was toppled by de la Guardia, with help from U.S. intelligence agents, Panama adopted a policy of moderation and collaboration with U.S. military personnel, signing a defense sites agreement in 1942 that pleased the United States. The war had a major impact on Panama's economy as President de la Guardia, with significant financial commitments from Washington for highway construction, increased purchases of Panamanian supplies, a third locks expansion plan, and the extension of the Pan American Highway, a road system stretching from Alaska to Chile that was completed in 1963, except for the Darién Gap between southern Panama and northern Colombia. With Panamanian collaboration, the United States was able to tighten security around the canal, eliminate Axis intelligence activities in the country, and continue policies to preserve Panama as a convenient protectorate, but with most of the benefits clearly in favor of the United States and Americans living in the Canal Zone.

PANAMA AND THE UNITED STATES DURING THE COLD WAR

U.S.-Panamanian collaboration during World War II served to postpone a large number of Panamanian demands for greater independence, equality, and control over the canal itself. After the war these issues were pursued aggressively by the Panamanian government but largely resisted by the United States. Of particular interest to the Panamanians was the question of whether the changing nature of race relations in the United States would also be implemented in Panama (at the time, the Canal Zone was segregated by race). Labor and race relations began to improve in Panama after 1945, but when the Cold War erupted in the late 1940s union leaders came under attack for being communist tainted. The advent of atomic weapons produced a heightened sense of security among policymakers in Washington, who worried about how to protect the canal while realizing the security value of the canal was declining owing to the growing size of the navy's newest ships. In 1946 the U.S. Army founded a training center for Latin American military personnel in Panama that after several decades was named the U.S. Army School of the Americas (SOA). Funded by the U.S. government, the SOA-training programs emphasize counter-terrorism, counter-insurgency warfare training, and multinational military relationships. Since moving to Ft. Benning, Georgia in 1984, the School of the Americas has taught courses related to counter-narcotics matters. The substantial number of graduates from the SOA who have been involved in military takeovers and human rights violations has earned it the title of "School for Dictators" and the scorn of members of Congress and private citizens in the United States and elsewhere throughout the Americas.

Panama's growing assertiveness against the forced alliance eventually produced a meeting between President Eisenhower and José Antonio Remón, Panama's pro–United States and anticommunist president, in 1955. Remón's demands on the United States were explicit recognition of Panama's sovereignty in the Canal Zone and the right to display the two countries' flags side by side. The Treaty revisions signed in January 1955 produced some gains for Panama, but most were economic rather than political because the United States would not alter the 1903 sovereignty rights and refused to give Panama a share in canal tolls. Secretary of State John Foster Dulles rejected every Panamanian demand to obtain sovereignty in the zone.

By the mid-1950s the canal had lost most of its military value due to its narrowness and vulnerability to foreign attack; however, Panama's value for counterinsurgency training, intelligence, and projecting U.S. influence during the Cold War increased. Most Panamanians considered the concessions in the 1955 Treaty meaningless, and by the late 1950s public dissent raged against the United States. In a surge of public outcry called "Operation Sovereignty," Panamanian students planted Panamanian flags in the Canal Zone and demanded the government provide more schools and financial aid. Riots continued in 1958–1959 as student and labor leaders derived inspiration from Castro's successful revolution in Cuba. To improve relations with Latin America and Panama, President Eisenhower helped create the Inter-American Development Bank (IDB), a centerpiece for the Alliance for Progress. By 1960 the National Security Council (NSC) had decided to propose the construction of a new sea-level canal across Central America by 1980, a project that never came to pass.

The Diplomacy of Treaty Revision

Pressure for recognition of Panamanian sovereignty in the Canal Zone increased during the 1960s. After student-led rioting in 1964 left 24 people dead in a campaign—Flag Riots—to have Panama's flag flown in the Canal Zone, alongside the U.S. flag, and demands that the Canal's toll profits be shared, President Lyndon B. Johnson negotiated a new treaty with Panama that would have recognized Panamanian sovereignty in the Canal Zone, but it failed in the U.S. Senate. Several years later Presidents Richard M. Nixon and Gerald Ford began talks with the Panamanians on a new treaty that would relinquish U.S. sovereignty; but after Nixon became embroiled in the Watergate scandal, treaty negotiations came to a standstill until 1976, when presidential candidate Ronald Reagan made U.S. control over the Panama Canal a serious campaign issue. Once Jimmy Carter became president in 1977, he reversed his position (he had campaigned against relinquishing control over the Canal Zone) and negotiated two new canal treaties—one to govern the canal during the transition period, the other beginning in the year 2000. Conservative opponents of the treaties, led by Ronald Reagan and Congressman Daniel Flood, lobbied hard for their defeat in the U.S. Senate, but after the longest treaty debate in history, the Senate ratified the two treaties by only one vote.

THE NORIEGA YEARS

The Central American Crisis

With the election of Ronald Reagan as president in 1980, U.S. Latin American policy shifted to Central America where Washington hoped to stop the "communists" in El Salvador and remove the Sandinistas from power in Nicaragua. To this end, the Reagan administration enlisted the assistance of General Manuel Antonio Noriega, a former intelligence chief of the National Guard who came to power after General Torrijos died in a plane crash in 1981. At first Noriega assisted both sides of the Central American crisis. He cooperated with U.S. intelligence and military agencies but also participated in the Contadora Group, an ad hoc association of four states—Colombia, Mexico, Panama and Venezuela—to settle the conflicts in Central America. After Noriega was implicated in the death of his chief political opponent—Dr. Hugo Spadafora—in 1987, the United States suspended millions of dollars in aid to Panama and started pressuring Noriega to resign from office. Over the next several years, U.S.-Panamanian relations soured as it became increasingly apparent that Noriega was not interested in democratization efforts, combating drugs, and treaty implementation efforts.

Noriega's involvement in drug trafficking started early in his military career. By 1968 he had graduated from the Peruvian Military Academy and was a paid informant of the U.S. Central Intelligence Agency. In 1972 a high-level U.S. drug official proposed to President Nixon that the White House "plumbers" (undercover operatives hired to stop leaks of sensitive political information, often using illegal methods) assassinate Noriega, but Nixon refused to approve the idea. Noriega's reluctance about extending the Pentagon's lease on Fort Gulick (home of the U.S. Army School of the Americas since 1946) under the 1977 treaties frustrated the U.S. military and contributed to the school being moved in 1984 to Ft. Benning, Georgia. When it became known in 1986 that Noriega was a double agent who passed U.S. secrets to Fidel Castro and had connections to Colombian drug mafias (which were smuggling tens of millions of dollars of cocaine into the United States), the Reagan administration decided it was time to get rid of Noreiga—but not until the Sandinistas were removed in Nicaragua and George Bush was safely in the White House. After all, Noriega was instrumental in smuggling guns to the Contras and allowing the CIA to establish a Contra training camp in Panama. As long as the United States considered the defeat of the Sandinista government in Nicaragua a priority, Noriega was somewhat insulated from criticism over his governing style and drug smuggling.

With a prime location, good communications, and the necessary financial infrastructure, Panama has served as a major center of money laundering and transshipment of Andean cocaine into the United States. With more than 600 banks ready to help with drug smuggling and money laundering, some $600 million in drugs were reported to have passed through Panama annually during the mid-1980s. General Noriega learned the drug and weapons business from his predecessor; but after Torrijos died in a plane crash in 1981, Noriega's knowledge of this nefarious activity helped him to greatly expand the trafficking of drugs.

Operation Just Cause

The 1989 invasion of Panama by U.S. forces was the first post–Cold War invasion of a Latin American country that was not justified (at least explicitly) on the basis of a global-ideological threat to the security of the United States. Washington's decision to invade was preceded by two years of diplomatic bungling by the Reagan and Bush administrations, as well as increasing vilification of General Noriega in the American press for his illegal drug trafficking, money laundering, and brutal suppression of polit-

"Lets Try Rocking It Back and Forth"

ical dissent. At first the United States suspended millions of dollars in aid to Panama in hopes that economic sanctions would force Noriega's removal. But General Noriega only became more defiant, and relations deteriorated through 1988 and 1989.

With each attempt by the United States to increase the pressure on Noriega—two U.S. grand juries indicted him on drug violations in 1988—he became more defiant of U.S. policy to rid Panama of his presence. With Noriega shaking his fist at the Bush administration for several months, and personal attacks on President Bush by members of his own party and the press for vacillating (*Time* magazine accused him of being a wimp), George Bush ordered an invasion called "Operation Just Cause." Although Bush justified the invasion on the grounds that he needed to protect U.S. citizens in Panama, help restore democracy, and bring an end to a brutal dictatorship, the real reasons had more to do with domestic politics in the United States at the time. President Bush needed to do something that would lay to rest the image of indecisiveness that had dogged him during the 1988 campaign and his difficulty in figuring out how to conduct foreign policy during his first year in office. Domestic politics would not allow the president to wait for economic sanctions to work, as critics within his own party relentlessly accused him of being a coward who lacked the necessary resolve to deal with the dictator Noriega.

The December 1989 invasion was denounced by the Organization of American States in a resolution that was approved by 20 to 1, largely on the basis of the nonintervention language in the OAS Charter. However, the invasion was supported by both political parties in the U.S. Congress and by 80 percent of the U.S. public despite the absence of national security alarms concerning communist influence, intrusion by rival superpowers, or Cuban-inspired Marxist guerrillas operating in Central America. Operation Just Cause had nothing to do with the Monroe Doctrine, but it constituted the largest U.S. military force to be used in combat since the Vietnam War and the largest U.S. military operation in Latin America since the Spanish-American War of 1898. After several weeks of U.S. occupation, Noriega finally surrendered (after taking refuge in the residence of the papal nuncio) and was taken by U.S. drug enforcement officials to Miami to stand trial on drug-trafficking charges. Noriega's surrender was facilitated by U.S. military officials, trained in psychological operations, who blasted the papal nuncio's home with music from Bobby Fuller ("I Fought the Law and the Law Won") and Linda Ronstadt ("You're No Good") on a twenty-four-hour basis.

The intervention achieved its objective—the capture of Noriega—but it cost the United States $163 million in military operations expenditures, 23 American lives and over 350 casualties, and the enmity of its Latin American neighbors and others around the world. Hundreds of Panamanians lost their lives, and thousands were injured and lost their homes. After a showy and controversial trial, Noriega was convicted and sentenced to 40 years in a U.S. prison for racketeering, money laundering, and violations of drug laws. As he languishes in a Miami jail, General Noriega accepts little of the blame for the invasion and damage to his homeland. He blames George Bush—with whom he met in Washington on several occasions to discuss counterinsurgency activities in El Salvador and Nicaragua—and others in the Reagan administration for his plight.

CONCLUSION

Recent polls conducted in Panama indicate that a huge majority of Panamanians want U.S. troops to remain in Panama after 2000. With 16,000 existing U.S.-provided jobs related to the operation of the canal, as well as the recognition of the importance of U.S. assistance to fight powerful drug cartels, Panamanians are again engaged in a process of rethinking their national identity. The United States and Panama reached a formal agreement in late 1997 that will create (after U.S. Senate approval) a "multilateral counter-drug center" at Howard Air Force base in Panama, which has been a U.S. facility for many years. However, language in the accord that allows American soldiers to engage in "other missions," giving the United States what some critics see as legal grounds to intervene militarily in the region, prompted President Ernesto Pérez Balladares in 1998 to denounce the agreement as "an ill-conceived pile of paper." As such, the drug wars have provided the motivation for retaining a U.S. military presence on Panamanian turf.

Panama remains important to the United States, and the hemisphere, less as an interoceanic waterway than as a geographic foothold to deal with a plethora of issues that have little to do with security, economic investments, and predatory foreign powers within the context of maintaining U.S. influence. Despite its quasi-obsolescence the Panama Canal is still a valuable source of revenue, and the canal watershed is valuable for scientific research on tropical systems important to hemispheric survival. Thus, the future of the Panama Canal may lie more in land-use planning and ecosystem protection than in maintaining U.S. sovereignty and protecting against the possible encroachment of extra-hemispheric powers. The notorious School of the Americas, where thousands of Latin American military officers were trained in security practices, is being turned into a five-star hotel catering to eco-tourists by a Spanish-Mexican consortium of venture capitalists.

NOTES

1. Quoted in David McCullough, *The Path between the Seas: The Creation of the Panama Canal, 1870–1914* (New York: Simon and Schuster, 1977), p. 392.

2. Quoted in Walter LaFeber, *The Panama Canal: The Crisis in Historical Perspective* (New York: Oxford University Press, 1978), p. 9. Emphasis in original.

3. Little in the way of political philosophy influenced the technicians and administrators who labored to build the Panama Canal. However, the construction of the canal was such an efficient and successful *government* enterprise that it worried those who feared that such a prosperous project might serve as a demonstration of the advantages of socialism over capitalism.

SUGGESTED READINGS

Armony, Ariel, and Thomas W. Walker. *Repression, Resistance, and Democratic Transition in Central America.* Wilmington, DE: Scholarly Resources, 1999.

Buckley, Kevin. *Panama: The Whole Story.* New York: Simon and Schuster, 1991.

Collins, Richard H. *Theodore Roosevelt's Caribbean: The Panama Canal, the Monroe Doctrine, and the Latin American Context.* Baton Rouge: Louisiana State University Press, 1990.

Conniff, Michael L. *Panama and the United States: The Forced Alliance.* Athens: University of Georgia Press, 1992.

Dinges, John. *Our Man in Panama: How General Noriega Used the United States, and Made Millions in Drugs and Arms.* New York: Random House, 1990.

Farnsworth, David N., and James W. McKinney. *U.S.-Panamanian Relations, 1903–1978.* Boulder, CO: Westview Press, 1983.

LaFeber, Walter. *The Panama Canal: The Crisis in Historical Perspective*, Expanded Edition. New York: Oxford University Press, 1978.

21

Paraguay

TIMELINE OF U.S. RELATIONS WITH PARAGUAY

1811	Paraguay declares independence from Spain
1861	U.S. diplomatic relations are established
1865–1870	Triple Alliance War
1932–1935	Chaco War
1940–1948	Pro-Axis military dictatorship of General Higinio Morínigo
1954	General Alfredo Stroessner takes power in a coup d'état
1958	Vice-President Nixon visits Asunción
1962–1966	United States provides almost $47 million in economic and military aid
1965	Stroessner supports President Johnson's Dominican intervention
1972	Stroessner extradites heroin boss Auguste Ricord
1977	President Carter pressures Stroessner on human rights
1977–1978	Ambassador Robert White pressures Stroessner on human rights
1979	World Anti-Communist League holds biannual congress in Asunción; Stroessner calls Carter a communist
1981	President Reagan reverses some of Carter's anti-Stroessner initiatives
1985–1988	National Endowment for Democracy assists with democratization efforts
1989	Stroessner is overthrown in coup by General Andrés Rodríguez
1993–1997	President Clinton continues Bush administration policies
1993	Juan Carlos Wasmosy is elected president
1996	Attempted coup against Wasmosy by General Lino Oviedo

1997	General Oviedo elected Colorado candidate for 1998 presidential elections; is jailed later in the year for insulting the president
1998	President Clinton warns President Wasmosy of serious consequences if he tries to stop presidential elections scheduled for May 1998; General Oviedo is sentenced to 10 years in prison for 1996 coup attempt
	Raúl Cubas Grau (General Oviedo's running mate until his jail sentence was upheld), candidate for the ruling Colorado Party, elected president

INTRODUCTION

Paraguay's landlocked status, distant location, and negligible strategic and economic important to the United States have been important factors in explaining the sporadic and limited involvement of the United States in Paraguay. Positioned between two major South American powers—Argentina and Brazil—Paraguay has fought two of the three major Latin American wars and numerous minor conflicts. One war was fought in the 1930s to restore its national honor and territory after a devastating war against a triple alliance of Argentina, Brazil, and Uruguay in the 1860s in which it lost two-thirds of its population and 25 percent of its territory. According to Riordan Roett, "Had Paraguayans not fought so often and so well, their nation would probably not exist today."[1]

Paraguay's history of boundary conflicts has engendered a constant fear of attack by its close neighbors. Since gaining independence in the early part of the nineteenth century, Paraguay has emphasized the value of internal security and relied on a powerful military apparatus. Whether it is being run by civilians or army officers, Paraguay has experienced an unbroken chain of dictatorships. Between 1811 and 1967 there was only one contested election for president, and even then the incumbent won handsdown. Between 1870 and 1954 the average president stayed in power for less than two years, unable to govern for long periods due to intense rivalry between the Colorados and Liberals (Paraguay's two major political parties) and the predatory nature of the military. During the dictatorship of General Alfredo Stroessner (1954–1989), Paraguay overcame this malady by combining an obedient military with a heavy emphasis on anticommunism and a well-disciplined party (Colorado) organization during the Cold War.

PARAGUAY AND THE UNITED STATES IN THE NINETEENTH CENTURY

During most of the nineteenth century, U.S. involvement in Paraguay was minimized by the foreign policy of three presidents-for-life (Dr. José Gaspar

Rodríguez de Francia, Carlos Antonio López, and Francisco Solano López) whose most important goal was the protection of Paraguay's sovereignty and independence. Until the death of Rodríguez de Francia in 1840, Paraguay was so isolated that no nation had recognized its independence and world trade with it was almost nonexistent. The United States did not recognize Paraguay until 1861, fully 50 years after its independence from Spain. Consumed by the fear of powerful neighbors, Paraguay's military dictators used state control of the economy for self-reliance and to repel foreign invaders. The Monroe Doctrine had little impact on U.S.-Paraguayan relations; it was never invoked by the United States to prevent foreign powers from colonizing or intervening in Paraguay's internal affairs, and Paraguayans failed to see it as something that could enhance their security or national survival.

The *Water Witch* Affair

With little sustained interest in Paraguay, either for economic or security reasons, the United States maintained cordial relations with Asunción until the arrival of the USS *Water Witch* in 1854. The U.S. naval voyage was complicated by the economic interests of Edward Augustus Hopkins, an entrepreneur and former naval officer who was also U.S. consul in Asunción during the regime of Carlos Antonio López. Intent on amassing a fortune by promoting his navigation company, Hopkins soon found himself in conflict with Paraguay's president because of his indiscretions and diplomatic blunders. After proceeding up the Paraná River—in violation of Paraguayan law and contrary to the orders of President López—to determine the potential for commerce and to carry out scientific investigations, the *Water Witch* was fired on by Paraguayan gunners, killing one helmsman. Three years later, in a belated effort to punish López, the United States decided to send a flotilla of 19 ships and 2,500 men to Paraguay. After López agreed to pay $250,000 to the helmsman's survivors in the United States, the crisis was averted. Relations improved in 1859 when Paraguay and the United States signed a treaty of friendship and commerce, a gesture that brought some dividends during the Triple Alliance War.

Triple Alliance War, 1865–1870

In the Triple Alliance War (1865–1870), fought against Argentina, Brazil, and Uruguay, Paraguay lost two-thirds of its population (only 29,000 male Paraguayans survived the war) and surrendered 25 percent of its national territory to Brazil and Argentina. One of the bloodiest wars in the history of the Western Hemisphere, the Triple Alliance War (the conflict is also known as the Paraguayan War) had much to do with the ruthless Francisco Solano López, a mentally unstable and ambitious dictator in search of glory and military prestige. With a well-trained army of 80,000, López envisioned becoming the Napoleon of South America until he was killed in battle by Brazilian soldiers in 1870.

Once Argentina was drawn into the Brazil-Uruguay alliance fighting against Paraguay in 1865, the U.S. minister in Buenos Aires wrote to Secretary of State Seward about the possibility of U.S. mediation. Seward's response indicated a willingness to assist with settling the dispute in the interest of hemispheric peace, but the differences were too profound to be settled by mediation. There was considerable sympathy in the United States for Paraguay's plight during the war, despite the fact that the conflict was provoked by Paraguayan dictator Francisco Solano López. New York newspapers sided with underdog Paraguay, and top officials in Washington were strong supporters of López. As the decimation of Paraguay continued after the end of the U.S. Civil War in 1865, some former Confederate officers offered to prepare a fleet of six ships to fight against the alliance waging war against Paraguay.

After the defeat, Paraguay faced the daunting task of rebuilding its economy after one of the greatest military disasters in modern history. With a succession of military leaders at the helm, Paraguay courted thousands of immigrants from Italy, Spain, Germany, and Argentina. Paraguay continued to be plagued with border disputes, dependency on foreign capital, and authoritarian rule. After a territorial dispute with Argentina in 1878, the president of the United States was called on to arbitrate the right of sovereignty over the disputed territory between the two countries. President Rutherford B. Hayes ruled in favor of Paraguay; both sides approved of the outcome and expressed their thanks to the United States. Paraguay went even further with its appreciation, naming a city Villa Hayes and one of 19 provinces after the American president.

PARAGUAY AND THE UNITED STATES DURING THE EARLY TWENTIETH CENTURY

The dawn of the twentieth century brought the Liberal Party to power in 1904 with promises to guide the nation toward prosperity, stability, and peace. The Liberals were not successful, and internal struggles of one kind or another contributed to the pressures that set in motion the war against Bolivia in 1932. With revolution and political turmoil in Central America (including the canal project in Panama) and the Caribbean, the United States had little time to devote to Paraguay.

The Chaco War, 1932–1935

The Chaco War was the consequence of two previous conflicts—the Triple Alliance War, and the War of the Pacific—stretching back seven decades. After the disastrous loss in the Triple Alliance War in the 1860s, Paraguay was better equipped for war in the 1930s. The Chaco area had been in dispute for many generations, and Paraguay was anxious to eliminate the memories of its painful defeat in 1870. Having lost its outlet to the sea in the War of the Pacific (1879–1883), Bolivia was intent on securing a port on the Paraguay River that would enable it to transport goods to the Atlantic (see Chapter 3). After several skirmishes provoked hostilities between both nations between 1927 and 1932, Paraguay prepared for battle but did not formally declare war until 1933. The Chaco War drained Paraguay's meager resources, and although the war ended in victory over Bolivia, the cost (36,000 dead and $125 million in expenditures) was extremely high for a poor country. The inability of the League of Nations and the other major hemispheric powers to settle the dispute peacefully was a setback to hemispheric cooperation, and the utility of international organizations in conflicts of this nature lost legitimacy. Collective efforts to solve the dispute peacefully were compounded by the belief that U.S. petroleum interests were lending support to Bolivia, whereas Argentina and Great Britain were behind Paraguay's forces. Both countries experienced a wave of nationalism and agitation for political reform after the war was settled by a peace treaty in 1938, and in the case of Bolivia the war was a contributing factor to its revolution in 1952.

Paraguay and the Good Neighbor Policy

President Roosevelt's Good Neighbor Policy coincided with the Great Depression, the Chaco War, the great-power rivalry with Britain and Germany, and the expanding power of the military in Paraguay. Hitler's aggressive foreign policy in southeastern South America raised the possibility of security threats to the United States as war clouds hovered over Europe. Because there were numerous authoritarian nationalists in Paraguay during the 1930s, top officials in Washington worried about the possibility of pro-German politicians coming to power and opposing the United States. As a counteroffensive to German expansion in the Western Hemisphere, the Roosevelt administration initiated an effort to bring all the Latin American countries within the political and economic sphere of the United States through several hemispheric conferences between 1938 and 1940. Roosevelt also embarked on a propaganda campaign designed to undermine Nazi influence, and he promoted closer military cooperation, including air- and naval-base rights to counter German influence.

U.S. efforts to propose collective security pacts against outside aggression were opposed by Paraguay because they implied hostile references to Germany. With the United States and Germany competing for influence in South America, it behooved countries like Paraguay to accept funds from both powers without committing themselves unequivocally to one or the other. The German presence in Paraguay by 1940 was substantial, the result of liberal immigration policies after the nation's near annihilation during the Triple Alliance War. Out of a total population of less than one million in the late 1930s, there were some twenty-six thousand Germans living in Paraguay, including Hugo Stroessner, the father of future dictator Alfredo Stroessner (1954–1989). Hitler's agents had great success in preaching the gospel of National Socialism, and until a few months before the end of the war Paraguayan presidents consistently rejected U.S. complaints against the widespread Nazi presence in the country.

Paraguay and World War II

The outbreak of World War II brought the United States and Paraguay together in a concerted effort to expand the U.S. sphere of influence and draw Paraguay away from the influence of Nazi Germany. The task of bringing Paraguay around to the Allied cause during the war was made all the more difficult because of the pro-Axis dictatorial regime of General Higinio Morínigo (1940–1948), a skillful opportunist who did not declare war against Germany until February 1945 in a last-ditch gesture designed to assure Paraguay's membership in the United Nations and guarantee war-indemnity claims against the defeated Axis powers. Relying heavily on the army for his support, Morínigo ruled with a heavy hand, jailing opponents, silencing the press, and banning political parties. In addition to economic aid at the beginning of the war, the United States provided $11 million in Lend-Lease (U.S. matériel and services provided to its allies) military equipment to Paraguay in 1941, and it made loans for public works projects to counter German/Nazi influence. Paraguayan trade with the United States increased dramatically during the war years, and U.S. influence over Paraguay expanded significantly. Paraguay also received vast amounts of economic and material assistance for its international alignment during the war. Until the final years of the war, the Roosevelt administration tolerated the pro-Axis dictator Morínigo in order to maintain the façade of hemispheric solidarity. Ultimately U.S. ambassador Wesley Frost convinced Paraguay to break with the Axis powers and support the Allies. Frost considered Morínigo a "white-glove dictator," less harsh than other pro-Fascist Latin American dictators, patriotic, and free of corruption. This attitude toward so-called benevolent dictators would serve the United States as a useful rhetorical prop to justify support for rulers who violated human rights and opposed any form of democracy during the Cold War.

PARAGUAY AND THE UNITED STATES DURING THE COLD WAR

After using economic and military aid to "purchase" Paraguay's alignment against Germany during World War II, the United States continued to influence Paraguayan affairs during the Cold War. Between 1945 and 1947, Morínigo succumbed to a shift in U.S. policy in which the State Department began a campaign to encourage democracy and freedom in Paraguay in exchange for continuing foreign aid. Under intense pressure from U.S. ambassador Willard Beulac, Morínigo had no choice but to modify the nondemocratic aspects of his government; but the ambassador's efforts often led to heated protests against "foreign intrusion" from his military supporters. Nevertheless, U.S. pressure to "democratize" Paraguay soon led to a destructive civil war led by a coalition of communists, Liberals, and Febreristas (cadres of the February 1936 Revolution) against the Asunción government. During the intense conflict the United States remained neutral, a maneuver that some interpreted as support for Morínigo and the Colorado Party. With the use of barefoot peasant reserves and an artillery regiment under the command of Alfredo Stroessner, the Colorados prevailed. Paraguay's new foreign minister, Federico Chaves, informed the United States that Paraguay would remain a close friend and ally in the Cold War and that in return he hoped that the Truman administration would be forthcoming with economic assistance. Despite the absence of democracy, U.S.-Paraguayan relations improved from 1948 to 1953, with dramatic increases in U.S. trade, private investment, technical assistance, military aid, economic aid, and loans. By using aid, loans, trade agreements, and military/security pacts, the United States forged a close friendship with Paraguay that lasted for most of the Stroessner era.

The Tyrannosaur: Alfredo Stroessner and the United States

Alfredo Stroessner rose through the ranks of the Paraguayan military to rule Paraguay longer than any chief executive, from his seizure of power in a coup in 1954 until his regime's overthrow in 1989. Known in Paraguay as the *stronato* (the dictator's extreme form of tyranny), General Stroessner used "preventive repression" and a well-established political party to dominate Paraguayan politics. Unlike other military dictatorships in Latin America during the Cold War, Stroessner cultivated the Colorado Party (the primary instrument of patronage) as a popular base for his regime. After Stroessner visited the United States in 1953, the Eisenhower administration saw him as a valuable asset in the war against communism. It also regarded Paraguay's government, then under Federico Chaves, as an important ally in dealing with Argentina's anti-U.S. president, Juan Domingo Perón. In the following year Stroessner seized power in a military coup but received assurances from the Eisenhower administration that relations would remain cordial. In a meeting with U.S. president Dwight Eisenhower in 1956, Stroessner assured him that "Paraguay was one-hundred percent anti-communist."[2] With a privileged military and secret police to guarantee his grip on power, Stroessner had no trouble suppressing internal revolts, defeating invasions by Paraguayan exiles living in Brazil and Argentina, and acquiring the backing of the U.S. government. After arriving in Paraguay in 1958, Vice-President Richard Nixon told Paraguayan officials that "In the field of international affairs, I do not know of any other nation which has risen more strongly than yours against the threat of communism and this is one reason why I feel especially happy to be here."[3] In return for generous amounts of aid and political legitimacy, Stroessner became a staunch defender of American foreign policy. For example, he severed relations with Castro's Cuba and supported the U.S.-backed expulsion of Cuba from the Organization of American States, and he agreed to collective armed action during the Cuban missile crisis in 1962. In 1968 he offered the Johnson administration the use of Paraguayan troops to fight in Vietnam, but the offer was rejected. Paraguay outlawed the Communist Party and refused to establish diplomatic relations with the Soviet Union, as did other right-wing governments in Latin America.

The offspring of a German father and a Paraguayan mother, Stroessner spent his early years following a military career in which he acquired the values of order and discipline. During the 1930s he developed an admiration for fascism and Nazi ideology and later a deep hatred of communism. Home of the first Nazi Party in South America (1932–1946), Paraguay under Stroessner became a sanctuary for former Nazis like Josef Mengele (known as the "Angel of Death" at Auschwitz) and hundreds of other Nazis and fascists from other parts of Europe. In August 1979 Nicaragua's deposed anticommunist dictator, Anastasio Somoza Debayle, arrived in Paraguay, where he was well protected and lived in comfort until he was assassinated by Argentine-based guerrillas in 1980.

In 1965 the U.S. House of Representatives passed the Seldon Resolution authorizing unilateral military intervention in Paraguay to counter the threat of "international communism, directly or indirectly." Washington's perception of a Paraguayan security threat evolved from a belief that its location—situated close to the economic heartland of South America where American investments are much larger—would make it ideally suited for left-wing guerrillas to use to export revolution throughout the southern South American region (Southern Cone). In return for using Paraguay for mostly military and security purposes, the United States supported the Stroessner dictatorship with economic and military aid, despite tensions over heroin smuggling (1971), child prostitution (1977), and human rights violations (1978). U.S. military forces maintained a large military mission in Asunción, constructed an air force base, and carried out training exercises on Paraguayan turf. In sum, U.S.-Paraguayan relations during the *stronato* were cordial and reliable for the first two decades, but they became characterized by conflict and tension over drug trafficking, democracy, and human rights from 1975 to the end of the dictatorship in 1989.

The United States and Paraguay: From Nixon to Reagan

The Nixon administration was forced to confront Paraguay over one of the largest drug smuggling operations in Latin America, the work of August (André) Ricord, a member of the "French Connection," a heroin smuggling ring based in Marseilles, France. With a reputation for rampant corruption and contraband, Ricord used Paraguay to smuggle between 50 and 75 percent of all the heroin brought into the United States between 1967 and 1973. As Nixon attempted to pressure the Paraguayan government over the protection it seemed to be offering to international drug rings, and the extradition of Ricord after he was arrested in 1972, Stroessner resisted until President Nixon suspended credit lines and military aid. Once Stroessner relented to Ricord's extradition, U.S.-Paraguayan relations returned to normal (that is, acquiescence to the excesses of the dictatorship) until the inauguration of Jimmy Carter in 1977.

After President Carter announced that he would no longer ignore human rights violations and the absence of democracy in Paraguay, U.S.-Paraguayan relations deteriorated rapidly. Using threats of cuts in military sales, economic aid, and trade, the United States tried to pressure Stroessner to liberalize his dictatorship. Carter sent Robert White as U.S. ambassador to Paraguay in 1977 to lead a campaign against Stroessner's abysmal human rights record. He managed to get almost one thousand political prisoners released during his first year and played a pivotal role in creating the National Accord, the first organized opposition to the Stroessner regime. Stroessner responded by attacking the United States for intervening in its internal affairs, and he characterized the U.S. government as "Carter-communism" during an address before the Congress of the World Anti-Communist League in 1977.

Paraguay expected bilateral relations to improve with the election of Ronald Reagan in 1980, an assumption based on Reagan's Cold War rhetoric and determination to combat international communism. However, Carter's changes in U.S.-Paraguayan relations continued under Reagan, with added pressure on Stroessner's right-wing dictatorship designed to offset criticism of the administration's war against leftists in Nicaragua. In an effort to confront Paraguay on the drug issue, Reagan appointed Clyde Taylor, former assistant secretary of state in the Bureau of International Narcotics Matters in the State Department, as ambassador to Paraguay. Taylor's public human rights diplomacy earned him insults and threats from the Paraguayan government. Despite executive-legislative conflicts over efforts to decertify Paraguay as a candidate for U.S. aid, the Reagan administration obtained full certification for it on "national security grounds." Reagan's Paraguay policy was not encumbered with serious internal divisions within the presidential advisory system (Department of State, CIA, and the National Security Council), and Stroessner lacked the support that other right-wing dictators enjoyed in Washington. Both factors played a minor role in Stroessner's downfall shortly after Reagan left office.

PARAGUAY AND THE UNITED STATES DURING THE POST–COLD WAR ERA

The United States and the End of the Stroessner Dictatorship

With growing protests, domestic and foreign, and cracks in the foundation of the dictatorship, Stroessner won his eighth reelection to the presidency in 1988. To the surprise of many, the dictatorship ended on February 3, 1989, when army commander General Andrés Rodríguez, father-in-law of the dictator's youngest son, overthrew Stroessner in a palace coup that resulted in the deaths of close to 200 people. After 35 years in power, the multimillionaire Stroessner had been toppled from within. He was then allowed to spend his remaining years in exile in Brasilia, Brazil.

After promising a war against drugs as a high priority, the Bush administration faced the problem of recognizing the new government when Rodríguez was reputed to have strong ties to drug traffickers and money launderers. Despite the obvious pleasure that Stroessner was gone, it took the White House two weeks to affirm Rodríguez as the legitimate heir to Stroessner. Convinced of the importance of U.S. recognition and international support, the new government in Asunción promised a prompt return to democracy (new elections were held in May 1989), the protection of human rights, and a commitment to do something about drug trafficking. After having himself reelected three months after the coup, Rodríguez promised not to seek reelection and keep the presidential election timetable on schedule. Under the *stronato*, General Rodríguez became one of the richest men in Paraguay. After a 40-year military career with a top salary of $500 a month, he owned several ranches, currency exchange shops, an import-export business, and the nation's largest brewery. To have amassed this much wealth on such a small salary attests to the depth of corruption and cronyism during General Stroessner's long rule.

U.S.-Paraguayan Relations, 1989–1993

With the end of the dictatorship and pledges of cooperation from Paraguay's new president, U.S.-Paraguayan relations improved considerably. Top officials in Washington, both governmental and military, traveled to Asunción to praise the positive changes in the government, increase the amount of technical and economic assistance, and wring concessions out of the Paraguayans of interest to domestic constituents in the United States. In 1990, Vice-President Dan Quayle traveled to Paraguay to praise the president's commitment to democracy and human rights, and later that year President Rodríguez met with George Bush at the White House. To combat drugs, the Bush administration demanded that Paraguay agree to the establishment of an anti-drug agency in the capital to carry out national anti-drug policy. The United States awarded Paraguay U.S. trade preferences, provided substantial amounts of economic aid, and welcomed its decision to join the Southern Cone Common Market (MERCOSUR) in 1992. Despite efforts from Stroessner loyalists in the military, and from members of his family, to restore Stroessner to power, Rodríguez managed to finish his full term without being toppled by the military. His successor, businessman-turned-president Juan Carlos Wasmosy, had to assume his role with less than 40 percent of the national vote. To many observers, however, his was the "cleanest, dirty" election in 48 years.

The Clinton Administration and Paraguay

President Clinton, faced with the realization that Wasmosy's election did not represent a real transition to democracy in Paraguay, nevertheless supported it. After all, the inauguration of Wasmosy in August 1993 represented the first civilian president in Paraguay in almost 40 years. With strong remnants of the Colorado/military alliance still visible in Paraguayan politics, moving from the *stronato* to some type of democratic system was not easy, as evidenced by the thwarted coup attempt against President Wasmosy in April 1996. In a showdown with General Lino Oviedo, Wasmosy was forced to take refuge in the U.S. embassy until the General was made to capitulate by a massive demonstration of diplomatic clout by the Clinton administration, the Organization of American States, and the MERCOSUR governments of Argentina, Brazil, and Uruguay. Threatened with economic and diplomatic isolation, General Oviedo backed down and the first democratically elected Paraguayan government in half a century was saved. Political crisis erupted again in 1997 when the ruling Colorado Party picked General Oviedo as its candidate for the presidential elections in 1998, despite internal opposition and the negative reaction among top officials in Washington.

With General Oviedo in jail for conspiring to overthrow the government in 1996, President Wasmosy provoked a preelection crisis in April 1998 by trying to annul his party's primary and keep front-runner Oviedo from winning the May presidential elections. The crisis was averted after the courts upheld Oviedo's 10-year prison sentence and President Clinton warned Wasmosy of serious international repercussions if the elections did not take place on schedule. In a horse race election, Raúl Cubas Grau

(General Oviedo's vice-presidential candidate until he was blocked from running), candidate for the ruling Colorado Party, was elected president by a narrow vote margin in May 1998.

Paraguay's long history of smuggling and contraband has generated a bitter dispute between American companies that are trying to protect their patents, licenses, and trademarks and thousands of Paraguayan entrepreneurs selling cheap imitations of American products. Under pressure from pharaceutical, recording, and software industries in the United States, Washington has started a campaign to threaten Paraguay with economic sanctions if it does not do something about protecting intellectual property from financial losses attributed to widespread counterfeiting. For example, in 1998 the U.S. recording industry estimates that it lost $125 million over the preceding year from fake products sold in Paraguay's thriving border towns such as Ciudad del Este.

CONCLUSION

U.S.-Paraguayan relations have been based on mutual concern over hemispheric security—defined as the removal of "foreign" ideologies, threats from neighboring countries and dissident exiles, and hemispheric drug trafficking—and Paraguay's need for constant doses of economic and military assistance from the United States. Although at times the relations with the United States have been strained, particularly during World War II and the last decade of the Cold War, relations with the United States have remained cordial despite differences on issues that are sensitive to both countries. Since the end of the Stroessner tyranny, Paraguayan leaders have attempted to initiate needed reforms, including free-market overhauls and membership in the Southern Cone Common Market; but cleansing the state of its corrupt and inefficient habits has been difficult, even with the support of the United States. Paraguay remains a headache for policymakers in Washington because of drug trafficking, commercial pirating, and recent evidence that it has become a staging ground for Muslim guerrillas with links to the Iranian-backed Hezbollah terrorists.

NOTES

1. Riordan Roett, "Paraguay's Fledgling Democracy: Precarious Progress," in Howard J. Wiarda and Harvey F. Kline, eds., *Latin American Politics and Development*, 4th ed. (Boulder, CO: Westview Press, 1996), p. 287.

2. Stephen G. Rabe, *Eisenhower and Latin America: The Foreign Policy of Anticommunism* (Chapel Hill: University of North Carolina Press, 1988), p. 86.

3. Quoted in Latin American Bureau, *Paraguay Power Game* (London: Latin American Bureau, 1980), p. 44.

SUGGESTED READINGS

Latin American Bureau. *Paraguay Power Game*. London: Latin American Bureau, 1980.

Lewis, Paul H. *Paraguay under Stroessner*. Chapel Hill: University of North Carolina Press, 1980.

Miranda, Aníbal. *United States–Paraguay Relations: The Eisenhower Years*. Washington, DC: Latin American Program, The Wilson Center, 1990.

Miranda, Carlos R. *The Stroessner Era: Authoritarian Rule in Paraguay*. Boulder, CO: Westview Press, 1990.

Mora, Frank O. "Paraguay and International Drug Trafficking." In Bruce M. Bagley and William O. Walker, eds., *Drug Trafficking in the Americas*. Coral Gables, FL: North-South Center/Transaction, 1994.

Roett, Riordan, and Richard Sacks. *Paraguay: The Personalist Legacy*. Boulder, CO: Westview Press, 1991.

22

Peru

TIMELINE OF U.S. RELATIONS WITH PERU

1824	Peru achieves independence from Spain
1826	U.S. diplomatic relations are established
1846–1847	President Castilla organizes military alliance to counter threat from Ecuador's exiled president
1840–1870	Guano trade links Peru and United States
1850	W. R. Grace Company opens for business
1865	Andean countries request U.S. intervention in defense of Monroe Doctrine
1879–1884	War of the Pacific
1888	Grace Contract is signed
1908–1912	Augusto B. Leguía serves as elected president (first term)
1919–1930	Leguía seizes power and slavishly supports United States (second term)
1920–1930s	Víctor Raúl Haya de la Torre organizes a new political party to attack Leguía and the United States
1941–1942	Peru-Ecuador border conflict
1942	Rio Protocol settles border war
1948	General Manual A. Odría seizes power; rules until 1956
1954	President Eisenhower awards Odría the Legion of Merit
1956–1962	Manuel Prado's presidency faces anti-American hostility
1963–1968	Fernando Belaúnde Terry serves as president (first term)
1968	The military overthrows Belaúnde over International Petroleum Company (IPC) affair

1968–1980	Military rules under banner of "Institutional Revolution"
1980–1985	Fernando Belaúnde Terry serves as elected president (second term)
1985–1990	Alan García serves as elected president
1987	Operation Snowcap begins
1990–1995	Alberto Fujimori serves as elected president (first term)
1992	Comrade Gonzalo, head of Sendero Luminoso, is captured
	President Fujimori dissolves Congress in April; a new Congress is elected in November
1995–2000	Fujimori serves as reelected president (second term)
1996	Túpac Amaru rebels seize 720 hostages at Japanese ambassador's residence in Lima
1997	Fujimori orchestrates dramatic rescue; all rebels are killed

INTRODUCTION

Peru and the United States have had a perplexing relationship—characterized by periods of cordiality and friendship, but tempered occasionally by diplomatic tensions and outright hostility—stretching back to the wars of independence. Boundaries with Ecuador, Colombia, Brazil, Bolivia, Chile, and the Pacific Ocean have drawn Peru into important international conflicts with its neighbors and the United States. Its mountainous terrain and long coastline have attracted foreign investors in search of minerals and other economic resources. From the early interest in whaling, guano fertilizer, and nitrates, to copper and silver mining in the nineteenth century, to petroleum exploration and tuna fishing in the twentieth century, Peru has provided a powerful magnet for U.S., South American, European, and Asian investors. Beginning in the 1950s, Peru's efforts to exercise national sovereignty and jurisdiction over a 200-nautical-mile maritime zone adjacent to its coast to protect its fishing industry generated a U.S.-led international effort to force a change in Peruvian policy—an unsuccessful one that harmed bilateral relations. Peruvians tried to use the Monroe Doctrine during two significant conflicts in the nineteenth century, but they turned against it after realizing Washington would not invoke it as Peru wanted.

The gradual expansion of U.S. economic control over Peru's natural resources, combined with a close working relationship with Peru's oligarchy, contributed to the radicalization of Peruvian politics and bouts of intense conflict with Washington beginning in the twentieth century. Since the Cold War, U.S.-Peruvian relations have been seriously strained by nationalistic and socialistic governments that threatened U.S. hegemony in the Western Hemisphere. A staggering foreign debt and the rise of the narcotics trade and terrorism also challenged relations with the United States. To pursue a more independent foreign policy, and to protect its national interests, Peru has emphasized a multilateral approach to regional economic and security issues through the Organization of American States and the United Nations, along with an active search for new markets through regional trade pacts designed to reduce its dependency on the United States. The election of Alberto Fujimori in 1990 increased tensions between Peru and the United States over human rights, constitutional governance, and narcoterrorism, but his neo-liberal economic policies (reducing the size of government and privatizing major industries) also brought praise from Washington.

PERU AND THE UNITED STATES IN THE NINETEENTH CENTURY

The United States and Peruvian Independence

U.S. representatives were in Peru even before it achieved its independence from Spain in 1824. Between 1817 and 1826, John B. Prevost, Jeremy Robinson, and William Tudor were instructed by the U.S. government to foster the commercial interests of the United States, oppose conservative European monarchies, and stress the importance of a more open democratic system than the one Simón Bolívar favored. Tudor became the first commercial representative of a foreign power to be granted recognition by Peru, and this helped pave the way for U.S. diplomatic recognition of Peru in 1826. The liberator of Peru, Venezuelan Simón Bolívar, distrusted the U.S. expansionist desires and interest in dominating the entire hemisphere.

Peru and the Monroe Doctrine

Monroe's message of 1823 received only passing interest in Lima and played a minor role in the history of U.S. involvement in Peru. Since Peru's independence in 1824, there have been only two occasions when the Monroe Doctrine influenced diplomatic relations. The first occurred in 1846–1847 in response to the efforts of Ecuador's exiled dictator, Juan José Flores, to plot with European governments to assist him in his efforts to regain power in Ecuador. Peruvian president Ramón Castilla (1845–1851; 1855–1862) tried to counter the Flores expedition by crafting a military alliance with Bolivia, Chile, and Ecuador. Castilla's diplomatic campaign also included efforts to convince the United States to sell him warships in the name of the Monroe Doctrine, but the Polk administration refused. In the end, neither the U.S. government nor the Monroe Doctrine was a factor in squashing the antics of former dictator Flores or in pushing for an inter-American conference.

The second instance evolved from Spanish intervention in Latin American politics from 1829 to 1865, often with other European powers, aimed at settling various types of claims or reestablishing the Spanish monarchy. Peru's insecurity was compounded by the fact that the Spanish government had never formally recognized Peruvian independence, and in 1864 a Spanish naval force seized and occupied the Chincha Islands, a source of valuable guano, a fertilizer made from the dried excrement of seabirds. This dispute between Spain and Peru brought the two countries to war in 1865 and an Andean appeal for U.S. intervention. The brief war produced a Quadruple Alliance—Peru, Chile, Ecuador, and Bolivia—and a request to Secretary of State William Seward for direct intervention in defense of the Monroe Doctrine. Seward rejected the plea on the grounds that Spain was no longer interested in acquiring territory; hostilities continued for a short while, and a peace agreement was signed in Washington in 1871. Washington's refusal to intervene—the first explicit request by any Andean power for such service—and the inability of the Monroe Doctrine to provide much protection from foreign encroachments gave rise to distrust and hostility toward the United States and contributed to future conflicts over boundaries and economic resources. The Monroe Doctrine declined in importance for Peru and the United States until the pro-U.S. Augusto B. Leguía (1908–1912; 1919–1930) governed Peru and used the Monroe Doctrine as a way to win favors from Washington.

Guanopreneurs and Railroad Builders in Peru

Peru experienced some degree of economic prosperity during the middle of the nineteenth century due to European demand for guano fertilizer to increase agricultural production. With numerous coastal islands and millions of birds, Peru was the world's best source of guano. Contracts were signed with British and French merchants, Chinese laborers were imported to harvest the caustic guano, and a new group of guano profiteers gained power in Peru. By the 1870s, one European company—Dreyfus and Company—controlled the entire guano trade, from harvesting to banking. Flush with guano profits and loads of borrowed money, Peru contracted with Henry Meiggs, a daring and unscrupulous railroad builder from New York, to construct a line from the southern coast to the mines in the Andes between 1868 and 1870. His engineering skills earned him the name "Yankee Pizarro," but his business strategy included the use of Chinese laborers and bribes for Lima's top politicians. The cost of the railroad was too great for Peru's economy and antiquated financial system, and the nation was forced into bankruptcy in 1876, unable to pay interest on its foreign debt. With its guano deposits exhausted and the discovery that sodium nitrate was a superior fertilizer to guano (and also a necessary ingredient for gunpowder manufacture), Peru soon found itself at war with Chile over nitrate mining in the Atacama Desert (see Chapter 5).

Casa Grace and U.S. Control of Peru's Economy

Peru's humiliating defeat at the hands of more powerful Chilean forces contributed to civil war and the decision to sign the so-called Grace Contract in 1888, involving a powerful U.S. business and British creditors. The Grace Contract opened the door for foreign capitalists and established a close business relationship with Peru's oligarchy until the 1930s. In exchange for cancellation of Peru's huge foreign debt, the Grace Contract granted foreigners control over its railroads, a steamer franchise, guano, and jungle land as well as annual payments of 80,000 English pounds for a period of 30 years. Many Peruvians hated the Grace Contract for its assault on national pride, but it marked the beginning of Peru's postwar economic recovery. Coming so soon after the loss of Tacna and Arica in the War of the Pacific, and causing lingering animosity toward U.S. diplomats, the relationship with Grace meant that Washington had to deal as much with those who owned Peru's extractive industries as with its top officials in charge of the government.

W. R. Grace Company played a major role in the economic development of Peru—and the expansion of U.S. influence—during the second half of the nineteenth century with interests in shipping, arms, guano, silver mining, and railroads. By the end of the 1880s the Grace brothers (William R. and Michael P.) exerted so much influence over U.S. foreign policy that they managed to engineer the downfall of Charles W. Buck, U.S. minister to Peru, to protect their company's business interests at the expense of existing property rights of U.S. citizens. The Casa Grace (the name most commonly used in Peru) was able to manipulate the State Department, circumvent U.S. diplomats, and persuade the U.S. government to abandon a fundamental principle of its foreign policy in dealing with Peru. The Grace brothers "became the de facto representatives of the United States in Peru, controlling the flow of information to Washington and directing what policy to pursue."[1] The fate of Charles Buck, and the willingness of the U.S. government to accede to the power of private interests in Peru, demonstrates the importance of nonstate actors (individuals and ideas) in the formulation of U.S. foreign policy during the nineteenth century. The power of W. R. Grace Company continued well into the twentieth century, expanding its economic empire (and good will under the banner of Casa Grace) with a policy of identifying itself with Peruvian national interests. In business since 1850, W. R. Grace has the longest history of all U.S. firms operating in Peru.

PERU AND THE UNITED STATES IN THE EARLY TWENTIETH CENTURY

Peru's frustrations with the United States gradually gave way to more cordial diplomatic relations after the late 1880s, due in large part to the growing North American participation in the expanding Peruvian economy. Growing investments in copper and silver mining by the giant Cerro de Pasco Copper Corporation after its founding in 1901 helped to improve both diplomatic and commercial relations. During the first three decades of the twentieth century, Washington enjoyed normal and friendly relations with Peru while events in Central America and the Caribbean contributed to U.S. Marine intervention and occupation, diplomatic blundering, and the expansion of the Monroe Doctrine. Peru supported the United States on such key events as the acquisition of the Panama Canal rights, World War I, the League of Nations, and U.S. occupation of Nicaragua. In return, Peru hoped to receive assistance from the United States in the form of loans, investments, administrative advisors, and support for local foreign policy questions. By the beginning of World War I, the Peruvian economy had moved away from European trade and investment into the political and economic orbit of the United States.

Peru's Monroeist President

U.S.-Peruvian relations were influenced by Augusto B. Leguía, an autocratic president (1908–1912; 1919–1930) for some 15 years, a tenure longer than any other chief executive's in Peru's history. Leguía's tight control over the government enabled him to bring Peru under the influence of the United States; settle territorial disputes with Bolivia, Brazil, Chile, and Colombia; and provide a dramatic increase in the role of foreign capital in Peru's economy. President Leguía welcomed U.S. economic involvement—despite the fact that U.S. financial interests almost monopolized copper mining, petroleum production, and communications—because he believed it would help turn Peru into a modern capitalist country.

Despite his illegal seizure of power in 1919, Leguía's government was soon recognized by Woodrow Wilson because of his friendly attitude toward the United States and the importance of U.S. investment in Peru. The Leguía administration did everything possible to attract trade, capital, loans, and technology from the United States between 1919 and 1930. President Leguía's "Yankeephilism" (love of the Yankee) ranged from repressing all dissent to the lavish entertainment of key American businessmen and diplomats. In a string of controversial policies Leguía supported U.S. intervention in Nicaragua, proclaimed the Fourth of July a Peruvian national holiday, and recruited U.S. citizens to head numerous governmental agencies. At one point he stressed that his goal was "to put an American in charge of every branch of our Government's activities."[2] For good measure, Leguía hung a portrait of President James Monroe in the National Palace to symbolize the close bonds of friendship between Peru and the United States. The North Americans placed in charge of the customs service, tax bureau, and the Department of Education and Central

Reserve Bank were mostly Protestant administrators who spoke little Spanish and angered members of the Roman Catholic Church. "It is little wonder," according to Ronald Bruce St. John, "that critics of Leguía later charged that by 1930 Peru was directed, governed, and supervised by the U.S. Secretary of State."[3] It would take the disastrous effects of the Great Depression, populist agitation under the leadership of Víctor Raúl Haya de la Torre, and a popular military figure, Luis M. Sánchez Cerro, to rid Peru of the anti-nationalist Leguía. However, the United States would never find a chief executive in Latin America as ingratiating as Augusto B. Leguía, a Monroeist president of the first order.

Víctor Haya de la Torre and the APRA Movement

One of the most important figures to emerge in Peru in the 1920s and 1930s was Víctor Raúl Haya de la Torre, head of the most successful mass-based political party in Peru. Haya came from Peru's oligarchy but was impressed by the Marxism of José Carlos Mariátegui that stressed anti-imperialist revolution to solve the situation in Peru. He founded the Alianza Popular Revolucionaria Americana (APRA) while in exile in Mexico, a party that emphasized anti-imperialism, nationalization of land and industry, internationalization of the Panama Canal, and solidarity with all oppressed people. Haya parted company with Mariátegui after a while but continued to criticize U.S. capitalism and dominance, blaming the United States for Peru's impoverishment and underdevelopment and calling for drastic reforms.

However, by the late 1930s APRA ideology shifted toward a more moderate stance, ending the old invectives against Yankee imperialism and praising the merits of Franklin Roosevelt's Good Neighbor Policy. In turn, Peruvian politicians became more tolerant of *Aprismo*, although this was not the case with the military. After the military and APRA militants clashed in 1932, leaving numerous officers dead, Haya was exiled (not for the first or last time) and hundreds of his followers were arrested or executed in a massacre that occurred in Trujillo. Haya would continue to seek the presidency, but even when duly elected he was never inaugurated, due in large part to the military's hatred of APRA. When the youthful and flamboyant Alan García took charge of the party in the mid-1980s, APRA overwhelmed the opposition and ruled Peru for the first time in its history.

Peru-Ecuador Border Conflict, 1941–1942

During the presidency of Manuel Prado (1939–1945) Peru was a strong supporter of the war effort, allowing the United States to build an airfield in northern Peru to defend the Panama Canal, assisting the United States in tracking down enemy agents, and deporting Japanese-Peruvians to the

United States at President Roosevelt's request. Over 2,000 Japanese from 13 Latin American countries (mostly Peru and Brazil) were forcibly apprehended by the United States and shipped to internment camps in the United States during World War II. The Roosevelt administration—and Latin American government officials—considered the Japanese Latin Americans to be security threats, even though there was no reliable evidence of planned or contemplated acts of subversion, sabotage, or spying. The United States orchestrated and financed the operation, beginning in 1940 when FBI agents were instructed to spy on ethnic Japanese in Latin America. The FBI compiled blacklists of persons to be expelled and provided these to Latin American governments for their Japanese roundups. Washington officials also needed people of Japanese ancestry to exchange for U.S. civilians being held in Japan. In the end, more than 800 Japanese Latin Americans were used in two prisoner exchanges in the 1940s, one of the most bizarre, pathetic, and forgotten tales of U.S.-Latin American relations during World War II.

The major event for Peru during this period was the brief conflict with Ecuador over territorial claims to a disputed region. The hostilities escalated rapidly on both sides in 1941, but Peru's vastly superior military forces soon defeated the weak and unprepared Ecuadoran army on the battlefield. After Peru had occupied a large chunk of Ecuadoran territory, the governments of Argentina, Brazil, and the United States, later joined by Chile, organized a peaceful settlement in Rio de Janeiro in 1942. Known as the Rio Protocol of 1942, the settlement was a major diplomatic victory for Peru (it was allowed to retain most of the disputed territory) but a bitter disappointment for Ecuador. It continued to claim the status of an Amazonian state and repeatedly condemned the unfairness of the imposed settlement, despite the fact that it reluctantly signed and ratified the protocol. Both Peru and Ecuador continued to threaten and sometimes clash, including serious episodes in 1955, 1981, and 1995 (see Chapter 10).

PERU AND THE UNITED STATES DURING THE COLD WAR

The harmony that prevailed in U.S.-Peruvian relations during World War II continued during the first decade of the Cold War. However, by 1948 Peruvian General Manuel A. Odría, a hero of the 1941 war with Ecuador, had assumed power in a revolution supported by a variety of military and civilian elements of society. Despite his illegal seizure of power and alleged human rights violations, Odría enjoyed strong support in Washington for his administration's political stability, conservative economic policies, and anticommunism. Peru signed a bilateral aid and mutual defense pact with the United States in 1952 that established close ties with the Peruvian military. The Eisenhower administration gave Peru's dictator a Legion of Merit award in 1954 for dutifully following the anticommunist policies of the United States. The U.S. policy of supporting tyrants like Odría angered Peruvian nationalists and damaged U.S.-Peruvian relations during the rest of the decade.

Peru and the Alliance for Progress

Manuel Prado's presidency (1956–1962) spanned the last years of the Eisenhower administration and the first year of the Kennedy administration. In the aftermath of General Odría's eight-year dictatorship, Prado faced a growing domestic animosity toward the United States, fueled by anger over Eisenhower's support for right-wing authoritarian regimes, maritime zone disputes, and U.S.-imposed import quotas on Peruvian exports. Vice-President Richard Nixon's visit to Lima in May 1958 contributed further to the tensions between Peru and the United States. Nevertheless, Prado still depended on the U.S. government for millions of dollars in military aid. In an effort to reduce Peru's dependency on the United States, Prado developed closer ties to Europe, took a more active role in regional issues, and explored alternative sources of financial and technical assistance.

Peru's search for greater leverage and autonomy in its foreign relations coincided with the Alliance for Progress and continuing civil-military-APRA conflict. After a rapid-fire series of political events in 1962–1963—including a close presidential election, a brief military takeover, a break in diplomatic relations with the United States, and a new election—Fernando Belaúnde Terry (1963–1968) assumed the presidency. Despite charges from Peruvians accusing the United States of interfering in Peru's internal affairs, Belaúnde linked development and reform in accordance with Kennedy's goals of the Alliance for Progress. Educated at the University of Texas, Belaúnde spoke good English and maintained friendly relations with the United States during the Kennedy and Johnson years. At the same time, tensions between Washington and Belaúnde arose over Peru's claims against the International Petroleum Company (IPC) and against the U.S. fishing fleet operating off the Peruvian coast. Belaúnde's promise to settle the IPC dispute in Peru's favor was undermined by U.S. interference (Washington suspended or slowed payments of economic assistance) and domestic political opposition. After President Belaúnde thought he had negotiated a satisfactory settlement—IPC ceded its subsoil rights to the government in return for eliminating its tax claims against the company—in August 1968, two months later the Peruvian military, charging *vende patria* (selling out Peru to the IPC), took over the government and sent the president into exile in the United States.

The Institutional Revolution of 1968

With a reformist military in power under General Juan Velasco Alvarado, Peru's government embarked on an Institutional Revolution (1968–1978) that emphasized the themes of national sovereignty, developmentalism, and anti-imperialism to generate domestic political support. In an attempt to reverse the course of Peruvian politics, the military portrayed themselves as part of a new wave of Latin American militarism—honest, patriotic, and efficient—capable of directing national reform and economic development. Stressing Peru's Inca roots, including the glorification of rebel Túpac Amaru, an Indian leader who led anti-Spanish revolts, the Institutional Revolution became intensely nationalistic, taking over many U.S. corporations and challenging U.S. dominance in the Americas. The revolutionary government established diplomatic and commercial relations with the Soviet Union (including the purchase of weaponry in the early 1970s), Cuba, China, and other socialist states. The Velasco administration also ventured into radical proposals to reorganize the inter-American system, including resolutions in the Organization of American States (OAS) to relocate its headquarters to Latin America and Charter alterations to reflect the right of ideological pluralism in the Americas. Of course, each of these foreign policy initiatives served to heighten tensions between the United States and Peru.

By the late 1970s Peru was confronted with large foreign debts, which were worsened by the massive expansion of the state under military rule. As economic problems mounted, Velasco became more autocratic. This contributed to his replacement by General Francisco Morales Bermúdez, who promised a less radical version of the earlier program. Fernando Belaúnde returned for a second term (1980–1985), but his lackluster performance contributed to the election of APRA leader Alan García in 1985. By declaring that Peru would pay up to only 10 percent of national income on its debt, he both angered the Reagan administration and generated a deep recession and pushed inflation rates to record levels. The García administration also clashed with the United States over Nicaragua and Panama: Peru opposed U.S. support for the Contras, supported all regional peace efforts to settle the conflict in Central America, and denounced the United States for invading Panama by recalling its ambassador from Washington. García's confrontational style and rhetoric, often designed primarily for internal consumption, produced considerable tension as both countries realized the growing threat from the narcotics trade and terrorism.

Operation Snowcap

As the world's leading producer of coca, Peru found itself involved in international efforts to counter the rise in the narcotics trade and terrorism in the 1970s and 1980s. With the increasing demand for illicit drugs in the United States and Europe fueling the demand for cocaine, Peru and the United States faced the troublesome decision of how to confront the problem in hemispheric drug trafficking (see Table 22.1). After President Reagan signed a secret directive establishing international drug trafficking as a national security threat to the United States, the rules of the drug game changed. Now the U.S. military was used in the Andes to fight the battle against drug production and trafficking. Presidents Reagan, Bush, and Clinton have continued the policy of using small numbers of U.S. troops and increased military aid to the Andean countries involved in the anti-drug efforts. Under the name Operation Snowcap, the Pentagon and the Drug Enforcement Agency (DEA) have conducted anti-cocaine activities in 12 Latin American countries since 1987. DEA agents receive months of military training and Spanish-language courses before they are assigned to three- to four-month rotations accompanying police forces in Latin American countries.

The United States and the Shining Path (Sendero Luminoso)

U.S. efforts to fight a war against cocaine in Peru have been compounded by the existence of one of the most violent terrorist movements in twentieth-century Latin America, the Shining Path (Sendero Luminoso). Operating mostly in the countryside, Shining Path guerrillas took more than 20,000 lives between 1980 and 1995. U.S.-Peruvian relations have been strained by conflicting strategies of how to deal with drug trafficking and anti-government guerrilla activities. The United States favors control and eradication, whereas the Peruvians believe in direct confrontation with leftist guerrillas and narco-traffickers. Although they don't always agree, members of the Peruvian military and police see a much larger threat to Peru's major institutions and have often carried the war to extremes, retaliating with the same level of brutality as their enemies use. The United States and Peru continue to have fundamental disagreements about the source of the drug problem (Peru blames the demand in the United States; the United States blames the supply) and how best to reduce or eliminate it.

PERU AND THE UNITED STATES AFTER THE COLD WAR

President Fujimori and the Terrorists

U.S.-Peruvian relations under Alberto Fujimori, Peru's president of Japanese ancestry, have been rife with ambiguities over his anti-democratic methods of rule, the war against drug trafficking and guerrillas (and as-

Table 22.1
Illicit Drug Production in Latin America, 1987–1995 (in estimated metric tons)

Drug/Country	1987	1988	1989	1990	1991	1992	1993	1994	1995
Opium									
Colombia	--	--	--	--	--	--	--	--	65
Guatemala	3	8	12	13	17	--	--	--	--
Mexico	50	67	66	62	41	40	49	60	53
Coca Leaf									
Bolivia	79,200	78,400	77,000	77,000	78,000	80,300	84,400	89,800	85,000
Colombia	20,500	27,200	33,900	32,100	30,000	29,600	31,700	35,800	40,500
Peru	191,000	187,700	186,300	196,900	222,700	155,000	155,500	163,000	181,600
Ecuador	400	400	270	170	40	100	100	--	--
Marijuana									
Mexico	5,933	5,655	30,200	19,715	7,775	7,795	6,280	5,540	3,650
Colombia	5,600	7,775	2,800	1,500	1,650	1,650	4,125	4,138	4,133
Jamaica	460	405	190	825	641	263	502	208	206
Belize	200	120	65	60	49	0	0	0	0

Source: *International Narcotics Control Strategy Report*, March 1996. U.S. Department of State.

sociated human rights violations by the Peruvian army), and economic liberalization policies. His economic austerity program (sometimes referred to as "Fujishock") contributed to a drastic reduction in inflation, and the opening of the economy again to foreign investment pleased the Bush administration. During his first term (1990–1995), Fujimori was successful in countering political violence with the capture of the principal leaders of the Shining Path (Abimael Guzmán—"Comrade Gonzalo") and the Túpac Amaru Revolutionary Movement. However, in April 1992 he suspended Congress and the judicial branch in a self-coup (*autogolpe*) designed to help restore governmental authority over the economy and to carry on the struggle against terrorists; these actions were strongly criticized by the OAS and the United States for derailing Peru's democratic system. After some constitutional maneuvering that enabled him to run for a second term, Fujimori was reelected in 1995 in what was interpreted as a vindication of his economic security measures, human rights violations, and authoritarian schemes. In 1997 he orchestrated a spectacular rescue of more than 700 hostages held by members of Túpac Amaru guerrillas inside the Japanese ambassador's residence for over five months. The United States has expressed pleasure with Fujimori's neo-liberal economic reforms, but it disagrees with his autocratic style of governing Peru.

CONCLUSION

U.S.-Peruvian relations have been characterized by sharp contrasts between public and private interests since the early part of the nineteenth century. Peru's valuable minerals and other resources attracted significant numbers of foreign investors who developed close ties with Peru's oligarchy, contributing over time to the radicalization of Peruvian politics and intense conflicts with private companies and the U.S. government. This ambiguous relationship was epitomized by the economic and political power of W. R. Grace Company and the International Petroleum Company, two economic giants that displayed an impressive domination over the Peruvian economy until well into the twentieth century.

In the public realm, the U.S. government tried to ignore Peru until the middle of the twentieth century when international fascism and communism raised concerns about U.S. security in the hemisphere. In response to increasing levels of U.S. hegemony, Peru's politics changed beginning in the 1930s from the servile presidents like Augusto Leguía who wanted Peru tied as closely as possible to the United States, to those who tried to forge a more independent foreign policy. The Cold War period was particularly contentious, with the United States and Peru periodically locked in conflict over how best to deal with communism, economic reform, terrorism, and democracy; in the post–Cold War period the United States and Peru have drawn closer together as both countries have recognized the value of cooperation in dealing with drug trafficking, economic reform, and democratization. Yet the bilateral relationship is also strained by historical legacies rooted in economic domination and the lingering effects of authoritarianism in Peru's politics.

NOTES

1. William V. Bishell, "Fall from Grace: U.S. Business Interests versus U.S. Diplomatic Interests in Peru, 1885–1890," *Diplomatic History* 20, no. 2 (Spring 1996): 182.

2. Quoted in Steve Stein, *Populism in Peru: The Emergence of the Masses and the Politics of Social Control* (Madison: University of Wisconsin Press, 1980), p. 54.

3. Ronald Bruce St. John, *The Foreign Policy of Peru* (Boulder, CO: Lynne Rienner, 1992), pp. 159–160.

SUGGESTED READINGS

Poole, Deborah, and Gerardo Rénique. *Peru: Time of Fear*. New York: Monthly Review Press, 1992.

Skaggs, Jimmy M. *The Great Guano Rush: Entrepreneurs and American Overseas Expansion*. New York: St. Martin's Press, 1994.

St. John, Ronald Bruce. *The Foreign Policy of Peru*. Boulder, CO: Lynne Rienner, 1992.

23

Trinidad and Tobago

TIMELINE OF U.S. RELATIONS WITH TRINIDAD AND TOBAGO

1802	Spain cedes Trinidad to Great Britain
1814	Great Britain acquires Tobago
1889	The two islands become a single colonial unit
1941–1945	U.S. military base is established at Chaguaramas
1958	Caribbean Federation is formed
1962	Trinidad and Tobago achieve independence
	Caribbean Federation is terminated
	Eric Williams becomes prime minister
1970	Black Power Movement is established
	Islands join Non-Aligned Movement (NAM)
1976	Trinidad and Tobago becomes a republic
1977	United States returns Chaguaramas
1981	Prime Minister Williams dies; his People's National Movement (PNM) party continues to rule until 1986 under leadership of George Chambers
1983	Trinidad opposes U.S. invasion of Grenada
1984	President Reagan establishes Caribbean Basin Initiative
1986–1991	A.N.R. Robinson governs as prime minister
1990	Abu Bakr, head of Islamic Jamat al Muslimeen, attempts coup against Robinson government
1991–1995	Patrick Manning governs as prime minister
1995	Basdeo Panday is elected prime minister

| 1996–1998 | Drug trafficking expands to fill gap after a 90 percent drop in U.S. aid to Caribbean nations since the mid–1980s |
| 1997 | Prime Minister Panday signs series of comprehensive anti-drug measures with the United States |

INTRODUCTION

The twin-island nation of Trinidad and Tobago is located in the extreme southeastern Caribbean Sea, nine miles off the coast of Venezuela. Like Jamaica, Trinidad is a major economic and political player in the English-speaking Caribbean. Rich in oil, and a producer of steel and petrochemicals, Trinidad and Tobago has one of the highest per capita incomes in the Caribbean. Although most of its population is made up of the descendants of African slaves and East Indian indentured laborers, the two-island nation has managed to live in relative racial harmony. The move to independence in the 1950s and early 1960s was shaped by the work of labor leaders and British-trained nationalist politicians who mobilized opposition to British colonialism. One of the first of the English-speaking Caribbean nations to gain independence, Trinidad and Tobago made the transition from colonialism rather peacefully, unlike the politically turbulent and coup-prone Latin American nations. Constitutional government and competitive party systems have helped prevent military takeovers and other forms of extra-constitutional changes of administration.

The United States has enjoyed a number of advantages in its relations with the English-speaking Caribbean. First, throughout the nineteenth and most of the twentieth century, Caribbean islands like Trinidad and Tobago have been the responsibility of the British, a close ally of the United States. Second, the preparation for self-rule included some tutoring in the mechanics of parliamentary rule, a legacy that has brought stability, democracy, and the protection of individual rights. Third, the former British colonies, with the exception of Grenada, have been devoid of revolutions. Finally, with the British engaged in providing the security and political tutelage for its possessions in the Caribbean, the United States was free to concentrate on carving out its own sphere of influence.

THE NINETEENTH CENTURY

Originally a Spanish colony (Columbus claimed the islands in 1498 during his third voyage to the Americas), Trinidad provided a safe haven for French royalists fleeing Haiti, Martinique, and Guadeloupe during the French Revolution. Between 1626 and 1814, Tobago changed hands 22 times as predatory European powers fought for possession of its safe harbors. In 1802 the Kingdom of Spain turned over Trinidad to Great Britain, and in 1814 Tobago was acquired after 100 years of French occupation—but as a separate colonial unit. The site of two centuries of imperial struggles, Trinidad absorbed cultural and political influences from Europe (Spain, France, and Great Britain), Africa, and the East Indies. After the French Revolution in 1789, it remained a Spanish colony until it was taken over by the British in 1797. For a while the French ran the sugar plantations with African slaves, who had been forcibly transported to the island to provide labor for the European-owned estates. After a phase-out or "apprenticeship" period beginning in 1833, slavery was abolished entirely in 1838. Soon thereafter East Indian (Indian, Chinese, and Madeiran) indentured laborers were brought to the island to sustain the supply of cheap agricultural labor. In 1889 Great Britain joined the two islands as a single colonial unit in order to economize on government expenses.

There was little contact between the United States and Trinidad during the nineteenth century, with the exception of post-emancipation efforts to stimulate black immigration to the island in the 1860s. By the late nineteenth century the islands were becoming less profitable colonies because sugar was being produced more cheaply elsewhere, particularly in Cuba, Haiti, and the Dominican Republic. The decline in sugar income contributed to widespread unemployment and the early stirrings of national leadership, a labor movement, and opposition to colonialism. The process of twentieth-century political development in Trinidad and Tobago was greatly influenced by nationalist leaders who fought against colonialism and racism in Trinidad and Tobago, the Caribbean, and the United States.

TRINIDAD AND TOBAGO AND THE UNITED STATES IN THE TWENTIETH CENTURY

During the early part of the twentieth century oil replaced sugar as Trinidad's major export, but because of its capital-intensive nature the new industry did little to alleviate the chronic unemployment among former sugar workers. The arrival of U.S. oil companies after World War I to exploit Trinidad's southern oil fields led to the development of a radical trade union movement and the infusion of North American influence. The labor movement gained inspiration from Andrew Arthur Cipriani, a white man of Corsican descent who organized the masses while teaching them national pride and anticolonialism. Until his death in 1945, Cipriani struggled against racial discrimination and fought for political reforms and labor rights. The labor disturbances among oil and sugar workers in the 1930s contributed to the militancy of labor unions, which, in turn, developed into political parties intent on achieving national ownership of industries and independence from the British.

Cyril L. R. James: Writer and Revolutionary

C.L.R. James was born (1901) in Trinidad and became a powerful cultural critic and revolutionary throughout most of the twentieth century. As an intellectual and political activist, James provided the backbone of West Indian self-government with his historical analysis of the Caribbean and slavery. During his years in England (1932–1938) he discovered Marxism and Trotskyism, and he later addressed "the negro problem" during his long speaking tours of the United States (1938–1953) and elsewhere. James believed that blacks in the Caribbean and the United States were endowed with a fundamentally revolutionary spirit, but he also criticized African and Caribbean independence movements for their pro-Western stance. By the early 1950s James considered himself an independent Marxist, convinced that communism was the only salvation for the black masses. During the anticommunist "witch-hunts" of the McCarthy era in the United States, James was arrested for his anti-American activities but was not detained long before he was deported to England. He taught Eric Williams (prime minister of Trinidad and Tobago, 1962–1981) in the 1920s and served as his mentor during the final years of struggle for Trinidad and Tobago's independence, but eventually he broke with Williams on ideological and other grounds in the early 1960s. His lectures on literature and politics influenced the civil rights movement in the United States, and many black leaders in Africa involved in anticolonial struggles found inspiration in his writings on race and politics.

World War II and the "American Era"

World War II expanded the military presence of the United States in the English-speaking Caribbean and also brought American culture and oil companies. The "American Era" began in 1941 and ended in 1945, but the influx of U.S. military personnel and the construction of a large military base left a lasting impact on the island. While Trinidad and Tobago was still a Crown Colony, the British government in 1941 leased the Chaguaramas area (32 square miles of the northwestern peninsula) to the United States for a period of 99 years.

With thousands of American soldiers stationed on Trinidad during World War II, "Yankee dollars" fostered prostitution, high-paying jobs servicing the base, and a get-rich-quick mentality among Trinidadians. The racial prejudice of those from the United States added to the anti-foreign feelings of those who found themselves subjected to domination by Great Britain and the United States. When the United States showed no intention of giving up the area after the war, Eric Williams became the voice of national control by demanding that Washington return Chaguaramas to Trinidad to be used for the capital site for the West Indies Federation.

Insisting on its 99-year treaty rights, the United States refused to surrender the territory. Williams used the Chaguaramas conflict to organize the "Return Charaguamas" movement in which he led thousands of anti-American demonstrators in the nation's capital, Port-of-Spain, in 1960. Although the U.S.-Trinidadian conflict over Chaguaramas dragged on until 1977 when the United States finally gave up control, the intensity of the struggle, together with Trinidad's oil wealth, helped maintain the popularity of Williams's People's National Movement (PNM) for close to 30 years.

TRINIDAD AND TOBAGO AND THE UNITED STATES DURING THE COLD WAR

World War II brought pressure upon the British to relinquish its colonial empire. After the war, the British Labour Party with its brand of democratic socialism offered to "guide" its possessions in the Caribbean to self-government, a promise that proved to be more a delaying strategy than a faithful commitment to independence. As the Cold War progressed, some Caribbean leaders cooperated with the United States and Britain to contain Marxist influence in the labor movement. In need of foreign capital, the small islands of the Caribbean faced demands from multinational corporations to provide generous tax breaks, low wages, and guarantees of labor peace to attract investors.

The Rise of Dr. Eric Williams

The key figure in the drive toward Trinidad and Tobago's independence was Dr. Eric Williams, a West Indian scholar-politician who studied history at Oxford University and taught at Howard University in Washington, D.C., before joining the Caribbean Commission in 1952. He founded the People's National Movement (PNM) in 1956, a political party that would become his main weapon for achieving full independence in 1962. A brilliant thinker and scholar, Dr. Williams could be arrogant and at times eccentric, but he became Trinidad's first prime minister and guided the country during its first 25 years of PNM rule. During his tenure as prime minister (1962–1981) he pursued a nonalignment policy and defied both the United States and the Organization of American States by establishing relations with Cuba in 1972. Following Williams's death in 1981, the PNM continued its dominance of Trinidadian politics under George M. Chambers. His decision to publicly condemn the Reagan administration's invasion of Grenada in 1983–a move that put him at odds with the Trinidadian press and the public, who supported the invasion—seemed to reflect the anti-American legacy of the Chaguaramas conflict and the desires of the deceased former prime minister and revered leader.

Independence and the United States

The leaders who helped achieve independence adopted the parliamentary system of government and continued the traditional pattern of economic and political ties to the United Kingdom and the United States. By the time Trinidad became independent in 1962, the United States was confronted by challenges to its influence in the Caribbean, especially the rise of Fidel Castro and the revolutionary ferment in the Dominican Republic. Despite the fact that Trinidad and Tobago's independence leaders had advanced their cause by condemning the American presence since World War II, the United States promptly established diplomatic relations. However, the islands' conservative strategies of accommodation with the United States during the 1960s changed in the 1970s as Third World and nonaligned ideas permeated the Caribbean. After Trinidad experienced significant increases in its national income due to the actions of OPEC price increases, it assumed a new role as aid donor to the rest of the Caribbean.

The United States and Trinidad's Black Power Uprising

Black nationalists and the Black Power movement that developed in the United States in the 1960s influenced the politics of race in Trinidad and Tobago, spurred by unemployment, anti–trade union legislation, foreign control over the economy, and prime minister Eric Williams's perceived "Afro-Saxonism."[1] Led by Geddes Granger, protest and strikes broke out in February 1970 that led the government to declare a state of emergency followed by an army mutiny. With U.S. and Venezuelan warships waiting offshore, Prime Minister Williams managed to put down the uprising, but the movement on which it was based contributed to more strident opposition movements, black consciousness and regional identity, and the government's decision to speed up national ownership of foreign firms.

The United States and Trinidad during the 1980s

The Caribbean Basin became a focus of U.S. security interests during the 1980s as the politics of change in some parts of the Caribbean clashed with the Reagan administration's efforts to focus its foreign policy on events in El Salvador, Nicaragua, Jamaica, and Grenada. Between 1977 and 1981, Trinidad put the Chaguaramas conflict to rest and improved diplomatic relations with the United States, but the Grenadian revolution that brought Maurice Bishop and the New Jewel Movement to power served to renew tensions in the Caribbean. The death of Eric Williams in 1981 raised further questions about the direction of Trinidadian foreign policy during a time of doubt about conducting an independent foreign policy. Trinidad became increasingly uneasy with the military-security orientation of the

United States in the Caribbean, opposed the U.S. invasion of Grenada in 1983, and disapproved of the U.S.-financed regional security system in 1985 that incorporated a number of smaller Caribbean nation-neighbors.

George Chambers, the successor to Prime Minister Eric Williams, damp-ened bilateral relations further with the nationalization of Texaco in 1984, creating the Trinidad and Tobago Oil Company (TRINTOC). Trinidad and Tobago began to face declining oil prices and pressures for economic re-form from international lending agencies such as the International Mone-tary Fund (IMF). To address its economic/financial troubles, the government of A.N.R. Robinson (1986–1991) carried out IMF-imposed structural adjustment reforms in line with the prevailing free-market poli-cies sweeping the region. The IMF strategy—particularly the reductions in government expenditures and price increases—proved to have harmful side effects, including the rise of the Jamaat al Muslimeen Islamic sect headed by Yasin Abu Bakr. By 1990, four years of economic and social tensions contributed to an attempted coup by Bakr's group against the Robinson government—an unprecedented action that led to the occupation of par-liament, 23 dead, and 500 wounded before the rebels surrendered. The Jamaat rebellion undermined the government's legitimacy and contributed to the PNM victory of Patrick Manning in the 1991 parliamentary elec-tions.

TRINIDAD AND TOBAGO AND THE UNITED STATES AFTER THE COLD WAR

Security concerns within Trinidad and Tobago, and the growing impor-tance of drug trafficking and trade in the hemisphere in the aftermath of the Cold War, helped to improve relations with the United States beginning in 1990. In 1994 the government backed the U.S.-led, UN-sanctioned in-vasion of Haiti to remove the military government and return the demo-cratically elected president-in-exile Jean-Bertrand Aristide. Concerns about being left out of preferential trade arrangements have inspired calls for Caribbean Community (CARICOM) participation in the increasingly con-troversial North American Free Trade Agreement (NAFTA), but Trinidad and Tobago opposed the CARICOM agreement whereby no member can join or negotiate separately to obtain future NAFTA membership. The at-tempted coup by Muslim rebels in 1990 paved the way for the controversial election of November 1995 that brought Basdeo Panday to power, the first non-African prime minister in Trinidad's history. However, the strains of governing biracial Trinidad and Tobago have not ceased, as Panday has struggled to convince blacks—now in the opposition for the first time—of the fairness of his public policies. The Clinton administration remained aloof from the stresses and strains during this time, preferring to leave the mediation efforts and outcome in the hands of Caribbean leaders.

Trinidad and Tobago and the War on Drugs

Trinidad and Tobago has not been able to escape the problem of the illicit production, consumption, and transshipment of drugs in the Americas. In Trinidad and Tobago there is a long history of accepted use of marijuana (often referred to as *ganja*, a Hindi word for marijuana) dating from the importation of indentured workers from India following the abolition of slavery in 1838. Rastafarians, Afrocentric socioreligious sects found throughout the Caribbean, claim a religious justification for smoking marijuana. Nevertheless, illicit drug production and money laundering is less of a problem in Trinidad and Tobago than in other parts of the Caribbean, particularly in Jamaica and the Bahamas. The saliency of the drug issue in the Caribbean has also contributed to the view among top officials that security is multidimensional—military, political, economic, and environmental—rather than one-sided, as it was according to the Cold War definition that focused almost exclusively on the communist threat. As U.S. aid to the Caribbean region dropped precipitously in the aftermath of the Cold War, drug trafficking expanded to bridge the economic gap. To counter this trend, Prime Minister Panday signed several anti-drug measures with the Clinton administration.

CONCLUSION

The major concerns that Caribbean governments confront in the 1990s generally involve the questions of political fragmentation and economic viability. The challenges of globalization impose tremendous difficulties on small island countries throughout the Caribbean. St. Kitts and Nevis, the smallest two-island country in the hemisphere, is now contemplating separation of the islands. Although the spat can be traced to the decision by the British in 1882 to join the two islands, the recent animosity is tied to the declining sugar industry on St. Kitts and the thriving offshore banking activities on Nevis, which are used to launder money for drug traffickers. Those who govern Trinidad and Tobago face similar issues, adding to increasing emigration to the United States (particularly New York) in search of employment, less crime, and greater economic opportunities. The rapid expansion of drug trafficking in Trinidad and Tobago—resulting from a shift in transshipment tactics by the Colombian drug cartels—has contributed to a surge in murders and kidnappings and raised fears of a government takeover by narcos. While the government in Port-of-Spain has pushed ahead with vigorous anti-drug initiatives, its vulnerability to drug corruption is substantial and countermeasures will require greater involvement with the United States.

NOTE

1. *Afro-Saxons* is a term used in the English-speaking Caribbean to refer to foreign and local whites, who are resented for their elitism and control over economics and politics.

SUGGESTED READINGS

Anthony, Michael. *Historical Dictionary of Trinidad and Tobago*. Lanham, MD: Scarecrow Press, 1997.

Meditz, Sandra W., and Dennis M. Hanratty, eds. *Islands of the Commonwealth Caribbean: A Regional Study*. Washington, DC: U.S. Government Printing Office, 1989.

Williams, Eric. *Capitalism and Slavery*. 2nd ed. Chapel Hill: University of North Carolina Press, 1996.

24

Uruguay

TIMELINE OF U.S. RELATIONS WITH URUGUAY

1828	Uruguayan independence from Spain is achieved
1865–1870	Triple Alliance War
1900	José Enrique Rodó publishes *Ariel*, an anti-American polemic
1903–1907	José Batlle y Ordóñez serves as elected president (first term)
1911–1915	Batlle serves as elected president (second term)
1941	United States builds naval and air bases
1945	Foreign Minister Eduardo Rodríguez Larreta advances collective intervention doctrine
1958	Colorado Party ends 86 years of uninterrupted rule
1961	Tupamaros guerrilla movement is formed
1962–1972	Tupamaros engage in armed struggle
1967–1972	Uruguay moves from democracy to military dictatorship
1970	U.S. AID official Dan Mitrione is executed by Tupamaros
1972–1976	Juan María Bordaberry serves as president
1972	"State of Internal War" act is approved, granting unlimited powers to the military
	Tupamaro movement ends with capture of leaders
1973–1985	Uruguay is ruled by military dictatorship
1974	U.S. Congress terminates AID public safety program
1976	President Bordaberry is forced to submit resignation to the military

1985	Tupamaros renounce armed struggle to become a legal party
	Democracy returns with election of Julio María Sanguinetti (first term)
1989–1993	Luis Albert Lacalle serves as president
1990	Uruguay agrees to assist United States with anti-narcotics efforts
1991	Uruguay joins Southern Cone Common Market (MERCOSUR)
1994–1998	Julio María Sanguinetti serves as elected president (second term)

INTRODUCTION

Uruguay is the second smallest republic in South America (after Suriname). It is situated between Brazil and Argentina, two rival giants of the region. Its official name, La República Oriental del Uruguay, is derived from its geographical position on the eastern shore of the Uruguay River. U.S.-Uruguayan relations have been influenced by three critical but overlapping characteristics. First, Uruguay is situated beyond the immediate (Central America and the Caribbean) sphere of U.S. influence and has placed considerable emphasis on remaining aloof from great power rivalries, including interference from the United States. Second, the United States has never had a major economic or financial stake in Uruguay because of its size and agricultural economy. Third, Uruguay's democratic status and political stability during most of the twentieth century served the interests of the United States, and in turn Uruguay has tried to maintain a cooperative but independent stance toward Washington.

Uruguay experienced at least 60 years of relatively stable democratic rule during the twentieth century, longer overall than Costa Rica, Colombia, or Venezuela. During the Cold War, Uruguay became increasingly dependent on U.S. economic and military aid but resisted U.S. pressures to support intervention in the internal affairs of other hemispheric states. Although small and weak, Uruguay is bound to the United States through U.S.-sponsored hemispheric defense treaties, U.S. military missions and training, economic aid and technical assistance, private investment, and cultural exchanges. The economic and political strains that emerged after 1930 led to a period of sustained economic decline, political violence, and, ultimately, an authoritarian military dictatorship between 1973 and 1985. Uruguay has since joined the rest of Latin America in efforts to democratize and initiate anti-statist and free market economic reforms while at the same time protecting its well-established welfare state that provides generous benefits to the citizenry.

URUGUAY AND THE UNITED STATES IN THE NINETEENTH CENTURY

The United States and Uruguayan Independence

Uruguay's location between Brazil and Argentina led to its creation in 1828 as a buffer state, one that could provide a cushion to absorb potential hostilities from its two large neighbors. Although this role has sometimes been exaggerated or failed to stem interregional conflict, Uruguay's domestic and foreign policies have been greatly influenced by its association with more powerful adjoining states. The leader of the independence movement was José G. Artigas, part of a wealthy landowning family, who fought for Uruguay's autonomy within the Argentine Confederation between 1810 and 1820. After the Portuguese monarchy (established in Rio de Janeiro at the time) invaded Uruguay in 1817, Artigas continued to seek autonomy but was defeated in 1820 and fled to Paraguay. Therefore he was not present when independence was finally achieved in 1828, the result of British mediation of the war between the Brazilian Empire and the Argentine Confederation. Of paramount importance to the British was to provide for uninterrupted trade and access to shipping in the Río de la Plata region.

Uruguay and the Monroe Doctrine

Those who formulated U.S. policy toward Latin America in the 1820s and 1830s alluded to Monroe's message of 1823 but rarely cited it or referred to it as doctrine. For 15 years after Monroe's address, the nations of Europe paid little attention to the essence of the Latin American policy of the United States, did not refrain from meddling, and in some cases even acquired new territory in the region. Top officials in Washington were strikingly indifferent to the encroachments of France and Great Britain in the Río de la Plata region. For example, there was no protest in 1833 when the British seized the Falkland Islands from Argentina and when the French and British intervened on several occasions to maintain access to trade in Uruguay and Argentina.

With the growth of the concept of Manifest Destiny (a belief in the superiority of the United States that served as a basis for territorial expansion) and the Mexican War in the 1840s, the Polk administration—with or without the Monroe Doctrine—was helpless in stopping a joint French and British blockade of Buenos Aires (and Uruguay, since it was then under siege by Argentine forces) between 1845 and 1848. In a note to the U.S. ambassador in Buenos Aires in 1846, Secretary of State James Buchanan asserted that Great Britain had "flagrantly violated" the Monroe declaration but that "existing circumstances render it impossible for the United States to take a part in the present war."[1] The Monroe Doctrine lay dormant in U.S.-Uruguayan affairs until the 1920s, when Uruguay's president proposed an expanded version of the Monroe Doctrine for purposes of mutual defense of the hemisphere and as a counterweight to unilateral declarations by the United States that provoked such "Yankeephobia" in Latin America.

José Enrique Rodó and the Anti-*Yanqui* Movement

The dramatic defeat of Spain by the United States in 1898 and the seizure of Cuba and Puerto Rico deeply troubled many Latin Americans, fearful of a resurgence of expansionism beyond the Caribbean region. How far would the Yankees go to achieve their economic and strategic interests? The U.S. imperial offensive of the 1890s prompted a strong reaction by Latin American intellectuals, led by José Enrique Rodó, a Uruguayan writer and ethical philosopher who helped mobilize a generation of anti-American sentiment throughout Latin America. In a reaction to the outcome of the Spanish-American War, Rodó published *Ariel* in 1900, a short essay praising Latin America's cultural and spiritual superiority in contrast to North America's excessive materialism and moral inferiority. By employing Shakespearean images to demonstrate how American materialism can lead to spiritual mediocrity, *Ariel* contributed to a literary outcry and intellectual support for anti-Yankee polemics by other Latin American writers.

URUGUAY AND THE UNITED STATES DURING THE TWENTIETH CENTURY

Twentieth-century Uruguay has been profoundly influenced by President José Batlle y Ordóñez (1903–1907; 1911–1915), a non-Marxist social democrat who established the welfare state and plural presidency or *colegiado*, two innovations that helped to end the political instability and coup-prone characteristics of the region in the previous century.[2] The export economy expanded under Batlle, largely the result of the invention of refrigeration plants (*frigoríficos*) that allowed frozen beef to be shipped to European markets. The meat-processing industry also served as a magnet for the influx of foreign capital from the United States and Britain. Foreign economic penetration would have to face Batlle's economic nationalism and political reforms, but it was a moderate form of national control over economic enterprises, allowing U.S. meat-packing companies like Swift and Armour to operate alongside national producers. Uruguay experienced some remarkable achievements under Batlle, but the Great Depression, changes in the international economy beginning in the 1930s, and the influence of European fascism ultimately produced both internal strains and greater reliance on the United States and Europe. Two military presidents ruled Uruguay from 1931 to 1943, upsetting the liberal reforms instituted by Batlle and his Colorado Party followers over the previous three decades.

During World War I, Uruguay became extremely dependent on the United States for oil and coal deliveries, which may have accounted for the favorable views that Uruguayan leaders expressed about President Wood-row Wilson's interventionist Latin American policy. There was also the feeling in Uruguay that it was far enough away from the Panama Canal and the Caribbean to be out of range of the "big stick" being wielded elsewhere. After World War I, Uruguay espoused a policy of internation-alism and Pan-Americanism. In 1920, President Baltásar Brum proposed that the Monroe Doctrine be expanded and an American League of Nations be established. When the Uruguayan delegation submitted the Brum prop-osition to an International Conference of American States in 1923, the proposal received no support from the United States or the other Latin American states. With no interest in developing a global league (League of Nations) devoted to international security, the United States was not about to submit to Brum's idea of a regional league that might diminish its influ-ence and limit its ability to intervene to protect its security. The Latin Amer-ican delegates at the conference were not in a mood to pledge mutual defense of the Americas either. "The Latin American delegations," accord-ing to G. Pope Atkins, "were [more] intent on attacking the interventionist policies of the United States, which were being justified in the name of the Monroe Doctrine" than in negotiating a mutual defense pact with the United States.[3]

The United States and Uruguay during World War II

In contrast to the strains in U.S.-Argentine relations during World War II, relations with Uruguay were mostly cordial and cooperative. General Alfredo Baldomir (1938–1943) declared Uruguay's neutrality in 1939 but was forced to assume a pro-Allied stance after the Battle of the Río de la Plata involving the German battleship *Graf Spee* late that year. Baldomir permitted the United States to build naval and air bases for the war effort in 1941, and he broke relations with the Axis powers in 1942. Uruguay gained international prominence for its collective peace initiatives during the last three years of the war, including the efforts of Alberto Guaní (1943) and Eduardo Rodríguez Larreta (1945). Both proposed formulas that of-fered collective strategies for dealing with governments that attempt to es-tablish themselves by force and ignore democratic principles and human rights.

In 1941, President Roosevelt established the Office of Coordinator of Inter-American Affairs (OCIAA), a U.S. government agency to promote inter-American trade, counter Nazi propaganda, foster mutual understanding and appreciation, and obtain Latin American backing for the war aims of the United States. The OCIAA was directed by Nelson Rockefeller and strongly endorsed by the Latin Americanists in the Roosevelt administration who were adamant about preserving the Good Neighbor Policy. With strong pro-Nazi sentiments in Argentina, Sumner Welles, undersecretary of state for Latin American affairs, instructed the OCIAA in 1941 to build a long-range radio station in Uruguay to broadcast anti-Axis propaganda to Argentina in order to convince it to break relations with Nazi Germany. However, the heavy-handed nature of the OCIAA propaganda—replete with efforts to extol the virtues of the United States—failed to convert the Argentines and produced a backlash against the United States within other countries.

URUGUAY AND THE UNITED STATES DURING THE COLD WAR

After World War II a new style of populism emerged under the leadership of Luis Batlle Berres, nephew of José Batlle. President Luis Batlle (1947–1951, and head of the *colegiado* or plural presidency in 1955–1956) pushed forward with import substitution programs in order to expand Uruguay's industrial base. However, as world prices for agricultural products declined and the cost of technology imports grew, Uruguay's political economy ran into serious problems—decreased production and high inflation—that slowly eroded much of the economic gains and social benefits. After achieving one of the highest standards of living in Latin America, Uruguay found itself unable to sustain economic growth and financial liquidity and generous welfare benefits, particularly the burdensome social security system. In this downward cycle of political unrest and labor strikes—with strong leftist overtones—the collegiate system of governance, the United States, and international financial institutions were blamed for the political and economic maladies.

The United States and the Tupamaros

The growing frustration with Uruguay's sagging economy, its weak and unresponsive political apparatus, and the futility of legal channels of protest were critical factors in the formation of the Movement of National Liberation, or Tupamaros. Named after the famed Inca rebel Túpac Amaru, who tried to free his people from Spanish rule in eighteenth-century Peru, the Tupamaros created an urban guerrilla force without equal in the history of Latin America. Tupamaro guerrillas were mostly middle-class young adults who gained inspiration from the Cuban Revolution and Marxism. The leader of the Tupamaros, Raúl Sendic, 36-year-old law student, was convinced that change in Uruguay would require operating outside the law since the legal system was flawed and corrupt. For the Tupamaros, violence—bank robberies, political kidnappings, sabotage, jail breaks, seizures of government property, and executions—was considered a legitimate means to destroy the power of the local oligarchy, eliminate foreign capitalists, and ultimately create a socialist system for all.

After the Tupamaros carried out some notable military actions and succeeded in earning a significant amount of popular support and respect, the National Police—supplied and trained by the U.S. AID Office of Public Safety—were given the assignment of combating the group. Later, as Uruguay drifted toward military dictatorship under the presidency of Jorge Pacheco Areco (1967–1972), the police were placed under military rule. After the Tupamaros succeeded in abducting Dan Mitrione in 1970 (a U.S. AID official who was involved in the training of the police in harsh interrogation of political prisoners), aborted ransom-for-prisoners talks led to his execution on August 8, 1970 (this was the subject of the widely acclaimed Costa Gavras film *State of Siege*). President Pacheco responded by giving the armed forces carte blanche in their dealings with the urban guerrilla movement. Although the Tupamaros must share some responsibility for the violence that expanded the political influence of the armed forces, they cannot be strapped with the blame for the doctrine of national security employed by Uruguay's faceless junta during the 11 years it ran the country. Furthermore, Uruguayan police and military officers often ordered murders and bombings in order to create public fear and then make it appear as though the urban guerrillas were responsible.

With the help of a captured guerrilla leader, the military was instrumental in eliminating the Tupamaros by 1972; however, the task of removing the Tupamaros' influence required a declaration of internal war that severely undermined civil-military relations and democracy long after the end of the military dictatorship in 1985. After serving long prison terms or being forced into exile, the Tupamaros were freed under an amnesty decree in 1985, renounced armed struggle, and committed themselves to left-wing party politics. It is important to point out that while the Tupamaros did pose a physical threat to individual military officers, politicians, business leaders, and foreign diplomats, at no time did they ever possess the capacity to overthrow the government and establish a regime of their own.

The Rockefeller Report and the Transition to Dictatorship

Washington's policies toward Uruguay (and Latin America) had at least an indirect role in paving the way for the military takeover that occurred in the 1970s. During the Nixon and Ford administrations (1969–1977), Latin America was viewed as having little importance to the United States, with the exception of Castro's Cuba and the Marxist-socialist government of Salvador Allende. Governor Nelson Rockefeller of New York traveled to Latin America for President Nixon in 1969 but was met by anti-American demonstrations and violence, and some of his recommendations concerning the military startled those who favored democracy and dialogue. On the basis of his "study missions," Rockefeller found that

> a *new type of military man* is coming to the fore and often becoming a major force for constructive social change in the American republics. Motivated by increasing impatience with corruption, inefficiency, and a stagnant political order, the new military man is prepared to adapt his authoritarian tradition to the goals of social and economic progress.[4]

Under the right-wing presidencies of Pacheco and Bordaberry (1967–1976), Uruguay saw U.S. economic and military aid increase dramatically. Thousands of Uruguayan military personnel were trained under U.S. programs, and U.S. officials traveled to Uruguay to provide assistance with strategies of repression for the "new type of military man." The startling revelations of human rights abuses in a 1974 Amnesty International report on torture in Uruguay forced the U.S. Congress to terminate AID's public safety–police training program in the same year. In 1977 the United States terminated military aid. Although the United States never considered direct military intervention in Uruguay necessary during this period, it did endorse the Uruguayan military's antisubversive campaigns—supplying advice, equipment, training, and financial assistance. Moreover, U.S.-backed civic action programs helped spread a more popular image of the military in society.

Uruguay and the Carter Administration

By the time Jimmy Carter arrived at the White House in 1977, Latin America was a graveyard of democracies. Intent on shaping a new approach to inter-American relations, Carter relied on the recommendations found in the Linowitz Commission (an independent bipartisan group of private citizens), particularly those stressing the importance of human rights and democracy. This dramatic shift in policy served to isolate the United States from much of Latin America, and relations with Uruguay were reduced to diplomatic tensions and low levels of activity. President Carter's efforts to inject morality in foreign policy produced strong rivalries between the National Security Council and the State Department, but clearly the references to a "new type of military man" cited by Nelson Rockefeller were no longer part of Washington's hemispheric vision.

Uruguay and the Reagan Administration

The election of Ronald Reagan brought a new group of foreign policy advisors to Washington who were determined to reverse what they perceived as weakness in the previous administration of Jimmy Carter: "soft" on communism in the Third World, weak on defense, and "wishy-washy" in protecting U.S. interests and values around the world. Reagan's team of conservative policy advisors viewed the insurgencies in Central America and the increasing number of Marxist or leftist governments in the Caribbean region as the major threat to U.S. security interests. With right-wing military dictatorships in power in South America (in Argentina, Brazil, Chile, Paraguay, and Uruguay), the ardent anticommunists who made up the Reagan team placed little emphasis on small countries like Uruguay.

The decline in the legitimacy of military dictatorships and the resurgence of democracy in Uruguay puzzled the Reagan administration during its first term (1981–1985). Convinced that the ideas of well-known scholar and UN ambassador Jeanne Kirkpatrick regarding the necessity of accepting anticommunist, authoritarian government were sound foreign policy, the Reagan administration saw no problem in backing "moderate" authoritarians in Uruguay, particularly when it could be demonstrated that there was even the slightest influence from Cuba and the Soviet Union. To pursue these new strategies the Reagan administration decided that criticizing friendly anticommunist governments on human rights grounds was counterproductive to U.S. security interests. Reagan's security-oriented approach to a policy of rapprochement with South American militaries fizzled after a few years as democracy slowly returned to the region. After democracy was restored in 1985, President Julio M. Sanguinetti was invited to the White House (the first visit by a Uruguayan president in more than 30 years) and U.S. government assistance with democracy restoration efforts was offered. Despite little evidence to suggest that U.S. policies had much to do with the democratic trend in Uruguay, Reagan administration officials went to great pains to take credit for the resurgence of democracy.

Despite the more friendly tone established after the return to civilian rule, Uruguay opposed much of what the Reagan administration was doing in Central America. As a member of the Contadora Support Group, Uruguay was critical of U.S. aid to the anti-Sandinista rebels (Contras) in Nicaragua and opposed unilateral military intervention in Honduras and El Salvador. Sanguinetti opposed Operation Just Cause in Panama in 1989, characterizing the military intervention to capture General Noriega a "step backward." As a sign of further independence from the United States, Uruguay resumed commercial, cultural, and diplomatic ties with Cuba in 1985.

URUGUAY AND THE UNITED STATES AFTER THE COLD WAR

Despite the return of democracy in the 1980s, Uruguayans continue to worry about how much social and economic benefits are being sacrificed by emphasizing "democracy at any cost." A reluctance to punish the military, out of fear of enticing them from the barracks, was evident in the

1989 defeat of a referendum that would have subjected the army and police to trials for human rights abuses committed under the rule by the generals. President Lacalle's (1989–1993) cooperation with the United States on its antinarcotics efforts, and its push for free trade, improved relations with the Bush administration. Uruguay joined the Southern Cone Common Market (MERCOSUR) in 1991 in an effort to reduce mounting trade deficits with Brazil and Argentina.

Despite the neo-liberal economic reforms sweeping Latin America in the 1990s, Uruguayans defeated (72 percent voted against) President Lacalle's economic privatization plan to sell off Uruguay's state-controlled industries, turning again to the welfare-state traditions of the past. This sentiment was a severe setback for the president and contributed to the party's loss to former president Julio M. Sanguinetti's Colorados in the November 1994 elections. With three democratic elections in the past decade, it now appears that Uruguay is back on a somewhat democratic track; but the military remains a powerful institution, corruption continues to undermine political legitimacy, and the two-party stability that proved so valuable in the early part of the twentieth century has all but ended.

CONCLUSION

U.S. involvement in Uruguay, since establishing full diplomatic relations in 1867, have been characterized by cooperation more than conflict. During times of rivalry between Uruguay's two giant neighbors, the United States cultivated Uruguayan cooperation in an effort to resolve the conflict. Uruguay sided with the United States during both world wars and joined the United States in establishing a collective bulwark against communism during the early years of the Cold War. However, between the Cuban Revolution and 1990, sharp disagreements emerged over the best way to treat Fidel Castro, the use of force to resolve hemispheric disputes and controversies, and democracy promotion and human rights violations. Still, Uruguay is a relatively powerless player in the hemisphere and remains dependent on the United States for trade, loans, and other forms of international financial assistance.

NOTES

1. Quoted in Dexter Perkins, *A History of the Monroe Doctrine*, rev. ed. (Boston: Little, Brown, 1963), p. 86.

2. Uruguay's plural presidency consists of a collegial (*colegiado*) executive system composed of a president (responsible for foreign policy and national security) and a small number of ministers from both of the major political parties—Colorados and Blancos. This constitutional design emphasized co-participation in governing, offering the main opposition party the opportunity to play an active role in the

policy-making process. It was modeled after the Swiss system, and its primary purpose was to weaken the authoritarian tendencies associated with *caudillismo* (dictatorial rule).

3. G. Pope Atkins, "Uruguay," in Harold Eugene Davis and Larman C. Wilson et al., *Latin American Foreign Policies: An Analysis* (Baltimore, MD: Johns Hopkins University Press, 1975), p. 284.

4. *The Rockefeller Report on the Americas*, New York Times edition (Chicago: Quadrangle Books, 1969), pp. 32–33. Emphasis added.

SUGGESTED READINGS

Gillespie, Charles. *Negotiating Democracy: Politicians and Generals in Uruguay.* New York: Cambridge University Press, 1991.

Kaufman, Edy. *Uruguay in Transition: From Civilian to Military Rule.* New Brunswick, NJ: Transaction, 1979.

Latin American Bureau. *Uruguay Generals Rule.* London, England: LAB, 1980.

Weinstein, Martin. *Uruguay: Democracy at the Crossroads.* Boulder, CO: Westview Press, 1988.

25

Venezuela

TIMELINE OF U.S. RELATIONS WITH VENEZUELA

1811	Venezuelan independence from Spain is proclaimed
1821	Spanish forces are defeated in Battle of Carabobo
1830–1848	José Antonio Paéz serves as president
1895–1896	Venezuela–British Guiana boundary dispute
1899–1908	Cipriano Castro assumes power
1902–1903	German-Britain-Italian blockade
1908	Juan Vicente Gómez seizes power
1914	First commercial oil well is started
1930	U.S. oil companies gain control of Venezuelan production
1935	Juan Vicente Gómez dies; is succeeded by López Contreras
1940	Isaías Medina Angarita assumes presidency
1945	Medina is overthrown
1945–1947	Rómulo Betancourt leads civilian government
1947	Rómulo Gallegos is elected president
1948	Gallegos is overthrown by the military
1949–1957	Military rule
1954	Dictator Pérez Jiménez is awarded the Legion of Merit by the United States
1958	Pérez Jiménez is overthrown
	President Nixon is attacked by angry mobs in Caracas
1959–1964	Rómulo Betancourt serves as elected president
1961	Venezuela becomes model of Alliance for Progress
1969–1974	Rafael Caldera serves as elected president (first term)

1974–1980	Carlos Andrés Pérez serves as elected president (first term)
1976	Petroleum industry is nationalized
1989	Carlos Andrés Pérez is elected president (second term)
1993	Pérez is removed from office on charges of corruption
1993–1998	Rafael Caldera serves as elected president (second term)

INTRODUCTION

Venezuela has the distinction of being the only Latin American nation never to have gone to war with its neighbors, and it has managed to escape U.S. military intervention and coercive economic sanctions, a rarity in U.S.-Latin American relations. Venezuelan dictators have not been immune from the common blunders that provoked the wrath of the United States, but they often enforced an orderly peace during times of international crises, and the generous petroleum concessions and favorable economic policies they provided to U.S. corporations greatly diminished any pretext for intervention.

Since the middle of the twentieth century, Venezuela has been a supporter of the principles of the inter-American system—diplomatic dialogue, nonintervention, and democratic governance—and the protection of human rights. Caracas accepted, and used, the Monroe Doctrine when it served its national interests but resented the United States when it was invoked unilaterally and undermined Venezuelan sovereignty. Venezuela endorsed the Calvo (1868) and Drago (1902) doctrines, both of which addressed the importance of national sovereignty and nonintervention. During the Cold War, aid to dictatorships, anticommunism, and economic nationalism affected U.S.-Venezuelan relations, often producing diplomatic tensions and bitterness between the two nations. Unlike other Latin American republics in the twentieth century, Venezuela never experienced a revolutionary confrontation with the United States, a tribute to its leadership, vast petroleum resources, and distant location.

VENEZUELA AND THE UNITED STATES DURING THE NINETEENTH CENTURY

With the United States preoccupied with continental expansion and the problem of slavery, relations between Venezuela and the United States were fairly routine and internationally insignificant throughout most of the nineteenth century. Venezuela's economic problems were compounded by intense military conflict between 1810 and 1909. It was a violent political era dominated by local strongmen (caudillos) from hostile regions. Until the first commercial oil well began operation in 1914, Venezuela relied on cacao and coffee exports, but the coffee boom at the turn of the century left Venezuela dependent on foreign loans, mostly from Britain and Germany.

The United States and Venezuelan Independence

The Creole elite of Caracas proclaimed independence on April 19, 1811, but final liberation from Spanish colonialism did not occur until 1821. Under the leadership of Simón Bolívar ("the Liberator") and José Antonio Paéz, a former royalist and brilliant military tactician, Venezuela won its War of Independence and established the century-long dominance of wealthy landlords and merchants. Preoccupied with the War of 1812 and the task of pressuring the Spanish to cede Florida, officially the United States did not recognize Venezuela until 1822. The long delay in formal recognition and U.S. false claims of neutrality bothered the Venezuelans, who had put a great deal of emphasis on emulating U.S. institutions.

Bolívar's dream of Pan-American unification soon disintegrated into rule by warring caudillos, with emphasis on strong government, personalism, and macho heroism. The 1820s was a period in which the United States and Venezuela shared liberal values—Bolívar's idea of a republican identity for the Americas paralleled President James Monroe's proclamation of a U.S. sphere of influence—but this harmony soon gave way to periods of neglect, filibustering, and other conflicts.

Venezuela and the Monroe Doctrine

The Monroe Doctrine did not impact Venezuela until the middle of the nineteenth century when foreign powers, including the United States, sent their warships to Venezuela to back the financial claims of their citizens who were engaged in commerce and trading (mostly cacao, but later gold and coffee). By the 1870s, Venezuela tried to revive the internationalist legacy of Bolívar and take a more active approach to hemispheric and Caribbean affairs. Venezuela used the Monroe Doctrine to its own advantage but was not always consistent in how it interpreted Monroe's message. For example, between 1876 and 1887, Venezuelan ministers in Washington appealed to the Monroe Doctrine on seven different occasions to warn of foreign encroachments, but these warnings seem to have gone unheeded.

Venezuelans criticized Washington for heavy-handed involvement in its internal affairs. After the United States reprimanded Venezuela for using French capital to exploit its natural resources, a Venezuelan newspaper in 1880 responded by telling Washington that it would not close off economic "progress because it happens to not suit your 'Monroe Doctrine' or any other idea of a protection you wish to exercise at a distance of two thousand miles." To do so "would be the height of folly on our part."[1] During the 1889 Inter-American Conference in Washington orchestrated by James G. Blaine, Venezuela challenged U.S. control over the agenda, arguing that more attention should be devoted to peaceful arbitration of boundary disputes and joint (or collective) efforts to protect the hemisphere from European aggression.

Between the Spanish-American War (1898) and World War I, the United States used a variety of techniques to put teeth in the Monroe Doctrine in an effort to protect the hemisphere from the rapacious Europeans. This era of protective imperialism also carried noble intentions by U.S. policymakers: helping countries solve development problems and determine how to become more civilized, teaching the South Americans the virtues of democracy and electoralism, and providing the necessary security under the tutelage of the United States. After the British deferred to the Monroe Doctrine during the Venezuela–British Guiana boundary dispute (1895–1896), and Spain was defeated in Cuba in 1898, Germany offered the only security threat to the hemisphere. From the days of William McKinley to Woodrow Wilson, U.S. presidents viewed Germany as the major threat to the region. The perception of a German threat was based on an ambitious and an erratic leader, an expanding military, and Germany's refusal to bow gracefully to the Monroe Doctrine. At the time, the German press referred to the Monroe Doctrine as nothing more than a "special manifestation of American arrogance."[2] The threat to Venezuela stemmed from Germany's use of military power to settle claims and debts, and the possibility of foreign occupation.

José Antonio Paéz and the United States

U.S.-Venezuelan relations were generally harmonious between 1830 (the death of Bolívar) and 1848. During this time Venezuela's independence hero, José Antonio Paéz, and his close political and economic followers, cultivated warm relations with U.S. representatives in Venezuela. Paéz was good at putting down rebellions, and the United States admired him for his strong-arm methods of containing racial and regional tensions. Confidence in Paéz's political authority and his military power relieved Washington of having to intervene in Venezuela, while the Paéz oligarchy recognized the value of having U.S. warships offshore to intimidate domestic opponents. This early form of gunboat diplomacy also helped to frighten European predators.

After the Liberal opposition came to power in 1848, U.S.-Venezuelan relations slowly deteriorated when the new leadership began to form a militia consisting of lower class blacks. In order to convince Washington of the necessity of intervention, U.S. representatives in Caracas emphasized the parallel fears of race and revolution. U.S. chargé Benjamin Shields engaged in constant demands for U.S. forces to assist his Venezuelan friends to keep the blacks in submission, but his requests were rebuffed by Washington. Convinced that Shields had overstepped his bounds in representing the United States in Venezuela, the State Department removed him in 1849 for having compromised the interests of the United States. The constant meddling of U.S. representatives in Venezuelan affairs did little to foster good relations during the later half of the nineteenth century.

The Age of Guano Filibustering

U.S.-Venezuelan relations during the second half of the nineteenth century suffered from conflicts over U.S. citizens' claims—many of which were fraudulent or exaggerated—against the Venezuelan government. It didn't help that many of the claimants to whom the United States provided protection were Venezuelans by birth who demanded U.S. government intervention if their business interests were threatened. The whole process of settling claims became so enmeshed with bureaucratic delays and questionable claims that it took decades of litigation to settle some of them. When several guano (bird dung fertilizer) entrepreneurs from the United States laid claim to the guano on Aves Island off the Venezuelan coast and started mining the fertilizer, Venezuelan soldiers removed the U.S. flag and ordered the U.S. citizens to leave. This irritating venture led to 40 years of legal wrangling, with Venezuela finally agreeing to make compensation. Assuming a vastly superior set of values and goals, U.S. representatives often developed a missionary zeal to teach Venezuelans the virtues of American political culture and efficient governance. Two events—a boundary dispute and a European naval blockade—between 1895 and 1903 became part of the U.S. drive for hegemony in the Americas.

Venezuela–British Guiana Boundary Dispute, 1895–1896

Conflicting claims over the boundary between Venezuela and British Guiana gave rise to a significant extension of the Monroe Doctrine under the presidency of Grover Cleveland and his secretary of state, Richard Olney. On the basis of a line drawn by British explorer and surveyor Sir Robert H. Schombürgk in the early 1840s, the British claimed a significant portion of Venezuela. The Venezuelans claimed a different boundary line. Confronted by continual encroachments into Venezuelan territory, they made little headway in resolving the dispute through international arbitration. In order to force a settlement of the growing dispute, Venezuela appealed to the Cleveland administration to invoke the Monroe Doctrine.

Fearing the possibility of war with the British over a territorial dispute, and the necessity of preventing new or expanded European colonies in the Western Hemisphere, the United States entered the controversy by taking Venezuela's side and insisting on settlement by arbitration. The showdown with the British over territorial claims in northern South America was no small matter for the Cleveland administration. In President Cleveland's mind, not only was Venezuela's claim just but the Monroe Doctrine, international morality, and U.S. honor and influence throughout Latin America were all at stake in the dispute. In a letter of instruction to Thomas F. Bayard, U.S. ambassador to Great Britain, Secretary of State Richard Olney invoked the Monroe Doctrine and extended its interpretation with extraordinary disregard for the sentiments of the Latin American states. In what became known as the Olney Corollary to the Monroe Doctrine, the U.S. secretary of state asserted on July 20, 1895, that:

> Today the United States is practically sovereign on this continent, and its fiat [decree] is law upon the subjects to which it confines its interposition. Why? It is not because of the pure friendship or good will felt for it. It is not simply by reason of its high character as a civilized state, nor because wisdom and justice and equity are the invariable characteristics of the dealings of the United States. It is because, in addition to all other grounds, its infinite resources combined with its isolated position render it master of the situation and practically invulnerable against any or all other powers.
>
> All the advantages of this superiority are at once imperiled if the principle be admitted that European powers may convert American states into colonies or provinces of their own.[3]

It was about as blunt and arrogant a statement of the reach of American imperial power as one can find in the annals of U.S.-Latin American relations. Olney's famous note—designed to remind Great Britain of continuing U.S. opposition to further encroachments in the Western Hemisphere—angered some Latin American officials, provoked an outcry from the British, and almost caused war between the United States and Great Britain. Fearing a precedent that might extend to other British possessions in the Western Hemisphere, British foreign secretary Lord Salisbury, after receiving the note, challenged the United States by refusing to give the Monroe Doctrine the equivalent of international law, accused Venezuela of refusing any reasonable settlement, and denied the right of the United States to insist on arbitration.

As war clouds loomed over Venezuela and British Guiana, President Cleveland called for an arbitration commission to begin work in 1896 to settle matters. After complicated negotiations that stretched into 1899, an arbitration tribunal awarded most of the disputed territory to Great Britain, except for land around the mouth of the Orinoco River (see Chapter 14). In negotiating with Britain, Olney did not consult Venezuela and ignored certain Venezuelan claims on his own authority, making Caracas furious but leaving it little leverage to counter Olney's ploy. By compelling Britain to submit to arbitration and bow to the Monroe Doctrine, Olney's bold message amounted to a declaration that the United States was the sole hegemonic power in the Western Hemisphere. It marked the most significant explication of the Monroe Doctrine since 1823, and it paved the way for further corollaries to the Doctrine during the first three decades of the twentieth century.

As the century ended, Venezuela fought with creditor nations over financial claims, many of which stemmed from property damage that occurred during periods of civil strife. In what became a common practice throughout the nineteenth century, European powers sent warships to collect debts that Venezuela either could not or would not pay. Faced with frequent incursions into the Western Hemisphere by foreign powers to secure repayment, the United States addressed the dilemma of how to preserve the Monroe Doctrine and prevent the acquisition of territory by a nonhemispheric power.

VENEZUELA AND THE UNITED STATES IN THE EARLY TWENTIETH CENTURY

During the early part of the twentieth century, Venezuelan trade and commerce shifted away from Europe to the United States, but Caracas continued to have problems with the use of force by creditors to collect debts. By carefully assuring the U.S. government that it had no intention of acquiring or permanently occupying Venezuelan territory, the European nations demonstrated their acceptance of the Monroe Doctrine.

The Venezuela Blockade of 1902–1903

After years of political turmoil and the difficulties of dealing with Venezuelan dictators, numerous countries were disturbed about debt default, unsettled claims, and the erratic antics of Venezuelan president Cipriano Castro. To force Castro to pay his government's debts, Germany, England, and Italy imposed a naval blockade on Venezuela in December 1902. Germany's gunboat diplomacy was carried out by Reich Chancellor Bernard von Bülow, who saw the chance for a quick victory and an opportunity to improve Germany's position in the growing Latin American market. Italy was a minor player in the affair, having been invited to join the blockade by the British, not the Germans.

The informal alliance between Germany and Great Britain stemmed from similar interests in Venezuela and the perception that a U.S. response to European activity in the hemisphere would cause no uproar, despite the language of the Monroe Doctrine. After all, the United States had remained calm when the European powers strong-armed Guatemala in 1901 and 1902 (see Chapter 13), and President Roosevelt's words seemed clear as to the meaning of "misconduct" and "punishment" in the Western Hemisphere. In December 1901 he explicitly stated that "We do not guarantee any [American] state against punishment if it misconducts itself, provided that *punishment does not take the form of the acquisition of territory by any non-American power*."[4] By 1902 the Europeans had good reason to believe that there could not be a misunderstanding of the Roosevelt administration's meaning of the Monroe Doctrine, despite the fact that Britain accepted the Doctrine and Germany did not.

Once the joint European intervention got under way, President Roosevelt realized that the Venezuelan crisis could arouse the U.S. public and lead to events beyond the control of Washington. Did Germany actually threaten U.S. interests in the Americas? The actions that led policymakers in Washington to conclude that Germany posed a threat to the region proved to be a strong mixture of German bravado and American suspicion, more than a serious effort to challenge the Monroe Doctrine and a first step toward the conquest of South America. Eventually the crisis ended with Germany's acceptance of arbitration talks in Washington. In the end each of the three blockading powers received compensation from Venezuela, and the crisis over debt collection helped clarify the privileged position of the United States in the Western Hemisphere. The German threat was groundless, but anxiety over Germany (and other foreign powers) continued. President Roosevelt gained confidence by taking Panama, stopping disturbances in the Dominican Republic, and announcing the Roosevelt Corollary in 1904. In response to the Venezuelan crisis, Argentine foreign minister Luis María Drago sought to make illegal the use of armed intervention to force payment of foreign governmental debts (he referred to it as an "economic corollary to the Monroe Doctrine"), but the United States was vehemently opposed on economic grounds and refused to rule out the possible necessity of armed force.

Cipriano Castro and the United States

The diplomatic crisis that erupted in 1902 coincided with the triumph of General Cipriano Castro, a regional tyrant from the Andean state of Táchira, who assumed power through a series of battles with other regional strongmen and reestablished the authority of the central government. His open defiance of the United States—he severed diplomatic relations twice during his dictatorship—and Venezuela's European creditors contributed to the challenge to the Monroe Doctrine stemming from the European blockade of 1902–1903. Roosevelt's experience with the naval blockade led him to formulate a new policy for the United States; it would exercise an "international police power" to maintain order and ensure that Latin American nations paid their European creditors. However, Roosevelt's new Latin American policy did not stop Castro's irritating behavior, including his brutal treatment of the opposition and his threats to U.S. economic interests. In 1901–1902, the New York and Bermúdez Company (a U.S. company organized in 1885 that extracted natural asphalt from eastern Venezuela) paid General Manuel A. Matos to overthrow Castro. The private U.S.-backed revolt failed, but it cost the Venezuelan government $5 million and the nation twelve thousand casualties. Unable to tolerate Castro's chronic wrongdoing, Roosevelt gave the orders to plan for a military invasion of Venezuela to topple the recalcitrant Castro and "show those Dagos that they will have to behave decently."[5] Secretary of State Elihu Root advised the president against the use of force, and the United States was left with no choice but to wait for Castro's failing health to solve the problem. In 1908, Castro sailed for Europe for medical treatment. He never ruled Venezuela again. The government came under Juan Vicente Gómez, a trusted aide who ruled Venezuela until his death in 1935.

Juan Vicente Gómez and the United States

Shortly after Cipriano Castro's departure from Venezuela, Juan Vicente Gómez announced he was taking over, informed the State Department he was willing to settle all outstanding claims, and requested the assistance of U.S. warships to help maintain order. Gómez consolidated his power and developed close relations with the United States that lasted throughout World War I and the Great Depression. During his 27 years in power, Gómez helped change Venezuela from a predominantly agricultural country to the second-largest oil producer in the world. To avoid foreign intervention, Gómez built a national army to maintain order, settled foreign claims as quickly as possible, and used oil revenues to modernize Venezuela and put its financial house in order. He made sure that foreign investors were safe from revolutionaries and the danger of nationalization. He became one of the first of the twentieth century's "friendly dictators" toward the United States. Despite the brutality and corruption of his administration, Gómez evolved into one of the many "benign" and long-standing autocratic rulers, "the last of the caudillos on the Porfirio Díaz model and the first of the 1930s policemen like Rafael Trujillo and Anastasio Somoza."[6]

The United States and Venezuelan Oil

After World War I the United States recognized the necessity of finding new sources of energy to fuel new technologies that were of major economic—and eventually, military—importance. Venezuela was one of the new production centers; the first commercial oil well began operation in 1914, and by 1929 four U.S. oil companies had transformed Venezuela into one of the world's leading producers of petroleum. By 1930, thanks to lucrative contracts from Juan Vicente Gómez, U.S. petroleum companies gained 99 percent control of Venezuelan oil production, investing relatively little while taking billions of dollars out of the country. For the first three decades of oil production in Venezuela, foreign investors could count on generous concessions since the producer government had nothing to lose and a great deal to gain. Over time, however, foreign ownership of natural resources and domestic pressure for national control contributed to strained relations between the United States and Venezuela. Although Venezuela followed the U.S. lead during the major wars of the twentieth century, the bilateral disputes that emerged inevitably focused on the ownership of oil.

Numerous oil barons from the United States became wealthy through their Venezuelan oil investments. One of the best known was William F. Buckley Sr., a Texas petroleum executive who first invested in Mexico during the Mexican Revolution (see Chapter 18) but was forced out by Mexican authorities for his anti-revolutionary activities in 1917. With concessions from the dictator Gómez, William Buckley used underhanded methods with his local allies to obtain oil-drilling monopolies, which angered both the State Department and the oil companies. It wasn't long before Gómez figured out the ploy and vetoed Buckley's plan for a transshipment monopoly.

With growing investment and generous revenue from the oil concessions, Gómez was able to balance his budgets, reduce Venezuela's large foreign debt, control political opposition, and avoid invasion by the United States. Moreover, the Venezuelan dictator won over the oilmen by allowing them to dictate oil legislation. President Wilson's State Department tolerated Gómez's despotism and declaration of neutrality toward Germany and even suppressed news of his crimes in order to forestall demands from the American public for his removal. Until his death in 1935, Gómez was insulated by the changing views of policymakers in Washington toward the Monroe Doctrine and the use of U.S. troops to restore order and protect American lives and property. When thousands of students revolted in Caracas in 1928, U.S. diplomats recognized the importance of a dictator like Gómez to keep communism and subversion out of Venezuela. Like many Latin American dictators during the twentieth century, Gómez employed clever propaganda in the United States to portray his country as a model of stability, progress, and order; in light of U.S. concerns about communism, Gómez labeled nearly all his opponents indiscriminately as either communists or subversives, thus easily justifying his authoritarian abuses. Of most importance to the United States, Gómez (often called the "tyrant of the Andes" by his critics) managed to eliminate the chronic wrongdoing of his predecessor that had justified U.S. intervention throughout the Caribbean and Central America during his 27 years in power.

Venezuela and the Good Neighbor Policy

After the death of Gómez in 1935, U.S.-Venezuelan relations changed significantly, assisted by Franklin Roosevelt's Good Neighbor Policy, World War II, and the growing demands inside Venezuela for democratic rule. The prevailing view in Washington, however, was that Venezuela was still underdeveloped and needed political guidance. Roosevelt's Good Neighbor Policy disavowed the right to intervene with military forces to correct "uncivilized" behavior, and it served to remove a major source of irritation between the United States and Latin America. However, since Gómez had been one of the few Latin American leaders who supported U.S. military intervention and rule in the Caribbean, the Good Neighbor Policy had little effect on U.S.-Venezuelan relations. The oil companies had the most to lose from minimal diplomatic contact with the dictator, since their business activity depended on bribes and praise for the tyrant, as well as the assumption that the U.S. Marines would protect American investments. Moreover, the resistance to change among U.S. oil executives contributed to Venezuela's growing hostility toward foreign ownership of its major source of revenue.

During the reign of Eleazar López Contreras (1935–1940), Venezuela raised the taxes on foreign oil profits in order to push ahead with public works projects and improve services to the poor. Although there was no talk of expropriating U.S. properties, Washington worried about loss of control over an economic and strategic resource. Tensions mounted after the Mexican oil expropriation of 1938 as U.S. oil companies suffered continual attacks from nationalists of all persuasions. With a keen sensitivity toward Latin American socioeconomic aspirations, Laurence Duggan, chief of the Latin American division in the State Department, led the bureaucratic struggle for a new policy. In a memorandum to U.S. Secretary of State Cordell Hull and U.S. Under Secretary of State Sumner Welles, Duggan argued that a clash between the Venezuelan government and U.S. oil companies would have a negative effect on American investments throughout Latin America. In Duggan's view, "American petroleum companies . . . must not be permitted . . . to jeopardize our entire good neighbor policy through obstinancy and short-sightedness. Our national interests as a whole far outweigh those of the petroleum companies."[7] Duggan's memo emphasized the strategic significance of Venezuelan petroleum and helped to further his goal of achieving a unified hemisphere in the event of a war in Europe. Fearful that Nazi Germany might jeopardize access to Venezuelan petroleum and threaten its security interests, the United States worked hard to gain Venezuela's support during the war. The United States agreed to a new oil law giving Venezuela more revenue from the foreign oil industry, and this had the effect of expanding U.S. influence in Venezuela after the war.

VENEZUELA AND THE UNITED STATES DURING THE COLD WAR

The rapid growth of the petroleum economy from the 1920s through the time of World War II resulted in a more powerful national government and the growth of a small middle class demanding greater participation in Venezuelan politics. The emergence of new political parties, trade unions, and peasant leagues during the liberal dictatorship of General Medina Angarita (1941–1945) set the stage for more than a decade of civil-military turmoil (including military dictatorship between 1948 and 1958) before a somewhat shaky democratic regime was put in place in 1958.

Venezuela and the Poor Neighbor Policy

In his campaign for the presidency in 1952, Dwight Eisenhower criticized the Truman administration for turning Roosevelt's Good Neighbor Policy into a "poor neighbor policy."[8] Eisenhower's rhetorical efforts to return to good neighbor principles were commendable, but the issues of the Cold War and anticommunism often required that the democratic idealism engendered by World War II give way to national security and a return to interventionism. When military rulers in Peru and Venezuela replaced the democratic governments there in the late 1940s, the United States had no trouble recognizing these governments, particularly when they promised to oppose communism and support the United States at the United Nations.

The promises of U.S. economic assistance for Latin America after World War II did not materialize, and the State Department answered all complaints by telling Latin Americans that the only way they could expect foreign capital was by creating the proper climate for foreign investment. This meant technical cooperation and free trade and investment strategies, not foreign aid from the United States. Unlike its stance in World War II, Latin America did not rally behind the United States during the Korean War because of the Truman administration's stingy economic aid policy. The Truman administration also sought to redefine the Monroe Doctrine, claiming that the interventionism of past U.S. presidents had been "protective" in nature and necessary for the security of the hemisphere. In what became known as the "Miller Doctrine" (named after Assistant Secretary Edward G. Miller Jr.) the United States argued "that collective intervention against communism was an 'imperative' of the Monroe Doctrine and the OAS charter."[9]

Dictators and Double Standards

During the early Cold War period, Venezuela became the focus of a policy debate in Washington over the nature of intervention, aid to dictatorships, and support for democracy. The last of the twentieth-century Venezuelan dictators was Marcos Pérez Jiménez, a military figure who believed the armed forces were the most competent to bring national unity, as well as material and technological progress, to Venezuela. At first part of the military junta that governed after 1948, Pérez Jiménez stole the 1952 election and announced he would solve Venezuela's problems with a "New National Ideal." During the 1950s oil production more than doubled, and Venezuela soon became a foreign investor's dream. Creole Petroleum announced that its 1957 profits approached 50 percent. Opponents of the dictatorship were treated with torture and imprisonment, while Pérez Jiménez and his friends enriched themselves at the nation's expense. U.S. military officers instructed Venezuelan officers on the importance of Cold War ideology and accepted rampant corruption, the absence of civil liberties, and human rights abuses as one of the necessary evils in keeping the Soviets out of the hemisphere and protecting Venezuela's oil supply. Those who represented the United States in Venezuela during the 1950s either ignored the excesses of the dictatorship or offered old shibboleths about "immature" voters needing further tutelage in operating a fully democratic system. Chargé Franklin W. Wolf, in one of his bouts of "wisdom," asserted that "the people of Venezuela are not yet ready nor adequately prepared for democracy."[10]

To demonstrate their anticommunist credentials, Pérez Jiménez, Venezuelan military officers, and Pedro Estrada, head of the brutal national security police force, conspired with their counterparts in Peru and the Caribbean in a plan to overthrow the elected governments of Jacobo Arbenz (in Guatemala) and José Figueres (in Costa Rica). U.S. secretary of state John Foster Dulles intervened and warned the conspirators that an OAS conference would be preferable; moreover, the United States (and the United Fruit Company) had their own leader-removal operation for Arbenz, although not for Figueres. Pérez Jiménez stayed out of the covert CIA effort to remove Arbenz in Guatemala, but the Eisenhower administration offered recognition, praise, and honorific medals to him and Peru's dictator at the time, General Manuel Odría. In November 1954 the Venezuelan dictator was awarded the Legion of Merit by the United States for "special meritorious conduct in the fulfillment of his high functions, and anti-Communistic attitudes." This single act of embracing dictators would haunt Monroe's ghosts for years to come, but it served short-term economic interests by allowing new petroleum concessions to be awarded to U.S. investors in 1956 and protecting U.S. exports to Venezuela. As the Eisenhower administration came to a close, Democrats used Pérez Jiménez as a symbol of brutal dictatorship and a failed Republican policy toward the region as a whole. Dictator Pérez Jiménez was deposed in 1958.

Nixon's Venezuelan Visit

Vice-President Richard Nixon's visit to Latin America in 1958 coincided with the rapidly deteriorating relations between the United States and Latin America. In his 18-day journey throughout the hemisphere, Nixon encountered riotous displays of anti-Americanism motivated by Eisenhower's support for repressive dictatorships, the CIA's removal of Arbenz in Guatemala in 1954, the U.S. refusal to provide economic assistance, and the imposition of tariff barriers against Latin American exports. Nixon attributed *all* anti-American protests to an international communist conspiracy aimed at the destruction of the United States, and he refused to acknowledge the legitimacy of Latin American demands.

Nixon was warned of angry demonstrators planning for his arrival in Caracas and received word of an assassination plot from U.S. intelligence sources. After being assured by the Venezuelan government of its ability to handle the situation, Nixon decided to go to Caracas because he considered it his most important stop on the tour. In his motorcade from the airport, he was confronted with shouts of *Muera Nixon!* (death to Nixon) and was nearly killed by a howling mob determined to "punish" the United States for its past connivance with the recently deposed dictator Pérez Jiménez and his notorious chief of secret police.

The ugly incident in Caracas sparked a debate within the Eisenhower administration over how to best reform inter-American relations. Several suggestions came from Nixon himself, including a revised recognition policy based on a tepid distinction between dictators and democrats. Following what he had heard from Teodoro Moscoso, who later headed President Kennedy's Alliance for Progress, Nixon suggested that the United States offer "a formal handshake for dictators; an *embraso* [sic] for leaders in freedom."[11] As military dictators fell from power between 1958 and 1960, the Eisenhower administration found it much easier to modify its rhetoric in favor of democracy and respect for human rights, but military aid programs expanded to protect the fledgling democracies of the region.

Rómulo Betancourt and the Betancourt Doctrine

With the overthrow of dictator Marcos Pérez Jiménez, Venezuelans tried political democracy for only the second time in the twentieth century. At the forefront of this effort was Rómulo Betancourt, a young lawyer and veteran of previous efforts to combat dictatorships and install democratic rule. Betancourt played a major role in Venezuelan politics, starting with his early protests against the dictator Juan Vicente Gómez in 1928, to his death in 1981. He took charge of the revolutionary government that ruled Venezuela from 1945 to 1948, and later he was elected president (1959–1964). Betancourt championed the promotion and protection of representative democracy and human rights in Latin America. Venezuela provided many of the ideas of economic development and social change that became part of the Alliance for Progress and a model for democratic reform governments in Latin America. Betancourt's unwavering commitment to democracy, social reform, economic development, and anticommunism made him, and Venezuela, a model regime during the Alliance years. To solidify the cordial relationship, President Kennedy visited Caracas in 1961 and President Betancourt made an official visit to Washington in 1963. Yet Venezuela and the United States continued to clash over how to handle all forms of dictatorship in Latin America.

While he was president, Betancourt formulated what became known as the Betancourt Doctrine. In this he contended that intervention might be necessary under the Rio Treaty to eliminate Latin American dictatorships. He was not successful in getting the Organization of American States (OAS) to adopt the Betancourt Doctrine in the sense of active intervention to remove a dictatorial regime, but he did utilize nonrecognition as a diplomatic tool to condemn 10 Latin American governments during his time in office. The most noteworthy application of the Betancourt Doctrine occurred in 1960 following the attempted assassination of Betancourt by Dominican strongman Rafael L. Trujillo. Although the Dominican case provided some legitimacy to Betancourt's policy of dealing with dictatorships, Latin Americans across a wide political spectrum still regarded the Doctrine as a dangerous interventionist policy with little justification. In return for his alignment with U.S. efforts to isolate Castro's Cuba, the Kennedy administration showered Betancourt with economic assistance to underwrite economic and social change, and with military aid to help him defeat political radicals.

The Politics of Petroleum

After the harmony of U.S.-Venezuelan relations during the Kennedy years, tensions developed over global perspectives and regional priorities. Relations with the United States continued to be important for Venezuela, but it expanded its ties to the world through international organizations that provided new opportunities for weak nations to expand their political visions and solve pressing economic problems.[12] Venezuela had a major role in the formation of the Organization of Petroleum Exporting Countries (OPEC) in 1960 in an effort to raise oil prices, and it nationalized its iron and oil industries in 1975 and 1976. U.S.-Venezuelan relations were more a mixture of cooperation and conflict than what had prevailed in the 1950s and 1960s. After joining OPEC, Venezuela continued to supply large amounts of petroleum to the United States during periods of disruptions and shortages in world oil markets in the late 1960s and early 1970s. Yet it also pushed OPEC to quadruple world oil prices in 1973 and continued to play a major role in global energy strategies. The two Latin American members of OPEC—Venezuela and Ecuador (which withdrew in 1992)— enjoyed the benefits of the dramatic increases in oil prices in 1974 but saw fewer benefits from the second round of production cuts by the OPEC cartel in 1978–1979. The Ford administration and the U.S. Congress made no distinction between OPEC members and the countries that had joined the embargo against the West, and it passed punitive legislation in retaliation that did great harm to Venezuela and Ecuador despite the fact that they did not cooperate with the embargo. Regardless of the short-term gains by the oil producers in the 1970s, the real losers were the Latin American and Third World importers of petroleum that spent most of the decade of the 1980s struggling to extricate themselves from large foreign debts.

Venezuela and the Reagan Era

During the 1980s Venezuela clashed with the Reagan administration over U.S. support for the Nicaraguan Contras, the application of the Reagan Doctrine, and the UN debate over the limits to the expanse of territorial sea that a nation could claim. Venezuela opposed U.S. policy in Central America by joining the Contadora Group in its efforts to pursue a peaceful settlement to the conflict (see Chapter 19). U.S. efforts to isolate and condemn Cuba also generated controversy and hostility between the United States and Venezuela. In the United Nations and the OAS, Venezuela has been consistent in either abstaining or voting against U.S. resolutions aimed at censuring Castro's Cuba. Along with other Latin American governments, Venezuela opposed U.S. legislation implemented in the 1990s to extend hostile U.S. legislation toward Cuba beyond the shores of the United States.

VENEZUELA AND THE UNITED STATES AFTER THE COLD WAR

Venezuela suffered from mounting economic problems and political instability in the late 1980s and early 1990s that opened up serious domestic divisions after 30 years of continual democratic rule. A massive international debt brought the Bush and Clinton administrations to Venezuela's rescue, but the austerity measures needed to win the approval of U.S. investors caused public rioting in February 1989, two attempted military takeovers in 1992, and the forced resignation of President Carlos Andrés Pérez (on charges of rampant corruption and embezzlement) during his second term (1988–1993). The Clinton administration was instrumental in reversing a coup attempt against Pérez, but the president's removal and arrest did not stop the political and economic problems.

After Rafael Caldera returned to the presidency for a five-year term (1993–1998), Venezuela's economic slide continued until he managed to encourage foreign oil companies to reinvest to bolster the petroleum sector. These initiatives were difficult for Venezuelan nationalists to swallow, but they made Venezuela the number one foreign supplier of petroleum to the United States. In 1996, Venezuela replaced Saudi Arabia and Mexico as the biggest oil supplier to the United States, due in large part to the fact that Venezuela provided U.S. oil companies with lucrative production-sharing agreements. On arriving in Caracas, Venezuela, on October 12, 1997, President Clinton invoked the legacy of Christopher Columbus, telling his audience that a "new world" was being forged throughout the hemisphere by new explorers interested in a pan-American free trade zone for the new millennium. Recognizing the importance of Venezuela—the largest exporter of oil to the United States and a $15 billion-a-year revenue source—President Clinton also mentioned other issues, such as the environment and efforts to combat drug trafficking in the Americas.

CONCLUSION

Since the time of the Monroe Doctrine, U.S. involvement in Venezuela has fluctuated according to the economic, political, and security needs of the United States. When international crises provoked fears of foreign intrusion, the United States assumed the right to control Venezuela's destiny, although Washington never ordered the invasion or occupation of the country. Venezuela's involvement in two conflicts at the turn of the century had a major impact on U.S. Latin American policy, paving the way for the expansion of the Monroe Doctrine and the drive to achieve dominance in the Caribbean region after the decision to build a transoceanic canal in Panama. With a long string of "friendly" dictators during the early part of the twentieth century, U.S. investors reaped huge profits from Venezuela's oil, policymakers in Washington needed little arm-twisting to obtain Venezuela's compliance with major U.S. interests. Accustomed to easy wealth, and firm in the conviction that democracy is firmly implanted in national soil, Venezuelans have been perplexed by democracy's failure to produce a more egalitarian and just society that is free of corruption and predatory militarism. Venezuela's troubles are mostly homegrown, but the history of U.S. involvement there is also a factor.

NOTES

1. Quoted in Judith Ewell, *Venezuela and the United States: From Monroe's Hemisphere to Petroleum's Empire* (Athens: University of Georgia Press, 1996), pp. 87–88.

2. Quoted in Nancy Mitchell, "The Height of the German Challenge: The Venezuelan Blockade, 1902–3," *Diplomatic History* 20, no. 2 (Spring 1996): 185.

3. Quoted in Samuel Flagg Bemis, *The Latin American Policy of the United States: An Historical Interpretation* (New York: W. W. Norton, 1971), p. 120.

4. Quoted in Mitchell, "The Height of the German Challenge," p. 190. Emphasis added.

5. Quoted in Stephen G. Rabe, *The Road to OPEC: United States Relations with Venezuela, 1919–1976* (Austin: University of Texas Press, 1982), p. 10.

6. Ewell, *Venezuela and the United States*, p. 117.

7. Quoted in Rabe, *The Road to OPEC*, p. 64.

8. Stephen G. Rabe, *Eisenhower and Latin America: The Foreign Policy of Anticommunism* (Chapel Hill: University of North Carolina Press, 1988), p. 6.

9. Ibid., pp. 24–25.

10. Quoted in Ewell, *Venezuela and the United States*, p. 159.

11. Quoted in Rabe, *Eisenhower and Latin America*, p. 104.

12. Venezuela joined the Andean Pact (1973), the Latin American Economic System (1975), and the Group of Three (1995, with Mexico and Colombia) in an effort to distance itself from the United States and forge closer ties throughout Latin America and the Caribbean.

SUGGESTED READINGS

Braveboy-Wagner, Jacqueline Anne. *The Venezuelan-Guyana Border Dispute: Britain's Colonial Legacy in Latin America.* Boulder, CO: Westview Press, 1984.

Ewell, Judith. *Venezuela and the United States: From Monroe's Hemisphere to Petroleum's Empire.* Athens: University of Georgia Press, 1996.

Haggerty, Richard A., ed. *Venezuela, a Country Study*, 4th Edition. Washington, DC: U.S. Government Printing Office, 1993.

Hood, Miriam. *Gunboat Diplomacy, 1895–1905: Great Power Pressure in Venezuela*, 2nd Edition. Boston: Allen & Unwin, 1983.

Rabe, Stephen G. *The Road to OPEC: United States Relations with Venezuela, 1919–1976.* Austin: University of Texas Press, 1982.

Rudolph, Donna Keyse, and G. A. Rudolph. *Historical Dictionary of Venezuela*, 2nd Ed. Lanham, MD: Scarecrow Press, 1996.

Appendix

The Monroe Doctrine: Excerpts from Monroe's Original Message, December 2, 1823

At the proposal of the Russian Imperial Government, made through the minister of the Emperor residing here, a full power and instructions have been transmitted to the minister of the United States at St. Petersburg to arrange by amicable negotiation the respective rights and interests of the two nations on the northwest coast of this continent. A similar proposal had been made by His Imperial Majesty to the Government of Great Britain, which has likewise been acceded to. The Government of the United States has been desirous by this friendly proceeding of manifesting the great value which they have invariably attached to the friendship of the Emperor and their solicitude to cultivate the best understanding with this Government. In the discussions to which this interest has given rise and in the arrangements by which they may terminate, the occasion has been judged proper for asserting, as a principle in which the rights and interests of the United States are involved, that the American continents, by the free and independent condition which they have assumed and maintain, are henceforth not to be considered as subjects for future colonization by any European powers. . . .

It was stated at the commencement of the last session [of Congress] that a great effort was then making [*sic*] in Spain and Portugal to improve the condition of the people of those countries, and that it appeared to be conducted with extraordinary moderation. It need scarcely be remarked that the result has been so far very different from what was then anticipated. Of events in that quarter of the globe, with which we have so much intercourse and from which we derive our origin, we have always been anxious and interested spectators. The citizens of the United States cherish sentiments the most friendly in favor of the liberty and happiness of their fellow-men on that side of the Atlantic. In the wars of the European powers in matters relating to themselves we have never taken any part, nor does it comport with our policy so to do. It is only when our rights are invaded or seriously menaced that we resent injuries or make preparation for our defense. With the [independence] movements in this hemisphere we are of necessity more immediately connected, and by causes which must be obvious to all enlightened and impartial observers. The political system of the allied powers is essentially different in this respect from that of America. This difference proceeds from that which exists in their respective Governments; and to the defense of our own, which has been achieved by the loss of so much blood and treasure, and matured by the wisdom of their most enlightened citizens, and under which we have enjoyed unexampled felicity, this whole nation is devoted. We owe it, therefore, to candor and to the amicable relations existing between the United States and those powers to declare that we should consider any attempt on their part to extend their system to any portion of this hemisphere as dangerous to our peace and safety. With the existing colonies or dependencies of any European power we have not interfered and shall not interfere. But with the Governments who have declared their independence and maintained it, and whose independence we have, on great consideration and on just principles, acknowledged, we could not view any interposition for the purpose of oppressing them, or controlling in any other manner their destiny, by an European power in any other light than as the manifestation of an unfriendly disposition toward the United States. In the war between those new Governments and Spain we declared our neutrality at the time of their recognition, and to this we have adhered, and shall continue to adhere, provided no change shall occur which, in the judgment of the competent authorities of this Government, shall make a corresponding change on the part of the United States indispensable to their security. . . .

The late events in Spain and Portugal shew that Europe is still unsettled. Of this important fact no stronger proof can be adduced than that the allied powers should have thought it proper, on any principle satisfactory to themselves, to have interposed by force in the internal concerns of Spain. To what extent such interposition may be carried, on the same principle, is a question in which all independent powers whose governments differ from theirs are interested, even those most remote, and surely none more so than the United States. Our policy in regard to Europe, which was adopted at an early stage of the wars which have so long agitated that quarter of the globe, nevertheless remains the same, which is, not to interfere in the internal concerns of any of its powers; to consider the government *de facto* as the legitimate government for us; to cultivate friendly relations with it, and to preserve those relations by a frank, firm, and manly policy, meeting in all instances the just claims of every power, submitting to injuries from none. But in regard to those continents circumstances are eminently and conspicuously different. It is impossible that the allied powers should extend their political system to any portion of either continent without endangering our peace and happiness; nor can anyone believe that our southern brethren, if left to themselves, would adopt it of their own accord. It is equally impossible, therefore, that we should behold such interposition in any form with indifference. If we look to the comparative strength and resources of Spain and those new Governments, and their distance from each other, it must be obvious that she can never subdue them. It is still the true policy of the United States to leave the parties to themselves, in the hope that other powers will pursue the same course.

Glossary

Act of Chapultepec. A formal declaration made at the Chapultepec Conference in Mexico City in 1945 by representatives from 21 American republics providing for a collective response against any aggressor from outside or inside the region. It expanded the Monroe Doctrine from a unilateral guarantee against intervention into a mutual security system, included provisions that would prohibit aggression by one American state against another, and called for the negotiation of a treaty of reciprocal assistance, foreshadowing the creation of the Rio Treaty in 1947.

Alliance for Progress. An ambitious U.S. policy in regard to Latin America established during the administration of John F. Kennedy that included a massive assistance program tied to U.S. economic aid, a concerted effort to build democratic institutions, and a slightly veiled hope that such actions would undermine Fidel Castro's radical revolution in Cuba. The Alliance was terminated by the U.S. Congress in 1973 after it concluded that the policy's main objectives had not been achieved.

Ambassador. The highest-level diplomatic representative of a foreign government in a host country. In the United States, ambassadors are appointed by the president and require confirmation by the U.S. Senate before assuming duties abroad. Throughout the twentieth century, U.S. ambassadors in Latin America have often been powerful figures, deeply involved in the internal politics of the countries where they are appointed to serve.

Banana Republic. A disparaging reference to poor and politically incompetent Central American countries whose economies at one time depended solely on the export of tropical fruits (mainly bananas) and run by corrupt dictators. Dominated by multinational fruit companies that liked doing business with dictators, banana republics often epitomized both economic and political dependency on the United States.

Betancourt Doctrine. A policy of commitment to democratic reforms and opposition to dictatorships of both the Marxist and right-wing types named after popular Venezuelan president Rómulo Betancourt during the early 1960s.

Braden Corollary. An interpretation of the Monroe Doctrine named after U.S. diplomat Spruille Braden—a wealthy mining entrepreneur from Montana—for his aggressive and controversial efforts to prevent Argentina's Juan Perón from coming to power in 1946. Braden, like many of his counterparts, tried to justify his strong anti-fascist and anticommunist views in the name of democracy, inter-American security, and the Monroe Doctrine. The Braden Corollary contributed to the rise of Yankeephobia in Latin America during the 1940s and 1950s.

Calvo Clause. A principle of international law named after Argentine diplomat and jurist Carlos Calvo; it challenged the position of European countries that said they had a right to intervene on behalf of their nationals when claims arose over civil wars, revolutions, breaches of contract, and the like.

Caudillo. A type of leader who exercises dictatorial powers with little concern for democracy, constitutionalism, and human rights. Many caudillos were military men whose main interests were in centralizing power, maximizing personal gain, and eliminating political rivals.

Clark Memorandum. An important U.S. State Department document on the Monroe Doctrine prepared by J. Reuben Clark in 1928 (published in 1930) in an effort to improve relations between the United States and Latin America by rejecting the Roosevelt Corollary as a false and counterproductive interpretation of Monroe's principles. Its publication symbolized a major shift in American foreign policy and paved the way for the Good Neighbor Policy.

Cold War. A crucial period of world history from 1947 to 1990, marked by intense ideological, political, and economic hostility between the United States and the Soviet Union, that had a major impact on U.S.-Latin American relations. The Cold War contributed to numerous forms of U.S. intervention in Latin America and the Caribbean and support of counter-revolutionaries who carried out foreign policy initiatives backed by Washington. Inside Latin America, the Cold War contributed to the perpetuation of harsh dictatorships, military takeovers, massive human rights violations against opposition forces, and the expansion of the military, all as a bulwark against various kinds of communism.

Containment. The major foreign policy of the United States during the Cold War designed to prevent the expansion, or perceived expansion, of the Soviet Union, its major adversary. While containment's major regional focus was on Europe (Marshall Plan and the North American Treaty Organization—NATO), it was often tragically misapplied to Latin America and the Caribbean. Communist threats were often misdiagnosed or exaggerated, frequently asserting a connection between revolutionary upheavals and the Soviet Union or Cuba, its Caribbean ally from 1960 to 1990. The father of containment was George F. Kennan, but his views generated many "sons" who were ardent believers in the containment doctrine.

Coup d'État *(Golpe de Estado)*. A common technique of attaining governmental power in Latin America, usually the result of an action by a military or political group within the existing system. Coups are commonly designed to overturn election results, protect economic and perceived security interests, or undertake a revolution.

Dictator. See **Caudillo.**

Dollar Diplomacy. A policy of financial reform directed principally at the Caribbean and Central America by President William H. Taft and Secretary of State Philander C. Knox, designed to bring political stability and financial solvency. Although it originated as a more acceptable replacement for military intervention, it was frequently criticized as a device to protect American bankers and as another way to facilitate U.S. economic exploitation of the region.

Domino Theory. A foreign policy metaphor attributed to President Dwight D. Eisenhower in 1954 as a rationale for U.S. commitment to a noncommunist Vietnam. According to this theory, if one nation becomes communist-controlled, communism will spread, and neighboring states will fall (like a row of dominoes), thus having a profound effect on the security of the United States. Although not articulated as such, President Wilson's Latin American policy rested on the necessity of intervention to prevent "bad" revolutions (Mexico and Russia) from "infecting" neighboring countries. President Reagan's interventionist policies in Central America and the Caribbean were influenced by domino analogies and related thinking in dealing with El Salvador and Nicaragua. Although many considered it a crude and false analogy, it provided policymakers in Washington with a powerful metaphor in which to present foreign policy in simplistic terms to the American people.

Drago Doctrine. A principle of international law advanced by Argentine foreign minister Luis M. Drago in 1902 stating that—in the spirit of the Monroe Doctrine—the existence of a public debt cannot serve as a justification for armed intervention or occupation of an American state by a European power. After the United States agreed to renounce its interventionist policies in the 1930s, the Drago Doctrine was adopted as a fundamental principle of inter-American relations.

Filibuster or *filibustero*. A mercenary or adventurer from the United States, many of whom went to Latin American and Caribbean countries in the nineteenth century for the sake of acquiring territory, glory, and financial enrichment. Many were devout believers in Manifest Destiny and were financially backed by Southerners anxious to expand slave territory. William Walker's exploits in Nicaragua were the most notorious.

Good Neighbor Policy. A period (1930–1945) in U.S.-Latin American relations in which Washington formally abandoned the policy of intervention, called for the recognition of equality among American states, and emphasized collective and individual responsibilities for inter-American affairs.

Gunboat Diplomacy. A form of aggressive diplomacy used by the United States in Latin America and the Caribbean that involved dispatching naval gunboats to hostile ports or coastlines to display force and resolve with the intention of coercing obedience. It was particularly important from 1895 until 1934, although it has been employed by policymakers in Washington ever since.

Hegemony. A state of affairs in which one nation dominates others regionally or globally through economic, political, and military power. With hegemony in Latin America and the Caribbean, the United States possessed unrivaled leadership at times and the capacity to influence the Western Hemisphere by imposing its economic system, social and cultural values, and political ideology. Many scholars argue that with the end of the Cold War, the hegemony of the United States in Latin America and the Caribbean has either waned or no longer exists.

Iran-Contra Affair. A scandal that came to public attention during the Reagan administration in which it was revealed that American arms had been sold secretly to Iran (then defined as a "terrorist state") and the profits used to support (after funding was stopped by Congress) the Contras fighting against the Sandinista government in Nicaragua.

Junta. A Spanish word that refers to a small governing clique, usually military, that takes charge and attempts to govern while at the same time lacking any legal or constitutional authority. Because of the absence of legitimate authority, juntas often rule in an authoritarian manner, restricting civil liberties and undermining popular participation in politics.

Kennan Corollary. Named after State Department official George F. Kennan, who developed the policy of containment against the Soviet Union during the early stages of the Cold War, and extended the meaning of the Monroe Doctrine in the early 1950s by suggesting that U.S. support for brutal Latin American dictatorships was justified in the name of anticommunism and U.S. security.

Manifest Destiny. A belief in the superiority of the United States and its institutions and values during the nineteenth and early twentieth centuries that served as the basis for U.S. continental expansion and the seizure of territory from Spain, including a major war with Mexico, the annexation of Puerto Rico and the Panama Canal Zone, and protectorates over Cuba and other Caribbean countries.

Money Doctors. Foreign financial advisors and economic consultants—mostly from the United States—who designed sweeping economic and monetary reform programs and offered guidance for placating foreign lenders and investors. Money doctors, or monetary medics as they are sometimes called, treated many ailing economies in Latin America and the Caribbean, often hired voluntarily by host countries. The United States supported these economic missions because they provided the appearance of a "hands-off" foreign policy and served to defuse anti-interventionist criticism at home and abroad. At times, money doctors were accompanied by "election doctors," political scientists with expertise in elections, political parties, public administration, and constitutional design.

Multilateralism. A form of diplomacy or negotiations conducted by large numbers of states, often in public with the help of international organizations. The Organization of American States (OAS), with 34 participating members (Cuba is a member but does not participate), has been the primary instrument for conducting multilateral diplomacy in the Americas since its inception in 1948. At times multilateral negotiations include interested nongovernmental organizations (NGOs).

Neoliberal Economic Reforms. Economic policies that emerged in the late 1970s based on anti-government and free-market reforms designed to lower inflation, attract foreign investment, reduce the size and role of government, and push for freer trade. Neoliberalism has been controversial despite its economic success in some parts of Latin America and the Caribbean.

North American Free Trade Agreement (NAFTA). A 1994 agreement establishing a free trade area among Canada, Mexico and the United States. The main provisions of NAFTA include the almost total removal of trade and investment restrictions over a 15-year period. NAFTA creates a trade area second in size to Europe and is often mentioned as a precursor to an FTAA (Free Trade Agreement of the Americas). Opposition to NAFTA in the United States is one factor in the expansion of other economic integration efforts such as the Southern Cone Common Market (MERCOSUR) in South America.

Oligarchy. A government in which a small number of powerful elites (public and/ or private) exercises tight control, often for personal gain at the expense of the rest of the nation.

Olney Corollary. An arrogant and boastful statement made to the British in 1895 by U.S. secretary of state Richard Olney; it expanded the meaning of the Monroe Doctrine by stating that Latin America is part of a U.S. sphere of influence. It is sometimes referred to as the "Olney note" because it was presented in written diplomatic communication.

Organization of American States. An inter-American organization in the Americas composed of the United States, Canada, and 33 Latin American and Caribbean states. Established in 1948, it has played a key role in collective security, peaceful settlement of disputes, democracy promotion and protection of human rights, economic development, and regional integration.

Pan Americanism. A movement forged in the early nineteenth century to bring about greater cooperation among the American states. Through numerous Pan American conferences, the American states tried to establish mechanisms to deal with security, trade, and cultural relations on a collective basis. The inability to reach agreement on the definition and implementation of the nonintervention principle undermined the spirit of cooperation that lay at the heart of the movement. Pan American Day is celebrated throughout the Americas every April 14.

Reagan Doctrine. A component of President Ronald Reagan's foreign policy of supporting guerrillas and other opposition forces fighting Soviet- and Cuban-backed regimes in Latin America, Africa, and Asia. The doctrine emerged from Reagan's anticommunist speeches during his first term and was used to justify (1) the creation of the Contra forces to overthrow the Sandinista government in Nicaragua and (2) U.S. intervention in Grenada in 1983.

Rio Treaty. The first of several treaties, signed in Rio de Janeiro, Brazil, in 1947 (ratified in 1948), that were to serve as the basis for collective security in the Western Hemisphere. It contains the provisions of the Act of Chapultepec, providing that any attack on an American nation will be met by collective sanctions in line with Article 51 of the United Nations Charter. Also known as the Inter-American Treaty of Reciprocal Assistance, the Rio Treaty is implemented by the Organization of American States (OAS). It was invoked by the OAS against Cuba in 1962 (including prohibitions against participation in the OAS) and in the Dominican civil war in 1965.

Roosevelt Corollary. A statement of U.S.-Latin American policy made by President Theodore Roosevelt in 1904 that asserted the right of the United States to intervene in a Latin American country in order to prevent forceful European intervention, often motivated by debt collection. By expanding the interpretation of the original Monroe Doctrine from a defensive to an offensive doctrine of foreign policy in the Caribbean and Central America, Roosevelt's corollary became a justification for U.S. intervention for several decades thereafter.

Sandinistas. Members of a Nicaraguan guerrilla/revolutionary movement (Frente Sandinista de Liberación Nacional—FSLN) named after Augusto Sandino (1896–1934), a Nicaraguan rebel and symbol of resistance to U.S. imperialism in Central America. After overthrowing the Somoza Dynasty in 1979, the Sandinistas tried to carry out a socialist revolution that was opposed by the Reagan administration. The FSLN was forced to give up power in 1990 after being defeated by a broad coalition of opposition parties headed by Violeta Barrios de Chamorro.

School of the Americas. See **U.S. Army School of the Americas.**

Southern Cone. A geographical region encompassing countries located in southern South America. Shaped like a cone, it refers mostly to Argentina, Chile, Paraguay, and Uruguay. There are times when it also includes Brazil (particularly its southern region) and Bolivia.

U.S. Army School of the Americas. A training school for Latin American military personnel (all instruction is in Spanish) funded by U.S. government military programs. The School of the Americas (SOA) originated in Panama in 1946, but under the provisions of the 1977 Panama Canal Treaty it was moved to Fort Benning, Georgia in 1984. It offers over 50 different training programs, and its major mission has been low-intensity warfare training, counter-terrorism, counter-drug operations, professional development, and greater knowledge of U.S. customs and traditions. Since its inception, the school has graduated more than 59,000 officers, cadets, and noncommissioned officers from 22 Latin American countries and the United States. The substantial number of graduates from the SOA who have been involved in military takeovers and human rights violations has earned it the title of "School for Dictators" and the scorn of members of Congress, U.S. ambassadors, and private citizens in the United States who have tried in vain to close the SOA.

Washington Policymakers. Top government officials in the United States with responsibility for the conduct of foreign and domestic decision making. In dealing with Latin America, many have found the Monroe Doctrine useful as a rhetorical prop for advancing U.S. interests in Latin America and the Caribbean, especially when extrahemispheric powers have been involved. Its simplicity and reverence enabled foreign policy bureaucrats to more easily justify the use of force and intervention if a foreign threat could be asserted.

Yankeephobia. A fear and resentment of the United States on the part of Latin Americans, beginning in the nineteenth century, based on chronic U.S. political, economic, and military interventions in their internal affairs. This widespread feeling of outrage toward the United States lessened during the Good Neighbor period but resurfaced again during the Cold War when anticommunism contributed to persistent forms of covert intervention.

Index

Panama to see canal construction, 301; and Venezuela, 368
Roosevelt Corollary to Monroe Doctrine, 24, 25, 54, 57, 135, 136, 138–39, 168, 368
Root, Elihu, 57–58, 119, 270
Rosas, Juan Manuel de, 22
Rosenberg Jagan, Janet, 211, 214
Rostow, Walt W., 45
Royal Navy, 184
Rusk, Dean, 10 (Table 1.1)
Russell, John B., 224
Russell, Richard, 143
Russia, 2, 68

Saavedra Lamas, Carlos, 42
Sachs, Jeffrey, 47
Saint-Domingue, 221
Saint Patrick's Battalion, 262
Salinas de Gortari, Carlos, 258, 273–74, 275
Salinas de Gortari, Raúl, 275
Salisbury, Robert, third marquis of, 366
Sam, Vibrun Guillaume, 223
Samaná Bay, 138
Samper, Ernesto, 86, 94–95
Sánchez Cerro, Luis M., 331
Sánchez de Lozada, Gonzálo, 37
Sánchez Hernández, Fidel, 241
Sandinista National Liberation Front (FSLN), 279, 290, 294
Sandinistas. See Nicaragua
Sandino, Augusto César, 170, 268, 279, 285, 287
Sandino's rebellion, 170
Sandoval Alarcón, Mario, 206
Sanguinetti, Julio María, 350, 357, 358
Santamaría, Juan, 103
Santana, Pedro, 137, 149
Santos, Eduardo, 91
Saudi Arabia, 377
Schlesinger, Arthur, 215
Schley, Winfield Scott, 76
Schombürgk, Robert H., 365
School of the Americas. See U.S. Army School of the Americas

Schuler, Robert, 65
Schwartzkopf, Norman, Jr., 187
Seaga, Edward, 249, 250, 253, 254, 255
Second Hague Peace Conference (1907), 24
Second Summit of the Americas (1998), 83
Seldon Resolution, 318
Sendero Luminoso. See Shining Path guerrillas
Sendic, Raúl, 354
Serrano Elías, Jorge Antonio, 207
Seward, William H., 8 (Table 1.1), 23, 74, 137–38, 154, 196, 263, 328
Shields, Benjamin, 364
Shining Path guerrillas, 326, 335, 337. See also Peru
Shultz, George, 11 (Table 1.1)
Siles Zuazo, Hernán, 46
Smith, Walter Bedell, 201, 203
Soccer War (1969), 172
Social Christian Party, 110
Socialist International, 253
Solano López, Francisco, 23, 313, 314
Soldiers of Fortune. See Filibusters or filbusteros
Solomon, Étienne, 221
Solórzano, Carlos, 286
Somoza Debayle, Anastasio "Tachito" (son), 243, 279, 288, 290, 291, 318, 369
Somoza Debayle, Luis (son), 279, 288, 289, 290
Somoza Dynasty, 288–89, 291
Somoza García, Anastasio "Tacho" (father), 107–8, 201, 239, 279, 280, 287, 288, 289
South Africa, 129, 205
South America, 21, 41, 57
South American Commission, 21
Southern Cone, 21, 318
Southern Cone Common Market (MERCOSUR), 34, 68, 83, 321, 322, 350, 358
Soviet Union, 34, 78, 88, 120, 121, 123, 127, 128, 146, 158, 175, 198, 201, 206, 207, 215, 253, 357

About the Author

DAVID W. DENT is Professor of Political Science at Towson University in Baltimore, Maryland. He is the co-author of *Historical Dictionary of Inter-American Organizations* (1998) and the editor of *U.S. Latin-American Policymaking: A Reference Handbook* (Greenwood, 1995) and *Handbook of Political Science Research on Latin America: Trends from the 1960s to the 1990s* (Greenwood, 1990). He is the author of numerous articles and chapters, and for the past twenty-five years he has been a contributing editor for the *Handbook of Latin American Studies*, a biannual reference book published by the Hispanic Division of the Library of Congress.

DATE DUE

SEP 11 201			
NOV 12			
JUN 13 03			
DEC 19 03			
NOV 06			
APR 17 2007			
MAY 28 2007			
MAY 01 2008			
GAYLORD			PRINTED IN U.S.A.